eKNOW 2018

The Tenth International Conference on Information, Process, and Knowledge Management

March 25 – 29, 2018

Rome, Italy

eKNOW 2018 Editors

Roy Oberhauser, Aalen University, Germany
Samia Aitouche, University Batna 2, Algeria
Martijn Zoet, Zuyd University of Applied Sciences, the Netherlands
Zermane Hanane, University Batna 2, Algeria
Koen Smit, HU University of Applied Sciences Utrecht, the Netherlands

Printed from e-media with permission by:

Curran Associates, Inc.
57 Morehouse Lane
Red Hook, NY 12571

CURRAN ASSOCIATES INC. proceedings.com

Some format issues inherent in the e-media version may also appear in this print version.

Printed by Curran Associates, Inc. (2018)

International Academy, Research, and Industry Association (IARIA)
412 Derby Way
Wilmington, DE 19810

Phone: (408) 893-6407
Fax: (408) 527-6351

petre@iaria.org

Additional copies of this publication are available from:

Curran Associates, Inc.
57 Morehouse Lane
Red Hook, NY 12571 USA
Phone: 845-758-0400
Fax: 845-758-2633
Email: curran@proceedings.com
Web: www.proceedings.com

eKNOW 2018

Forward

The tenth edition of the International Conference on Information, Process, and Knowledge Management (eKNOW 2018) was held in Rome, Italy, March 25 - 29, 2018. The event was driven by the complexity of the current systems, the diversity of the data, and the challenges for mental representation and understanding of environmental structure and behavior.

Capturing, representing, and manipulating knowledge was and still is a fascinating and extremely useful challenge from both theoretical and practical perspective. Using validated knowledge for information and process management and for decision support mechanisms raised a series of questions the eKNOW 2018 conference was aimed at.

eKNOW 2018 provided a forum where researchers were able to present recent research results and new research problems and directions related to them. The topics covered aspects from knowledge fundamentals to more specialized topics such as process analysis and modeling, management systems, semantics processing and ontology.

We take this opportunity to thank all the members of the eKNOW 2018 Technical Program Committee as well as the numerous reviewers. The creation of such a broad and high-quality conference program would not have been possible without their involvement. We also kindly thank all the authors who dedicated much of their time and efforts to contribute to the eKNOW 2018. We truly believe that, thanks to all these efforts, the final conference program consists of top quality contributions.

This event could also not have been a reality without the support of many individuals, organizations, and sponsors. We are grateful to the members of the eKNOW 2018 organizing committee for their help in handling the logistics and for their work to make this professional meeting a success.

We hope that eKNOW 2018 was a successful international forum for the exchange of ideas and results between academia and industry and for the promotion of progress in knowledge management research.

We also hope that Rome provided a pleasant environment during the conference and everyone saved some time for exploring this beautiful city.

eKNOW 2018 Chairs

eKNOW Steering Committee
Roy Oberhauser, Aalen University, Germany
Conceição Granja, Norwegian Centre for eHealth Research | University Hospital of North Norway, Norway
Andrzej M.J. Skulimowski, AGH University of Science and Technology - Krakow, Poland
Dirk Malzahn, Dirk Malzahn Ltd. / HfH University, Germany
Peter Bellström, Karlstad University, Sweden
Susan Gauch, University of Arkansas, USA
Edy Portmann, Institute of Information Systems - University of Bern, Switzerland
Nitin Agarwal, University of Arkansas at Little Rock, USA

eKNOW Industry/Research Advisory Committee
Gil Ad Ariely, Interdisciplinary Center Herzliya (IDC), Israel
Daniel Kimmig, solute GmbH, Germany
Mauro Dragoni, Fondazione Bruno Kessler, Italy
Dayu Yuan, Google Inc., USA
Ming Zhou, Microsoft Research Asia, China
Faisal Azhar, HP UK LTD, UK

eKNOW 2018

COMMITTEE

eKNOW Steering Committee

Roy Oberhauser, Aalen University, Germany
Conceição Granja, Norwegian Centre for eHealth Research | University Hospital of North Norway, Norway
Andrzej M.J. Skulimowski, AGH University of Science and Technology - Krakow, Poland
Dirk Malzahn, Dirk Malzahn Ltd. / HfH University, Germany
Peter Bellström, Karlstad University, Sweden
Susan Gauch, University of Arkansas, USA
Edy Portmann, Institute of Information Systems - University of Bern, Switzerland
Nitin Agarwal, University of Arkansas at Little Rock, USA

eKNOW Industry/Research Advisory Committee

Gil Ad Ariely, Interdisciplinary Center Herzliya (IDC), Israel
Daniel Kimmig, solute GmbH, Germany
Mauro Dragoni, Fondazione Bruno Kessler, Italy
Dayu Yuan, Google Inc., USA
Ming Zhou, Microsoft Research Asia, China
Faisal Azhar, HP UK LTD, UK

eKNOW 2018 Technical Program Committee

Gil Ad Ariely, Interdisciplinary Center Herzliya (IDC), Israel
Chris Adetunji, University of Southampton, UK
Nitin Agarwal, University of Arkansas at Little Rock, USA
Faisal Azhar, Hewlett Packard (HP), UK
Zbigniew Banaszak, Koszalin University of Technology, Poland
Gianni Barlacchi, University of Trento, Italy
Peter Bellström, Karlstad University, Sweden
Martine Cadot, LORIA - University Henri Poincaré Nancy I, France
Ali Çakmak, Istanbul Sehir University, Turkey
Enrico Caldarola, Università di Napoli "Federico II", Italy
Ricardo Campos, Polytechnic Institute of Tomar / LIAAD INESC TEC, Portugal
Massimiliano Caramia, University of Rome "Tor Vergata", Italy
Shayok Chakraborty, Arizona State University, USA
Dickson Chiu, The University of Hong Kong, Hong Kong
Ritesh Chugh, Central Queensland University, Australia
Paolo Cintia, University of Pisa / KDDLab Isti Cnr, Italy
Marco Cococcioni, University of Pisa, Italy
Cláudio de Souza Baptista, Federal University of Campina Grande, Brazil
Chiara Di Francescomarino, Fondazione Bruno Kessler (FBK), Italy
Giuseppe A. Di Lucca, University of Sannio - RCOST (Research Center on Software Technology), Italy
Mauro Dragoni, Fondazione Bruno Kessler, Italy
Schaumlechner Erwin, Tiscover GmbH, Austria

Jørgen Fischer Nilsson, Technical University of Denmark, Denmark
Joan-Francesc Fondevila-Gascón, UPF | Blanquerna-URL | UdG (Escola Universitària Mediterrani) | UCJC, UOC, UAB & UB | CECABLE, Spain
Susan Gauch, University of Arkansas, USA
László Grad-Gyenge, Creo Group, Hungary
Conceição Granja, Norwegian Centre for eHealth Research | University Hospital of North Norway, Norway
Fabrice Guillet, Polytech Nantes - University of Nantes, France
Mena Habib, Maastricht University, Netherlands
Daniela Hossu, University Politehnica of Bucharest, Romania Andrei Hossu, University Politehnica of Bucharest, Romania
Zhisheng Huang, Vrije University Amsterdam, Netherlands
Anca Daniela Ionita, University Politehnica of Bucharest, Romania
Alfred Inselberg, Tel Aviv University, Israel / San Diego Supercomputing Center, USA
Lili Jiang, Umeå University, Sweden
Mouna Kamel, Institut de Recherche en Informatique de Toulouse (IRIT), France
Michael Kaufmann, Lucerne University of Applied Sciences and Arts, Switzerland
Daniel Kimmig, solute GmbH, Germany
Efstratios Kontopoulos, Information Technologies Institute (ITI) / Center for Research & Technology Hellas (CERTH), Greece
Chinmay Kumar Kundu, KIIT University, Bhubaneswar, India
Andrew Kusiak, University of Iowa, USA
Franz Lehner, University of Passau, Germany
CP Lim, Deakin University - Institute for Intelligent Systems Research and Innovation, Australia
Haibin Liu, China Aerosp. Eng. Consultation Center, Beijing, China
Carlos Alberto Malcher Bastos, Federal Fluminense University, Brazil
Dirk Malzahn, Dirk Malzahn Ltd. / HfH University, Germany
Mohammed Amin Marghalani, King Abdul Aziz University, Saudi Arabia
Nada Matta, Universite de Technologie de Troyes, France
Christine Michel, Liris (INSA de Lyon), France
Roy Oberhauser, Aalen University, Germany
Daniel O'Leary, University of Southern California, USA
Jonice Oliveira, Federal University of Rio de Janeiro (UFRJ), Brazil
João Paulo Costa, INESC Coimbra | CeBER and Faculty of Economics - University of Coimbra, Portugal
Ludmila Penicina, Riga Technical University, Latvia
Lukas Pichl, International Christian University, Japan
Edy Portmann, Institute of Information Systems - University of Bern, Switzerland
Lukasz Radlinski, West Pomeranian University of Technology in Szczecin, Poland
German Rigau, UPV/EHU, Spain
Ígor Rodríguez Iglesias, Universidad de Huelva, Spain
Aitouche Samia, University Batna 2, Algeria
Dobrica Savić, International Atomic Energy Agency | Vienna International Centre, Austria
Stefan Schulz, Medizinische Universität Graz, Austria
Hong-Han Shuai, National Chiao-Tung University, Taiwan
Andrzej M.J. Skulimowski, AGH University of Science and Technology - Krakow, Poland
Efstathios Stamatatos, University of the Aegean, Greece
Lubomir Stanchev, California Polytechnic State University, USA
Cristian Stanciu, University Politehnica of Bucharest, Romania

Copyright Information

Table of Contents

What Do Sub-second Price Data Tell Us about the Arrowhead Stock Market?

Mieko Tanaka-Yamawaki
Dept. Math. Sciences, School of Interdisciplinary Math.
Meiji University, 1-21-4, Nakano, Nakano-ku,
Tokyo, 164-8525, Japan
e-mail: mieko@meiji.ac.jp

Masanori Yamanaka
Dept. Physics, School of Science and Engineering
Nihon University, 14-8-1, Kanda-Surugadai, Chiyoda-ku
Tokyo 101-8308, Japan
e-mail: yamanaka@phys.cst.nihon-u.ac.jp

Abstract—**In this paper, we study ultrafast stock time series of the newly developed arrowhead trading system in Tokyo Market, in order to investigate the statistical nature of the stock time series under sub-second time scales. We also compare the current result to the past study on longer time scale up to a few minutes. It is shown that the empirical distributions obtained in this study follow the scaling law of the Lévy stable distribution of index α ranging from 1.4 to 2.0.**

Keywords-stock time series; arrowhead market, statistical distribution, scaling phenomena.

I. INTRODUCTION

The science of price fluctuation was initiated by a French Mathematician Luis Bachelier, who recognized the nature of price fluctuation as the random walk (Brownian motion) in 1900 [1], which was five years earlier than Albert Einstein's formulation of random walk in physics. This tradition is still carried over in the basic theory of financial technology to evaluate the derivative prices, such as Black-Sholes-Merton (BSM) formula [2]-[5].

However, it is well-known that the BSM formula often fails to describe the real world. While the important parameter σ (volatility) is assumed to be a certain constant in the above formula, there is no reliable way to compute its value theoretically.

Two empirical ways are often used to obtain the value of σ: One is the 'historical volatility', or the realized volatility', to compute the average values of the standard deviation over the historical price data over a fixed length, such as 2 weeks. Another is the 'implied volatility' to obtain σ by inversely solving the BSM formula from for the actual price time series of the option prices. However, the obtained values σ are not a constant but varies as a function of K (the target price of each option) of the same option for different terms T. This is known as the 'smile curve' because the σ-K plot shapes concave and resembles the 'smile' mark. Considering the importance of the derivation of the BSM formula in financial engineering, it is essential to solve the problem of σ.

Another problem of the BSM formula is the basic assumption of Gaussian nature of price fluctuation, which is incompatible with the observed 'fat-tail', or 'narrow-neck' nature of the actual statistics of the price fluctuation. Moreover, it is widely accepted that the price fluctuation has the scale invariant property, which is incompatible with the Gaussian distribution, since Gaussian distribution is bounded by the scale of variance, or standard deviation, σ. In order to remedy this situation, a scale-invariant distribution called Lévy stable distribution is proposed and the index α=1.4 was discussed widely [6][7]. Although the infinite variance in Lévy stable distribution is not mathematically compatible to framework of option pricing theory, actual price fluctuations behave more like Lévy stable distribution than Gaussian. Thus, it is a highly challenging problem to clarify the statistical nature of price fluctuation in various range of time resolutions.

In this work, we investigate the new world of arrowhead stock market [8], not only to determine the shape of the statistical distribution, but also to examine various results obtained so far, such as cross correlation between different stocks using random matrix theory-oriented principal component analyses and related techniques [9]-[11], for the stock market of normal speed to the results on this newly developed arrowhead market.

In this paper, we report the statistical distributions of price fluctuation obtained from the sub-second range to a few minutes, in order to show their scale invariant property.

The rest of the paper is structured as flows. In Section II, we summarize the formulation of price dynamics. In Section III, we show the result of our former analysis [12] using five-second sampled prices of 100 companies of Tokyo market in 2013, in which the average stock prices per 5 second are well described by Lévy stable distribution of index α=1.4, based on the fact that the distribution follows the scale invariance for a wide range of time scale Δt=1 to 12. In Section IV, we analyze newly obtained full arrowhead stock price data of the years 2015-2016 [12] to show that the scale invariance seems to hold in the range of 0.8 second to one hour, although the estimated range of index α is rather broad ($1.4<\alpha<2.1$). Finally, Section V is devoted to the conclusion.

II. FORMULATION OF PRICE DYNAMICS

We are interested in the statistical distribution of the price increment, which is often called log-return

$$Z(t) = logX(t + \Delta t) - log\,X(t) \quad (1)$$

of the asset price $X(t)$ at time t and the same price $X(t+\Delta t)$ at $t+\Delta t$, to clarify whether the statistical distribution of the price returns is not purely Gaussian but has fat-tails and narrow necks. Several decades ago, it was pointed out by Mandelbrot [6] then followed by Mantegna and Stanley [7] that the probability distribution of asset returns follow Lévy stable distribution, defined as

$$f_{\alpha,\beta}(Z) = \frac{1}{2\pi}\int_{-\infty}^{\infty} e^{ikZ-\beta|k|^{\alpha}}\, dk \quad (2)$$

which is the Fourier transform of the kernel *F(k)* given by

$$F_{\alpha,\beta}(k) = e^{-\beta|k|^{\alpha}} \quad (3)$$

The first parameter α characterizes the distribution and is called Lévy index, taking the range of $1 \le \alpha \le 2$, and the second parameter β is proportional to the time interval Δt, as follows.

$$\beta = \gamma\Delta t \quad (4)$$

Equation (4) can be understood as follows. The stable distribution holds the same index α under convolution of two stochastic variables following the same stable distributions: *i.e.*, $z=x+y$ follows Lévy stable distribution of index α if both x and y follow Lévy stable distribution of the same index α. This means that the distribution of asset returns at 5 seconds ($\Delta t=1$) follows the same distribution as the same asset returns at 10 seconds ($\Delta t=2$).

$$f_{\Delta t=2}(z) = \int_0^z f_{\Delta t=1}(x) f_{\Delta t=1}(z-x)dx \quad (5)$$

In the Fourier space, a convolution is reduced to a product of the Fourier kernels.

$$F_{\Delta t=2}(k) = (F_{\Delta t=1}(k))^2 \quad (6)$$

which can be generated to the case of n steps to have

$$F_{\Delta t=n}(k) = (F_{\Delta t=1}(k))^n \quad (7)$$

A series of n steps yields β to be multiplied by n, without changing the Lévy index α. However, this model of price movements naturally assumes a limitation on the maximum number of steps, n.

Note that (2) can be integrated for two special cases, $\alpha=1$ and $\alpha=2$, first of which is the Lorentz distribution,

$$P_{\alpha=1,\beta}(Z) = \frac{\beta}{\pi}\frac{1}{\beta^2+Z^2} \quad (8)$$

and the second is the normal (Gaussian) distribution.

$$P_{\alpha=2,\beta}(Z) = \frac{1}{2\sqrt{\pi\beta}} exp\left(-\frac{Z^2}{4\beta}\right) \quad (9)$$

For general values of α, the distribution is computed by numerically integrating Eq. (2).

The scale invariant property of Lévy stable distribution is derived from Eq. (2),

$$P_{\alpha,\beta}(Z/(\Delta t)^{1/\alpha}) = (\Delta t)^{1/\alpha}\ P_{\alpha,\beta\Delta t}(Z) \quad (10)$$

Setting $Z=0$ in Eq. (10), Lévy index α is estimated by comparing the height of the distribution $P_{\Delta t}(0)$ for various values of Δt.

$$log(P_{\alpha,\beta\Delta t}(0)) = -\frac{1}{\alpha}log(\Delta t) + log(P_{\alpha,\beta}(0)) \quad (11)$$

The above scenario was applied on American stock index S&P500, per 1 minute for 1984-1985, and per 15 seconds for 1986-1989, which was well-fitted to Lévy stable distribution around the center of the distribution, and the scale invariant property was proved in the range of Δt =1-100 min [7].

The scale invariant property of Lévy stable distribution is derived from Eq. (2),

$$P_{\alpha,\beta}(Z_s) = (\Delta t)^{1/\alpha}\ P_{\alpha,\beta\Delta t}(Z) \quad (12)$$

$$Z_s = Z/(\Delta t)^{1/\alpha} \quad (13)$$

III. Preliminary Result by 5 Second Sampled Data

Although the arrowhead trading system was introduced in Tokyo Security Exchange (TSE) on January 4, 2010, it was hard for us to access to the full numerical data due to its huge size. Tokyo Market Impact View (TMIV) [13] offered us an opportunity to download sampled prices of 100 selected stocks per 5 seconds for a limited time from April to December, 2013 (Data-A).

We investigated the statistical property of the price increment of TMIV, and obtained the empirical probability distribution of the average of the 100 stock prices for various time intervals $\Delta t=1$, corresponding to the interval of 5 seconds, 3, 6, 12, 24, corresponding to the interval of 2 minutes, as shown in Fig.1 [8]. If the statistical distribution if the price increments $Z(t)$ is indeed the scale-invariant distribution, those histograms of five different values of Δt should overlap each other after the scaling transformations of Eq. (12) and Eq. (13).

As shown in Fig.2, histograms of various values of the scale parameter Δt in Fig. 1 overlap on a single distribution by rescaling acording to Eq.(12) if the parameter α is chosen to the value $\alpha=1.4$.

The scale invariance of the statistical distribution of price increments can be checked using two other methods. One way is to use Eq. (11) for checking the straightness of the log-log plot of P(0) vs. Δt and also to obtain the Lévy index α from the slope ($-1/\alpha$) of the plot. By means of the least square fit, the best fit line turns out

By using this data set, we investigated the statistical distribution of the price increment

$$log\ P(0) = -0.709\ log(\Delta t) + 2.56 \quad (14)$$

as shown in Fig.3. The Lévy index α obtained in this result is $\alpha=1/0.709=1.41$, which is consistent to in Fig. 2. [7]

So far, we have seen that our analyses on Data-A (5 seconds resolution of TSE arrowhead market) gave us a consistent result. However, a question remains. The price increments looked like purely random in early 20th century. However, it was shown that the price changes are governed by the scale invariance under high resolution analyses. Also, it became clear that the probability distribution of the price changes is featured by the fat-tails and a narrow neck. We have to clarify to what level of resolution this phenomenon goes on. We need to determine whether or not the scale invariant property is valid under the arrowhead market in which the assets are traded under ultra-high resolution shorter than a millisecond.

Before getting into the arrowhead market, we attempted to check our results to another independent data of 1 minute resolution, downloaded from Google Finance site [14] for the duration of June 16, 2015 to November 4, 2015. We call this data Data-B. However, the time resolution (frequency) of this Data set is not as small as the previous Data-A and the scaling method is not suitable to analyze this data. We need a different method for Data-B. Since we cannot compare the distributions of different time resolutions, we adopt another method to search for the best value of α to minimize Kulbuck-Leibler divergence (K-L divergence) between two probability distributions $p(x)$ and $q(x)$ defined by

$$D(p||q) = \sum_{x \in X} p(x) log \frac{p(x)}{q(x)} \quad (15)$$

We compute $D(p||q)$ in Eq. (15) by setting $p(x)$ and $q(x)$, as the probability distribution of the 1- minute price increments (return) and the corresponding Lévy stable distribution for various values of α and β. The best fitted result for those parameters is consistent with the case of Data-A, as shown in Table 1 [12].

IV. FULL ARROWHEAD PRICE DATA

Recently, full arrowhead price data became available via the web page of JPX [8]. Compared to the Data-A, the data sizes are incredibly large. They are compared in Table 2. The most active stock in Nov. 2016 has over 36 million data points in one month, and the sum of Nov. and Dec. 2016 has comparable size to that of total 100 companies in Data-A. Moreover, the times of trades are utterly irregular in the case of arrowhead data, while Data-A has exactly 3600 points each day.

We began our analysis from the most active stock, code number 8306. We first pick up the stock prices every 100 millisecond interval to make a time series of the stock prices from October, 2015 to December 2016. Based on this data file, we draw the empirical probability distributions for various values of Δt. For the sake of simplicity, we focus on the graphs for Δt= 8, 16, 32, 64, 128, 256, 512,1024, 2048, 4096, and 8192 (×100ms). Those eleven histograms are simultaneously shown in Fig.4. The graph for Δt= 8 has the smallest width on the horizontal axis Z and the tallest height on the vertical axis $\log_2 P(Z)$, and the graph for Δt= 16 is slightly smaller width in Z and shorter height in the vertical axis. Those histograms of regularly increasing time scales seem to obey some regularity. If they obey a scale-invariant distribution such as Lévy stable distribution, we should be able to identify the scaling factor $c = (\Delta t)^{1/\alpha}$. For example, the graphs for Δt= 8 should overlap the graph for Δt= 16 by multiply Z by the factor $c=2^{1/\alpha}$ and divide the vertical axis by the same factor c. Applying the same rule on all the eleven histograms, they should be able to overlap on a single distribution if the factor c is properly chosen. This is done by choosing c=1.5 as shown in Fig.5. All the eleven histograms corresponding to Δt= 8, 16, 32, 64, 128, 256, 512,1024, 2048, 4096, and 8192 (×100ms) can be scaled to a single curve by choosing c=1.5 and the corresponding index is around α=1.7. Unfortunately, the resolution of this estimate is not high and the accuracy of the factor c varies in the range of $1.4 < c < 1.6$ according to the estimation of P(0). This uncertainty of c implies the uncertainty of the index α, in the range of $1.4 < \alpha < 2$, as shown in Table III. The uncertainty of P(0) comes from the nature of the price data, since the observed number of unchanged price contains numerous counts of the 'absence of trade' on top of the 'trade with the same price'. It is hard to distinguish those two by the data. However, it is possible to estimate the true value of P(0) in such a way for the probability P(Z) to satisfy a smoothness by removing excess P(0) from the data.

V. CONCLUSION

We focused in this work to discover possible new elements to characterize the price changes under ultrafast market transactions of sub-millisecond intervals in the arrowhead market, operated in Tokyo market from 2010. In particular, we investigated the shape of the statistical distribution of the price increments. Especially, we obtained the probability distribution of the asset returns and examined the central part of the distribution utilizing its scale-invariant property.

In our previous work using 5 second resolution data [12], however, the distribution turned out to be the same as the result of one-minute resolution data in [7]. In this paper we show, using the new data of 100ms resolution, that the same kind of scale-invariant statistical distribution holds for the sub-second motion of price changes, although the index to characterize the scale invariance comes out to be α=1.7. Considering various uncertainties, this value is roughly consistent to our previous result in [12].

REFERENCES

[1] L. J. B. Bachelier, Theory of Speculation, 1900.
[2] F. Black and M. Scholes, Journal of Political Economy, Vol. 81, pp. 637-654, 1973.
[3] R. Merton, The Review of Economics and Statistics, Vol. 51 pp. 247–257, 1969.
[4] R. C. Merton, The Bell Journal of Economics and Management Science, Vol. 4, pp. 141–183, 1973.
[5] R. C. Merton, "Option Pricing When Underlying Stock Returns Are Discontinuous", Journal of Financial Economics, Vol. 3, pp. 125-144, 1976.
[6] B. B. Mandelbrot, "The variation of Certain Speculative Prices", J. Buisiness, Vol. 36, pp.394-419, 1963.
[7] R. N. Mantegna and H.E. Stanley, Nature Vol.376, pp.46-49, 1995.
[8] www.jpx.co.jp/english/corporate/news-releases/0060/20150924-01.html; [retrieved March 2018]
[9] S. Nagata and K. Inui, "Does high-speed trading enhances market efficiency?", Journal of Trading, Vol.3, pp.75-81, 2014
[10] M. Tanaka-Yamawaki et al.;"Trend-extraction of Stock Prices in the American Market by Means of RMT-PCA"; Intelligent Decision Technologies,SIST10, pp.637-646, 2011.
[11] X.Yang, Y.Mikamori, and M. Tanaka-Yamawaki, Procedia Computer Science, Vol.22, pp.1172-1181, 2013.
[12] M. Tanaka-Yamawaki, Procedia Computer Science, Vol. 112, pp. 1439–1447, 2017.

[13] www.tse.marketimpactview.com [retrieved March 2018]
[14] finance.google.com/finance [retrieved March 2018]

TABLE I. THE K-L DIVERGENCE OF THE BEST FIT INDICES OF LÉVY STABLE DISTRIBUTION AND DATA-B

data (1 min return)	α	β	K-L DIV.
Ave. of 440 returns	1.40	5.4×10^{-6}	0.039
9503	1.55	10.0×10^{-6}	0.286
7201	1.65	3.9×10^{-6}	0.423
6502	1.55	8.8×10^{-6}	0.156

TABLE II. THE DATA SIZES OF ACTIVE COMPANIES ARE COMPARED TO DATA-A

Stock code	Data-A	Nov. 2016	Dec. 2016
# of companies	100	3806	3820
8306	0	36,330,455	31,418,450
7203	640,800	13,430,448	10,297,008
9984	0	9,984,780	14,009,724

TABLE III. THE SCALE FACTOR AND THE VALUES OF LÉVY INDEX

$c = (\Delta t)^{1/\alpha}$	1.4	1.5	1.6
α	2.06	1.71	1.47

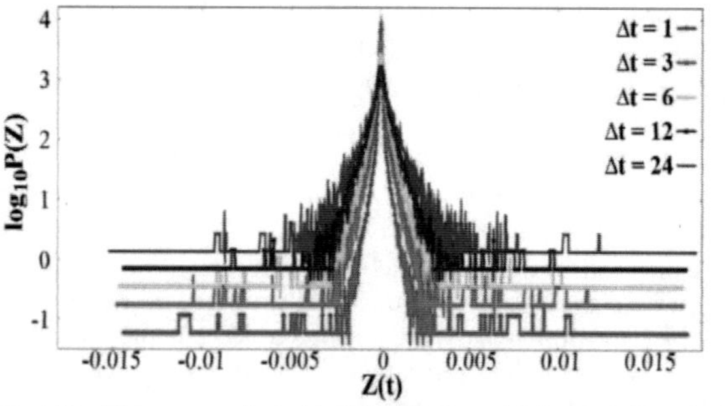

Fig.1 The histograms of statsitical distribution of Z for Δt=1 (5 sec), 3 (15 sec), 6 (30 sec), 12 (1 min), and 24 (2 min).

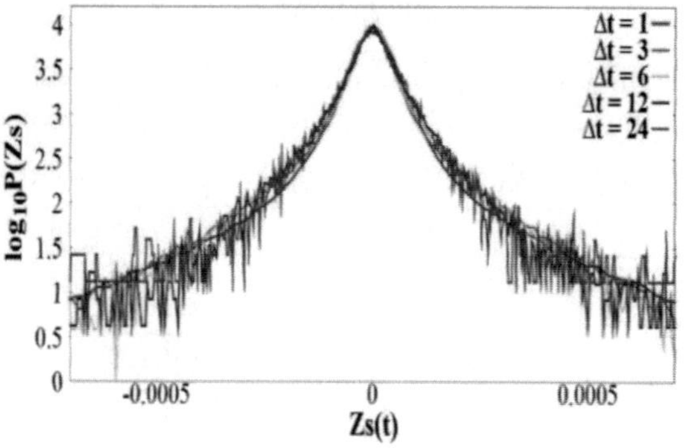

Fig.2 The histograms in Fig.1 are well scaled by Zs vs. $\log_{10}P(Zs)$ for Δt=1(equivalent to 5s), 3(15s), 6(30s), 12(1 min), and 24(2 min) for the case of $\alpha = 1.4$.

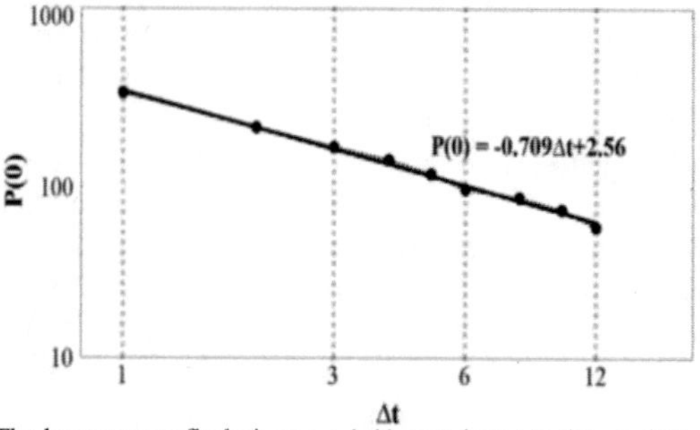

Fig. 3 The least square fit derives α =1.41, consistent to the result from Fig. 2.

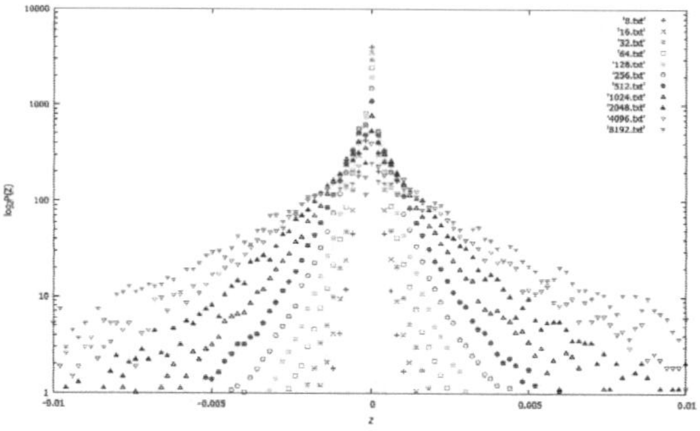

Fig. 4 The histograms of 100ms returns of stock code 8306 are compared for various levels of coarse graining, 8.txt, 32.txt,.., 8192.txt, corresponding to the time scales, Δt =8-8192 (unit 100ms).

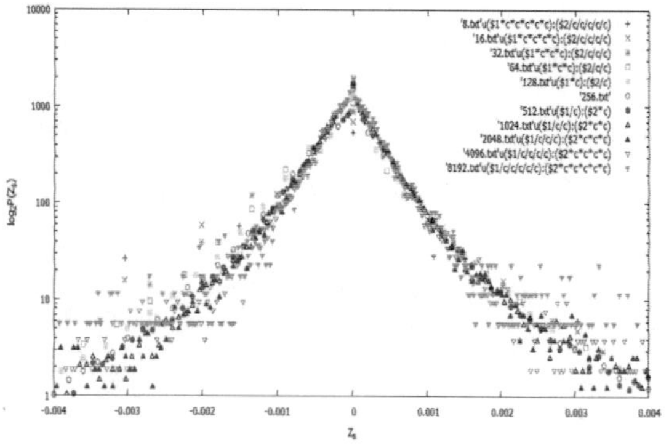

Fig. 5 The six histograms in Fig. 2 of different time resolutions, Δt =8, 32, 128, 512, 2048, 8192 (unit 100ms) can be rescaled to overlap on a single curve by properly choosing the scaling factor $c = (\Delta t)^{1/\alpha}$. This figure shows the case of c=1.5 which derives the index α – 1.7.

Control Metrics Evaluation Model for Business Processes using Process Mining

Rodrigo Alfonso García Oliva, Jesús Javier Santos Barrenechea, Jimmy Alexander Armas Aguirre
Universidad Peruana de Ciencias Aplicadas, Perú
e-mails: u201310705@upc.edu.pe, u201312919@upc.edu.pe, Jimmy.armas@upc.pe

Santiago Aguirre Mayorga
Pontificia Universidad Javeriana
Bogotá D.C, Colombia
e-mail: saguirre@javeriana.edu.co

Abstract— **Process mining is considered a discipline that contains a set of techniques, algorithms and methods for discovering, monitoring and optimizing business processes through event logs extracted from transactional systems. Based on this discipline, a model is proposed that allows the evaluation of the performance and behaviour of business processes through a set of control metrics. As a result of the model evaluation, six control metrics were analyzed in the logistic process of a Peruvian retail enterprise using ProM Tools for the application of Process Mining techniques and Qlikview for the implementation of the Process Cube and results presentation.**

Keywords- Process Mining; Event Logs; Business Process Intelligence; Process Cubes.

I. INTRODUCTION

It is not new that companies are currently in a continuous search for improvements for the execution of their processes. Therefore, they are immersed in the choice of new technologies that provide tools and techniques to improve the control of their operations The current approaches for process improvement have a high probability of failure, as is the case of process re-engineering where there is a probability of failure of between 60 and 70% [1]. It is in response to this need that Process Mining emerged. This field of research is defined as a discipline that uses event logs generated by information systems to discover, analyze and improve business processes [2]. However, as an emerging technology, it still presents many challenges for its application. These include: poor understanding of inexperienced users, integrating Process Mining with other types of analysis and the complexity of using existing tools [2]. These challenges are reflected in the lack of reports and visualizations that clearly reflect to the end user the outcome of the process analysis, which is extremely important because transforming data into valuable information requires an understanding of the data context and the ability to visualize large volumes of data [3]. On the other hand, it should be considered the complexity of replicating the workflow, which requires analysts to perform many analysis steps in a specific order [4], despite the fact that multiple iterations are usually required in order to fine-tune the report so that it provides the highest level of understanding for the end user. Therefore, with the objective of addressing these challenges, a solution is developed to meet the obstacles involved in the execution of this technique, allowing a greater ease in the application and interpretation of results by using business process control metrics that provide the user a clear view of the current situation of behavior and execution of their processes.

The rest of the paper is structured as follows. Section 2 presents the state of the art. In Section 3, we present the proposed model. Section 4 presents the results of the implementation of the proposal in a real scenario. We conclude the work in Section 5.

II. STATE OF THE ART

In this section, we address the state of art wich has been divided in three sub-sections based on the explored topics:

A. Process Cubes

A Process Cube can be defined as a collection of events or process models organized through different dimensions (e. g. time, resources, roles, etc.) [6] allowing to manipulate the collection of events with traditional OLAP (On-Line Transactional Processing) operations (Slice, Dice, Drill Down, etc.) as commonly used in Business Intelligence [5]. Different approaches have been explored on the subject, giving positive results. The work of Ribeiro and Weijters demonstrates the advantages of developing an Event Cube (a similar term to refer to a Process Cube) where it allowed process analysts to apply Process Mining from different perspectives of the process in a simple way [7]. Similarly, the work of Bolt and Van der Aalst implements the Process Cube concept in a practical way in an application called "Process Mining Cube" that demonstrated good performance results compared to previous approaches [8].

B. Process Mining: Methods and Metrics

Process Mining has received great attention in recent years from the academic community, resulting in a large number of process discovery techniques, techniques for event log data analysis, techniques for trace classifications, process control metrics and specific application areas [1]. In the area of metrics, Minsu Cho proposes a methodology which focuses on the investigation of process metrics. This methodology includes two sets of indicators. The first group mentions a set of BPI best practice metrics, which were already proposed by Reijers and Mansar in 2005. The second set of indicators is designed to measure process performance (Process Performance Indicator) taking time, cost, quality and process flexibility as the main factors [9]. On the other hand, one of the main problems observed in the Process Mining application was the integration of Event Logs related to the process to analyze. Under this precedent, Claes and Poels developed a rules-based algorithm for merging Event Logs implemented in ProM Tools that allows to overcome one of the obstacles when applying Process Mining with multiple Event Logs [10].

As far as quality metrics are concerned, Kherbouche, Laga and Masse propose a model to ensure the quality of the Event Logs, to subsequently apply the algorithms of Process Mining. For this purpose, the model comprises a set of metrics based on complexity, precision, consistency and completeness [11]. Janssenswillen et al. present a comparative study on various quality metrics in the discovery phase of Process Mining based on Fitness, Precision, Generalization and Simplicity criteria [12].

In the discovery phase, we can highlight the work of Wang, Wong, Ding, Guo and Wen where a scalable solution capable of evaluating algorithms of Process Mining is detailed. In particular, it attempts to investigate how we can choose an effective Process Mining algorithm without extensive evaluation of each algorithm, allowing us to obtain the most optimal and reliable results based on the analysis process [13]; in the Conformance Checking phase, Adryansyah et al. present a compliance method based on measuring the precision of the observed behaviour in the event log and the process model generated previously in the discovery phase, the particularity of its approach stands out in that it allows to work with incomplete event logs and reduce the propensity to incorrect discoveries [14].

From another point of view, Conforti, La Rosa and ter Hofstede address the challenge of discovering high-quality process models in the presence of noise in event logs, through a technique to remove the infrequent behavior of these records [15]. The technique was implemented in ProM Tools as a plugin under the name of "Infrequent Behavior Filter". The plugin gives the user the freedom to select Gurobi or LPsolve as ILP solver.

C. PM2 Methodology

The PM2 methodology seeks to provide a guide for the implementation of Process Mining projects, which, unlike other existing methodologies, stands out for its scope to be applied to different types of projects [16]. PM2 consists of six phases: planning, extraction, data processing, mining and analysis, evaluation and finally, process improvement and support. The main contribution of the methodology is the data processing phase, which specifies various tasks such as filtering, adding different types of perspectives, among others, which together aim to have information that can allow optimal analysis in later phases [16].

III. Control Metrics Evaluation Model

A. Background

The proposed model takes concepts from the PM2 methodology for its design, since its approach seeks to evaluate performance and compliance with the rules and regulations of the process, and also covers a wide range of Process Mining techniques and other types of analysis techniques useful for the study of structured and unstructured processes in an iterative way [16]. The phases of the methodology that represented the greatest contribution were Extraction, Data Processing, Mining and Analysis and Evaluation. It is important to consider the minimum requirements to apply Process Mining. The first consideration is that the information of the process to be analyzed must be hosted in some data repository (database, csv file, transaction log, business suite, etc), from which the event logs will be extracted. The second one is that, with respect to the extracted event log, in order to apply Process Mining it must contain at least the following fields: Case identifier, Activity name and Time stamp.

In addition, the model makes use of Qlikview 12 for the visualization of data and ProM Tools 6.7 for the processing of event logs.

B. Model Phases

The main objective of the model is to evaluate control metrics to provide a diagnosis of the analyzed process. The model consists of six phases that can be grouped into two main groups (Pre-processing and execution). Each of them is detailed below, as shown in Figure 1.

- *Extraction:* The objective of this phase is to extract Event Data from the information systems that support the process to be analyzed under the format of an Event Log, so that Process Mining techniques can be applied. The minimum Event Log requirement must be a process instance identifier (CaseID), activity name and time stamp.
- *Integration:* The aim of this phase is to integrate the Event Logs obtained in the extraction phase into a single Event Log, so that a holistic approach is taken to the process (end-to-end).
- *Cleansing:* This phase aims to ensure that the Event Log information is consistent. To do this, the Event Log is filtered by removing the information that may negatively affect the analysis (lack of data, null values, etc.), in the same way incomplete or infrequent traces are eliminated.
- *Discovery:* This phase aims to discover a process model based on the Event Log already processed.
- *Conformance:* In this phase the model generated in the previous phase is compared with the model that currently follows the process, in addition the deviations and control metrics are calculated in this phase.

- *Diagnose:* The objective of this phase is to evaluate previously calculated control metrics and provide visual representation of the results for the end users understanding.

C. *Structural and Control Metrics*

For the structural analysis of the event log, the model contemplates metrics proposed in Kherbouche work, of which the following are used to calculate the level of complexity and variability of the process based on the information contained in the Event log [11]. The metrics are Average Trace Size (ATS), Average Trace Lenght (ATL), Average Loops per Trace (ALT), Density (DN) and Trace Heterogeneity Rate (THR).

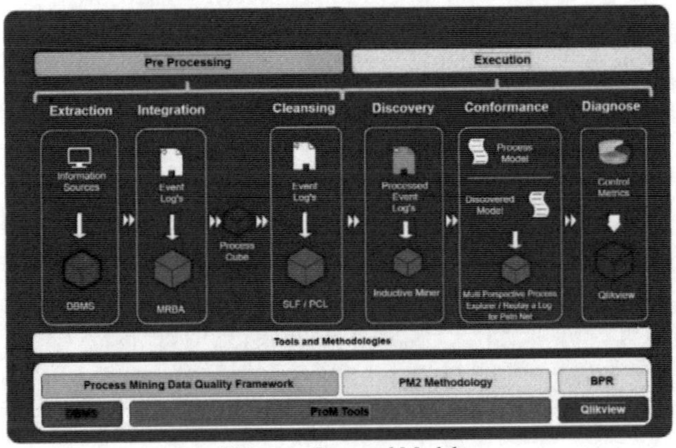

Figure 1. Proposed Model

IV. RESULTS

The developed model is validated in a logistics process, particularly the management of purchase orders of a Peruvian company in the retail sector. The evaluation of the model allows to measure its performance and behavior through the previously explained phases.

A. *Extraction Phase*

For the extraction of the event data, the master tables were identified in the system database used by the organization, along with the help of the database administrator; the information from the tables was then interrelated through a query in SQL language to extract the event records. The extracted information from the system decanted in the generation of three Event Logs that contemplate the information of the management of purchase orders, generation of the invoice and the inventory receipts.

Table I shows the structural characteristics of the extracted Event Logs:

TABLE I STRUCTURAL CHARACTERISTICS OF EVENT LOGS

Structural Characteristics of Event Logs			
Metric	***EvLog1***	***EvLog2***	***EvLog3***
# Events	26515	4367	12303
# Instances	4669	2414	3795
# Activities	8	5	5
# Resources	42	37	40

B. *Integration Phase*

In this phase, the three previously extracted Event Logs are unified into a single Event Log with the complete process information (end-to-end approach). The procedure carried out through the application of ProM Tools plugin is described below:

1) Analysis of Identifiers: In this step it is analyzed that the Event Logs share the instance identifier field (CaseID), so that the activities based on this field can be integrated. If you do not have such a shared common field, CaseIDs must be transformed in such a way that they are related to the other Event logs to be integrated. For the present case of application, the organization manages its processes through an RMS information system divided into modules, so this phase manages the same CaseID.

2) Running the plugin: To unify the Event Logs, the "Merge two Event Logs using a rule based algorithm" plugin is used in ProM Tools [10]. The results of the integration phase are shown in Table II:

TABLE II. BASIC STRUCTURAL CHARACTERISTICS OF THE INTEGRATED EVENT LOG

Basic structural characteristics of the Integrated Event Log	
Metric	***Integrated Event Log***
# Events	43185
# Instances	4669
# Activities	18
# Resources	71

If the total number of events and activities is the sum of all the events logs, it indicates that the process was successful since this means that all the executed events are included, on the other hand for the instances the maximum value observed in the events logs should be obtained, otherwise this would mean that there are executions of the process that are not being considered because a CaseID represents an execution of the process.

C. *Application of the Process Cube*

It is important to analyze the basic process information in the unified Event Log, in order to help the user define which will be the points relevant to the process for review. For this purpose, the Process Cube will allow us to analyze the Event Log of the retail company based on the following perspectives shown on Figure 2. It is important to note that the dimensions were defined based on the information available to extract. However, it is possible to include as many dimensions as considered necessary according to the user's need for analysis and they are, in that sense, not mandatory and only allow to enrich the analysis. The Process Cube application was implemented in Qlikview, the results of structural metrics can be seen in Table III:

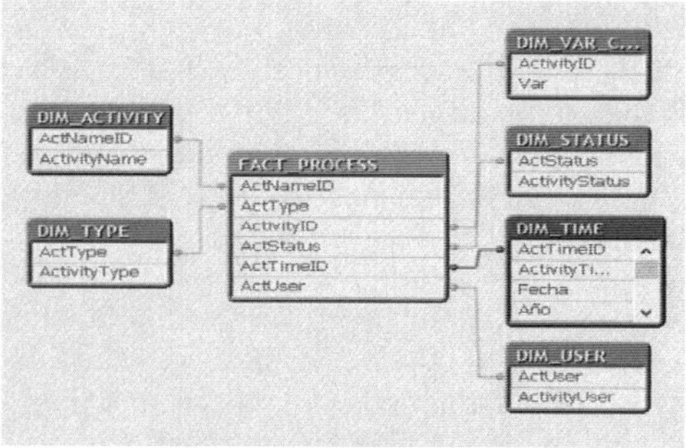

Figure 2. Process Cube Model

TABLE III. RESULT OF THE STRUCTURAL METRICS OF THE INTEGRATED EVENT LOG

Result of the structural metrics of the integrated Event Log	
Metric	***Result***
ATL	9.25
ATS	9.07
ALT	0.11
DN	0.98
THR	0.66

The results of the structural metrics, specifically density (DN) and trace heterogeneity ratio (THR), indicate that this is a process with a low level of loops, i. e. the activities for a process execution are not repeated. However, if we analyze the THR, we can see that it is traced from a process of high variability.

D. Cleansing Phase

In order for the results of the Discovery and Conformance phases to generate reliable results, filtering tasks need to be performed. For filtering tasks, the SLF (Filter Log on Simple Heuristics) and PCL (Filter log using Prefix-Closed Language) plugins are applied in ProM Tools. The first plugin is used for filtering incomplete traces. The second one seeks to eliminate the infrequent behavior in the process, removing traces of little frequency from the log. In addition, when performing the filtering task taking into account the activity PO CREATION as initial and PO MODIFICATION (purchase order closing) as final, one can get a new event log with the characteristics as reported in Table IV.

TABLE IV. STRUCTURAL CHARACTERISTICS OF FILTERED EVENT LOG

Structural characteristics of filtered Event Log	
Metric	***Filtered Event Log***
# Events	9565
# Instances	1047
# Activities	12
# Resources	58

To measure the effectiveness of this phase, the precision metric was evaluated before and after applying the filtering tasks with the "Multi-Perspective Process Explorer" plugin wich analyses how many events can be replayed correctly on the generated model given a dataset. The results can be observed in Table V:

TABLE V. PRECISION RESULTS IN THE CLEANING PHASE

Precision results in the cleaning phase			
Metric	***Pre***	***Post***	***Δ P.P***
Precision	83.50 %	97.40 %	13.9
# Correct Events	85.00 %	97.30 %	12.38
# Incorrect Events	15.00 %	2.70 %	12.38
# Missing Events	8.9 %	1.20 %	-7.76

The results were positive, achieving 97.40% accuracy.

E. Discovery Phase

In order to generate the model, the Inductive Miner method is used. It is important to configure the process start and end activities in advance. By default, the method will analyze the possible activities. However, it also gives the possibility to perform the selection manually.

F. Conformance Phase

In the Conformance phase, we will test the model discovered in the previous phase with the model currently implemented in the company. The plugin used for this task is the "Multi Perspective Process Explorer", which indicates the degree of deviation of the process activities.

- Metric #1: Percent Transition Fitness: Percent of instances that are reproducible in a Petri net [17].

Measurement Method: Multi Perspective Process Explorer plugin was used to calculate this metric, which uses the data attributes associated with events to analyze processes from multiple perspectives [18]. In this case, the conformity perspective will be used, which will show us the percentage of instances of the event log that are reproducible in the Petri net of the company process model based on the number of reproducible events, non-reproducible events and the number of missing events.

- Metric #2: Inconsistency Ratio Activity frequency with respect to the total instances of initial activity.

Mesaurement Method: For the calculation of this metric, the Log Inspector was used with its Log Summary utility, which shows the activity, the number of instances that count each one and their respective relative frequency. The Explore Event Log utility was also used to find the sequence pattern and initial process activity. Additionally, a calculation was made to find the metric. This calculation is composed of the following formula:

$$IR = \frac{AIN}{NIA} \times 100 \qquad (1)$$

In (1) AIN is the activity instance number, NIA is the number of initial activity and IR is the Inconsistency Ratio metric.

- Metric #3: Arrival rate per hour: Number of case arrivals into the process per time unit [17].

Mesaurement Method: To calculate this metric, the Replay a Log for Petri Net plugin was used, which uses a

Petri Net and an event log to create advanced alignments between each trace in the registry and the network [13]. It is possible to obtain from the execution of this plugin the waiting time, the sojourn time and the frequency occurrence by activity. Based on these values, the average duration of the process is computed. The arrival rate per hour is then computed as the number of instances divided by the sojourn time.

- Metric #4: Percentage of execution duration per activity: Shows the percentage of the execution duration of each activity with respect to the total duration of the process.

Mesaurement Method: The Replay a Log for Petri Net plugin was also used to calculate this metric, making use of the Waiting time, sourjourn time and frequency of occurrence by activity variables, calculating the total duration time of the process, and the Percentage of execution duration by activity with respect to the total execution time.

- Metric #5: Resource Saturation: It will calculate the number of instances executing a resource per hour.

Mesaurement Method: For the calculation of this metric, the Inductive Visual Miner plugin was used, which given an event log, the Inductive Visual Miner automatically discovers a process model, compares this model with the event log and displays several improvements such as performance measures, queue lengths [20]. Obtaining from this execution the variables instance frequency and the sourjourn time in hours.

- Metric #6: Percentage of execution duration per resource: It shows us the percentage of time it takes a resource to execute its activities with respect to the total time of the process.

Mesaurement Method: The Inductive Visual Miner plugin was also used to calculate this metric, obtaining from its execution the variable sourjourn time in hours. It is on the basis of this variable that the total duration time is calculated, and then we proceed to calculate the percentage of duration per resource using the formula:

$$PED = \frac{DPR}{TD} \times 100 \qquad (2)$$

In (2) DPR is the execution duration per resource, TD is the total execution duration and PED is the percentage of execution duration per resource metric.

G. Diagnose Phase

As a result of the application of the model, the following control metrics and their respective evaluation of results could be obtained:

- Metric #1: Transition Fitness

The low level of transition fitness is a sign of a deviation in the process execution flow. Looking at the result obtained, it can be seen that the activities: 1ST BOX OF PO AND CREATION OF THE INVOICE / LAST BOX OF PO present deviations in their execution. Performing a more in-depth analysis it could be concluded that currently, the main cause of disagreement of the process is given in activity 1ST BOX of OC with the registration of events given is due to the fact that, as can be seen in the image, it is usual to start receiving products without having completed the flow of approvals.

- Metric #2: Inconsistencies with respect to the total instances of the initial activity:

The initial activity of the process is CREATION OF PO, which has a total of 1047 instances and refers to 1047 orders created in the analyzed process, which is expected to generate the same invoice amount in this process, but as can be observed this activity only has a frequency of 14.42% with respect to the initial activity, as well as income creation activity that presents a frequency of 53.20%.

- Metric #3: Arrival rate per hour:

The average number of instances per hour that the process executes is 2.50 and when comparing this figure with that of each activity, it can be observed that there are 4 activities below this ratio. This would be a clear indication that there is a possibility of bottlenecks in these activities.

- Metric #4: Percentage of execution duration per activity:

Since the average percentage of total execution duration is 9.09%, when comparing this with the percentage of each activity, it can be observed that there are four activities below this ratio. This would be a clear indication that there is a possibility of bottlenecks in these activities since they have a higher percentage of duration than the calculated average.

- Metric #5: Resource Saturation:

By having on average 6.25 executions per hour in the process, we compare this figure with the result of the metric for each resource, evidencing that the Head of category, Head of warehouse, GG. DIV. RETAIL and the Commercial P. Analyst perform fewer activities per hour than the average. This is an indication that these resources are saturated due to the high demand for execution of the instances they execute.

- Metric #6: Percentage of execution duration per resource:

Since the average percentage of total execution duration is 14%, when comparing this figure with the percentage of each resource, it can be seen that there are 2 resources below this ratio. This would be a clear indication that there is the possibility that these resources generate a bottleneck in the process and complemented by metric 5, we can deduce that in the case of the category head this delay is due to the overload presented by the resource.

V. CONCLUSIONS

This article presents a model that allows the evaluation of business process performance and behavior through a set of control metrics using Process Mining techniques. It was developed to facilitate the evaluation of metrics that are useful for the analysis and detection of bottlenecks, deviations and resources involved in the analyzed process. The proposal was validated in a company in the retail sector where the event log of the purchasing management process was analyzed giving as a result of the application of the model and the evaluation of the proposed metrics, the identification of anomalies. The model was capable of assuring the quality of the analysis in the pre-processing phase, at the same time the application of the Process Mining methods for discovery, diagnose and conformance analysis were derived in control metrics through the application of the algorithms and plugins implemented in the open source tool ProM Tools and the use of Qlikview for the presentation of results and application of the Process Cube.

VI. REFERENCES

[1] Y. Wang, F. Caron, J. Vanthienen, L. Huang, and Y. Guo. "Acquiring logistics process intelligence: Methodology and an application for a Chinese bulk port", Expert Systems with Applications, vol. 41, pp. 195–209. 2014

[2] W. van der Aalst. "Process Mining: Overview and Opportunities". ACM Trans. Manage. Inf. Syst.,vol. 3, pp. 7:1--7:17, 2012.

[3] W. M. P. van der Aalst, J. L. Zhao, and H. J. Wang. "Business Process Intelligence: Connecting Data and Processes", ACM Transactions on Management Information Systems, vol. 5, pp. 1–7, 2015.

[4] A. Bolt, M. de Leoni, W. M. P. van der Aalst, and P. Gorissen. "Business Process Reporting Using Process Mining, Analytic Workflows and Process Cubes: A Case Study in Education", Data-Driven Process Discovery and Analysis: 5th IFIP WG 2.6 International Symposium, vol. 244, pp. 28–53, 2017.

[5] M. Castellanos, A. K. Alves de Medeiros, J. Mendling, B. Weber, and A. J. M. M. Weijters, "Business Process Intelligence". Handbook of Research on Business Process Modeling, pp. 456–480, 2009.

[6] W. M. P. van der Aalst. "Process Cubes: Slicing, Dicing, Rolling Up and Drilling Down Event Data for Process Mining". Asia Pacific Business Process Management: First Asia Pacific Conference, Lecture Notes in Business Information Processing, vol 159, pp. 1–22, 2013.

[7] J. T. S. Ribeiro, and A. J. M. M. Weijters. "Event Cube: Another Perspective on Business Processes", On the Move to Meaningful Internet Systems: OTM 2011, Lecture Notes in Computer Science, vol 7044 ,pp. 274–283, 2011.

[8] A. Bolt, and W. M. P. van der Aalst, "Multidimensional Process Mining Using Process Cubes", Enterprise, Business-Process and Information Systems Modeling: 16th International Conference, pp. 102–116, 2015.

[9] M. Cho, M. Song, M. Comuzzi, and S. Yoo. "Evaluating the effect of best practices for business process redesign: An evidence-based approach based on process mining techniques", Decision Support Systems, vol. 104 , pp. 92-103, 2017.

[10] J. Claes, and G. Poels. "Merging event logs for process mining: A rule based merging method and rule suggestion algorithm", Expert Systems with Applications, vol. 41, pp. 7291–7306, 2014.

[11] M. O. Kherbouche, N. Laga, and P. A. Masse. "Towards a better assessment of event logs quality". 2016 IEEE Symposium Series on Computational Intelligence, pp. 1-6, 2016.

[12] G. Janssenswillen, N. Donders, T. Jouck, and B. Depaire. "A comparative study of existing quality measures for process discovery". Information Systems, vol. 71, pp. 1–15, 2017.

[13] J. Wang, R. K. Wong, J. Ding, Q. Guo, and L. Wen. "Efficient Selection of Process Mining Algorithms". IEEE Trans. Serv. Comput., vol. 6, pp. 484–496, 2013.

[14] A. Adriansyah, J. Munoz-Gama, J. Carmona, B. F. van Dongen, and W. M. P. van der Aalst. "Measuring precision of modeled behavior". Information Systems and e-Business Management. vol. 13, pp. 37-67, 2015.

[15] R. Conforti, M. La Rosa, and A. H. M. ter Hofstede. "Filtering Out Infrequent Behavior from Business Process Event Logs". IEEE Transactions on Knowledge and Data Engineering, vol. 29, pp. 300–314, 2017.

[16] M. L. van Eck , X. Lu, , S. J. J. Leemans, and W. M. P. van der Aalst. "PM 2 : A Process Mining Project Methodology", Advanced Information Systems Engineering, Lecture Notes in Computer Science, vol 9097, pp. 297–313, 2015.

[17] P. T. Hornix. "Performance analysis of business processes through process mining". Master's Thesis, Eindhoven University of Technology, 2007.

[18] F. Mannhardt, M. de Leoni, and H. A. Reijers. "The Multi-perspective Process Explorer". CEUR Workshop Proceedings, vol. 1418, pp. 130-134, 2015.

[19] F. Bezerra, J. Wainer, and W. M. P. van der Aalst. "Anomaly Detection Using Process Mining". Lecture Notes in Business Information Processing, vol. 29, pp. 149-161, 2009.

[20] S. J. J. Leemans, D. Fahland, and W. M. P. Van Der Aalst, "Process and deviation exploration with inductive visual miner," CEUR Workshop Proceedings, vol. 1295, pp. 46–50, 2014.

Evaluation of Experimental Station Potentials in a Shared Facility: Focus on the Combined Use of Stations

Keiichi Shinbe

Department of Social Intelligence and Informatics
Graduate School of Information Systems
The University of Electro-Communications/JASRI
Tokyo/Hyogo, Japan
Email: shinbe@spring8.or.jp

Kosuke Shinoda

Department of Social Intelligence and Informatics
Graduate School of Information Systems
The University of Electro-Communications
Tokyo, Japan
Email: kosuke.shinoda@uec.ac.jp

Hirohiko Suwa

Ubiquitous Computing Systems Laboratory
Graduate School of Information Science
NAIST
Nara, Japan
Email: h-suwa@is.naist.jp

Satoshi Kurihara

Department of Social Intelligence and Informatics
Graduate School of Information Systems
The University of Electro-Communications
Tokyo, Japan
Email: skurihara@uec.ac.jp

***Abstract*—The large synchrotron radiation facility SPring-8 in Japan is a shared research facility opened to domestic and foreign researchers of industry, government, and academia. It is used for research and development in a wide range of fields. This facility must be efficiently operated and must have substantial research outcomes because national grants are used to fund its operation. This paper creates a visual of how the experimental stations in the facility were used over time on the basis of the SPring-8 publication database. It aims to clarify which experimental stations are used in combination to create research outcomes. A network analysis showed that each experimental station can be classified into groups: a group with many research outcomes, a mediating group that supports research by other experimental stations, and a group specialized for combined use with specific experimental stations. It also became clear that there is a difference in the publication productivity of each group.**

Keywords–Shared Research Facility; Complex Network; Cluster Analysis; Visualization; SPring-8.

I. Introduction

Shared research facilities in Japan are financed by the national treasury. For this reason, such facilities must maximize their research outcomes and contribute to academic progress and social and economic development. Optimizing facility services with a limited budget and staff is also important. To improve facilities and their proposal systems, it is necessary to determine whether experiments conducted have had corresponding research results. In most cases, for shared research facilities that have only recently started operation, those in charge of the facility prioritize tracking usage trends such as the operation time of the facility and the number of users. The evaluation of research outcomes by facility-use is often conducted after the facility has been in operation for several years. Also, in many cases, those in charge of the facility evaluate mainly on quantitative values such as the number of published papers or citations. Therefore, there is not much analysis of research outcomes derived from the combined use of experimental stations in facilities.

This research aims to present a new perspective by evaluating experimental stations in addition to conventional quantitative indicators. We analyzed the database in which the results of research conducted at SPring-8 [1] are registered. SPring-8 is a shared research facility open to domestic and foreign researchers in the fields of industry, government, and academia.

This paper ' s main contributions are as follows: first, we closely examine how the interactions between experimental stations changed over time, and extracted some characteristic network structures; second, we visualize the publication productivity of each experimental station and classify them into several groups; third, we present the potential for creating research outcomes as a general indicator for each experimental station whose position cannot be evaluated by its number of associated publications alone.

In Section 2, we give an overview of SPring-8 and its publication database. We then discuss related work in Section 3. In Section 4, we explain how we visualized the potential for creating research outcomes. In Section 5, we focus on unique structures in the complex network of beamline interactions and classify the beamlines into four groups on the basis of publication productivity. By the analysis results, we discuss future subjects for research in Section 6.

II. Overview of SPring-8

SPring-8 is a large synchrotron radiation facility constructed in the west of Japan that started operation in October 1997. More than 15,000 researchers come to SPring-8 annually, and more than 2,000 experiments in a wide range of fields, such as material science, earth science, life science, environmental science, and industry (in other words, research proposals) are conducted every year.

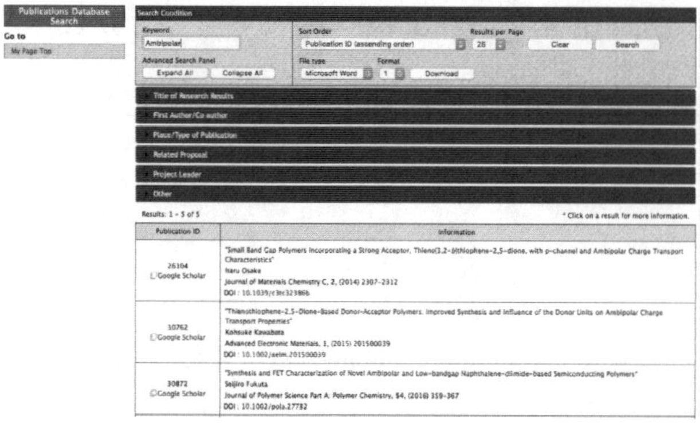

Figure 1. SPring-8 Publication Database.

This facility has multiple experimental stations with different characteristics; these experimental stations are called "beamlines" [2]. In a beamline, high-intensity light (radiation light) is spectroscopically divided (taken out into the light of a specific wavelength), and a measurement sample is irradiated with it. Researchers who want to use this facility prepare an application form describing which experimental station they wish to use, for what purpose. They need to submit their proposal on the user portal website "SPring-8 User Information" [3] before the deadline that is twice a year. The main items of the application form are shown below.

- Experimental Details
- Research Area
- Research Method
- Project Team Members
- Samples
- Requested Experiment Time
- Preferred Beamline

After the deadline, proposals are reviewed from the perspectives of scientific validity, technical feasibility, and experiment safety. After these assessments, the proposal review committee makes a final decision on whether or not to approve each proposal.

Beamlines are classified into three types depending on the researching party by whom they are intended to be used. In this research, we analyze the potential for creating research outcomes of 26 public beamlines that were built for researchers to use generally and 18 contract beamlines that were constructed by research proposers (consisting of domestic and foreign industries, academia, and government) for their own continuous use.

A beamtime fee corresponding to usage time is charged after each experiment. However, if researchers publish their research results in a refereed journal article, etc., within three years of the experiment and register information such as the article title in the SPring-8 publication database, the beamtime fee is waived.

The research result information of SPring-8 is open as a database on the User Information portal [4], and it is possible to search by specifying article title, author name, journal title, proposal term, and other such terms (Figure 1).

Although it is not possible to directly access the article content from each search result, if the article ' s digital object identifier (DOI) has been registered, users can navigate to the website of the corresponding publisher manually.

III. Related Work

As a precedent network analysis, Yamashita et al. predicted trends in the information of academic fields using information from applications for Grants-in-Aid for Scientific Research [5]. Also, Érdi et al. analyzed a temporal change in the structure of a cluster based on the citation information of US patents [6]. Cho and Shih identified core and emerging technologies in Taiwan from a patent-citation network in order to pursue competitive advantages [7]. In addition, studies that trace the transition of research trends and predict research domains expected to develop in the future by analyzing the network of cited works and references have been conducted in various research fields [8]–[11].

National Institute of Science and Technology Policy in Japan (NISTEP) extracts high-attention research areas on the basis of citations in other articles and depicts the results in a "Science Map" [12]. With this map, one can understand the changes over time in research trends around the world and domestically with a visual similar to a heat map. One can also visually compare the competitive research areas of each research institution. However, this is not suitable for analyzing the potential for creating research outcomes from experimental stations in a single facility because this map comprehensively shows competitive domains of an entire research institution.

Major synchrotron radiation facilities in the world publish a booklet summarizing research highlights every year [13]–[15]. From this information, it is possible to roughly understand the latest trends and outcomes in each research domain at each synchrotron radiation facility. However, there are few studies that analyze from multiple perspectives how experimental stations in a shared facility are used in combination and whether combined use creates research outcomes.

In this research, on the basis of the SPring-8 publication database, we conduct network analysis to clarify the mutual relationship between beamlines that contributed to research outcomes. In short, we arrange each beamline as a node in a network diagram and connect the nodes if there is combined use of the beamlines. This connection is depicted as an edge. By analyzing the temporal changes in this beamline network, we can evaluate each beamline not only by its number of associated publications but also by the presence of nodes that contribute to outcomes. Further, in order to visualize the differences in trends between public and contract beamlines, the node shape of the two beamline types is distinguished.

IV. Methodology of Visualization

Here, we present the procedure for visualizing the potential for creating research outcomes of each beamline using a network analysis of the data accumulated in the SPring-8 publication database. We analyzed the research results (9,126 records) and related proposals (21,277 records) published between January 1, 2006 and September 30, 2017 and registered in the database by 13 October 2017. Then, we prepared separate data for every three years from 2006 in addition to the overall data and analyzed the overall trend and the changes over time. All data used in this analysis are open information that can be found in the SPring-8 publication database.

A. Structure of SPring-8 Publication Database

The SPring-8 publication database consists mainly of the following items.

- Publication Title
- Type of Publication
- Place of Publication
- Author Information (First Author, Coauthor, Corresponding Author)
- Related Proposal Information

Besides publications in refereed journals, activities such as oral presentations, poster sessions, and invited talks can also be registered in the publication database. However, the beamtime fee is only waived when a publication is registered in the categories of "refereed journals, dissertation, refereed proceedings," "SPring-8 research report," or "corporate technical journal" [16]. In this research, we analyze the registration data of publications that satisfy these criteria for approval as a "dissemination of research results."

In the publication registration form, in addition to the publication title, there is a column for registering related proposal information corresponding to past research results, and multiple items of related proposal information can be registered for each research result. When doing so, it is necessary to enter the proposal number that uniquely identifies the research proposal to be used. From this number, it is possible to identify the beamline used in the experiment.

B. Calculation of Nodes and Edges

If a research result (article) is derived from multiple proposals, it is considered that a single beamline more than twice or different beamlines were used. In other words, by depicting a network with edge co-occurrence of beamlines used in research outcomes, the nature of each beamlines' contribution to research outcomes can be represented visually.

We calculated values of nodes and edges according to the following procedure (Figure 2).

1) Record beamline(s) from related proposals for each registered publication.
2) Enumerate combination(s) of beamlines included in the same registered publication.
3) Count total number of registered publications for each beamline. This value corresponds to node size.
4) Count total number of registered publications for each beamline-pair combination. This value corresponds to edge width.

C. Visualization of Combined Use with Beamlines

An undirected graph was created using the beamlines of related proposals as nodes and the combination of beamlines as edges. The graph-drawing algorithm used a spring model. We represented the number of publications registered for each beamline with the size of the node and the number of publications derived from the combined use of multiple beamlines with the width of the edge. Public beamlines were plotted as circles while contract beamlines were plotted as squares; this way, the difference in the interaction depending on the beamline type could be identified.

A weak connection between the nodes indicates that the frequency of combined use of the beamlines is low. Because

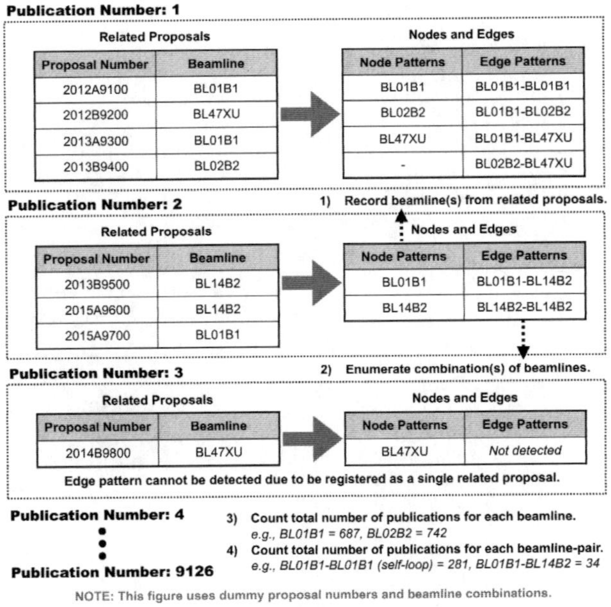

Figure 2. How to Count Nodes and Edges.

these networks have a low impact on research outcomes, we excluded edges with less than five publications over the entire period. However, in the network in which the aggregation period is divided into three years, the edges that are not included in the overall period are drawn on the network even if the number of registered publications in the beamline-pair is less than five.

D. Visualization of Publication Productivity

The proportion of articles associated with each beamline to the total number of registered publications is plotted on the x-axis. The ratio of the edge of each node (degree) to the maximum edge number, i.e. the edge co-occurrence rates of the beamline, is plotted on the y-axis. We define the coordinates of each beamline in this graph as publication productivity.

V. RESULTS AND DISCUSSION

Figure 3 shows the beamline network that is based on the related proposals of registered publications issued between 2006 and the end of September 2017.

From the total number of edges and registered publications, it can be seen that the mutual relationship between beamlines is stronger for public beamlines than for contract beamlines. Many public beamlines occupy the central part of the network while contract beamlines are satellites in the peripheral part. Further, some contract beamlines were isolated from the network of beamline connections, and most of the approved proposals were conducted with a single beamline. Figure 3 also shows that beamlines with little combined use with other beamlines have a relatively low number of publications. As for beamlines with a large number of publications, nodes with high degrees such as BL01B1 and BL02B2 are in the center of the network, while structures that use a small number of beamlines in combination intensively like BL38B1, BL41XU and BL44XU are also seen. In this way, the existence of a clique is recognized between beamlines that have relatively

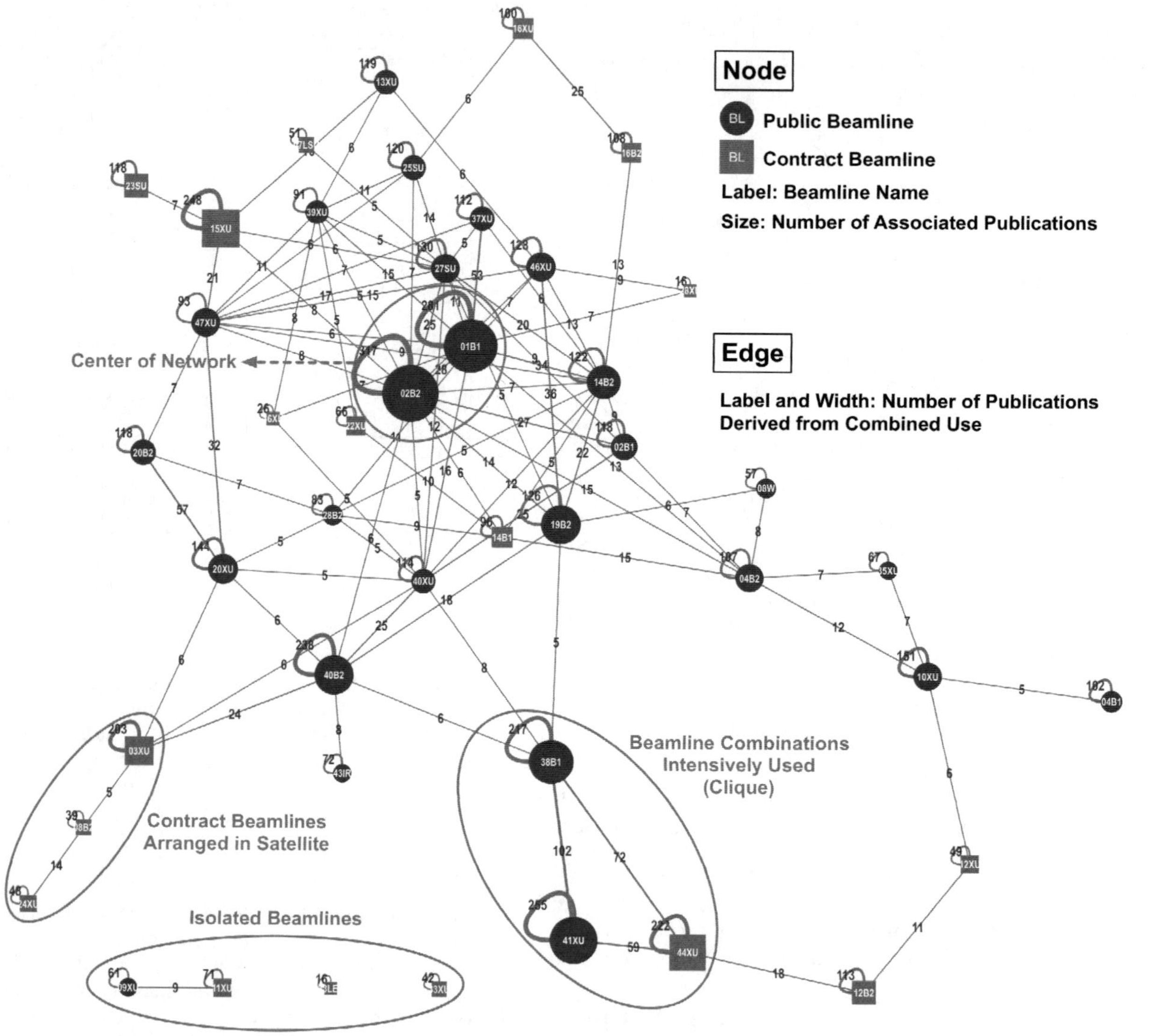

Figure 3. Beamline Network Based on Related Proposals of Registered Publications (Publication Year: 2006-2017).

low degrees but a large number of publications. In this case, "clique" means that the three nodes are connected to each other by edge. The clique in the beamline network seems to indicate compatibility of experimental equipment to some extent. These results suggest that when a specific beamline is crowded with proposals and the requirements of the measurement object are met, a change to another beamline may be possible. Therefore, if it is anticipated that a beamline in a clique has a high ability to produce outcomes and the demand in the future is expected to be strong, it will be possible to consider adding additional beamlines of the same specifications. The cliques in which the number of registered publications between each node by beamline-pair is 12 or more are listed in Table I.

TABLE I. TYPICAL CLIQUES IN BEAMLINE NETWORK

No.	*Beamline 1*	*Beamline 2*	*Beamline 3*	*Total Publication Count*[*1]
1	BL38B1	BL41XU	BL44XU	197
2	BL14B2	BL19B2	BL46XU	71
3	BL01B1	BL14B2	BL40XU	60
4	BL01B1	BL02B2	BL04B2	54
5	BL14B2	BL27SU	BL40XU	26

[*1] Calculated the unique number of publications including at least two beamlines related to each clique.

Additionally, we divided the aggregation period into every three years from 2006 on the basis of publication year in order to compare how beamline combinations changed over time. Table II shows the cluster coefficients by period, average degree, number of nodes, and number of edges (excluding self-loops). We computed these values by using the complex network visualization software Cytoscape [17] and built-in plugin NetworkAnalyzer [18].

From these indicators, the network showing the mutual relationship between beamlines is sparse as a whole from

TABLE II. CLUSTER COEFFICIENT, AVERAGE DEGREE, NODE AND EDGE COUNT FOR EACH PERIOD

Periods	*Cluster Coefficient*	*Average Degree*	*Node Count*	*Edge Count*[*1]
2006-2008	0.068	2.02	39	20
2009-2011	0.249	4.00	42	65
2012-2014	0.293	5.36	44	96
2015-2017[*2]	0.303	5.16	44	92
Entire Period	0.299	5.45	44	98

[*1] Self-loop edges were excluded from the Edge Count.
[*2] Based on calculated values until September 2017.

2006 to 2008, and there was only one clique corresponding to the No. 1 combination of Table I. However, in the 2009 to 2011 period, the network structure grew large, combined use of beamlines increased considerably, and cliques No. 2 and 4 appeared. The number of clusters and edges increased in 2012 to 2014, and the existence of all the cliques in Table I was visible at this point. However, in the last three years, the network structure saturated and no significant change was observed as an indicator. This is likely because the number of approved proposals, operation time of the facility, and beamlines in operation (nodes) have not changed significantly in recent years.

The proportion of the number of registered publications for each beamline to the total number of publications (9,126) is plotted on the x-axis. The percentage of combined use among other beamlines, i.e. the degree of each node divided by the maximum number of edges (43) in the network, is placed on the y-axis. Each point is drawn as a scatter diagram (Figure 4).

The graph of publication productivity shows that beamlines can mainly be classified into the following four groups.

- High-Performance Group
- Mediating Group
- Specialized Group
- Low-Performance Group

The triangular dotted line indicates beamlines for specialized applications. Some such beamlines include industrial-use beamlines and protein crystallography beamlines whose main application is a routine measurement of protein structure analysis.

The high-performance group is a beamline group with a large number of registered publications and nodes with high degrees. As can be seen from Figure 3, it is in the center of the network and is active in combined use with other beamlines, but there are also a large number of publications that come from multiple uses of the same beamline. In beamlines included in this group, a general-purpose measurement method called X-ray absorption fine structure (XAFS) is available. Its use for general purposes in a wide range of research fields is likely a factor leading to the group's high performance.

The mediating group has relatively few registered publications, but has active combined use with other beamlines, which suggests that this group supports the research outcomes of other beamlines. In this group, nodes have relatively high degrees, and it is difficult to identify cliques. In other words, the combined use of three or more beamlines is not common. Therefore, it is presumed that beamlines in this group are also utilized for preliminary experimental measurements in various research fields.

Beamlines included in the specialized group are highly capable of creating research outcomes, but they are characterized by limited combining with other beamlines. In other words, it is a group that easily creates cliques, such as the No. 1 beamline group in Table I. This beamline group is contained in a triangle dotted line indicating that it has a specific application type, and contains most of the beamlines capable of the routine measurement called protein crystal structure analysis. It is thought that the connection with beamlines used in other research methods and fields is sparse for this reason.

The low-performance group has few publications, and its association with other beamlines is weak. The fact that many contract beamlines are in this group is considered to be one reason that the publication productivity of contract beamlines is relatively lower than that of public beamlines. Contract beamlines were initially built by research proposers on the premise that they would be used for specific research, so this group is not generally considered for a wide range of use by researchers other than stakeholders. However, the installation space for beamlines is limited, and it is essential to continually create research outcomes commensurate with the beamtime because government grants are being used in the construction and operation of the entire facility. Because there are beamlines specialized for research in specific areas with few contact points with other fields, they should not be evaluated only by their associated number of registered publications. But, the potential for creating research outcomes in this group would be improved by promoting interaction with other beamlines.

VI. CONCLUSION

In this research, on the basis of data registered in the SPring-8 publication database, we visualized the correlations between beamlines and the potential for creating research outcomes from each beamline. As a result, the edges in the network increased with time, and we found that new outcomes were created as a result of using various beamlines in combination. We also found that the beamline network includes some clusters such as a group with a large number of publications, a group that indirectly supports the outcomes of other beamlines, and a group that forms a clique structure with strong connections between specific beamlines. It is essential to consider measures for improving the performance of beamlines (nodes) with low degrees and few registered publications. Our research will be helpful as one method for deciding which beamlines to renew when planning a SPring-8 upgrade program.

However, in this research, we do not mention the differences in beamtime required for creating publishing results for each research area and the quality of the research outcomes. Therefore, to deepen the evaluation of individual beamlines, it will be necessary to consider the impact that research outcomes conducted using each beamline has had on academia and society and the adaptability of the beamlines to high-growth-potential fields in the future. We aim to further this analysis by including external indicators such as the ranking of academic journals (e.g., impact factor) and the number of cited articles for each registered publication. We also intend to analyze the similarities between registered publications using the metadata of the publication database and adding the originality of publications as a perspective to consider when evaluating the beamlines.

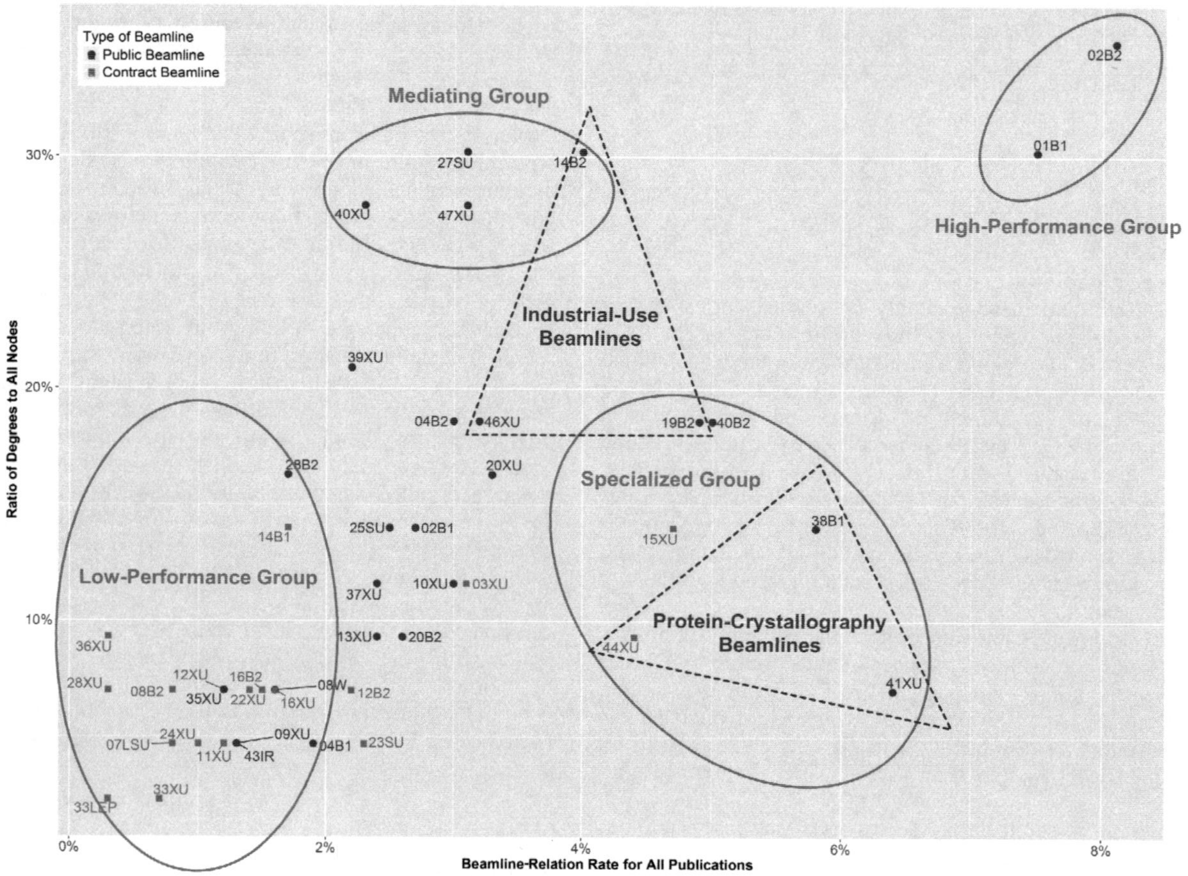

Figure 4. Relation Rate of Beamlines for All Registered Publications and Ratio of Degrees to All Nodes (Publication Year: 2006-2017).

REFERENCES

[1] "SPring-8," 2018, URL: http://www.spring8.or.jp/en/ [retrieved: February, 2018].

[2] "Beamlines," 2018, URL: http://www.spring8.or.jp/en/about_us/whats_sp8/facilities/bl/ [retrieved: February, 2018].

[3] "SPring-8 User Information," 2018, URL: https://user.spring8.or.jp/?lang=en [retrieved: February, 2018].

[4] "SPring-8/SACLA Publication Database," 2018, URL: https://user.spring8.or.jp/uisearch/publication2/en [retrieved: February, 2018].

[5] N. Yamashita, M. Numao, and R. Ichise, "Predicting Research Trends Identified by Research Histories via Breakthrough Researches," IEICE Transactions on Information and Systems, vol. E98-D, 2015, pp. 355–362.

[6] P. Érdi et al., "Prediction of emerging technologies based on analysis of the US patent citation network," Scientometrics, vol. 95, 2013, pp. 225–242.

[7] T.-S. Cho and H.-Y. Shih, "Patent citation network analysis of core and emerging technologies in Taiwan: 1997-2008," Scientometrics, vol. 89, 2011, pp. 795–811.

[8] C. Calero-Medina and E. C. Noyons, "Combining mapping and citation network analysis for a better understanding of the scientific development: The case of the absorptive capacity field," Journal of Informetrics, vol. 2, 2008, pp. 272–279.

[9] N. Shibata, Y. Kajikawa, Y. Takeda, and K. Matsushima, "Detecting emerging research fronts based on topological measures in citation networks of scientific publications," Technovation, vol. 28, 2008, pp. 758–775.

[10] S. Iwami, J. Mori, I. Sakata, and Y. Kajikawa, "Detection method of emerging leading papers using time transition," Scientometrics, vol. 101, 2014, pp. 1515–1533.

[11] T. Prabhakaran, H. H. Lathabai, and M. Changat, "Detection of paradigm shifts and emerging fields using scientific network: A case study of Information Technology for Engineering," Technological Forecasting and Social Change, vol. 91, 2015, pp. 124–145.

[12] A. Saka and M. Igami, Eds., Science Map 2010 and Science Map 2012 -Study on Hot Research Areas (2005-2010 and 2007-2011) by bibliometric method-. National Institute of Science and Technology Policy, Jul. 2014.

[13] N. Yagi, Ed., SPring-8/SACLA Research Frontiers 2016. Japan Synchrotron Radiation Research Institute (JASRI), Aug. 2017, ISSN: 1349-0087.

[14] G. Admans, Ed., ESRF Highlights 2016. European Synchrotron Radiation Facility (ESRF), Feb. 2017.

[15] APS Science 2016. Argonne National Laboratory (APS), May 2017, ISSN: 1931-5007.

[16] "After Experiment: Publications," 2018, URL: https://user.spring8.or.jp/?p=748&lang=en [retrieved: February, 2018].

[17] "Cytoscape: An Open Source Platform for Complex Network Analysis and Visualization," 2018, URL: http://www.cytoscape.org [retrieved: February, 2018].

[18] "Cytoscape App Store - NetworkAnalyzer," 2017, URL: http://apps.cytoscape.org/apps/networkanalyzer [retrieved: February, 2018].

The Effects of Social Capital on Individual Adaptation to New ICT

Kee-Young Kwahk
College of Business Administration / Graduate School of Business IT
Kookmin University
Seoul, South Korea
e-mail: kykwahk@kookmin.ac.kr

Abstract—**This study examines how the social capital derived from social networks influences individual adaptation to a new information and communication technology system and its related performance levels. On the basis of social capital theory, we establish a research model that combines social network variables with psychometric ones. The proposed research model was empirically tested using the Partial Least Squares method. The results reveal that individuals' adaptation mechanisms can be explained in terms of their positions within social networks. We conclude by discussing the implications of the research findings.**

Keywords-social networks; social capital; adaptation; ICT

I. INTRODUCTION

Most of today's organizations have used Information and Communication Technology (ICT) to achieve their competitive advantage as well as to operate daily work practices, which makes the effective use of ICT by organization members a necessary condition for successful business. As a consequence, a primary challenge facing organizations with the intent of introducing a new ICT for the business purposes is how to adapt organization members to the major technological changes that have an impact on their business operations and strategy.

Despite the growing attention to the effective utilization of the ICT system in the workplace, however, there is an accumulation of evidence from the literature indicating that organizations do not utilize newly introduced ICT systems to their full functional potential and a number of new implementations continue to fail [2][4]. We explore the reasons for the underutilization of new ICT by focusing on the two barriers related to individual's coping process for adapting to ICT-induced changes. On one hand, from the technical perspective, today's ICT is complex and raises significant challenges for organization members, particularly by overwhelming them with numerous features and the accompanying learning requirements [5]. Users thus face knowledge barriers to system adaptation even after a formal introduction of the system [3]. On the other hand, from the organizational and social perspective, the introduction of new ICT tends to bring a disruptive workplace change, for example, a new way of order fulfillment process induced by a new ERP (Enterprise Resource Planning) system, which might lead to a sense of anxiety and uncertainty about the future among organization members. Users thus face emotion barriers to system adaptation even though they are knowledgeable about the system. Therefore, understanding the effective use of ICT with a focus on an individual's coping mechanism towards knowledge and emotion barriers will help us in devising ways to manage individual adaptation processes and thereby achieve the enhanced performance.

With the aforementioned motivation and background, this paper has the following research objectives: First, this study develops a research model of system adaptation and how it affects performance and reflects on individual coping mechanisms. Second, this paper introduces key social network constructs into the research model, thereby extending the applicability of social network research into the information systems field. Third, the proposed research model demonstrates a role of social network perspective in explaining system adaptation by combining traditional psychometric constructs with ones from social network domain and empirically validating the model.

The rest of the paper is structured as follows. In Section 2, we present the research model and hypotheses. In Section 3, we describe the research methodology. Section 4 presents the analysis and results. Finally, we conclude the work in Section 5.

II. RESEARCH MODEL AND HYPOTHESES

We developed a research model to explain the coping mechanism towards ICT-induced changes based on the perspectives of social capital theory. We propose the following hypotheses.

H1a. Supportive network position has a positive effect on self-efficacy.
H1b. Supportive network position has a positive effect on absorptive capacity.
H2a. Informational network position has a positive effect on self-efficacy.
H2b. Informational network position has a positive effect on absorptive capacity.
H3. Self-efficacy has a positive effect on absorptive capacity.
H4. Self-efficacy has a positive effect on individual adaptation.
H5. Absorptive capacity has a positive effect on individual adaptation.

H6. Individual adaptation has a positive effect on individual performance.

III. Research Methodology

The questionnaire administered in this study largely consisted of two parts, which investigated social network constructs and traditional psychometric constructs. We collected social network data using a two-step name generator/name interpreter method that elicits and then characterizes respondents' (egos') relationships with others (alters). In this study, a social network is seen as a set of individuals and the relationships between them in which the relationships represent communication or interaction directed towards exchanging task-related information (informational networks) or gaining emotional support (supportive networks). Traditional social network studies have devised various measures to assess the extent to which individuals have such kinds of relationships [6][7]. Based on those studies, we propose that individuals' social network positions are determined by size, closeness, frequency, and density derived from individuals' social networks. The items used to operationalize the psychometric constructs included in this study were adopted and modified primarily from previous studies, with necessary changes for the research context. All question items except for the performance measurement were measured using a seven-point Likert-type scale with anchors ranging from strongly disagree (=1) to strongly agree (=7).

IV. Analysis and Results

The proposed hypotheses were tested using PLS (Partial Least Squares) [1]. We selected PLS for the following reasons. First, PLS simultaneously explains the theoretical relationships between latent variables and indicators. Second, PLS does not assign the same weight to all indicators of a latent variable; it assigns different weights according to the indicators' degrees of contribution to the latent variable [8]. Third, PLS does not impose strong constraints on sample size compared with other structural equation modeling techniques, such as LISREL [1].

According to the two-step analytical procedure, we first conducted confirmatory factor analysis in order to evaluate the measurement model, and then we examined the structural model. The results of the structural model analysis are described with standardized path coefficients and t-values. The significance values of all the paths in this model were generated using the bootstrap resampling procedure. Self-efficacy was significantly influenced by supportive network position ($\beta = 0.263$; $t = 4.176$) but not informational network position ($\beta = 0.021$; $t = 0.284$), which accounted for 7.4 percent of the variance in self-efficacy. Absorptive capacity was significantly related to informational network position ($\beta = 0.227$; $t = 4.274$) and self-efficacy ($\beta = 0.801$; $t = 26.302$) but not supportive network position ($\beta = -0.013$; $t = 0.367$), which explained 72.8 percent of the variance in absorptive capacity. Self-efficacy ($\beta = 0.193$; $t = 2.071$) and absorptive capacity ($\beta = 0.693$; $t = 8.027$) were significantly related to individual adaptation, and accounted for 73.8 percent of the variance in individual adaptation. Finally, individual adaptation was significantly related to individual performance ($\beta = 0.601$; $t = 13.500$), explaining 36.2 percent of the variance in individual performance.

V. Conclusion

This research has shown that the social capital derived from organization members' social network positions aids in our understanding of coping processes toward the introduction of a new ICT system. The proposed research model suggests that emotion-focused coping processes are associated with individuals' positions within supportive networks, while problem-focused coping processes are related to individuals' positions within informational networks. The empirical results show that individual adaptation is enhanced by organization members' self-efficacy and absorptive capacity, which in turn are influenced by their supportive and informational network positions, respectively. The results of this study also revealed that the social network perspective might play an important role in investigating various IS (Information Systems)-related issues by integrating with the traditional research perspective. Such an approach would provide an alternative lens through which to view the domain of IS research, as well as an alternative instrument for managerial intervention.

References

[1] Chin, W.W. The Partial Least Squares Approach to Structural Equation Modeling. In G. A. Marcoulides (Ed.), Modern methods for business research (pp. 295-336). Mahwah, NJ: Lawrence Erlbaum Associates. 1998.

[2] Davis, F. D., and Venkatesh, V. "Toward Preprototype User Acceptance Testing of New Information Systems: Implications for Software Project Management," IEEE Transactions on Engineering Management, Vol. 51, No. 1, 2004, pp. 31-46.

[3] Fichman, R.G. and Kemerer, C.F., "The Illusory Diffusion of Innovation: An Examination of Assimilation GAPs," Information Systems Research, Vol. 10, No. 3, 1999, pp. 255-275.

[4] Jasperson, J., Carter, P. E., and Zmud, R. W., "A Comprehensive Conceptualization of Post-Adoptive Behaviors Associated with Information Technology Enabled Work Systems," MIS Quarterly, Vol. 29, No. 3, 2005, pp. 525-557.

[5] Kanter, J., "Have We Forgotten the Fundamental IT Enabler: Ease of Use?" Information Systems Management, Vol. 17, No.3, 2000, pp. 70-77.

[6] Scott, J., Social Network Analysis: A Handbook, Sage Publications, London, 2000.

[7] Wasserman. S., and Faust, K., Social Network Analysis. Methods and Applications, Cambridge University Press, Cambridge, 1994.

[8] Wold, S. "Multivariate Data Analysis: Converting Chemical Data Tables to Plots," In Computer Applications in Chemical Research and Education, Heidelberg: Dr. Alfred Huetithig Verlag, 1989.

Connecting Source Code Changes with Reasons

Namita Dave, Renan Peixoto da Silva, David Drobesh, Pragya Upreti, William Erdly, Hazeline U. Asuncion
School of Science, Technology, Engineering, & Mathematics
University of Washington, Bothell
Bothell, WA, USA 98011
e-mail: {namitad, rpeixoto, ddrobesh, pupreti, erdlyww, hazeline}@u.washington.edu

Abstract—**Understanding the reasons behind software changes is a challenging task, as explanations are not always apparent or accessible. In addition, when third party consumers of software try to understand a change, it becomes even more difficult since they are not closely working with the code. To address these challenges, we propose a technique for explicitly connecting code changes with their reasons, referred to as Flexible Artifact Change and Traceability Support (FACTS). FACTS presents a holistic view of changes by (1) generating traceability links for code changes at different levels of abstraction and (2) tracing code changes to heterogeneously represented reasons. Our user experiment indicates that FACTS is useful in understanding code changes.**

Keywords-software evolution tools; software traceability; software maintenance.

I. INTRODUCTION

Changeability is one of the essential difficulties with software [1]. Developers know the reasons for changes they make in the source code. These reasons may be recorded, but they are not always explicitly connected to code changes. This situation is more difficult for Third Party Consumers of Software (TPCS) who wish to understand the reason for a specific code change but they lack access to developers who performed the change. We aim to cater to these TPCS.

There are different approaches to address the challenge of determining *what* source code changed between two versions (e.g., [2], [3]), but these generally provide only one level of granularity of changes (e.g., line, method only). This limited view of changes may be addressed by software maintenance techniques to connect code with other code [4]–[6]. More importantly, there are limited techniques in addressing *why* a change occurred. There are techniques that connect code to documentation [7][8], to assist with impact analysis [9], but these do not provide a holistic view of *past* changes. Our approach is also distinctive from other software traceability approaches [7][8][10] in that we focus on tracing code *changes* (i.e., not source code, but the change between two versions of software) to their reasons. Most closely related work connects code changes with reasons for change by using a document summarization technique [11], but this technique falls short in determining which documents to summarize.

We address these gaps with our technique, Flexible Artifact Change Traceability Support (FACTS). FACTS assists with understanding past changes by (1) explicitly connecting code changes (at different levels of abstraction) to heterogeneously represented reasons via a traceability link, (2) visualizing the generated connections in an understandable manner, and (3) providing a novel set of tools to support the technique.

We define **reasons** as insights into a code change, as these may not be complete explanations, but only clues that can be connected with other clues. Thus, we do not include descriptions of code changes. For example, move method or the addition of a Bridge pattern is not a reason for change, i.e., they do not attempt to answer ***why*** these changes were made. These are succinct summaries of ***what*** changed. Reasons may be extracted from a sprint task list, user stories, bug reports, commit descriptions, news, or other artifacts.

The contributions of this paper are as follows. First, FACTS generates traceability links based on any available artifacts present during software development. Second, it flexibly works with any software life cycle methods, including contexts that use minimal methods [12]. The only assumption of this technique is that a version control system is used [13][14] and that reasons for change are available. Finally, our user experiment indicates that our tracing technique is useful to TPCS. Our prior work involved collecting metrics for project management [15]. This paper elaborates on tracing code changes with reasons.

This paper is organized as follows. Section II provides a motivation behind our work and Section III briefly covers existing techniques. Section IV presents the FACTS approach. Section V covers the user experiment. We close the paper with avenues for future work.

II. MOTIVATION

TPCS who have two snapshots of source code generally ask the questions: Q1) What is the difference between these two versions? Q2) Why was this change made?

While there are numerous techniques that answer Q1 for software developers (see Section III), our approach caters to TPCS. For example, TPCS who see that a method moved from one source code file to another does not know *why* the move occurred, unlike developers who may have tacit knowledge about the change. TPCS include project managers (PMs), software engineers who build on top of another product, or Principal Investigators (PIs) of scientific software. The importance of Q1 & Q2 is described below.

Scenario 1: Scientific software development. In this context, software is used to solve a scientific problem and researchers generally have limited background in Computer Science (CS) or Software Engineering (SE)[16] A PI may rely on Research Assistants (RAs) (e.g., graduate students or post-doctoral researchers) to write software [12] These RAs may also have limited background in CS or SE [12]. Before the RAs leave, the PI has at least two versions of the software: the original version given to the RAs and the modified version. At this point, the PI examines the source code to determine the source code changes (Q1) and if the changes satisfied the tasks given to the RAs (Q2).

Scenario 2: Distributed software development. Software development occurs in multiple locations, which may have different time zones. Even though a development team follows software engineering practices, a PM may still encounter difficulties understanding all the changes that occurred from the last official release to the current version. This task is more difficult in organizations required to conform to government regulations, since code quality is paramount [15] Here, PMs must quickly locate the changes (Q1) (i.e., view coarse-grained changes first and fine-grained details as needed) [15]. They also need to determine if they satisfy the deliverables for a release (Q2).

III. Related Work

We discuss existing evolution techniques that FACTS leverages and compare FACTS to work in other areas.

A. Software Evolution

Determining code changes between two versions has been well studied, with techniques that compare changes at the line [3]class or package [2], or at the behavioral level [17]. Additional information can be provided by AST Diffs, such as location of the change or the type of change (e.g., add, move) [18]. FACTS leverages these types of tools and connects their output to provide coarse-grained (e.g., packages changed) and fine-grained (e.g., methods changed) changes (see "Connect CCD to CCD" in Section IV.D.3).

More recently, there are techniques that provide coarse-grained changes in the form of summary. ChangeScribe applies this summary as an automatically generated commit message [19], Another technique focuses on identifying structural code changes [20]. Again, these are focused on *what* changed, and may be folded into our framework.

B. Reasons for Code Change

A closely related work provides a reason for a code change by using natural language processing techniques to summarize documents such as bug reports and source code [11], [21]. This approach first creates a chain of documents, obtains summaries from those documents, and displays them with the code. This work falls short in determining *which* software artifacts to connect to source code changes, which we do with our technique. Another approach depends on embedded unique identifiers within commits, such as a bug or issue ID, to connect reasons to method changes [22], which we do not require. Another technique focuses on connecting code changes to requirements [23], while our approach takes a broader set of artifacts than requirements. Finally, classification of code changes based on categories of maintenance activities [24]. We aim to provide a richer set of reasons than categories of changes.

C. Software Traceability

Software traceability research aims to identify relationships between various software artifacts. We focus on traceability links between 1) code change to code change and 2) code change to documentation. A representative set of traced artifacts is in Table I along with their techniques and intended users. None of these techniques connect different granularities of code changes with heterogeneous artifacts, i.e., provide a holistic view of changes.

"Code changes to code changes" Traceability Links. There are various techniques for connecting related source code, including traditional information retrieval methods [4]–[6] and static analysis tools [24]. Our approach is not focused on locating related source code, but connecting code changes to other code changes.

"Code Changes to Documentation" Traceability Links. Techniques that connect source code to documentation [8], [10], [25] do not specify *why* a change occurred. There are also several traceability techniques that assist with impact analysis (*potential* view of change) (e.g., [9]). Our technique, meanwhile, focuses on the changes that occurred in the past and understanding them (*actual* view of changes). There are also techniques that create traceability links between code and other artifacts [26], [27] or between code, artifacts (in software repositories), and people [28]. However, these techniques do not connect code changes (at different levels of granularity) with heterogeneous artifacts.

D. Background on Random Forest

Random Forest classification involves a collection of several weak classifiers to create strong classifier [29]. A decision tree-learning algorithm on a subset of training data trains each of the weaker classifier. The random forest uses these multiple random trees classifications to vote on an overall classification for given input data set. We used Weka implementation of Random Forest with cosine similarities as features (see Section IV.D).

IV. Approach

FACTS is a systematic approach to tracing code changes with reasons, reasons with other reasons, and code changes to other code changes. Figure 1 shows the framework of our approach, with each layer performing the core steps in the approach. The blue dashed line in the middle distinguishes between code and reasons, and these steps can occur in parallel. We discuss from the bottom layer to the top, as each layer uses the output of the layer below it.

TABLE I. Sample of Exisitng Traceability Techniques

Traced Artifacts	*Techniques*	*User*
issue reports & commit [30]	ChangeScribe with undersampling Random Forest	Developer
Issue reports & commit [13]	Diff comparison, user specification	Developer, PM
Code, document, and people [28]	Directed graph & regular language reachability	Developer
test code & source code [31]	Slicing & Coupling tool (SCOTCH), Latent Semantic Indexing	Developer

A. Extractor Layer

The extractor layer is responsible for extracting software change information. There are two types of extractors in this layer: extractors that extract reasons from various artifacts and extractors that obtain specific code versions. These extractors are built on top of other third party tools.

1) Extracting Reasons

One can find reasons for changes in a repository, database, or embedded within artifacts [15]. Explicitly stored reasons, such as bug databases, is straightforward to extract. One simply uses public Application Programming Interfaces (APIs) to perform such extraction [32]. If APIs are not available, but reasons are accessible via a website, then reasons can be scraped off the project site [33].

To extract embedded reasons, we used keywords such as "history" or "change notes". We also leverage the APIs of various tools (e.g.[34][35]). The process of extraction is tool-specific and can be artifact-specific (e.g., the process of extracting an issue and changes notes may be different even though both may be extracted from web pages). We built an extractor for each tool and artifact type.

2) Extracting Code Versions

The code extractors allow us to obtain snapshots of the source code for two versions to obtain changes in the software. We obtain these versions via an API provided by a code repository (e.g., JGit [32]).

B. Detector Layer

The detector layer identifies the changes within two versions of source code. This layer leverages various differencing techniques, such as line diff, class diff, and package diff. This layer provides insight into changes at different levels of granularity, providing a holistic view of changes. Moreover, one could also complement these structural diffs with behavioral diffs, such as SymDiff [17].

In addition to these techniques, we also use a technique for mining refactoring patterns [36]. Refactoring patterns provide yet another view into the code changes that may be more succinct than can be provided by existing diffs.

C. Transformer Layer

Once extraction finishes, the transformer layer transforms reasons and code changes into their uniform representations.

1) Transforming Reasons

Reasons, which are extracted from various artifacts, are represented as an **Artifact Change Description (ACD).** Here is a sample ACD:

```
id: acd1
timestamp: 5/1/10 3:20pm
sourceType: Release Notes
author: John Doe
path: https://github.com/apache/cassandra/
      blob/trunk/CHANGES.txt</path>
description: Remove pre-startup check for
open JMX port (CASSANDRA-12074)
```

Figure 2. Example of Artifact Change Description (ACD).

The extracted ACDs (issue database, commit records, requirements specifications, design documents), contain the following elements: id, path, description, sourceType, author, and timestamp. ID is an auto-generated identifier. Path specifies the location of change description on the local machine, on the local network, or on the Internet. The path may also point to a specific location within the artifact to support accessibility at different levels of granularity [15]. Description is a free-form text that describes the change. This may be a commit comment or a user story. SourceType specifies the type of artifact. If the extractor is a web scraper of a bug database, source type is "bug" or the specific name of the bug database. The author is an optional element, since this may not always be available. Timestamp, also optional, indicates the time when a change description was created.

2) Transforming Code Changes

Code Change Description (CCD) is a representation of source code or other implementation change. Figure 3 shows an example of a CCD entry.

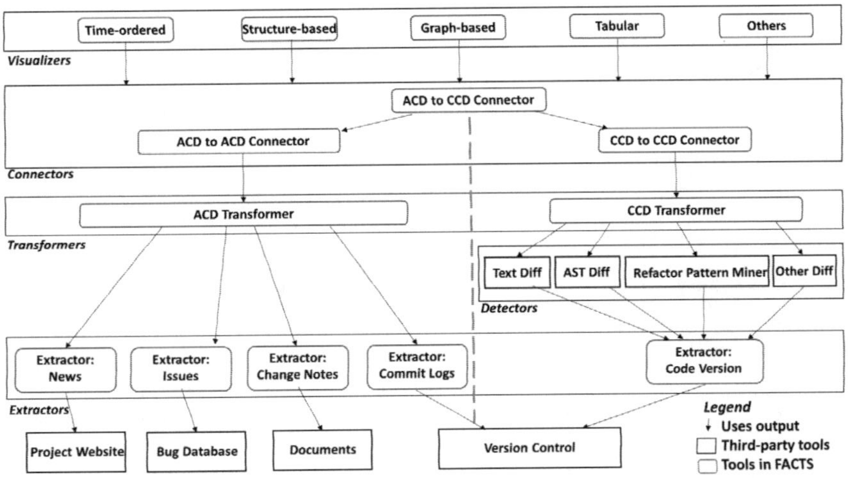

Figure 1. FACTS Framework.

```
id: ccd1
timestamp: 6/1/16 4:20pm
sourceType: package diff
sourcePath: acme/analysis/authDiff.txt
changeType: add
description: package auth
base-snapshot: 134a434f342347
compare-snapshot: 184a434f342959
```

Figure 3. Example of Code Change Description (CCD).

The extracted Code Change Description have the following elements: timestamp, the type of change (add, delete, edit), and the description of the change. The base- and compare-snapshot contain unique identifiers for the versions of the code that are compared, which may be commit identifiers, revision numbers, or release numbers. Description provides details about the changeType. The sourceType specifies the type of code differencing tool used. For example, the output of line diff has a sourceType "line diff". The output of the diff of a reverse engineered package diagrams has a sourceType "package diff".

D. Connector Layer

The connector layer is responsible for linking the extracted information. It connects information at the same level of abstraction (CCD to CCD and ACD to ACD) and across different level of abstraction (ACD to CCD).

Figure 4 shows an overview of the traceability links generated in FACTS. The blue dashed line in the middle separates the reasons for change, i.e., ACDs, from the code and other implementation change, i.e., CCDs. We use the Commit ACD as the focus of our traceability links to leverage the commit link already provided by a version control system. This allows us to bridge an abstraction gap between code and the explanations for change.

1) Pre-process

Before generating traceability links, we pre-process the data as follows. First, we remove all special characters. Then we split camel-cased words, words with underscore or hyphen, into individual words. Next, we transform all the words to lowercase. All these steps are performed prior to generating the traceability links.

For ACD-ACD traceability links, additional steps are performed. We lemmatize, remove stop words, and expand abbreviations. We expanded the abbreviations in order to normalize the vocabulary. We use the library JWKTL to lookup terms within the Wiktionary dump [37]. This utility translates abbreviations into a canonical, expanded and non-abbreviated word form.

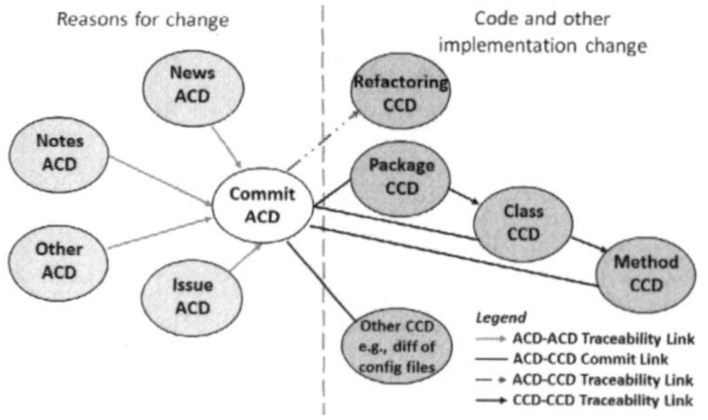

Figure 4: Traceability links in FACTS.

2) Same level of abstraction: Connect ACD to ACD

As we mentioned, reasons do not provide complete explanation for a change. Therefore, we connect different ACDs to better understand the reasons for change.

We can connect different ACDs using text similarity as description tag is free form text. We use a bag of words representation of documents and Random Forest implementation in Weka to create a prediction model capable of identifying traceability links.

Each classifier is built using the features described in Table II. Features F1-F4 are straight text comparisons. These features are insufficient, since they ignore important concepts that should be weighted more heavily. Thus, we identified the following groups of concepts that should receive more weights: features, architecture elements, tool operations (see F5-F10).

Sometimes, it is necessary to give more weight to terms that occur together in a document. This can be achieved by using N-grams with tf-idf (Term Frequency-Inverse Document Frequency) weighting (see F8-F10). N-grams can be calculated as follows: (1) the average N-gram distance between each term in the list of concepts and commit ACD; (2) the average distance between each term and other ACDs; (3) the N-gram distance between commit ACD and other ACDs. F8-F10 averages these three results.

Features F11-F13 are specific to connecting commit ACDs and issue ACDs. F11 checks if the commit was created between the issue report date and the update date of the same issue. F12 and F13 represent the number of days between the date of a commit and the issue report date, and the difference between the issue update date and the date that a commit was created, respectively.

3) Same level of abstraction: Connect CCD to CCD

Code changes are often provided at one level of granularity (e.g., line, class). Thus, understanding code change is limited at that level. To provide a holistic view of changes, CCDs at different levels of granularity can be connected. At the package level we trace changes from package CCDs to line diffs within packages, including changes to miscellaneous files (e.g., non-programming language programs, configuration files, scripts). For object-oriented languages, we trace package CCD to class CCD and to method CCD (see Figure 4). A traceability link is created by matching the fully qualified package names with the paths in the other diffs.

4) Different levels of abstraction: Connect CCD to ACD

Connecting code changes to reasons for changes is challenging since this requires bridging different levels of abstraction. The representation of concepts at the code level may be different from the representation of concepts at the reasons level. For example, the feature "elastic scalability" may have no matching terms in the source code.

To achieve this mapping, we leverage the developer action of committing code changes to the repository. When code changes are committed, we have a snapshot of the changes that occurred. In addition, developers generally enter a description for their changes.

TABLE II. ACD-ACD FEATURES LIST

Feature	Description
F1	number of terms in common
F2	cosine similarity
F3	maximum of cosine
F4	average of cosine
F5	weighted cosine for feature terms
F6	weighted cosine for architecture element terms
F7	weighted cosine for operation terms
F8	n-grams for feature terms
F9	n-grams for architecture terms
F10	n-grams for operation terms
F11	issueReportDate < commitDate < issueUpdate
F12	commitDate - issueReportDate
F13	issueUpdateDate - commitDate

Coarse-grained mapping: We leverage a commit ACD as a bridge between code and explanation. The connection between the commit ACD and the other ACDs are also provided by the technique we mentioned in the previous section. Thus, all the explanations for all the code changes within a given commit can be provided (see Figure 4). This connection is coarse-grained, at the level of a commit.

Finer-grained mapping: We can also achieve a more fine-grained connection between code changes and reasons by connecting refactoring pattern CCDs with commit ACD. Our approach to connecting mined refactorings with reasons for their occurrence consists of two main phases: *Training Phase* and *Test Phase*, and they share the following steps:

Step 1: Commit-Refactoring Pairing: Similar to creating ACD-ACD traceability links, we use Random Forest to build a model for connecting each commit ACD to refactoring CCD (output from Ref-Finder). This traceability link contains the following attributes: link (true or false), refactoring, commitID, commitDate, commitMessage, and calculated similarity features (discussed next).

Step 2: Similarity Analysis: After generating commit-refactoring links, we use similarity features (F1-F5) between refactorings and commit logs. Table III describes the features used, which were defined based on the information contained in refactoring changes and commit logs, including differences introduced in each commit, that could possibly enhance the process for growing decision trees within the classifier method. F1 checks if the refactoring activity is found in a commit log, by matching the full name of a package, class, method or parameter. F2 corresponds to the number of terms in common between a refactoring CCD and a commit ACD. F3 measures the cosine similarity between a refactoring CCD and a commit ACD. F4 and F5 are the maximum and the average of cosine similarity between commit ACD and refactoring CCD.

E. Visualizers Layer

This layer provides various visualizations, but we focus on two visualizations here: structure-based and graph-based visualizations.

Structure-based visualization allows users to view code changes to reasons. One can view coarse-grained changes (package view), then zoom-in to detailed changes (class and method view). Here users can see reasons for change.

The graph-based visualization allows users to view reasons with code changes. Users may select which concepts to view: features, architecture, operations. This displays the list of commits related to that particular concept. The user can view all code changes in a graph by selecting a commit. In addition, all the related reasons are displayed at the bottom, in this case news and issues ACDs.

F. Limitations of the approach

The limitations of the approach are as follows: dependence on a version control system, development of artifact/tool-specific extractors, and offline processing of artifacts. Since we focus our tracing technique on commit CCDs, we assume the usage of a version control system by a development team. This is not an unreasonable requirement as these tools are in widespread use in the software industry.

In order to obtain high quality reasons (i.e., minimal noise), the ACD extractors must be tool- and even artifact-specific. While this may require additional overhead in building extractors, this is a one-time overhead.

TABLE III. CCD-ACD FEATURES LIST

Feature	Description
F1	String of interest (yes/no)
F2	Number of terms in common
F3	Cosine similarity
F4	Maximum of cosine
F5	Average of cosine

Due to the sheer volume of change information obtained, we currently assume offline processing. This is also not unreasonable, as users can simply run the tool overnight and view the results the following day, similar to running a nightly build. It may be possible to parallelize the processing of all ACDs and CCDs, but this is currently beyond the scope of this paper.

Finally, while FACTS provides links to possible reasons, users have to read the linked documents (as automated techniques are not able to reach 100% accuracy). However, in the future, we plan to incorporate user feedback so that our classifier can learn from incorrectly classified links. In addition, while our approach is limited by the availability of artifacts, we believe it provides any available reasons to help uncover *why* a change was made.

V. EVALUATION

We conducted an experiment to assess (1) whether the FACTS approach is useful in understanding past code changes and (2) whether exposure to the FACTS tool support encourages developers to use it in their work. Answers to these Research Questions (RQ) were obtained using open-ended and multiple choice survey questions.

1) Method

Participants. In our study, we had a total of 36 participants, 22 of whom are Computer Science & Software Engineering graduate students and senior/junior level undergraduate students and 14 industry users. Half of the participants were assigned to the control group and the other half to the treatment group. The software industry users (experience range from 5 months to 18 years) included technical leads, developers, managers, analysts, and one patent lawyer. Limited exposure or background with traceability tools was most common between both groups, despite their having had on average 5.75 years of industry or comparable experience using Eclipse IDE.

Dataset. The experiment was performed using the Apache Cassandra project, which presented a realistic challenge: very large codebase and a high velocity of code change. Specifically, we used v2.1.0 (200K LOC) and v3.0.1 (350K LOC). Cassandra also has multiple, concurrent branches, and frequent tagging and merges. Thus, our codebase selection has many realistic aspects as a sample for a moderate- or large-sized software product.

Environmental setup. All experiments were conducted on two virtual machines on which the users remotely connected. One virtual machine contains the Eclipse Diff Tools while the other machine contains the FACTS tool as an Eclipse Plugin. In both environments, both versions of the Cassandra project were available to enable users to examine the differences between the two versions.

Procedure. Subjects were asked to do the following: (1) fill out a pre-experiment online survey, (2) perform a task, and (3) fill out a post-experiment online survey. The pre-experiment online survey gathered demographic information about the participants (e.g., roles, length of experience) with their interest in traceability and software maintenance tools.

With regards to their task, they were given the hypothetical scenario of ACME Corp upgrading from v2.1.0 to v3.0.1 of Cassandra. The subject was informed that this was their first day working for ACME, and then instructed to learn two things: (A) Cassandra's high level design and (B) recent code changes. The subjects were given a maximum of two hours to explore and compare codebases, and directed to be ready to receive their initial code modification tasks assignment at the end of that brief self-orientation period. This instruction fits TPCS type of users. The "Treatment" group used FACTS tool support to understand code changes, while the "Control" group used traditional Eclipse IDE tools.

The post-experiment survey consisted of two parts: a quiz and a set of questions regarding their task. To test their understanding, they were given a timed "quiz" regarding code changes. Similar to an industry work environment, the questions in the quiz are very difficult.

To minimize bias, several study controls were used. First, random group assignment was used. Subjects did not know if they were in the control or treatment group. Second, we used anonymous user-codes to shield subject identity. Additional care was taken that our researcher and subjects were "double-blinded" of each other's identity. Finally, the questions in the quiz were generated by an undergraduate student using Eclipse Compare/Diff tools and were checked by researchers in our group. This shows the questions are fair, and subjects in the Control have an equal chance to answer the questions as the subjects in the Treatment group.

2) Results

With regards to RQ1, we found evidences that the FACTS tool support is useful in understanding past code changes. First, on average the subjects in the treatment group answered more correct questions than the control group (Control=1.5 vs. Treatment=2.28 correct answers). One explanation to why there is not a much wider gap between the two groups is that, due to the visualizations being in their prototype stages, there were some tool errors that came up during the study. Also, the earlier versions of the visualizations, which are the structure-based and tabular visualizations, were the only ones presented to the users.

Second indication that the approach is useful is that 71% of the treatment group (a statistically significant result) indicated that the tool, i.e., the approach, helped with their understanding of the codebases, citing ease of tracking changes along with time savings as benefits. One of these subjects, an industry user who is responsible for overseeing distributed development teams (up to 25 people in four time zones), said, "*It is difficult to keep track of what changes in the project. This tool would save time, and make the process more useful as well.*"

With regards to RQ2, we also found that the subjects responded positively to using an improved version of the FACTS tool support in their work. When users in the treatment group were asked their level of interest in using the FACTS tool support to improve their current work process, 46% stated that they were "most interested" or "very interested", and 38% stated that they have "some interest".

3) Discussion

The sub-populations of industry subjects compared with student subjects showed some marked distinctions that are significant for the target population of TPCS. The industry developers showed a generally higher engagement and motivation rate, relative to the sub-population of student subjects, as measured by all of the following: (1) willingness to participate in future studies of FACTS traceability tools (64% industry vs. 50% students); (2) time you would invest in optimized versions of FACTS-IDE tool (13.7 hours industry vs. 10.96 hours student, when asked to base on 40 hour/week); (3) response to the question "Does the software tool help you link artifacts of change with actual code changes?" (Yes replies were 71% industry vs. 73% students). These results, when coupled with the participation rate (94% for industry subjects vs. 69% for student subjects) indicate a generally positive applicability trend of the FACTS tool to the actual population of developers.

VI. CONCLUSION

In this paper, we presented a novel framework for connecting code changes with reasons for change, with minimal requirements on the types of documents present or the software processes used. We systematically trace all the extracted changes and reasons within the same level of abstraction and across different levels of abstractions. Finally, the change information is visualized to assist with understanding reasons behind a code change. Our evaluation indicates that FACTS is useful for understanding code changes, especially for industry subjects.

In the future, we plan to assess the accuracy of our tracing techniques. We also plan to further improve the user interface, improve the scalability of our tool, and conduct additional experiments and case studies with industry users.

ACKNOWLEDGEMENTS

We thank Karen Potts, Nathan Duncan, Wenbo Guo, Andrew Byland, Jonathan Featherston, Haihong Luo for developing visualizations and other tools in the FACTS framework, Steve Kay and Hoa Vo for assisting with user studies, and Delmar Davis for his input on existing techniques. R.P. da Silva is sponsored by CAPES and the Science Without Borders program. This work is based in part by the US National Science Foundation under Grant No. CCF 1218266 and ACI 1350724.

References

[1] F. P. Brooks Jr., "No Silver Bullet Essence and Accidents of Software Engineering," *Computer*, vol. 20, no. 4, pp. 10–19, Apr. 1987.

[2] L. Bendix and P. Emanuelsson, "Diff and Merge Support for Model Based Development," *Proc Int'l Workshop on Comparison and Versioning of Software Models*, 2008, pp. 31–34.

[3] G. Canfora, L. Cerulo, and M. Di Penta, "Ldiff: An Enhanced Line Differencing Tool," *Proc Int'l Conf on Software Engineering (ICSE)*, 2009, pp. 595–598.

[4] N. Dave, K. Potts, V. Dinh, and H. U. Asuncion, "Combining Association Mining with Topic Modeling to Discover More File Relationships," *Intl J. Adv. Softw.*, vol. 7, no. 3 & 4, pp. 539–550, 2014.

[5] R. Oliveto, M. Gethers, D. Poshyvanyk, and A. De Lucia, "On the Equivalence of Information Retrieval Methods for Automated Traceability Link Recovery," *Proc Int'l Conf on Program Comprehension*, 2010, pp. 68–71.

[6] S. P. Reiss, "Semantics-based Code Search," *Proc ICSE*, 2009, pp. 243–253.

[7] G. Antoniol, G. Canfora, G. Casazza, and A. De Lucia, "Maintaining Traceability Links During Object-oriented Software Evolution," *Softw. Pract. Exper*, vol. 31, no. 4, pp. 331–355, 2001.

[8] K. M. Anderson, S. A. Sherba, and W. V. Lepthien, "Towards Large-scale Information Integration," *Proc ICSE*, 2002, pp. 524–534.

[9] S. Lehnert, Q. u a Farooq, and M. Riebisch, "Rule-Based Impact Analysis for Heterogeneous Software Artifacts," *Proc Conf Software Maintenance and Reengineering (CSMR)*, 2013.

[10] G. Antoniol, G. Canfora, G. Casazza, A. De Lucia, and E. Merlo, "Recovering traceability links between code and documentation," *Trans. Softw. Eng. (TSE)*, vol. 28, no. 10, pp. 970–983, Oct. 2002.

[11] S. Rastkar, "Summarizing software artifacts," PhD Thesis, University of British Columbia, 2013.

[12] S. Ahalt *et al.*, "Water Science Software Institute: Agile and Open Source Scientific Software Development," *Comput. Sci. Eng.*, vol. 16, no. 3, pp. 18–26, 2014.

[13] "Git version control." [Online]. Available: https://git-scm.com/. [Accessed: 05-Feb-2018].

[14] "Subversion." [Online]. Available: https://subversion.apache.org/. [Accessed: 05-Feb-2018].

[15] H. U.Asuncion, M. Shonle, R. Porter, K. Potts, N. Duncan, and W. J. M. Jr, "Using Change Entries to Collect Software Project Information," *Proc Int'l Conf on Software Engineering & Knowledge Engineering (SEKE)*, 2013.

[16] B. Yasutake *et al.*, "Supporting Provenance in Climate Science Research," *Proc Int'l Conf on Info, Process, & Knowledge Mgmt (eKNOW)*, 2015.

[17] S. K. Lahiri, C. Hawblitzel, M. Kawaguchi, and H. Rebelo, "SYMDIFF: A Language-Agnostic Semantic Diff Tool for Imperative Programs," in *Computer Aided Verification*, 2012, pp. 712–717.

[18] S. Raghavan, R. Rohana, D. Leon, A. Podgurski, and V. Augustine, "Dex: a semantic-graph differencing tool for studying changes in large code bases," *Proc Int'l Conf on Software Maintenance (ICSM)*, 2004, pp. 188–197.

[19] L. F. Cortes-Coy, M. Linares-Vasquez, J. Aponte, and D. Poshyvanyk, "On Automatically Generating Commit Messages via Summarization of Source Code Changes," *Int'l Working Conf on Source Code Analysis and Manipulation*, 2014, pp. 275–284.

[20] J. I. Maletic and M. L. Collard, "Supporting source code difference analysis," *Proc ICSM*, 2004, pp. 210–219.

[21] S. Rastkar and G. C. Murphy, "Why Did This Code Change?," *Proc ICSE*, 2013, pp. 1193–1196.

[22] A. S. Ami and S. Islam, "A Content Assist based Approach for Providing Rationale of Method Change for Object Oriented Programming," *Intl J. Info Eng. Electron. Bus.*, vol. 7, p. 49, 2015.

[23] E. B. Charrada, A. Koziolek, and M. Glinz, "Identifying outdated requirements based on source code changes," *Proc Int'l Requirements Engineering Conf*, 2012, pp. 61–70.

[24] M. Sharp and A. Rountev, "Static Analysis of Object References in RMI-Based Java Software," *TSE*, vol. 32, no. 9, pp. 664–681, 2006.

[25] X. Chen and J. Grundy, "Improving Automated Documentation to Code Traceability by Combining Retrieval Techniques," *Proc Int'l Conf on Automated Software Engineering*, 2011, pp. 223–232.

[26] D. Cubranic, G. C. Murphy, J. Singer, and K. S. Booth, "Hipikat: A Project Memory for Software Development," *IEEE Trans Softw Eng*, vol. 31, no. 6, pp. 446–465, 2005.

[27] M. Kersten and G. C. Murphy, "Mylar: A Degree-of-interest Model for IDEs," *Proc Int'l Conf on Aspect-oriented Software Development*, 2005, pp. 159–168.

[28] A. Begel, Y. P. Khoo, and T. Zimmermann, "Codebook: Discovering and Exploiting Relationships in Software Repositories," *Proc ICSE*, 2010, pp. 125–134.

[29] L. Breiman, "Random Forests," *Mach. Learn.*, vol. 45, no. 1, pp. 5–32, Oct. 2001.

[30] T. D. B. Le, M. Linares-Vasquez, D. Lo, and D. Poshyvanyk, "RCLinker: Automated Linking of Issue Reports and Commits Leveraging Rich Contextual Information," *Proc Int'l Conf on Program Comprehension (ICPC)*, 2015.

[31] A. Qusef, G. Bavota, R. Oliveto, A. D. Lucia, and D. Binkley, "SCOTCH: Test-to-code traceability using slicing and conceptual coupling," *Proc ICSM*, 2011, pp. 63–72.

[32] "JGit." [Online]. Available: https://eclipse.org/jgit/. [Accessed: 05-Feb-2018].

[33] "jsoup: Java HTML Parser." [Online]. Available: https://jsoup.org/. [Accessed: 05-Feb-2018].

[34] "Excel Services REST API." [Online]. Available: https://docs.microsoft.com/en-us/sharepoint/dev/general-development/excel-services-rest-api. [Accessed: 05-Feb-2018].

[35] A-PDF, "A-PDF Text Extractor," Aug-2016. [Online]. Available: http://www.a-pdf.com/text/. [Accessed: 05-Feb-2018].

[36] M. Kim, M. Gee, A. Loh, and N. Rachatasumrit, "Ref-Finder: A Refactoring Reconstruction Tool Based on Logic Query Templates," *Proc Int'l Symposium on Foundations of Software Engineering*, 2010, pp. 371–372.

[37] "Java Wiktionary Library." [Online]. Available: https://dkpro.github.io/dkpro-jwktl/. [Accessed: 05-Feb-2018].

Possible Interpretation of Mass-in-Mind: A Case Study Using SCRABBLE

Suwanviwatana Kananat Jean-Christophe Terrillon Hiroyuki Iida

Japan Advanced Institute of Science and Technology
Nomi, Ishikawa, Japan
e-mail: {s.kananat, terril, iida}@jaist.ac.jp

***Abstract*—This paper explores the possible interpretation of 'mass-in-mind,' which describes a shift in a perceived challenge due to experience. This work involves a measurement called 'game refinement,' which has been used to quantify the engagement of a game. It establishes an incomplete link between real-world physics and physics-in-mind, in which the acceleration and the distance, also known as game progress, have been identified. An existence of mass-in-mind, however, has just been established. The mathematical model of mass-in-mind is constructed based on the data interpretation, in which SCRABBLE matches between computer players were analyzed. The results reveal a significant gap between prior models, which is explainable once the mass-in-mind is considered.**

Keywords–Scrabble; game refinement theory; game progress model; boardgame model; physics-in-mind.

I. INTRODUCTION

Quantifying emotional excitement and mental engagement in games is the subject of game refinement theory [1]. Early work in this direction has been carried out by Iida *et al.* [1] while constructing a logistic model based on game outcome uncertainty to measure the attractiveness and sophistication of games [2]. Efforts have been devoted to the study of the acceleration of the game progress [3], [4], [5]. The mass part has just recently discussed [6], however, still remains unknown even it has been one of the most fundamental concept in classical mechanics [7].

SCRABBLE [8] has been played for several decades in various situations [9], for instance, as a competitive match between professional players [10], [11] or as a friendly match among family members or students [12]. Different players may have different vocabulary knowledge and supposed to have distinct playing experience. Besides, players can play SCRABBLE either for entertaining or educational purpose [12]. This paper focuses on an evaluation of SCRABBLE from the game designer's point-of-view, in which two original game refinement models are considered. However, the differences are observed then being discussed.

The term 'mass' originally came from Latin word 'Massa', which means accumulation, body, crowd or heap [13], [14]. Mass is one of the most fundamental concepts in both classical and modern physics [7]. Initially, the notion of inertial mass was brought to the consideration by Isaac Newton [15], [16]. The superficial definition is the tendency of a body to resist changes of acceleration. However, this might subject to misinterpretation in a case of modern physics [17]. The motion of an object is indeterminable without the consideration of mass [7]. Similarly, the acceleration of the game progress is unobtainable without the mass-in-mind.

Earlier works in game refinement theory successfully established two mathematical models, known as the boardgame model [1] and the game progress model [5], which correspond to the boardgame and the scoring game respectively. SCRABBLE, however, is the particular case where two models are applicable. The results are compared, then lead to the reconsideration of the precedent theory. This work is expected to enhance the completeness of game refinement theory and become one of the standard assessment tools in the future.

The paper structure is as follows. In Section II, we describe the brief history of the study of Game Refinement Theory. Section III explains the mass-in-mind concept, how it is established and its affect to the mathematical model of game refinement. Section IV presents related prior works. Section V presents the assessment and corresponding error from applying the newly proposed model, thus discusses the results of the analysis. Concluding remarks are given in Section VI.

A. Scrabble

SCRABBLE® is a registered trademark. All intellectual property rights in and to the game are owned in the United States of America by Hasbro Incorporated, in Canada by Hasbro Canada Corporation, and throughout the rest of the world by J.W. Spear & Sons Limited of Maidenhead, Berkshire, England, a subsidiary of Mattel Incorporated [8], [18], [19].

SCRABBLE has been used as the main test-bed of this study. It is a word anagram game which published in 1938 by Hasbro [18], one of the famous toys game company in the United States.

In opposition to a typical boardgame, SCRABBLE players should possess not only strategic skill but also a sufficient vocabulary size. This is because they are required to form legit words from randomly tiles given.

From earlier work [20], it is known that SCRABBLE possesses the stronger entertaining aspect compared to educational aspect. While many players generally play SCRABBLE for enjoyment purpose, only few players play it in an educational way. By developing artificial intelligent player, the direction to improve SCRABBLE is proposed using the feedback from the artificial intelligence [21].

Superficially, SCRABBLE might be considered as a boardgame. However, it contains the aspect of competitive scoring as well. Hence, we can observe the scoring rate, branching factor, and game length. Those are essential for the game progress model and the boardgame model of the game refinement measure.

II. GAME REFINEMENT MEASURE

This section gives a short description of game refinement theory. A general model of game refinement was proposed based on the concept of the rate of change in game information progress [5]. This model bridges a gap between boardgames and scoring sports games.

A. Game Progress Model

The term 'game progress' is twofold. One criterion is the game speed or scoring rate, while the other is game information progress, which focuses on the game outcome. Game information progress presents the degree of certainty of the game's results in time or steps. Having full information of the game progress i.e., after its conclusion, game progress $x(t)$ will be given as a linear function of time t with $0 \leq t \leq t_k$ and $0 \leq x(t) \leq x(t_k)$, as shown in (1).

$$x(t) = \frac{x(t_k)}{t_k}\ t \quad (1)$$

However, the game information progress given by (1) is unknown during the in-game period. The presence of uncertainty during the game, often until the final moments of a game, reasonably renders game progress exponential. Hence, a realistic model of game information progress is given by (2).

$$x(t) = x(t_k)(\frac{t}{t_k})^n \quad (2)$$

Here n stands for a constant parameter, which is given based on the perspective of an observer of the game that is considered. Then the acceleration of the game information progress is obtained by deriving (2) twice. Solving it for $t = t_k$, the equation becomes (3).

$$x''(t_k) = \frac{x(t_k)}{(t_k)^n} t^{n-2}\ n(n-1)\ |_{t=t_k} = \frac{x(t_k)}{(t_k)^2}\ n(n-1) \quad (3)$$

It is assumed in the current model that game information progress in any game is transported into and encoded in our brains. We do not yet know about the physics of information in the brain, but it is likely that the acceleration of information progress is subject to the forces and laws of physics. Therefore, we expect that the larger the value $\frac{x(t_k)}{(t_k)^2}$, the more exciting the game becomes, due in part to the uncertainty of the game outcome. Thus, we use its square root, $\frac{\sqrt{x(t_k)}}{t_k}$, as a game refinement measure for the game under consideration. We call it GR value for short, we also call $x(t_k)$ and t_k G and T respectively, as shown in (4).

$$GR = \frac{\sqrt{G}}{T} \quad (4)$$

The tendency of game refinement theory has been explained in [22]. We consider the trend between game refinement theory and the player skill. While an increasing relation leads to the entertaining experience, a decreasing relation leads to the serious or educational experience. However, two above ways may be utilized together to attract customers as shown in a case of business [23].

B. Early Works with Scrabble

The swing model [20], a derivation of the game progress model, is defined to solve the nonidentical scoring system in SCRABBLE. In this study, swing denotes a notion of phase

TABLE I. EARLIER GAME REFINEMENT MEASURE OF SCRABBLE

DS	G	B	$T = D$	$\frac{\sqrt{G}}{T}$	$\frac{\sqrt{B}}{D}$	*Difference*
0.1	7.30	14.202	35.79	0.075	0.105	-39.48%
0.2	13.21	28.468	43.77	0.083	0.122	-46.0.8
0.3	12.04	51.093	43.83	0.079	0.163	-106.00%
0.4	11.54	81.300	42.38	0.080	0.213	-165.43%
0.5	13.76	124.393	39.66	0.094	0.281	-200.67%
0.6	13.22	158.125	39.88	0.091	0.315	-245.85%
0.7	10.30	200.321	37.58	0.085	0.377	-341.01%
0.8	11.33	254.111	36.67	0.092	0.435	-373.58%
0.9	10.14	333.689	35.87	0.089	0.509	-473.65%
1.0	10.78	361.805	35.85	0.092	0.531	-479.33%

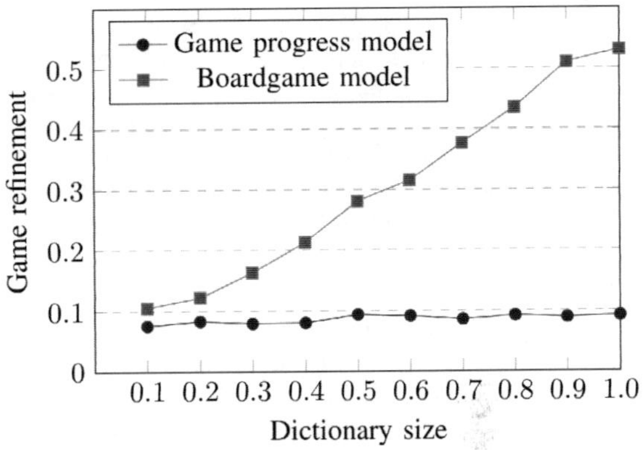

Figure 1. Comparison of two original game refinement measures

transition in mind from advantage to disadvantage and vice-versa. Let DS be the dictionary size represented in the zero-to-one normalized scale. The data are shown in Table I and Figure 1.

Next, we compare the value of the two approaches, thus display the observable difference. While the branching factor grows with the dictionary size as expected, there is only slight change in the number of swing occurrence and the game length.

Since game refinement theory has been used to quantify the engagement of the game regardless of the type of the game, we expected that the measures using two different approaches are identical. However, this is not necessarily true in a case of SCRABBLE.

The simple explanation is that the total branching factor B is overwhelmingly excessive in the case of SCRABBLE. Generally, SCRABBLE players cannot recognize all possible instances to human limitations. They might not be able to remember all the words in the standard dictionary or use them efficiently within the limited time. In particular, we must take the effective branching factor b into account. It was previously introduced in [24].

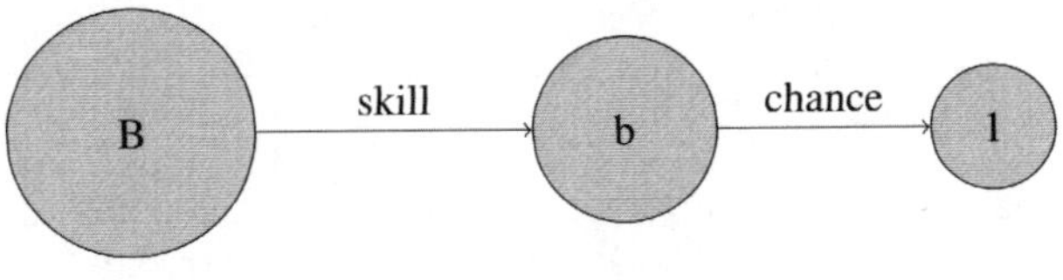

Figure 2. Player selection process

The branching factor B represents a number of all possible moves [1]. The effective branching factor b is the subset of the branching factor B which contains only instances satisfyingly perceived by a player [22]. The process to identify effective solutions among all possible moves is involved with individual skill. The generic single-step selection process is illustrated in Figure 2.

III. MASS-IN-MIND

A. Real-world Physics

In physics, kinetics is the branch of classical mechanics regarding motion. Newton's laws of motion [25], [26], [27], [28] are three fundamental laws which describe the relationship between forces acting upon a body, and its movement in response to those, as shown in Law 1, Law 2 and Law 3. More precisely, the first law defines the force qualitatively, the second law offers a quantitative measure of the force and the third postulates that a single isolated force does not exist.

In this study, we mainly focus on the second law, which describes the nature of mass, resistance to acceleration, or inertia, when a net force is applied.

Law 1: **Newton's first law** In an inertial frame of reference, an object either remains at rest or continues to move at a constant velocity in a straight line, unless acted upon by an external force.

Law 2: **Newton's second law** In an inertial reference frame, the vector sum of the forces F acting on an object is equal to the mass m of that object multiplied by the acceleration a of the object:

$$\mathbf{F} = m\mathbf{a} \tag{5}$$

It is assumed that the mass m is a constant.

Law 3: **Newton's third law** When one body exerts a force on a second body, the second body simultaneously exerts a force equal in magnitude and opposite in direction on the first body.

B. Game Refinement Theory Revisited

Although the study of the game refinement measure and the attempt to construct a link between real-world physics and physics-in-mind has been made, currently only the acceleration of the game progress is identified. However, mass, the essential part of real-world physics is not yet mentioned.

SCRABBLE is a scoring game played on a board, so it is the first domain, which two different game refinement approaches are applicable. Once two procedures were applied to SCRABBLE, we identified a significant gap between them, then realized that there might be an inconsistency in the original game refinement measure.

C. Establishment of Mass-in-Mind

Different objects react differently to the same net force due to their respective mass. For the same net force applied, an object with a higher mass will have a lower acceleration. We suppose that force-in-mind is the property of the game, and the mass-in-mind is the property of the player, then acceleration-in-mind is obtained by those two factors. Table II shows an intended mapping between real-world physics and physics-in-mind.

TABLE II. CORRESPONDENCE BETWEEN REAL-WORLD PHYSICS AND PHYSICS-IN-MIND

Notation	*Real-World Physics*	*Physics-in-Mind*
F	Force	Game Sophistication
m	Mass	Decision Complexity perceived by a player
$a = \frac{F}{m}$	Acceleration	Intuition of a player

Based on the perception described above, the definition of the mass-in-mind, or decision complexity perceived by a player, is given in Definition 2.

Definition 1: **Selection possibility** p is given as a proportion between selective instances which are satisfyingly perceived and the entire.

Definition 2: **Mass-in-mind** m is the inversion of the selection possibility of a player in a specific subject.

According to the definition given, we construct the mathematical model to make it more concretely for both game progress model and the boardgame model. Considering a boardgame, the possibility among a personal optimal selection is $\frac{b}{B}$, thus its inversion is $\frac{B}{b}$. In a case of the scoring game, however, is not directly obtainable. Therefore, the approximate model is introduced. By supposing that a player gets g scores out of Σg total score at the endgame, one score has the $\frac{g}{\Sigma g}$ possibility to be distributed to that player. Hence, the selection possibility is obtained by $\frac{g}{\Sigma g}$, thus its inversion is $\frac{\Sigma g}{g}$. Table III summarizes the mathematical model of game refinement considering mass.

TABLE III. GAME REFINEMENT MODEL CONSIDERING MASS

Notation	*Game Progress Model*	*Boardgame Model*
F	$\frac{G}{T^2}$	$\frac{B}{D^2}$
m	$\frac{\Sigma g}{g}$	$\frac{B}{b}$
$a = \frac{F}{m}$	$\frac{Gg}{T^2 \Sigma g}$	$\frac{b}{D^2}$

IV. RELATED WORKS

This section presents prior works done in this direction. How data is transferred within the human brain was explained using physics [29]. As opposed to our Newtonian physics analogy, the computational mechanism in the human brain is explained by quantum physics and information theory.

The arrow which points from the past to the future, known as the Time's arrow, was introduced to explain the consciousness and the awareness of the time. The time quantity used in most physics equations dealing with events is measurable. However, that is not necessarily equal to the time we sense. A human is subjected to lose track of time when concentrating on some medium.

In game refinement theory, the uncertainty of the game outcome is described with classical physics model. Game refinement measure reflects attractiveness of a game from the viewpoint of designers. A game is enjoyable when its challenge matches with preferences and skills of a player [30]. While deficiency leads to a tiresomeness, an extreme difficulty may lead to frustration. The high perceived challenge is one of the conditions in flow theory [31], which results in a loss of self-consciousness and track of the time.

The study of the $n(n-1)$ in (3) is explained in [22] as the C parameter. C_b and C_s are used for the boardgame and the scoring game respectively. They are defined in (6).

$$C_b = \frac{b}{B} \quad (\frac{1}{B} \leq C_b \leq 1) \qquad C_s = 1 \tag{6}$$

Through the effect of the C parameter, the acceleration part of the game refinement measure becomes (7)

$$R_b = \frac{\sqrt{b}}{D} \qquad R_s = \frac{\sqrt{G}}{T} \tag{7}$$

The result shows a similarity with this study. According to the mathematical formula, the C_b is as an inversion of the mass-in-mind. Thus R_b is the exact value of the square root of the acceleration from the boardgame model considering the mass. However, the mass-in-mind of game progress model does not share the same definition with C_s. Instead, it is likely constant. This method could enhance the completeness of the interpretation of the C parameter by redefining C_s, which would have some value, instead of being always 1.

V. Assessment and Discussion

We developed an artificial intelligent player to simulate multiple SCRABBLE matches. A hundred of distinct match settings are simulated with two hundred iterations each. Essential data, including individual score, total score, branching factor, game length were collected.

For the game progress model, we measure the individual score of a winner side and a loser side separately because they are obviously different. The data involving the force-in-mind is given in Table IV. Then, the acceleration-in-mind of each side are obtainable by considering their respective mass-in-mind, as shown in Table V and Table VI. Hence, the average is calculated and shown in Table VII and Figure 3.

TABLE IV. Game Progress Model Considering Mass

DS	G	T	F
0.1	7.30	35.79	5.70×10^{-3}
0.2	13.21	43.77	6.90×10^{-3}
0.3	12.04	43.83	6.27×10^{-3}
0.4	11.54	42.38	6.43×10^{-3}
0.5	13.76	39.66	8.75×10^{-3}
0.6	13.22	39.88	8.31×10^{-3}
0.7	10.30	37.58	7.29×10^{-3}
0.8	11.33	36.67	8.43×10^{-3}
0.9	10.14	35.87	7.88×10^{-3}
1.0	10.78	35.85	8.39×10^{-3}

For the boardgame model, the effective branching factor is considered. It was suspected to be close to B and 1 for beginners and experts respectively. However, determining the effective branching factor b for intermediate players is a challenging question. We then introduce approximate models, as shown in Table VIII.

Each approximate model is used with the boardgame model considering mass. The comparative results with the game progress model considering mass are shown in Figure 4.

TABLE V. Game Progress Model Considering Mass (Winner's Intuition)

DS	F	g_{winner}	Σg	m_{winner}	a_{winner}
0.1	5.70×10^{-3}	474.47	870.17	1.83	3.11×10^{-3}
0.2	6.90×10^{-3}	679.75	1277.66	1.88	3.67×10^{-3}
0.3	6.27×10^{-3}	734.77	1395.11	1.90	3.30×10^{-3}
0.4	6.43×10^{-3}	768.29	1440.30	1.87	3.43×10^{-3}
0.5	8.75×10^{-3}	767.80	1453.58	1.89	4.62×10^{-3}
0.6	8.31×10^{-3}	784.15	1489.60	1.90	4.38×10^{-3}
0.7	7.29×10^{-3}	773.26	1464.62	1.89	3.85×10^{-3}
0.8	8.43×10^{-3}	799.52	1508.04	1.89	4.47×10^{-3}
0.9	7.88×10^{-3}	807.81	1516.03	1.88	4.20×10^{-3}
1.0	8.39×10^{-3}	818.62	1541.31	1.88	4.45×10^{-3}

TABLE VI. Game Progress Model Considering Mass (Loser's Intuition)

DS	F	g_{loser}	Σg	m_{loser}	a_{loser}
0.1	5.70×10^{-3}	395.70	870.17	2.20	2.59×10^{-3}
0.2	6.90×10^{-3}	597.91	1277.66	2.14	3.23×10^{-3}
0.3	6.27×10^{-3}	660.33	1395.11	2.11	2.97×10^{-3}
0.4	6.43×10^{-3}	672.01	1440.30	2.14	3.00×10^{-3}
0.5	8.75×10^{-3}	685.77	1453.58	2.12	4.13×10^{-3}
0.6	8.31×10^{-3}	705.45	1489.60	2.11	3.94×10^{-3}
0.7	7.29×10^{-3}	691.36	1464.62	2.12	3.44×10^{-3}
0.8	8.43×10^{-3}	708.52	1508.04	2.13	3.96×10^{-3}
0.9	7.88×10^{-3}	708.22	1516.03	2.14	3.68×10^{-3}
1.0	8.39×10^{-3}	722.69	1541.31	2.13	3.93×10^{-3}

TABLE VII. Game Progress Model Considering Mass (Average Intuition)

DS	a_{winner}	a_{loser}	$a_{average}$
0.1	3.11×10^{-3}	2.59×10^{-3}	2.83×10^{-3}
0.2	3.67×10^{-3}	3.23×10^{-3}	3.43×10^{-3}
0.3	3.30×10^{-3}	2.97×10^{-3}	3.12×10^{-3}
0.4	3.43×10^{-3}	3.00×10^{-3}	3.20×10^{-3}
0.5	4.62×10^{-3}	4.13×10^{-3}	4.36×10^{-3}
0.6	4.38×10^{-3}	3.94×10^{-3}	4.14×10^{-3}
0.7	3.85×10^{-3}	3.44×10^{-3}	3.64×10^{-3}
0.8	4.47×10^{-3}	3.96×10^{-3}	4.20×10^{-3}
0.9	4.20×10^{-3}	3.68×10^{-3}	3.92×10^{-3}
1.0	4.45×10^{-3}	3.93×10^{-3}	4.18×10^{-3}

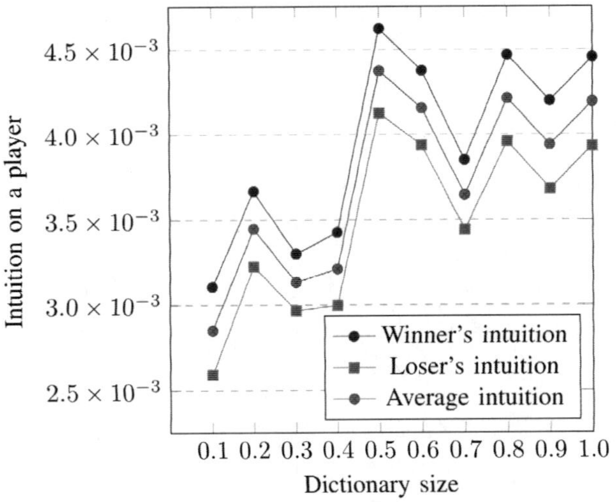

Figure 3. Comparison of the game progress model considering mass

The above figure shows that $\log B$ and $\sqrt[3]{B}$ yield a precise

TABLE VIII. EFFECTIVE BRANCHING FACTOR APPROXIMATION

Formula	*Interpretation*
1	Experts
$\log B$	Possible approximation for intermediate players
$\sqrt[3]{B}$	Possible approximation for intermediate players
$\sqrt{B}$	Possible approximation for intermediate players
B	Beginners

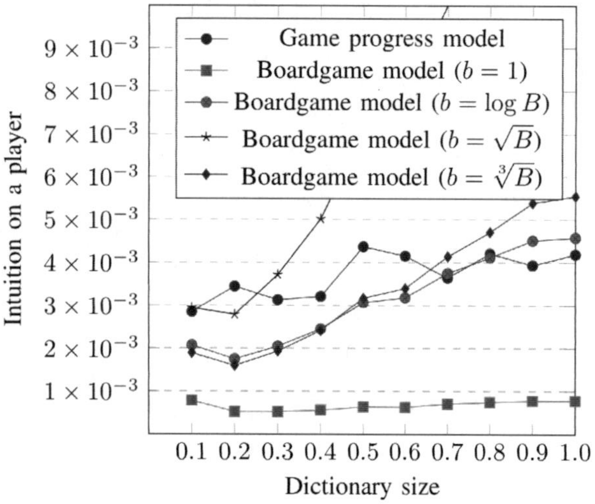

Figure 4. Comparison of GR measures considering mass

approximation for the effective branching factor b. For more precise comparison, the respective mean squared errors between the approximation and the average acceleration from the game progress model considering mass are shown in Table IX. The final comparative results using $\log B$, which is the current best known approximation are shown in Table X.

TABLE IX. MEAN SQUARED ERROR COMPARISON

Formula	*Mean Squared Error*
1	9.55×10^{-6}
$\log B$	8.42×10^{-7}
$\sqrt[3]{B}$	1.29×10^{-6}
$\sqrt{B}$	3.42×10^{-5}
B	2.13×10^{-2}

TABLE X. COMPARISON OF TWO GAME REFINEMENT MEASURES CONSIDERING MASS

DS	*Game Progress Model*	*Board Game Model*	*Difference*
0.1	2.83×10^{-3}	2.07×10^{-3}	27.30%
0.2	3.43×10^{-3}	1.75×10^{-3}	49.30%
0.3	3.12×10^{-3}	2.05×10^{-3}	34.66%
0.4	3.20×10^{-3}	2.45×10^{-3}	23.78%
0.5	4.36×10^{-3}	3.07×10^{-3}	29.89%
0.6	4.14×10^{-3}	3.18×10^{-3}	23.40%
0.7	3.64×10^{-3}	3.75×10^{-3}	-2.91%
0.8	4.20×10^{-3}	4.12×10^{-3}	2.25%
0.9	3.92×10^{-3}	4.52×10^{-3}	-14.60%
1.0	4.18×10^{-3}	4.58×10^{-3}	-9.30%

VI. CONCLUSION

Game refinement theory has been used to assess the engagement of a subject. Two earlier models, the game progress model and the boardgame model have been used for the scoring game and the typical boardgame respectively.

SCRABBLE, a game with a scoring system, which is played on a board, is the primary concern of this study. Two earlier models have been applied to this game. However, the significant difference has inspired us to investigate in particular and strengthen the link between real-world physics and physics-in-mind.

We revise game refinement theory after an analogy between real-world physics and physics-in-mind is considered, then the definition of mass-in-mind is established. The concrete mathematical model is constructed based on the type of the subject that is examined. The $\frac{\Sigma g}{g}$ and $\frac{B}{b}$ are introduced for the scoring game and the boardgame respectively. Our study shows that $\log B$ is a good approximation for b. After mass-in-mind is brought into consideration, there is a small difference in the measurement of the acceleration. The randomness of the raw data and the rough approximation of the effective branching factor b are possibly the cause of the apparent error.

In Newtonian mechanics, the concept of mass is based on the self-object only. As opposed to that, mass-in-mind is not just based on the player considered, but also on his experience or skillfulness in that particular subject. In the case of the boardgame, the effective branching factor b depends on the branching factor B and the skill of the player. Professional players tend to have a smaller b, which leads to a higher mass. However, they will have a lower mass in a scoring game. Also, the mass-in-mind of a winner is always less than that of a loser, which leads to a higher acceleration a, which exposes more emotional impact. This appearance is typical behavior as the game usually is more enjoyable to the winner.

Although this paper focuses on the artificial intelligence with perfect vocabulary knowledge, the proposed models fit well with the other cases, which is shown in Table XI.

TABLE XI. COMPARISON OF AVERAGE ERROR

Player Knowledge	*Mean Squared Error*	*Mean Absolute Percent Error*
0.1	1.65×10^{-6}	24.13%
0.2	1.65×10^{-6}	30.09%
0.3	1.19×10^{-6}	32.45%
0.4	1.17×10^{-6}	31.29%
0.5	7.78×10^{-7}	26.59%
0.6	7.68×10^{-7}	24.39%
0.7	8.37×10^{-7}	24.01%
0.8	7.14×10^{-7}	21.06%
0.9	6.26×10^{-7}	19.07%
1.0	8.42×10^{-7}	21.74%

In practice, mass-in-mind is not always a constant but depends on various uncontrollable causes. For instance, current mood and temper may affect the enjoyment of a game. Hence, player may not have the same intuition while playing the same game. We currently do not consider these factors and leave them for future work.

After mass-in-mind is proposed, it is possible to discuss later other physics-in-mind variables, for instance, energy-in-mind and momentum-in-mind, which will enhance the completeness of our theory and the explanation of the phenomenon of emotional impact.

Although the interpretation of mass-in-mind for the case of a time-limited sport is not yet addressed in this paper, we strongly affirm that the same result will be obtained as with the game progress model considering mass, which is $\frac{g}{\Sigma g}$. Further investigation and verification are also left for future work.

ACKNOWLEDGMENT

This research is funded by a grant from the Japan Society for the Promotion of Science, within the framework of the Grant-in-Aid for Challenging Exploratory Research (grant number 17K19968).

REFERENCES

[1] H. Iida, K. Takahara, J. Nagashima, Y. Kajihara, and T. Hashimoto, "An application of game-refinement theory to mah jong," in International Conference on Entertainment Computing. Springer, 2004, pp. 333–338.

[2] P. Májek and H. Iida, "Uncertainty of game outcome," in 3rd International Conference on Global Research and Education in Intelligent Systems, 2004, pp. 171–180.

[3] J. Takeuchi, R. Ramadan, and H. Iida, "Game refinement theory and its application to volleyball," Research Report 2014-GI-31 (3), Information Processing Society of Japan, 2014, pp. 1–6.

[4] N. Nossal and H. Iida, "Game refinement theory and its application to score limit games," in Games Media Entertainment (GEM), 2014 IEEE. IEEE, 2014, pp. 1–3.

[5] A. P. Sutiono, A. Purwarianti, and H. Iida, "A mathematical model of game refinement," in International Conference on Intelligent Technologies for Interactive Entertainment. Springer, 2014, pp. 148–151.

[6] H. Iida, "Where is a line between work and play?" Information Processing Society of Japan, Tech. Rep. 39(2018-GI-039), mar 2018.

[7] L. B. Okun, "The concept of mass," in Energy and Mass in Relativity Theory. World Scientific, 2009, pp. 11–16.

[8] "Scrabble — word games — board games — scrabble online," (Accessed on 1/30/2017). [Online]. Available: https://scrabble.hasbro.com/en-us

[9] "Scrabble history — making of the classic american board game," (Accessed on 1/13/2017). [Online]. Available: https://scrabble.hasbro.com/en-us/history

[10] "Wespa tournament calendar," (Accessed on 1/30/2017). [Online]. Available: http://www.wespa.org/tournaments/index.shtml

[11] "Official tournament rules - naspawiki," (Accessed on 1/30/2017). [Online]. Available: http://www.scrabbleplayers.org/w/Rules

[12] "Scrabble: An entertaining way to improve your child's vocabulary and spelling skills," (Accessed on 11/24/2017). [Online]. Available: http://mathandreadinghelp.org/articles/Scrabble/3A_An_Entertaining_Way_to_Improve_Your_Child/27s_Vocabulary_and_Spelling_Skills.html

[13] "Mass — define mass at dictionary.com," (Accessed on 11/24/2017). [Online]. Available: http://www.dictionary.com/browse/mass

[14] M. Jammer, Concepts of mass in classical and modern physics. Courier Corporation, 1997.

[15] E. Mach, The science of mechanics: A critical and historical account of its development. Open court publishing Company, 1907.

[16] O. Belkind, Physical Systems: Conceptual Pathways Between Flat Space-time and Matter. Springer Science & Business Media, 2012, vol. 264.

[17] "New quantum theory separates gravitational and inertial mass - mit technology review," (Accessed on 11/24/2017). [Online]. Available: https://www.technologyreview.com/s/419367/new-quantum-theory-separates-gravitational-and-inertial-mass

[18] "Hasbro official website — hasbro toys," (Accessed on 1/30/2017). [Online]. Available: https://www.hasbro.com/en-us

[19] "Corporate information about mattel, inc. — creating the future of play," (Accessed on 1/30/2017). [Online]. Available: https://corporate.mattel.com

[20] S. Kananat, J.-C. Terrillon, and H. Iida, "Gamification and scrabble," in Games and Learning Alliance. Springer, 2016, pp. 405–414.

[21] K. Suwanviwatana and H. Iida, "First results from using game refinement measure and learning coefficient in scrabble," arXiv preprint arXiv:1711.03580, 2017.

[22] S. Xiong, L. Zuo, and H. Iida, "Possible interpretations for game refinement measure," in International Conference on Entertainment Computing. Springer, 2017, pp. 322–334.

[23] L. Zuo, S. Xiong, and H. Iida, "An analysis of hotel loyalty program with a focus on the tiers and points system."

[24] H. Iida, "Fairness, judges and thrill in games." IPSJ-SIG-GI, 2008, pp. 61–68.

[25] M. Browne, Schaum's outline of theory and problems of physics for engineering and science. McGraw-Hill, 1999.

[26] S. Holzner, Physics I for dummies. John Wiley & Sons, 2016.

[27] I. B. Cohen, Introduction to Newton's" Principia". Harvard University Press, 1971, vol. 1971.

[28] I. Newton, "Axioms or laws of motion," The Mathematical Principles of Natural Philosophy, vol. 1, 1729, p. 19.

[29] W. Loewenstein, Physics in mind: a quantum view of the brain. Basic Books (AZ), 2013.

[30] C. Murphy, "Why games work and the science of learning," https://ntrs.nasa.gov/search.jsp?R=20130008648, 2012, accessed: 2017-07-22.

[31] O. Schaffer, "Crafting fun user experiences: A method to facilitate flow," Human Factors International, 2013.

Everything Was Good!

The Influence of Sentiment and Product Category on Aspect Choice in German Customer Reviews

Amelie I. Metzmacher[a], Verena Heinrichs[a], Björn Falk[a], Robert H. Schmitt[a]
[a] Laboratory for Machine Tools and Production Engineering (WZL), RWTH Aachen University, Aachen, Germany
E-mail: A.Metzmacher@wzl.rwth-aachen.de, V.Heinrichs@wzl.rwth-aachen.de, B.Falk@wzl.rwth-aachen.de, R.Schmitt@wzl.rwth-aachen.de

Abstract— **Studies dealing with the use of pronouns in customer reviews in social media against the background of sentiment analysis do not consider the role attributed to the pronoun within an evaluative sentence. The following paper addresses the question of when and why customers choose pronouns instead of nouns or proper nouns to function as aspects within an evaluative sentence. To this end, two influencing factors on aspect choice have been investigated: 1) The sentiment of the evaluative sentence (positive, neutral, negative); 2) The category of the evaluated aspect (product, service). The results reveal that, particularly within positive statements, there exist differences between customer reviews evaluating products to those evaluating services.**

Keywords-NLP; sentiment analysis; social media.

I. Introduction

With respect to the growing demand for individualized products and services, understanding the Voice of the Customer (VoC) becomes increasingly important for companies. To better survive competition and fulfill customer demands, it is crucial for companies to develop customer-oriented solutions based on precise knowledge about customer requirements [1].

Knowledge about customer requirements can be captured by studies, interviews, ethnographic research, customer visit teams, customer brainstorming, or lead user analysis [2]. However, these methods are most often time consuming and costly while suffering from low response rates.

Social media provide an alternative to gain knowledge about customer requirements. Information relating to customer requirements derived from social media is more authentic as customers in discussion forums usually uninhibitedly and immediately provide their opinion about products and services [3]. Moreover, the amount of data available online is steadily increasing.

In consideration of the steadily increasing number of available data, it is not possible to extract relevant information from customer reviews in social media manually. Thus, it is necessary to develop a method to automatically extract only the beneficial information from customer reviews, i.e., information about the perceived quality of products and services [4].

Aiming at a supervised machine-learning based solution, an annotation study was conducted to obtain an annotated corpus of German customer reviews from social media. Although there already exist such corpora, e.g., cf. [5], these corpora only include reviews relating to material products.

Within our approach, we focus on both, reviews relating to products and to services. The consideration of products and services is particularly helpful regarding the application for companies. Often reviews about products, as well as services need to be taken into account for customer-oriented product development and design. An example for this is a company producing domestic appliances while at the same time offering services for maintenance, repair and operations.

The corpus at hands consisted of 3,767 German customer reviews, which have been extracted from 38 different social media platforms. Three subjects were asked to annotate the sentiment of each given sentence (positive, neutral, negative) while labelling the aspect (the item that is evaluated, e.g., "room").

Developing a supervised machine-learning algorithm, we focus on the use of linguistic salience. Our approach comprises a detailed analysis of the language used within the reviews taking into consideration the differences with respect to the distribution of part-of-speech (POS) tags between product reviews and service reviews, as well as differences occurring with respect to the sentiment.

Concerning the annotated aspects, nouns and proper nouns constitute 82% of all POS tags:

- "Das Zimmer jedoch war sehr enttäuschend." (*Engl.* "However, the room was very disappointing.")
- "Nutella ist super lecker." (*Engl.* "Nutella is super yummy.")

The aspect category occurring second most was pronouns (5.5%):

- "Alles perfekt." (*Engl.* "Everything perfect.")
- "Er war noch pampig zu mir." (*Engl.* "He even was stroppy with me.")

This raises the question of when and why customers choose pronouns instead of nouns or proper nouns to function as aspects within an evaluative sentence.

Within our paper, we will examine the role of the following two influencing factors on aspect choice:

1) The sentiment of the evaluative sentence (positive, neutral, negative)

2) The category of the evaluated aspect (product, service)

In the following, Section 2 deals with related literature covering psychological and linguistic research relating to the use of pronouns including sentiment analysis. In Section 3, the procedure of the annotation study is presented, leading to the presentation and discussion of results in Section 4. Finally, Section 5 finishes this contribution with a brief conclusion and information about future research questions.

II. Linguistic And Psychological Research

As opposed to psychologically derived linguistic dimensions such as emotion words, pronouns constitute a closed class of standard grammatical units [6] [7]. The use of pronouns in verbal behavior has been studied from various linguistic and psychological viewpoints.

Substituting an anteceding noun or noun phrase, pronouns establish coherence in a text [8]. Crawley et al. [9] state that there is a preference for pronominal coreference if the antecedent is mentioned prominently (subjecthood, first position, clefted phrase). Bosch and Umbach [10] found out that for non-subject antecedents, the preference for demonstrative pronouns is stronger than for personal pronouns with subject antecedents.

With regard to personality measures, findings suggest that the use of first person singular pronouns (e.g., I, me, my) correlates with the degree of self-involvement and self-awareness of the speaker [11] [12]. A person who is focusing attention on himself is more likely to use first person singular pronouns [13]. For example, depression was found to be related to an increased use of first person singular pronouns in patients, reflecting a weakness in connecting to others [14]. However, the more the health of the patients improved, the more the individuals shifted in their use from first person to second and third person pronouns [15].

Following Sillars et al. [16], married couples who live in a satisfying and long lasting relationship are more likely to use first person plural pronouns (e.g., we, us, our) to demonstrate their sense of belonging.

Against the background of lying and truth-telling, studies found out that truth-tellers use a higher rate of first person singular pronouns than liars [17]. Liars use less first person singular pronouns to detach themselves from the lie being told [18]. Knowledge about the increased use of first person singular pronouns in truth-telling has led to the fact that liars and fake reviewers nowadays tend to overuse first person singular pronouns to persuade others [18][19].

Relating to research dealing with social interaction and politeness, Brown and Levinson state that in order to keep one's face while conveying a negative message, people impersonalize their opposite by avoiding the pronouns "I" and "you" [20]. In order to motivate others, people formulate statements, which are characterized by a low degree of first person singular pronouns emphasizing the spirit of collaboration needed [21].

Although pronouns carry no sentiment as such in [8], they function as linguistic markers for sentiment analysis. Ofek et al. [22] used pronouns to predict whether a statement contains objective or subjective content stating that subjective statements contain more personal pronouns than objective statements. Similar Moen et al. [23] found out that when angry, people use more second and third person pronouns to focus on others than themselves. However, studies dealing with the use of pronouns against the background of sentiment analysis do not consider the role attributed to the pronoun within an evaluative sentence.

III. Annotation Study

As described in our previous work [24], 38 different social media platforms have been chosen for data extraction. The open-source Java library jsoup [25] was implemented to extract 3,767 German customer reviews relating to products and services. The reviews were parsed into single sentences and tokenized using the Stuttgart-Tübingen TagSet (STTS) [26] and Stanford Parser [27].

Three German native speakers familiar with the process of annotation have been asked to annotate the customer reviews. Subjects were asked to annotate the sentiment of each given sentence (positive, neutral, negative) while labelling the aspect (the item that is evaluated, e.g., "room"). In case of ambiguous or sub-clause sentences, subjects were allowed to mark more than one aspect and sentiment value. For instance, within the sentence "Die Lage ist gut, aber der Raum sehr klein." (*Engl.* "The location is good, but the room is very small."), subjects were able to label two aspects and two sentiment values. The first part of the sentence was labelled positive ("good") relating to the aspect "location" and the second part dealing with the aspect "room" was labelled negative ("small"). This ensures that all information provided in a sentence are gathered.

Prior to annotation, the annotation process was explained to the subjects with three exemplary sentences. The sentences varied with respect to the level of complexity. This guarantees consistency amongst annotators, i.e., it should ameliorate the interrater reliability.

IV. Results And Discussion

Starting with analyzing the interrater reliability, Fleiss' Kappa values for aspect choice and sentiment values range between 0.5 and 0.8. Thus, they are located in moderate level of agreement [28].

Investigating the influence of sentiment on aspect choice, Figure 1 depicts the distribution of pronouns with respect to the sentiment. As the class for neutral sentiment value is with approximately 5% very low, we will not consider this class in our further analyses. Moreover, previous studies revealed that the class of neutral sentiment has to be examined separately [24].

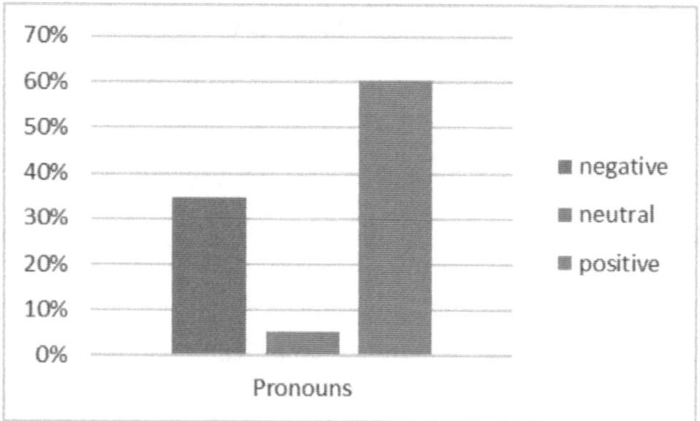

Figure 1. Distribution of pronouns as aspects with respect to the sentiment.

Figure 1 illustrates the distribution of pronouns denoting the aspect of an evaluative sentence against the sentiment of the sentence. Of all pronoun-as-aspect occurrences, 60% occur in positive sentences. The use of pronouns as aspects tends to be most prominent in evaluative sentences containing a positive sentiment. One first explanation could be that customers use more detailed forms of language, i.e., actual product parts or certain aspects of a service, if they formulate critique or evaluate the product with a negative outcome. In contrast to that, while formulating a positive review, customers tend to generalize.

Figure 2 depicts the distribution of pronouns denoting the aspect of an evaluative sentence against the sentiment of the sentence and the product category. It is striking that within the category service reviews, the number of pronouns-as-aspect occurrences is equal with respect to the sentiment of the sentence. When evaluating services, the sentiment of the sentence has no influence on the selection of the POS to represent the aspect. However, relating to reviews referring to products there exists a difference in the number of pronouns used as aspects between positive and negative sentiments. If a product is evaluated with a positive sentiment, the aspect is more likely to be realized by a pronoun.

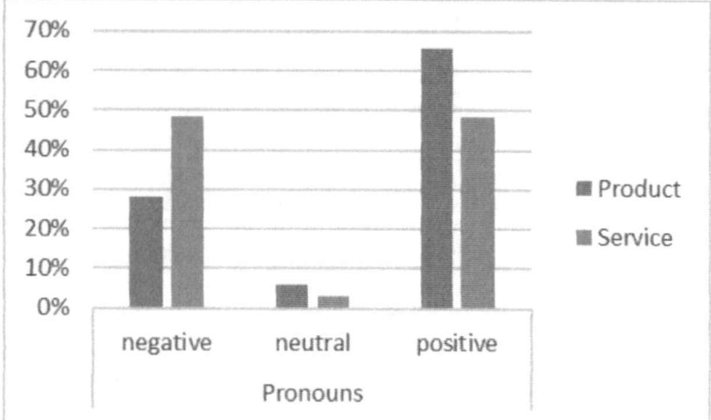

Figure 2. Distribution of pronouns as aspects with respect to sentiment and product category.

Taking a closer look at the actual pronoun tokens, which function as aspects within evaluative sentences, Figure 3 illustrates the words, which have been chosen to represent the aspect of an evaluative sentence. In most cases, 3rd person singular pronouns ("er, sie, es", "der, die, das") were attributed the role of the aspect.

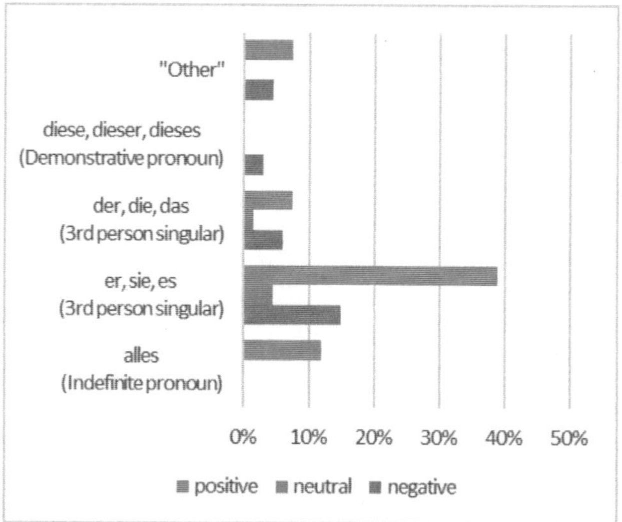

Figure 3. Distribution of used pronouns in product reviews with respect to the sentiment.

However, the indefinite pronoun "alles" (*Engl.:* "everything") is exclusively used in positive evaluative sentences. Our assumption is that when evaluating products with a positive sentiment, customers differentiate less and summarize their positive impression and experience using indefinite pronouns. On the other hand, when expressing anger within a negative evaluative sentence, customers reflect on single features and details describing precisely what has led to the negative impression and experience. Following this idea we cross-read the sentences labelled as positive and which contain the indefinite pronoun "alles" as aspect. As a result, more than 75% of the sentences contained the statement "everything was good" or words to that effect. Thus, one could argue that these pronouns functioning as aspects in product statements are representative for the general customer satisfaction regarding the given product.

V. Conclusion And Future Work

The results obtained in our study strengthen the assumption that there exists a difference in the use of pronouns as aspects for negative and for positive evaluative sentences within customer reviews relating to material products. However, customer reviews dealing with services do not show these differences.

Pronouns are more often chosen as aspects if the evaluative sentence is positive. Positive reviews have a tendency to be longer in text length and token number. Therefore, one might argue that pronouns functioning as aspects are mainly used in longer comments to establish coherence within a text. Although, it is very likely that this argument is not true for the indefinite pronoun “alles” (*Engl.:* “everything”), it might make sense to investigate the number of sentences per comment, too. In addition, while enlarging the database, the use of pronouns within service reviews should be examined as well.

Whereas there is still a lot of potential for further research from the linguistic point of view within customer reviews in social media, our results already reveal the necessity to use POS information in automatically analyzing these data. Thus, within our objective to develop a supervised machine-learning algorithm to extract relevant information, this information will be taken into account.

ACKNOWLEDGMENT

The support of the German National Science Foundation (DFG) through the funding of the research project “Entwicklung eines Sensors für ungerichtete Beschwerden aus Online Foren” (SCHM 1856/69-1) is gratefully acknowledged.

REFERENCES

[1] R. Schmitt, S. Schmitt, A. Linder, M. Rüßmann, and V. Heinrichs, “Fehlerinformationen nutzen – Produkte nachhaltig absichern (in English: The usage of failure information – safeguarding products sustainably).” In: 18. Business Forum Qualität. Daten für die Qualität von morgen - generieren, interpretieren und nutzen (in English: 18th Business Forum Quality. Data for tomorrow’s quality – generation, interpretation and usage). September 2014. Apprimus Aachen, pp. 2-22, 2014.

[2] R. G. Cooper and S. J. Edgett, “Ideation for product innovation: What are the best methods." PDMA visions magazine 1(1), pp. 12-17, 2008.

[3] F. T. Piller, A. Vossen, and Ch. Ihl, “From Social Media to Social Product Development: The Impact of Social Media on Co-Creation of Innovation.” Die Unternehmung, 65(1), pp.1 – 22, 2012.

[4] K. Schouten and F. Frasincar, "Survey on aspect-level sentiment analysis." IEEE Transactions on Knowledge and Data Engineering 28(3), pp. 813-830, 2016.

[5] K. Boland, A. Wira-Alam, and R. Messerschmidt, “Creating an annotated corpus for sentiment analysis of german product reviews.” GESIS - Leibniz-Institut für Sozialwissenschaften. Mannheim, GESISTechnical Reports 2013/05, May 2013.

[6] B. Hall Partee, “Opacity, coreference, and pronouns.” Synthese, 21(3), pp. 359-385, 1970.

[7] J. W. Pennebaker, M. R. Mehl, and K. G. Niederhoffer. "Psychological aspects of natural language use: Our words, our selves." Annual review of psychology 54(1), pp. 547-577, 2003.

[8] H. W. Cowles, "The influence of ‘aboutness’ on pronominal coreference." ZAS Papers in Linguistics, 48, pp. 23–38, 2007.

[9] R. A. Crawley, R. J. Stevenson, and D. Kleinman, "The use of heuristic strategies in the interpretation of pronouns." Journal of Psycholinguistic Research 19(4), pp. 245-264, 1990.

[10] P. Bosch and C. Umbach, "Reference determination for demonstrative pronouns." ZAS Papers in Linguistics 48, pp. 39 – 51, 2007.

[11] W. Ickes, S. Reidhead, and M. Patterson, “Machiavellianism and self-monitoring: as different as ‘me’ and ‘you’” Soc. Cogn. 4, pp. 58–74, 1986.

[12] L. Scherwitz and J. Canick, “Self reference and coronary heart disease risk.” In: Type A Behavior Pattern: Research, Theory, and Intervention, ed. K Houston, CR Snyder, New York: Wiley, pp. 146–167, 1988.

[13] D. Davis and T. C. Brock , “Use of first person pronouns as a function of increased objective self-awareness and performance feedback.” J. Exp. Soc. Psychol. 11, pp. 389–400, 1975.

[14] W. Bucci and N. Freedman, “The language of depression.”, Bull. Menninger Clin. 45, pp. 334–358, 1981.

[15] R. S. Campbell and J. W. Pennebaker, "The secret life of pronouns: Flexibility in writing style and physical health." Psychological science 14(1), pp. 60-65, 2003.

[16] A. Sillars, W. Shellen, A. McIntosh, M. Pomegranate, “Relational characteristics of language: elaboration and differentiation in marital conversations.” West. J. Commun. 61, pp.403–422, 1997.

[17] M. L. Newman, J. W. Pennebaker, D. S. Berry, and J. M. Richards, “Lying words: Predicting deception from linguistic styles.” Personality and social psychology bulletin, 29(5), pp. 665-675, 2003.

[18] B. Liu, “Sentiment analysis: Mining opinions, sentiments, and emotions”, Cambridge University Press, 2015.

[19] E. Cambria, D. Das, S. Bandyopadhyay, and A. Feraco, “Affective Computing and Sentiment Analysis.” In A Practical Guide to Sentiment Analysis, Springer International Publishing, pp. 1-10, 2017.

[20] P. Brown, and S. C. Levinson, “Politeness: Some universals in language usage.” Cambridge university press, 1987.

[21] J. W. Pennebaker & L. A. King, “Linguistic styles: language use as an individual difference.” J. Personal. Soc. Psychol. 77, pp. 1296–1312, 1999.

[22] N. Ofek, L. Rokach, C. Caragea, and J. Yen, “The Importance of Pronouns to Sentiment Analysis: Online Cancer Survivor Network Case Study.” Proceedings of the 24th International Conference on World Wide Web. ACM, pp. 83 – 84, 2015.

[23] M.- F. Moens, J. Li, and T.-S. Chua, “Mining user generated content.” CRC Press, 2014.

[24] A. I. Metzmacher, V. Heinrichs, B. Falk, and R. H. Schmitt, „Use of Negation Markers in German Customer Reviews“, The Eleventh International Conference on Advances in Semantic Processing (SEMAPRO 2017), IARIA, November 2017, pp. 37 - 41.

[25] J. Hedley “jsoup: Java HTML Parser”, 2009. [Online] Available from: https://jsoup.org/ [Retrieved: November, 2017].

[26] Insitut für Maschinelle Sprachverarbeitung, “German Tagsets”, 2013. [Online] http://www.ims.uni-stuttgart.de /forschung/ressourcen/lexika/GermanTagsets.html [Retrieved: November 2017].

[27] A. N. Rafferty and C. D. Manning, “Parsing three German treebanks: Lexicalized and unlexicalized baselines”. In Proceedings of the Workshop on Parsing German. Association for Computational Linguistics, pp. 40-46, 2008.

[28] M. L. McHugh, “Interrater reliability: the kappa statistic”, Biochemia medica, 22(3), pp. 276-282, 2012.

Discriminative Approach to Semi-Supervised Clustering

Marek Śmieja

Faculty of Mathematics and
Computer Science
Jagiellonian University
Lojasiewicza 6, 30-348 Kraków
Email: marek.smieja@ii.uj.edu.pl

***Abstract*—We consider a semi-supervised clustering problem, where selected pairs of data points are labeled by an expert as must-links or cannot-links. Basically, must-link constraints indicate that two points should be grouped together, while those with cannot-link constraints should be grouped separately. We present a clustering algorithm, which creates a partition consistent with pairwise constraints by maximizing the probability of correct assignments. Moreover, unlabeled data are used by maximizing their prediction confidence. Preliminary experimental studies show that the proposed method gives accurate results on sample data sets. Moreover, its kernelization allows to discover clustering patterns of arbitrary shapes.**

Keywords*–*semi-supervised clustering; pairwise constraints; discriminative model.

I. INTRODUCTION

Clustering is one of core branches of machine learning and data analysis, which aims to find homogeneous groups in data. Since cluster analysis is purely unsupervised technique, its results may be unsatisfactory for a given problem. Semi-supervised clustering allows to include side information (expert knowledge) about class labels into clustering to obtain more appropriate effects for the user [1]. Pairwise constraints (relations) are a typical form of additional class information used in semi-supervised clustering. They indicate whether two points belong to the same (must-link) or different groups (cannot-link). The aim of semi-supervised clustering is to use pairwise constraints in order to produce more accurate results [2][3].

To meet the user expectations revealed in pairwise constraints, we follow a discriminative approach, which is usually applied in classification, but is rarely used in clustering. Discriminative model is more natural and effective for semi-supervised task than typical generative approaches, such as k-means or Gaussian mixture model (GMM), because it directly focuses on the underlying classification problem. We formulate a clustering model, which maximizes the probability that pairwise relations are preserved. Unlabeled data are handled by maximizing their prediction confidence, which agrees with a typical paradigm of semi-supervised learning (cluster assumption) stating that decision boundary should fall in low density region.

Our method is easy to implement and can be optimized with use of a gradient approach. Moreover, it can be kernelized so that to fit arbitrary clustering structures, see Figure 1 for the illustration. Preliminary experimental results show that our method is promising and allows to obtain competitive results to the state-of-the-art models.

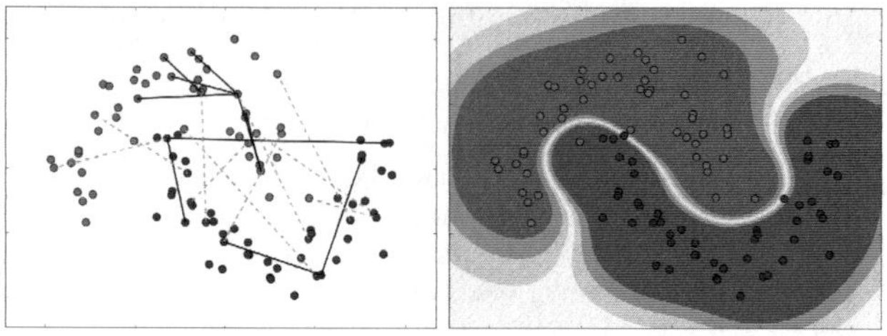

(a) (b)

Figure 1. Sample results of our method on two moons data set (b); must-links (solid black line) and cannot-link (dashed cyan) are shown in (a).

II. MODEL

We consider a data set $X \subset \mathbb{R}^D$, such that $N = |X|$, where every element $x \in X$ belongs to one of K unknown classes. By $\mathcal{X} = X \times X$ we denote the set of all pairs in X. Partial information about class labels is revealed in the form of pairwise constraints, which cover selected pairs of data points $\mathcal{L} \subset \mathcal{X}$. Pairwise constraints indicate whether two points originate from the same or different classes, thus $\mathcal{L}$ can be split into the sets of must-link and cannot-link constraints given by [1]:

$$\mathcal{M} = \{(x, y) \in \mathcal{L} : x \text{ and } y \text{ belong to the same class}\},$$
$$\mathcal{C} = \{(x, y) \in \mathcal{L} : x \text{ and } y \text{ belong to the different classes}\}.$$

Our clustering model follows a discriminative approach in which the assignments of data points to clusters are directly modeled by posterior probabilities. Let $p_k(x) = p(k|x)$ be a posterior probability that a data point $x \in X$ is assigned to k-th cluster, where $k = 1, \ldots, K$. Once these conditional probabilities are defined, we get a partition of X, in which a point $x \in X$ is assigned to this group that maximizes its posterior probability. More precisely, we get a partition of X into $C_1, \ldots, C_k \subset X$, where

$$C_k = \{x \in X : p_k(x) = \max_j p_j(x)\}.$$

We assumed that posterior probabilities are given by a logistic function:

$$p_k(x) = p_k(x; \mathcal{V}) \propto \exp(\langle v_k, x \rangle + b_k), \tag{1}$$

where the set of parameters $\mathcal{V} = (v, b)$ consists of weight vectors $v = (v_1, \ldots, v_K)$ and bias values $b = (b_1, \ldots, b_K)$.

Our model focuses on maximizing a probability that pairwise constraints are satisfied. Let us first observe that the probability that a clustering model assigns two points $x, y \in X$ to the same cluster equals:

$$p_{\mathcal{M}}(x, y) = \sum_{k=1}^{K} p_k(x) p_k(y). \quad (2)$$

Consequently, the probability that $x, y \in X$ are classified to different groups is given by:

$$p_{\mathcal{C}}(x, y) = 1 - p_{\mathcal{M}}(x, y). \quad (3)$$

To meet the expert knowledge, we maximize both terms over all pairwise relations.

In addition to pairwise constraints, we usually have the access to a large number of unlabeled data. Since there is no information about their classes, we cannot simply maximize their correct assignments. However, we can encourage the model to give the most confident answers about their classes. Let us consider a function

$$\sum_{k=1}^{K} p_k(x)^2, \text{ for every } x \in \mathcal{X}, \quad (4)$$

which attains a maximal value, if the prediction confidence is maximal, i.e., $p_l(x) = 1$ for specific l and $p_k(x) = 0$, for all $k \neq l$. On the other hand, if all classes are equally probable then its value is minimal. Thus, to maximize a prediction confidence of the model, we maximize (4) over unlabeled data.

Our clustering objective function gathers (2), (3) and (4) over all data points. Its maximization can be implemented with use of gradient approach. Moreover, due to the form of posterior probabilities (1) one can introduce kernel functions to detect arbitrary shapes of clusters.

III. EXPERIMENTS

We examined our method on two standard data sets retrieved from UCI repository [4]: Letter (1000 examples, 16 features, 5 classes) and Seeds (210 examples, 7 features, 3 classes). To acquire pairwise relations, we randomly selected a pair of points (x, y) and label it as must-link if both x, y belong to the same cluster or as cannot-link, otherwise. We vary the number of constraints from $0.1N$ to $0.5N$ with a $0.1N$ increment. The results were evaluated using adjusted rand index (ARI) [5]. ARI attains a maximal value 1 for a partition identical with a ground-truth, while for a random grouping gives score 0.

We compared our method with five state-of-the-art techniques:

- another discriminative framework proposed in [6], referred to as DCPR (discriminative clustering with pairwise constraints).
- recent semi-supervised spectral clustering [7], referred to as spec
- constrained GMM proposed in [2] (GMM)
- two metric learning algorithms: diag [8] and itml [9]

The results presented in Figure 2 show that our method usually obtained very high scores. Its performance gradually increases as the number of constraints grows. It can be observed that itml and DCPR also gave high resemblance with reference grouping, while the performance of GMM, spec and diag were usually worse.

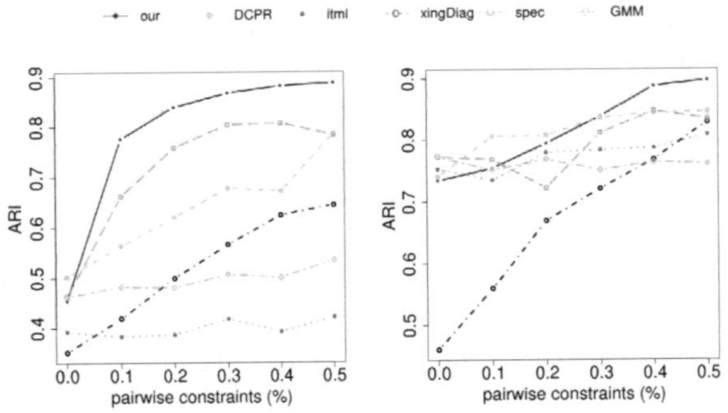

(a) Letter (b) Seeds

Figure 2. Adjusted rand index of examined methods two data sets retrieved from UCI repository.

IV. CONCLUSION AND FUTURE WORK

In this paper, we presented a new approach to clustering with pairwise constraints and demonstrated its usefulness on two data sets. In future, we plan to extend this model to handle unlabeled data in a more efficient way. In particular, we plan to use the information about data points' neighborhoods. We would also like to use different types of expert knowledge such partial labeling or relative constraints. Moreover, we will apply the proposed approach in real life problems.

ACKNOWLEDGMENT

This work was partially supported by the National Science Centre (Poland) grant no. 2016/21/D/ST6/00980.

REFERENCES

[1] S. Basu, I. Davidson, and K. Wagstaff, Constrained clustering: Advances in algorithms, theory, and applications. CRC Press, 2008.

[2] N. Shental, A. Bar-hillel, T. Hertz, and D. Weinshall, "Computing Gaussian mixture models with EM using equivalence constraints," in Advances in Neural Information Processing Systems (NIPS), Vancouver, British Columbia, Canada, December 2004, pp. 465–472.

[3] M. Bilenko, S. Basu, and R. J. Mooney, "Integrating constraints and metric learning in semi-supervised clustering," in Proceedings of the twenty-first international conference on Machine learning. ACM, 2004, p. 11.

[4] M. Lichman, "UCI machine learning repository," 2013. [Online]. Available: http://archive.ics.uci.edu/ml

[5] L. Hubert and P. Arabie, "Comparing partitions," Journal of Classification, vol. 2, no. 1, 1985, pp. 193–218.

[6] Y. Pei, X. Z. Fern, T. V. Tjahja, and R. Rosales, "Comparing clustering with pairwise and relative constraints: A unified framework," ACM Transactions on Knowledge Discovery from Data (TKDD), vol. 11, no. 2, 2016, p. 22.

[7] P. Qian et al., "Affinity and penalty jointly constrained spectral clustering with all-compatibility, flexibility, and robustness," IEEE transactions on neural networks and learning systems, vol. 28, no. 5, 2017, pp. 1123–1138.

[8] E. P. Xing, M. I. Jordan, S. J. Russell, and A. Y. Ng, "Distance metric learning with application to clustering with side-information," in Advances in neural information processing systems, 2003, pp. 521–528.

[9] J. V. Davis, B. Kulis, P. Jain, S. Sra, and I. S. Dhillon, "Information-theoretic metric learning," in Proceedings of the 24th international conference on Machine learning. ACM, 2007, pp. 209–216.

Using Grice Maxims In Ranking Community Question Answers

Abed Alhakim Freihat
University of Trento
Trento, Italy
Email: abed.freihat@unitn.it

Mohammed R H Qwaider
FBK, Trento
Trento, Italy
Email: qwaider@fbk.eu

Fausto Giunchiglia
University of Trento
Trento, Italy
Email: fausto@unitn.it

***Abstract*—Community question answering portals and forum Web sites are becoming prominent resources of knowledge and experience exchange and such platforms are becoming invaluable information mines. Getting to this information in such knowledge mines is not trivial and fraught with difficulties and challenges. One of these difficulties is to discover the relevant answers and/or to predict the best answer(s) among these. In this paper, we present a Grice cooperative maxims based approach for ranking community question answers.**

Keywords–Community Question Answering; Grice Maxims; Ranking Algorithms; Cooperative Principle.

I. Introduction

Community question answering Web sites are growing rapidly. Web portals, such as Google Answers [1], Yahoo Answers [2], and other community forums are becoming rich resources for knowledge and experience exchange [3]. Despite the richness of these resources, benefiting from them - that depends on the ability of discovering relevant answers and/or ranking them - is still limited [4]. In the last decades, dozens of approaches to solve the ranking problem have been proposed. These approaches usually depend on feature extraction by using machine learning techniques [5].

In this paper, we address the problem of answer ranking in a different way. Our hypothesis is that linguistics offer us a good opportunity to predict relevancy of answers and rank them accordingly. In particular, we think that Grice maxims [6] give us a way to score answers and thus rank them accordingly.

Originally, Grice maxims were presented mainly from a pragmatic point of view as a way to explain how a listener perceives the utterances of a speaker so that he can understand the intention of the speaker of a sentence which seems extensionally unrelated to the conversation. For example, using these maxims explains that the speaker B understands the intention of the speaker A. The same holds for A who understands the indirect answer. An important point here is that the extensional logic relation between A and B is missing or implicit.

A *What is the time?*

B *The bus left five minutes ago.*

In this work, we use Grice maxims from engineering point of view, where we interpret and use them as a way for measuring the extensional relevancy of what a speaker says. For example, we are interested in: Does answer$_i$ contain more information than answer$_j$ and interpret it as answer$_i$ is better than answer$_j$ if it contains more information and vice versa. Thus, our approach does not consider the pragmatic (intentional) interpretation of Grice maxims as in the previous example. Instead, we are focusing on the extensional relation(s) between a question and an answer, and the relation(s) between answer$_i$ and answer$_j$.

The paper is organized as follows. Section II describes community question answering portals and illustrates the problem statement. Section III gives an overview of related works. In Section IV, Grice maxims are presented. In this section, we show how they can be interpreted and used as criteria for scoring answers in community question answering portals. In Section V, the implementation of our approach is described, where we depict the used resources, some of the approach experiments, and the proposed scoring algorithm for answers ranking in community question answering portals. The paper is concluded with future work discussion in Section VI.

II. Problem Statement

In the last two decades, several types of question answering Web sites have emerged. These sites offer usually the possibility to post a question and get several possible answers to the posted question. In general, the community question answering Web pages can be classified into two main categories [7].

- **Closed professional Web pages**. Such Web pages are usually specialized in one or more related domains. Answering the questions in these Web sites is restricted to trusted experts who work in these domains. The answers in such Web sites are written in well written and standard language. For example, medical consulting pages belong to this category.
- **Open non professional Web pages**. The questions in such pages usually belong to different domains and answering the questions is not restricted to specialized persons or experts. In contrary to the former type, the answers in such pages may contain malformed or not well written answers and may contain noisy punctuations, such as *:)), !!??,:((*, or non standard abbreviations such as *plz, thnx, u r,...*
  Community forums belong to this type of Web sites which are more likely to the social media platforms such as Facebook and Twitter in that they do not put any constraints on used language, punctuations, morphology, or orthography rules.

In this work, we focus in our research on open community forms. In particular, we are going to test our approach on Qatar Living forum [8], which is an open domain community forum. This forum is used mostly by expats who live and work in Qatar.

Beside entertainment, this forum is a platform for knowledge and experience exchange about issues related to living and working in Qatar. This makes the forum besides its social side, a rich shared knowledge resource. Users who need advice or information about some issue related to living and working in Qatar, post their questions and they usually get several answers and comments from other registered users. The forum language is English though most of the forum members are non native speakers of English (which makes the task more challenging).

To summarize, given a question Q and a set of answers $\langle a_1, ..., a_n \rangle$, rank these answers according to their relevancy with respect to the question Q. The data sets, which we used for developing, and testing are taken from the SemEval 2016 Task 3 [9] competition.

III. Related Work

In this section, we give a brief review of community question answering approaches and a short overview of a similar approach that uses Grice maxims in computational approaches.

A. Community Question Answering Approaches

Question answers ranking is a task of great interest in both research and commerce. In the last couple of years, there were different shared tasks, in a wide contest in three SemEval editions [10], [9], and [11], also a more specific context of ranking a set of frequently asked questions for a given question [12].

In general, machine learning based approaches utilize a variety of features and techniques for solving the ranking problem, e.g., similarity features [12] such as cosine similarity applied to lexical, syntactic and semantic representations or distributed representations. In addition, machine learning approaches employ trigger words such as insulting, or degrading words, meta features such as user ID, or answer position in the list.

Other class of features is the class of automatically generated features, where these features are generated from syntactic structures using tree kernels [13]. The main classifiers used in these approaches are SVM (Support Vector Machine) classifiers [14] and Convolutional Neural Network [15].

The success of machine learning based ranking approaches depends on the learning platforms and the used set of features. For example, KeLP (Kernel-based Learning Platform) [16] had the best results on SemEval 2016 task 3, where they use KeLP machine learning platform [17] which learns the similarity of semantic representation between two given texts with the help of previously proposed features [18]. The second best results on SemEval 2016 task 3 belongs to ConvKN [18] which utilizes deep-learning techniques, by combining convolutional tree kernels and convolutional neural networks, together with text similarity and thread-specific features. The third best system is SemanticZ [19] that uses semantic similarity based on word embeddings and topics.

B. Grice Maxims Based Computational Approaches

Grice maxims have attracted many researchers who enriched the research community with variety of research proposals and articles about Grice theory. Most of these approaches are in the linguistics and pragmatics domains. In the following, we highlight few Grice maxims based computational approaches. We do not review Grice maxims theoretical approaches in the linguistics and pragmatics since they are worthy of dedicating one or more papers to review them.

In the current state of the art, we find interesting computational approaches that utilize Grice maxims for solving linguistic and other real world problems . For example, Vogel et al. [20] presented their approach that uses Grice maxims in multi-agent decision theory, where they suggest cognitively-inspired heuristics to reason about cooperative language resulting from Grice communication principle.

Another idea discussed a general game theoretic model of quantity implicature calculation [21], and proposed a procedure to construct interpretation games as models of the context of utterance from a set of alternative sentences, and a step-by-step reasoning process that selects the pragmatically feasible play in these games.

In another approach [22], Dale et al. used Grice maxims in generating referring expressions in natural language generating task. In another study, Kheirabadi et al. [23] consider news as a mutual conversational activity between the media and its audiences. Based on this observation, they introduce Grice pragmatic maxims as a set of linguistic criteria for news selectivity.

IV. Using Grice Maxims For Community Question Answers Ranking

Grice main idea is that communication between human beings is logic and rational. Following this idea, any conversation assumes cooperation between the conversation parties. This cooperation supposes in essence four maxims that usually hold in dialogues or conversations [6]. These maxims are:

1) **Quality**: Say only true things.
2) **Quantity**: Be informative as much as necessary.
3) **Relation**: Be relevant in your conversation.
4) **Manner**: Be direct and straightforward.

These maxims have been intensively researched in the domain of linguistics and pragmatics in the last decades, where the researchers focused on how to use Grice theory to explain speaker intention when he says some thing. In this work, we use these maxims partially to measure the appropriateness or relevancy of answer(s) of a given question. In this approach, we do not try to understand what the speaker (intentional) means. Instead, we try to understand if the speaker contribution contains (extensional) elements that comply with Grice maxims.

In the following, we explain how we interpret the quantity, relation and manner maxims in our approach. We do not use the quality maxim and it is beyond the scope of our research.

A. Quantity Maxim

Grice summarizes this maxim as "Speaker contribution is expected to be genuine and not spurious" and he gives criteria that indicate not violating the maxim.

1) Make your conversation as informative as required.
2) Avoid redundancy.

In our work, we use the first criterion in this maxim only. This means that we reward answers if they are informative and we do not penalize answers if they are redundant. In fact, we

do not have the mean to judge redundancy. We consider an answer as informative answer as follows.
Many of the Questions are usually inquiries about places, organizations, persons, or things. For example, the question *Is there any place where I can find scented massage oils in Qatar?* is asking about a place, the question *Does anyone have recommendations for which bank to use in Qatar?* is asking about an organization, the question *Can anybody give me details and information about where to find a very good dermatologist?* is asking about a person, and the question *What's the cheapest brand new car in Qatar?* is asking about thing.

Accordingly, answers for such questions are expected to contain information about the inquired entities or other entities that are in essence helpful for the user inquiry. For example, relevant answers for the question about the dermatologist may be names of hospitals rather than persons, such as the following answer *Try Apollo Clinic*.

In our approach, we interpret this maxim as How much an answer is informative as follows. Does the answer contain the following informative elements?

1) **Named entities**: A named entity here refers to person, organization, location, or product.
2) **References**: References here include Web urls, emails, and phone numbers.
3) **Currency**: We consider the presence of currency in an answer as informative element.
4) **Numbers**: In some cases, phone numbers, or currency are not recognized because they are implicit such as *20000 is a good salary*. For this reason, we consider the presence of numbers (2 digits or more) in answers as an informative element.

Of course, this list of informative elements is not exhaustive. However, these are the elements that we utilize in our approach.

B. Relation

Grice summarizes this maxim as "Speaker contribution is expected to be appropriate to immediate needs at each state of the transaction" and gives a very generic criterion to judge relevancy which is : Be relevant.
According to Grice himself and Grice theory researchers, this maxim is not well defined [24]

One of the problems related to defining answer relevancy in Grice theory is that while it can explain how the sentence B in the following conversation can be understood as the direct answer (*No, there is no milk left*), it does not give us a definition of what is a relevant answer, nor a way to compare the relevancy of direct answers such the answer shown above. This is very important since answers in community question answering are usually direct answers and according to our study, answers like B are extremely rare in community question answering portals.

A *Is there another pint of milk?*

B *Im going to the supermarket in five minutes.*

We think that defining what is a relevant contribution in the relation maxim and/or defining conversation relevancy in general is still an open issue that needs to be researched. At the same time, we try in this work to discover relevancy indicators and use them in our ranking algorithm. Accordingly, we can consider the following as relevancy indicators.

1) **Similarity**: Similarity between the question and the answer or at least overlapping between the question and the answer utterances.
2) **Imperatives**: Answers that contain imperative verbs such as *try*, *go to*, or *check* indicate that the answerer is explaining a way to solve a problem being discussed.
3) **Expression of politeness**: Expressions of politeness *I would*, *I suggest*, or *I recommend* are usually polite alternatives for imperatives. For example, *I suggest you to to do* is a polite way of saying *Do*.
Although this indicator overlaps with the manner maxim, we think that using such expressions indicates that answerer is serious in his answer and hence indicates relevancy.
4) **Factoid answer particles**: For factoid questions *is/are*, *does/do* the answer particles *yes/no* indicate the relevancy of the answer.
5) **Domain specific terms**: Domain specific terms indicate relevancy. For example, terms such as *CV*, *NOC (National Occupational Classification)*, *torrent*, etc. are domain specific terms. Using such terms indicates also that the answerer is trying to help or is explaining how to solve the problem being discussed.

Again, this list of relevancy indicators is not exhaustive and it would be much better for our approach if could use concrete criteria that indicates the relation maxim. Nonetheless, these indicators are helpful in indicating relevancy and using them is better than not using this maxim at all.

C. Manner

Grice summarizes this maxim as "a speaker contribution is expected to be clear" and he gives four criteria that indicate not violating this maxim:

1) **Avoid obscurity of expressions**
2) **Avoid ambiguity**
3) **Be brief**
4) **Be orderly**

We think that these maxims need more research to define them and give us the possibility to implement them in a computational approach. In fact, we need concrete criteria that we can use to determine whether a speaker contribution is obscure, ambiguous, brief, or orderly. For example, an expression which is ambiguous or obscure in some context may be unambiguous and clear in other contexts. The same holds for brief, since to our knowledge, there is no approach that can classify answers in concise and redundant answers. The last criterion also needs more explanation. In summary, these criteria are too generic and need to have more specific definitions.

In this work, we tried to give some criteria that can be used to judge that a speaker contribution complies with/ violates the manner maxim. These criteria are:

1) **Be positive**: By this criterion, we mean that the speaker contribution is expected to be tolerant and permissive.

2) **Avoid frustrating utterances**: Answers that contain such expressions are usually not useful in the conversation.
3) **Avoid ironic and humbling expressions**: We mean here that the answer tends to be formal and professional and that the answerer is aiming to give a direct useful contribution.
4) **Avoid insulting and degrading expressions**: Answers that contain such expressions are not expected to be be useful in any conversation.

We may also consider the grammatical and orthographic correctness as a criterion. We did not consider this because many of the members of Qatar Living are not native speakers of English.

V. IMPLEMENTATION

In the following, we present the ranking algorithm , where we start with explaining the used resources. Then, we illustrate some experiments that we have conducted in the framework of our approach, and finally we describe using Grice maxims in community question answers ranking.

A. Resources

In the following, we describe the resources that we used in our algorithm for each of Grice maxims.

Quality: No resources and this maxim was not used in the implementation.

Quantity: We have used an openNLP name finder [25] for Named Entity Recognition (NER). After testing state of the art name finders, we found that their performance is low in terms of precision and recall. This is due to the fact that the forum members usually do not follow English orthography in writing named entities. Named entity capitalization in the answers, which an important shape features for NER, is absent in many of the named entities in the answers. On the other hand, most of the used named entities in the forum are Arabic names (especially persons and locations), which makes the problem for the state of the art NER systems more difficult. To handle these two problems, we have trained the openNLP NER system on an annotated corpus which was taken from the training data set. The generated model reached, 91% precision, 83% recall, and 87% F measure. The annotated corpus and the model are available online [26] and can be freely used for both research and commercial purposes.

Relation: For the relation maxim, we have used four resources. These resources are:

a *Similarity*: For similarity, we used Word2Vec [27] and Brown and clark [28] embeddings.

b *Imperatives and Expression of politeness*: We have used an OpenNLP POS-tagger to detect imperatives and expressions of politeness. We reward answers that contains such expressions.

c *Domain specific terms*: Using the training data, a small dictionary that contains domain specific terms such as *router, CV, NOC, torrent...etc,* has been compiled. The terms in the dictionary are not classified and of course they are not exhaustive. Answers that contain such expressions are also rewarded.

Manner: We used here two resources for sentiment polarity lists [29], one positive sentiment word list and another negative sentiment words list.

a *Be positive*: For this criterion, we have used the positive sentiment list, which we use to reward answers that contain positive expressions.

b *Avoid frustrating expressions*: For this criterion, we used the negative sentiment list to penalize answers that contain frustrating expressions.

b *Avoid ironic and humbling expressions*: The negative sentiment list includes some of the ironic and humbling expressions. We have used the training data to extend the list with new ironic and humbling expressions that we found in the training data. Answers that contain such expressions are penalized.

c *Avoid insulting and degrading expressions*: The negative sentiment list includes some of the insulting and degrading expressions. We have extended the list with new expressions that we found in the training data. We penalize answers that contain such expressions.

B. Experiments

In the following, we describe some of the experiments that we conducted to compare their results with the results of our proposed algorithm which is described in the next section. We used the test data set taken from Semeval 2016 to evaluate the results of these experiments, where we used Mean Average Precision (MAP) as performance measure.

Experiment 1 (similarity run):

- **Method**: Rank the answers of a question using term frequencyinverse document frequency (Tf-IDF) [30] as a similarity function from the most similar answer to less relevant one.
- **Result**: The achieved result in this experiment was MAP=0.5839.

Experiment 2 (clusters / word representation 1):

- **Method**: We experimented mixing different combinations of word embeddings and similarity measure to rank the answers. We used Brown embedding with N-grams level, with a weight of 0.5 to embedding similarity and 0.5 to string similarity.
- **Result**: We got MAP=0.6089.

Experiment 3 (clusters / word representation 2):

- **Method**: Using Brown and Clark with weight of 0.3 to string similarity and 0.7 to cluster similarity.
- **Result**: we got MAP=0.5596.

Experiment 4 (clusters / word representation 3):

- **Method**: Including word2vec to Brown and clark, with a low-level features, like word shape with the same weight of 0.3 to string similarity and 0.7 to cluster similarity.
- **Result**: we got MAP=0.6422.

Experiment 5 (similarity rule based): In this experiment, we run the system in two phases:

1) Rank the comments depending on their token-based similarity score.

2) Re-rank it on background rules.
Having the first ranking clustered in three separated areas (good, potential useful, bad). Then we apply the following for each cluster. The answers of the same person were considered as duplicates.
Thus, we give priority to answers coming from different users. That means, we downgrade the answers of the same user if they are more than one answer.

In this experiment, the results were comparable with the previous experiments, where we got MAP=0.6403.

C. Grice Maxims Based Ranking Algorithm

In the following, we present our algorithm that uses Grice maxims to rank community question answers. The used abbreviations are explained as follows.

- SM: Similarity between question and answer.
- NE: Named entities.
- RE: Reference expressions.
- CN: Currency and numbers.
- IM: Imperative and polite expressions.
- DT: Domain specific terms.
- PS: Positive sentiment words.
- NS: Negative sentiment words.
- IR: Ironic and humbling words.
- ID: Insulting and degrading words.

Input:
Q: $\langle p, qText \rangle$, where p refers to the person who is asking, and $qText$ to the question text.
l: $\langle a_1, ..., a_n \rangle$, where $a_i = \langle p_i, aText_i, score_i \rangle$.
The variable p_i refers to the person who answered a_i, $qText_i$ to
the answer text, and $score_i$ to a number that represents the relevancy of a_i.
Output:
l: where l is the input list after sorting according to Grice Maxims.
algorithm GriceMaximxBasedRanking(q: $\langle p, qText \rangle$, l: $\langle ..., a_i = \langle p_i, aText_i, score_i \rangle, ... \rangle$)
begin
foreach answer a_i **in** l:
if $p_i = p$ **then** $score_i = i * -100$
else
$score_i = |SM_{qi}| + |NE_i| + |RE_i| + |CN_i| + |IM_i| + |DT_i| + |PS_i|$;
$score_i -= |NS_i| + |IR_i| + |ID_i|$;
sort l ;
return l;
end

The algorithm works in four steps as follows.

1) The algorithm checks whether the answerer is the same person who asked the question. The answers made by person who asked the question are downgraded such that they become the last answers in the list. Such answers according to our analysis are usually thanking messages or explanations of some aspects of their original question.
2) For the rest of the answers, the algorithm computes the similarity between the question Q and the answer a_i, where $0 \leq SM_{qi} \leq n$ $(n = |l|)$.
3) Then, based on Grice maxims, the answers are rewarded or penalized as follows.
   a The answer a_i is rewarded according to the number of entities, reference expressions, currency and numbers, imperatives, domain specific terms, and positive sentiment words.
   b On the other hand, a_i is penalized according to the number of negative sentiment, ironic, and insulting words.
4) After rewarding and penalizing all answers, we then sort the list of answers according to their achieved scores in descending order. Best answer is the first answer in the list and so on.

TABLE I. RESULTS OF SOME COMMUNITY QUESTION ANSWER RANKING APPROACHES IN SEMEVAL 2017.

System	MAP
Baseline	0.623
Best System	0.884
Our System	0.785
Worst System	0.633

The proposed approach participated at SemEval 2017 task 3, where our system [31] achieved a MAP=0.785 as shown in Table I.

VI. CONCLUSION

In this paper, we have presented a community question answers ranking approach based on Grice Maxims. In this approach, we gave extensional interpretation of Grice maxims rather than the intentional interpretation in pragmatics. We have demonstrated that Grice maxims indeed offer an effective method for solving challenging linguistic problems.

Although our approach did not reach the performance of machine learning based approaches, it gave a linguistic motivated solution which can be improved so that it reaches the performance of machine learning methods. We hope that the presented work will attract researchers to pay more attention to bridge the gaps in Grice maxims by defining solid criteria for these maxims. In particular, defining the criteria for what is informative, brief, redundant, obscure, ambiguous, or concise speaker contribution are very important for Grice based computational approaches such as the one presented in this paper.

We believe that more effort in this direction will offer us new powerful solutions that can achieve high quality results with significant performance.
In our planned future work, we plan to do more research on defining concrete criteria for the relation maxim. We think that defining the relation maxim can enhance the achieved results in the current work.

Another important concept that we plan to work on, is to explore the role of domain specific terms in community answers to classify questions and answers in domains. Our hypothesis is that domain specific classification of questions and answers improves the results of our current approach.

REFERENCES

[1] Google, "Google answers." https://answers.google.com/, 2018.

[2] Yahoo, "Yahoo answers." https://answers.yahoo.com/, 2018.

[3] M. S. Pera and Y.-K. Ng, "A community question-answering refinement system," in *Proceedings of the 22Nd ACM Conference on Hypertext and Hypermedia*, HT '11, (New York, NY, USA), pp. 251–260, ACM, 2011.

[4] X. J. Wang, X. Tu, D. Feng, and L. Zhang, "Ranking community answers by modeling question-answer relationships via analogical reasoning," in *Proceedings of the 32nd international ACM SIGIR conference on Research and development in information retrieval*, SIGIR '09, (New York, NY, USA), pp. 179–186, ACM, 2009.

[5] M. Nguyen, V. Phan, T. Nguyen, and M. Nguyen, "Learning to rank questions for community question answering with ranking SVM," *CoRR*, vol. abs/1608.04185, 2016.

[6] H. P. Grice, "Logic and conversation," in *Syntax and Semantics: Vol. 3: Speech Acts* (P. Cole and J. L. Morgan, eds.), pp. 41–58, San Diego, CA: Academic Press, 1975.

[7] D. Mollá and J. L. Vicedo, "Question answering in restricted domains: An overview," *Comput. Linguist.*, vol. 33, pp. 41–61, Mar. 2007.

[8] Q. Living, "Qatar living: best place for cars - properties - buying - selling - renting and Qatar news and events." http://www.qatarliving.com/, 2018.

[9] P. Nakov, L. Màrquez, A. Moschitti, W. Magdy, H. Mubarak, A. A. Freihat, J. Glass, and B. Randeree, "Semeval-2016 task 3: Community question answering," in *Proceedings of the 10th International Workshop on Semantic Evaluation (SemEval-2016)*, SemEval '16, (San Diego, California), pp. 525–545, Association for Computational Linguistics, June 2016.

[10] P. Nakov, T. Zesch, D. Cer, and D. Jurgens, eds., *Proceedings of the 9th International Workshop on Semantic Evaluation (SemEval 2015)*. SemEval '15, Denver, Colorado: Association for Computational Linguistics, June 2015.

[11] P. Nakov, D. Hoogeveen, L. Màrquez, A. Moschitti, H. Mubarak, T. Baldwin, and K. Verspoor, "SemEval-2017 task 3: Community question answering," in *Proceedings of the 11th International Workshop on Semantic Evaluation*, SemEval '17, (Vancouver, Canada), Association for Computational Linguistics, August 2017.

[12] E. R. Fonseca, S. Magnolini, A. Feltracco, M. R. H. Qwaider, and B. Magnini, "Tweaking word embeddings for FAQ ranking," in *Proceedings of Third Italian Conference on Computational Linguistics (CLiC-it 2016) & Fifth Evaluation Campaign of Natural Language Processing and Speech Tools for Italian. Final Workshop (EVALITA 2016), Napoli, Italy, December 5-7, 2016.*, 2016.

[13] A. Moschitti, "Making tree kernels practical for natural language learning," in *11th Conference of the European Chapter of the Association for Computational Linguistics*, pp. 113–120, 2006.

[14] M. Dinarelli, A. Moschitti, and G. Riccardi, "Re-ranking models based-on small training data for spoken language understanding," in *Proceedings of the 2009 Conference on Empirical Methods in Natural Language Processing: Volume 3 - Volume 3*, EMNLP '09, (Stroudsburg, PA, USA), pp. 1076–1085, Association for Computational Linguistics, 2009.

[15] K. Tymoshenko, D. Bonadiman, and A. Moschitti, "Convolutional neural networks vs. convolution kernels: Feature engineering for answer sentence reranking," in *NAACL HLT 2016, The 2016 Conference of the North American Chapter of the Association for Computational Linguistics: Human Language Technologies, San Diego California, USA, June 12-17, 2016*, pp. 1268–1278.

[16] S. Filice, D. Croce, A. Moschitti, and R. Basili, "Kelp at semeval-2016 task 3: Learning semantic relations between questions and answers," in *Proceedings of the 10th International Workshop on Semantic Evaluation (SemEval-2016)*, (San Diego, California), pp. 1116–1123, Association for Computational Linguistics, June 2016.

[17] M. Nicosia, S. Filice, A. Barrón-Cedeño, I. Saleh, H. Mubarak, W. Gao, P. Nakov, G. Da San Martino, A. Moschitti, K. Darwish, L. Màrquez, S. Joty, and W. Magdy, "Qcri: Answer selection for community question answering - experiments for arabic and english," in *Proceedings of the 9th International Workshop on Semantic Evaluation (SemEval 2015)*, (Denver, Colorado), pp. 203–209, Association for Computational Linguistics, June 2015.

[18] A. Barrón-Cedeño, G. Da San Martino, S. Joty, A. Moschitti, F. Al-Obaidli, S. Romeo, K. Tymoshenko, and A. Uva, "Convkn at semeval-2016 task 3: Answer and question selection for question answering on arabic and english fora," in *Proceedings of the 10th International Workshop on Semantic Evaluation (SemEval-2016)*, (San Diego, California), pp. 896–903, Association for Computational Linguistics, June 2016.

[19] T. Mihaylov and P. Nakov, "Semanticz at semeval-2016 task 3: Ranking relevant answers in community question answering using semantic similarity based on fine-tuned word embeddings," in *Proceedings of the 10th International Workshop on Semantic Evaluation (SemEval-2016)*, (San Diego, California), pp. 879–886, Association for Computational Linguistics, June 2016.

[20] A. Vogel, M. Bodoia, C. Potts, and D. Jurafsky, "Emergence of gricean maxims from multi-agent decision theory," in *Human Language Technologies: Conference of the North American Chapter of the Association of Computational Linguistics, Proceedings, June 9-14, 2013, Westin Peachtree Plaza Hotel, Atlanta, Georgia, USA*, pp. 1072–1081, 2013.

[21] M. Franke, "Quantity implicatures, exhaustive interpretation, and rational conversation," *Semantics and Pragmatics*, vol. 4, pp. 1–82, June 2011.

[22] R. Dale and E. Reiter, "Computational interpretations of the gricean maxims in the generation of referring expressions," *CoRR*, vol. cmp-lg/9504020, 1995.

[23] R. Kheirabadi and F. Aghagolzadeh, "Grice's cooperative maxims as linguistic criteria for news selectivity," *Theory and Practice in Language Studies*, vol. 2, no. 3, p. 547, 2012.

[24] R. Frederking, "Grice's maxims: do the right thing," *Proc. of AAAI SpringSymp. on Compl. Implicature: Computational Approaches to Interpreting and Generating Conversational Implicature*, 1996.

[25] Appache, "Apache opennlp." http://opennlp.apache.org/, 2018.

[26] A. A. Freihat, "Named entity recognizer for Qatar." https://www.researchgate.net/project/Named-Entity-Recognizer-For-Qatar, 2018.

[27] J. Turian, L.-A. Ratinov, and Y. Bengio, "Word representations: A simple and general method for semi-supervised learning," in *Proceedings of the 48th Annual Meeting of the Association for Computational Linguistics*, (Uppsala, Sweden), pp. 384–394, Association for Computational Linguistics, July 2010.

[28] R. Agerri and G. Rigau, "Robust multilingual named entity recognition with shallow semi-supervised features," *Artificial Intelligence*, vol. 238, pp. 63 – 82, 2016.

[29] J. Breen, "twitter-sentiment-analysis-tutorial-201107." https://github.com/jeffreybreen/twitter-sentiment-analysis-tutorial-201107, 2017.

[30] A. Rajaraman and J. D. Ullman, *Mining of Massive Datasets*. New York, NY, USA: Cambridge University Press, 2011.

[31] M. R. H. Qwaider, A. A. Freihat, and F. Giunchiglia, "Trentoteam at semeval-2017 task 3: An application of grice maxims in ranking community question answers," in *Proceedings of the 11th International Workshop on Semantic Evaluation, SemEval@ACL 2017, Vancouver, Canada, August 3-4, 2017*, pp. 271–274, 2017.

Fuzzy Supervision of an Industrial Production Process by Extracting Experts Knwoledge

Hanane Zermane, Naima Zerari, Rachad Kasmi, Samia Aitouche
Laboratory of Automation and Manufacturing,
Industrial Engineering Department
University Batna 2, Batna, Algeria
Emails: hananezermane@yahoo.fr, n.zerari@yahoo.fr, kasmiradwan08@gmail.com, samiaaitouche@yahoo.fr

Abstract— **The automation of production systems has been an answer to the changing and competitive industrial context and works by extracting data and experiences of experts. This automation is a double-edged sword; on one hand, it increases the productivity of the technical system (cost reduction, reliability, availability, quality), but, on the other hand, it increases the complexity of the system. This has led to the need of efficient technologies, such as Supervisory Control and Data Acquisition (SCADA) systems and techniques that could absorb this complexity such as artificial intelligence and fuzzy logic. In this context, we develop an application that controls the pretreatment and pasteurization station of milk localized in Batna (Algeria) by adopting a control approach based on expert knowledge and fuzzy logic.**

Keywords-Knowledge management; Data acquisition; Industrial process control; Fuzzy control.

I. INTRODUCTION

The overall process control objectives, such as the quality and the quantity of product, have been left in the hands of human operators in the past. Nowadays, computational intelligence has been used to solve many complex problems by developing intelligent systems, extracting expert's knowledge. Fuzzy logic has proved to be a powerful tool for decision-making systems, especially expert and pattern classification systems. Fuzzy set theory has been used in some chemical processes.

In traditional rule-based approaches, knowledge is encoded in form of antecedent-consequent structure. When new data are encountered, it is matched to the antecedent's clause of each rule, and those rules where antecedents match a data exactly are fired, establishing the consequent clauses.

This process continues until the desired conclusion is reached, or no new rule can be fired. In the past decade, fuzzy logic has proved to be useful for intelligent systems in chemical engineering. Most control situations are more complex than we can deal with mathematically.

In this situation, fuzzy control can be developed, providing a body of knowledge about the existing control process, in the form of a number of fuzzy rules. Fuzzy logic is used for the early detection of hazardous states and for the implementation of logic decision-making.

In this work, the expert's knowledge was extracted and fuzzy logic was integrated in the SCADA system to control an industrial process, milk production, to resolve problems and replace the old supervision system by a new architecture. The advantages of this architecture are its flexibility in control, its ability to process a lot of information in order to improve the productivity and to reduce maintenance costs. In Section 2, related works concerning fuzzy logic are presented. Section 3 is dedicated to the case study and the proposed approach. The implementation and the results of the developed system are discussed in Section 4. We conclude and discuss the results in a conclusion.

II. FUZZY LOGIC BASED WORKS

In reasoning about a complex system, humans reason approximately about their behaviors, thereby maintaining only a generic understanding about the problem. The generality and ambiguity are sufficient for human comprehension of complex systems. As the quote below from Zadeh's principle of incompatibility suggests, complexity and ambiguity (imprecision) are correlated: "the closer one looks at a real-world problem, the fuzzier its solution becomes" [1].

Complex industrial processes, such as a batch of chemical reactors, cement kilns and basic oxygen steel making, are difficult to control automatically. This difficulty is due to their non-linear, time varying behavior and the poor quality of available measurements. In such cases, automatic control is applied to those subsidiary variables which can be measured and controlled, for example temperatures, pressures and flows. The overall process control objectives, such as the quality and quantity of product, has been left in the hands of human operators in the past [2].

Security and reliability needs require the implementation of solutions such as artificial intelligence techniques. Expert systems and fuzzy logic are the most useful techniques to control industrial processes. Expert systems have the ability to process information with real time updating, deal with uncertain or incomplete knowledge, incorporate new knowledge into the program easily and put less pressure and responsibility on the human operator' they can evaluate the effects of different manufacturing parameters [3].

Fuzzy logic has rapidly become one of the most successful of today's techniques for developing sophisticated control systems. The reason is very simple, namely, fuzzy logic addresses such applications perfectly as it is similar to human decision making with the ability to generate accurate solutions from uncertain or approximate information. It fills an important gap in engineering design methods left vacant by purely mathematical approaches (linear control design), and purely logic-based approaches (expert systems) in system design [4].

Fuzzy logic offers several advantages that make it a particularly good choice for many control problems. It can control either linear or non-linear systems that are difficult or impossible to find a mathematical model. For this reason, fuzzy logic is integrated in several works and applied in different domains, in process control, decision making [5], as well as in failure mode and effect analysis [6].

III. CASE STUDY: MILK PRODUCTION

A. *Production milk process*

There are various products in the studied industrial system, pasteurized milk (milk for consumption), sterilized, fermented (called Laban), steamed yogurts, brewed and fresh cheese. To obtain a final milk product, the process is composed of several steps:

- Step 1: Milk receiving unit used to collect and analyze the milk.
- Step 2: Pretreatment unit contains 3 parts:
  - Plate Heat Exchanger: the goal is to exterminate the bacteria.
  - Degasser: used to remove the air present in the product.
  - Homogenizer: used to make the products more homogeneous, which helps to improve their quality and extend their duration of the conversation.
- Step 3: Pasteurization unit to exterminate the bacteria, and ensure the safety of the product.
- Step 4: Storage unit allows storing the milk before sending it to pasteurization.

The process of milk production passes through two principal workshops, i.e., Pretreatment and Pasteurization:

a) Pretreatment station

The process of the pretreatment station is composed of the following parts:

i. Plate Heat Exchanger:

It consists of a number of heat transfer plates, deposited in such a way that a passage between two plates is accessible to each of the two liquids (water and milk). It contains five sections:

- Section 1 (heating section): Composed of hot water from (60 to 71) C°.
- Section 2 (heating section): Composed of hot water (64 to 70) C° and milk, this section heats the milk from (58 to 68) C°.
- Section 3 (Recovery Section): Composed of hot milk and cold milk. This section allows for heat exchange with convection to conserve energy, and heat the milk gradually.
- Section 4 (cooling section): Composed of tap water from (30 to 42) C° and milk. This section allows the milk to cool from (42 to 30) C°.
- Section 5 (cooling section): Composed of cold water (2 to 4) C°.

ii. Degasser

The milk preheated to 68 ° C is introduced tangentially into the vacuum vessel. The steam gases rise up the chamber and are sucked by the vacuum pump, and the steam condenses in the condenser and returns to the milk.

iii. Homogenization

Homogenization step consists in passing the milk under high pressure to 60 bars through very narrow orifices, which reduce the size of the fat globules and partially destroy the casein micelles. All parts are presented in Figure 1 and the equipment is presented in Table I.

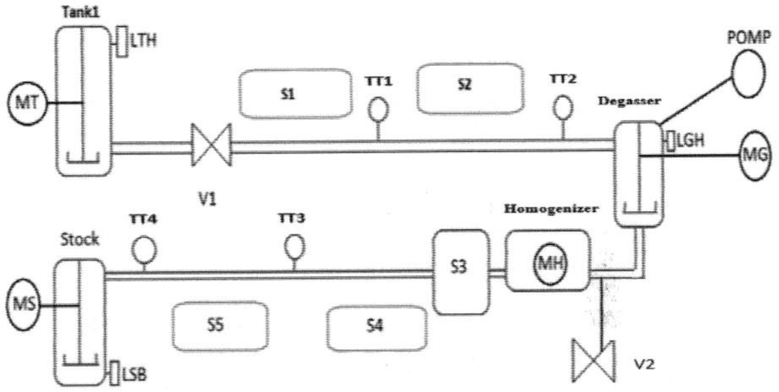

Figure 1. Schematic of the Pretreatment station.

TABLE I. EQUIPMENT IN THE DIFFERENT STATIONS.

Inputs		Outputs	
LTH	Tank 1 level sensor 1	MT	Tank 1 agitator engine
TT1	Temperature sensor S1	MG	Degasser agitator motor
TT2	Temperature sensor S2	MH	Homogenizing motor
TT3	Temperature sensor S4	MS	Stock tank agitator motor
TT4	Temperature sensor S5	POMP	Pump in the degasser for ejecting gases
LGH	Degasser level sensor	V1	Valve milk
LSB	Stock level sensor	V2	Steam valve

b) Pasteurization station

To carry out the pasteurization (Figure 2), a plate exchanger is used. The plate heat exchanger is composed of five stations, heating (S1P and S2P), recovery (S3P) and cooling (S4P and S5P).

- Section 1P (heating section): Composed of hot water from (60 to 70) C°.
- Section 2P (heating section): Composed of hot water (96 to 100) C° and milk, this section heats the milk from (90 to 95) C°.
- Section 3P (Recovery Section): Composed of hot milk and cold milk. This section allows for heat

exchange with convection to conserve energy, and heat the milk gradually.

- Section 4P (cooling section): Composed of tap water from (32 to 35) C° and milk. This section allows the milk to cool from (32 to 35) C°.
- Section 5P (cooling section): Composed of cold water (8 to 10) C°.

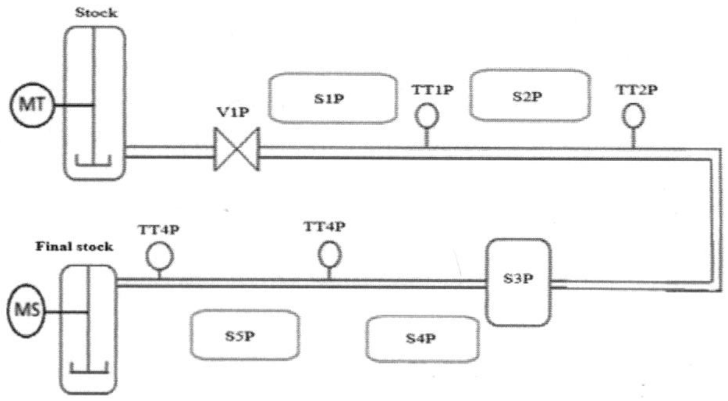

Figure 2. Schematic of the pasteurization station.

B. Problems and proposed solutions

During the internship within the company Aures Batna, and after the collection of the information, we observed the following shortcomings of the system:

- The production system of the unit is not automatized.
- Lack in the old system of supervision, which is not an HMI.
- There is no quality control feedback at the pretreatment and pasteurization stations.

Lack of control of different equipment pieces was due to most of them being very old and missing sensors for measurement.

To solve the above problems, we will try to build a powerful application that can correct the problems presented in the old system and that offers the services necessary to better supervise the stations. Our application offers the following advantages:

- Synthetic and dynamic representation, which has a graphical visualization of the behavior of the stations.
- Precise control of valves and actuators, taking into account several parameters, and at the same time the possibility of making the best decisions.
- Fuzzy control of the various equipment pieces of the stations.
- Diagnosis of alarms that inform the operator about the status and problems of the system.
- Display messages that help the operator to make decisions.
- History of alarm occurrence with the possibilities of printing and recording.
- Secure access to the supervision system with a password and a user name.

IV. Application of the Approach in Industry

To realize our approach, we divided it in two parts; the first one is the creation of the supervision system and the second is the creation of different fuzzy controllers in which we present one example.

A. Interface of the supervision system

After description of all steps parameters, we created a graphical programming in LabVIEW (Figure 3); we designed the supervision system that offers the following solutions:

- The system is no longer in half-automatic mode using solenoid valves and the implementation of fuzzy logic as a control technique.
- Now, we have a feedback circuit for quality control in the station to ensure the stability of the system.
- A system for generating alarms to identify and localize alarms.

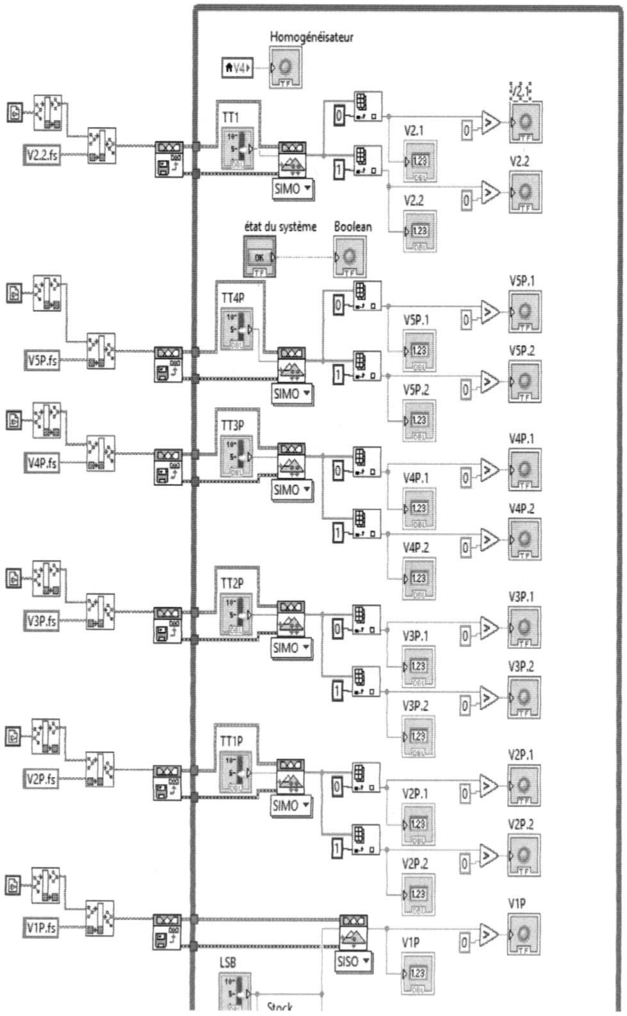

Figure 3. Part of the Block diagram of the control system.

Operators and engineers use HMIs to monitor and configure set points, control algorithms, and adjust and establish parameters in the controller. The HMI also displays process status information and historical information. Figure 6 shows the main interface of pretreatment station after the feedback circuit implementation in all the station.

To solve different problems in the workshop, we proposed to insert a feedback circuit in the process controlled by an HMI to control again the temperature of the product. This circuit is controlled by a fuzzy loop (Figure 4); it ensures the desired quality of the product and avoids its rejection like the situation in the installed system controlling different stations.

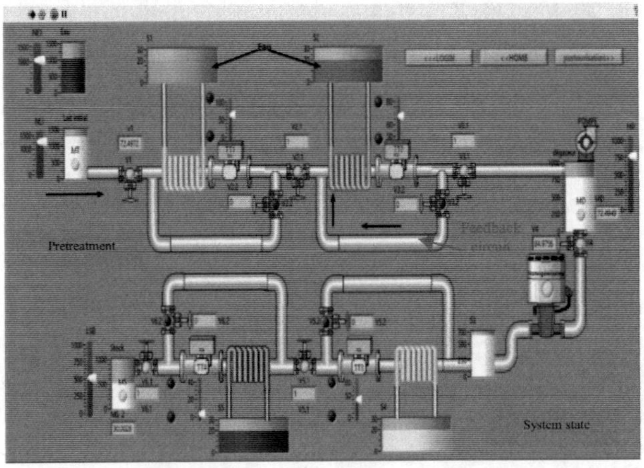

Figure 4. Implementation of the feedback circuit in the pretreatment station.

Diagnostics and maintenance utilities are used to prevent, identify and recover from abnormal operation or failures. In this reason, we created an interactive interface that locates exactly the alarm and its nature that signals the existence of an abnormal condition (for example, high pressure, max level in tank, etc.). To see all the generated alarms, a register of alarms was created. Figure 5 shows a block diagram that illustrates the system generating alarms and defaults.

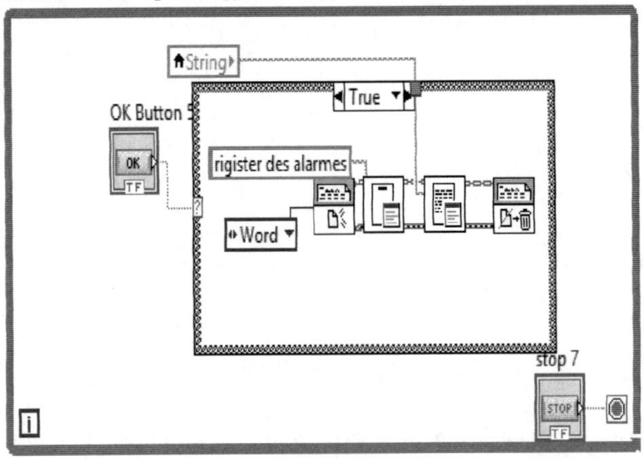

Figure 5. Block diagram of alarms generating system.

B. Creating Fuzzy Controllers

The creation of fuzzy controllers consists of two steps, establishing the relationship between inputs and outputs by fuzzy controller file Virtual Instrument (VI) and calling Fuzzy Controller files that contains the rules and membership functions of the fuzzy controller.

We presented in Table II some parameters used by the workshop, with their specifications, that will be used to control different stations.

TABLE II. DIFFERENT PROCESS'S PARAMETERS

Parameter	Definition	Type	Value
NE1	Main water tank level sensor	Input	0-15000L
NLI	Initial milk tank level sensor	Input	0-15000L
MT	Engine of the initial milk tank agitator	Output	0%-100%
V1	Solenoid valve of milk	Output	0%-100%
V2.1, V2.2	Solenoid valve of milk	Output	0 ;1
TT1	Section 1 Temperature Sensor	Input	0°C-100°C
TT2	Section 2 Temperature Sensor	Input	50°C-80°C
V3.1, V3.2	Solenoid valve of milk	Output	0 ;1
ND	Degasser Level Sensor	Input	0-10000L
PUMP	Pump in the degasser for ejecting gases	Output	0 ;1
MD	Engine of the degasser agitator	Output	0%-100%
V4	Solenoid valve of milk	Output	0%-100%
Homogenizer	Homogenizing motor	Output	0 ;1
TT3	Temperature sensor of section 4	Input	0°C-80°C
V5.1, V5.2	Solenoid valve of milk	Output	0 ;1
TT4	Section 5 temperature sensor	Input	0°C-40°C
V6.1, V6.2	Solenoid valve of milk	Output	0 ;1
MS	Stock tank agitator motor	Output	0%-100%
LSB	Stock level sensor	Input	0-10000L
V1P	Solenoid valve of milk	Output	0%-100%
TT1P	Temperature sensor of section 1P	Input	30°C-80°C
V2P.1, V2P.2	Solenoid valve of milk	Output	0 ;1
TT2P	Temperature sensor of section 2P	Input	50°C-110°C
V3P.1, V3P.2	Solenoid valve of milk	Output	0 ;1
TT3P	Section 4P Temperature Sensor	Input	0°C-50°C
V4P.1, V4P.2	Solenoid valve of milk	Output	0 ;1
TT4P	Temperature sensor of section 5P	Input	0°C-20°C
V5P.1, V5P.2	Solenoid valve of milk	Output	0 ;1

After determining all parameters, we need all conditions to control the process, which are presented in Table III.

TABLE III. RULES OF CONTROL

Rules
The valve V1 opens only if the level of the two tanks (water, initial milk) > 0, and the degree of opening depends on the level of these tanks
The MT motor only operates, if the level of the milk tank > 300 L
Valve V2.1 opens only if the temperature is between 60 C° and 71 C°
Valve V2.2 opens only if the temperature is not between 60 C° - 71 C°
Valve V3.1 opens only if the temperature is between 64 C° - 70 C°
Valve V3.2 opens only if the temperature is not between 64 C° - 70 C°
The pump only operates if the degasser level > 250 L
The MD motor operates only if the degasser level > 250 L, and the rotational speed is dependent on the degasser level.
The V4 valve opens only if the degasser level > 250 L and the degree of opening depends on the level of this tank
The Homogenizer motor operates only if the degasser level > 250 L
Valve V5.1 opens only if the temperature is between 30 C° - 42 C°
Valve V5.2 opens only if the temperature is not between 30 C° and 42 C°
Valve V6.1 opens only if the temperature is between 2 C° - 4 C°
Valve V6.2 opens only if the temperature is not between 2 C° and 4 C°
The MS motor operates only if the degasser level > 250 L, and its speed depends on the stock level
The valve V1P only opens if the stock level > 0, and the degree of opening depends on the level of this tank
The valve V2P.1 opens only if the temperature is between 65 C° - 70 C°
The valve V2P.2 opens only if the temperature is not between 65 C° - 70 C°
The valve V3P.1 opens only if the temperature is between 90 C° - 95 C°
The valve V3P.2 opens only if the temperature is not between 90 C° and 95 C°
The valve V4P.1 opens only if the temperature is between 32 C° and 35 C°
Valve V4P.2 opens only if the temperature is not between 32 C° and 35 C°
The valve V5P.1 opens only if the temperature is between 8 C° and 10 C°
The valve V5P.2 opens only if the temperature is not between 8 C° and 10 C°

We applied different rules to create fuzzy controllers. Figure 6 shows details of one of fuzzy controllers that controls the valve V1.

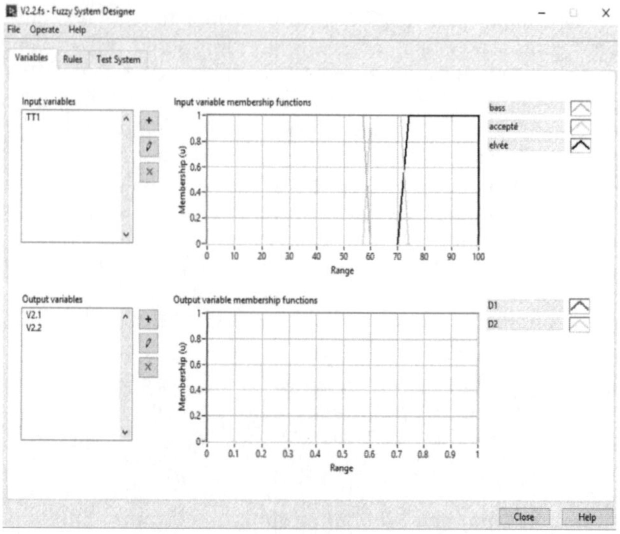

Figure 6. Inputs and outputs of the fuzzy controller of valve V2.1 and V2.2.

To integrate fuzzy control, we used some fuzzy rules (Figure 7), like:

- If 'TT1' is (low 'BAS') then 'V2.1' is 'D1' and 'V2.2' is 'D2'.
- If 'TT1' is (accepted 'accepté') then 'V2.1' is 'D2' and 'V2.2' is 'D1'.
- If 'TT1' is (high 'élevée') then 'V2.1' is 'D1' and 'V2.2' is 'D2'.

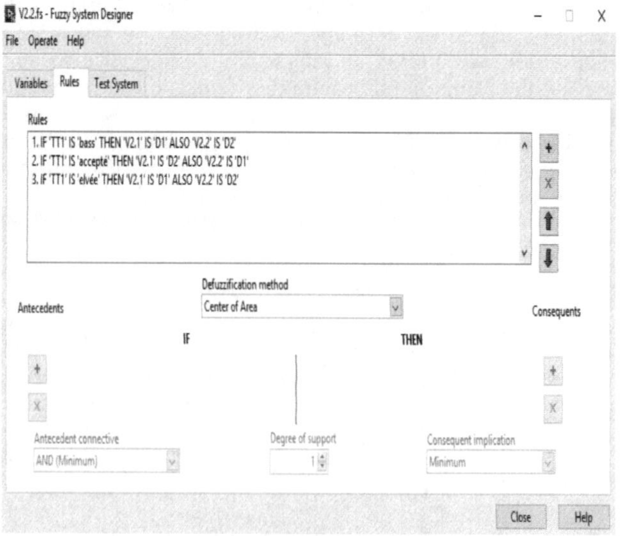

Figure 7. Inputs (TT1) and outputs (V2.1 and V2.2).

The results obtained according to variation in inputs, outputs and the surface generated after executing the fuzzy controller are shown in Figure 8.

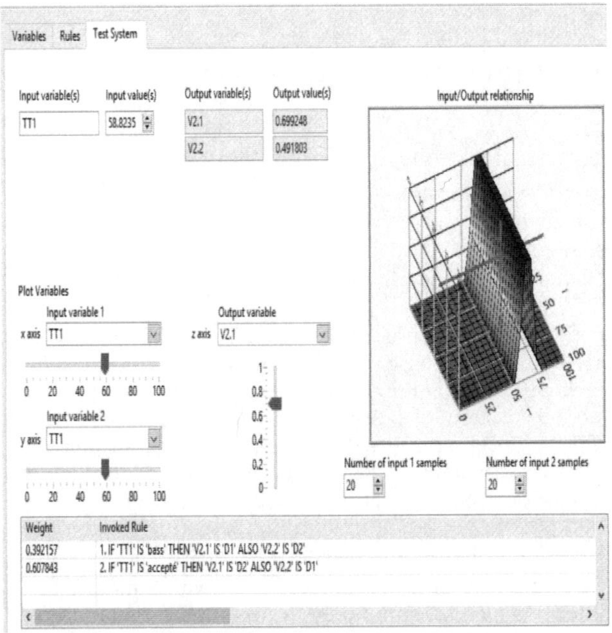

Figure 8. Relationship between inputs (TT1) and outputs (V2.1 and V2.2)

We tested the system response and its performance by comparing it with old controller using Matlab Simulink. The obtained results prove the advantages of the proposed method. The results comparison with a PID are shown in Figure 9, which indicates that the system is more stable.

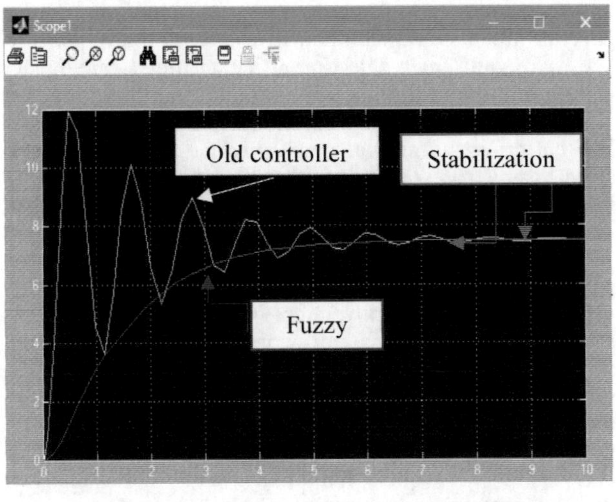

Figure 9. Performance of the new fuzzy controller.

As hardware application, S7-300 PLC saves on installation space and has a modular design. A wide range of modules can be used to extend the system centrally or to create decentralized structures depending on the task to be performed. To connect S7-300 with LabVIEW software, we used NI-OPC server to communicate between the PLC and LabVIEW interface.

V. CONCLUSION

Presently, companies often require innovative solutions to make their plant operating systems function at peak efficiency. Using latest in equipment technology, resources, and materials. However, complex industrial processes are difficult to control because of inadequate knowledge of their behavior. This lack of knowledge is principally a lack of structural detail and it is this, which prevents the use of conventional control theory. However, a human operator who makes decisions based on inexact and linguistic measures of the process state often controls these processes with great skill. Fuzzy logic is considered as a superset of standard logic, which is extended to deal with the partial truth. It has become one of the most successful technologies for developing complex control systems.

To improve control system reliability and availability, we implemented all solutions by creating a supervisory system, and we applicate different steps to ensure a fuzzy control of the system. The main objective of these solutions is to improve the old system. The solutions given are divided into two types. The first is a material solution and we proposed a feedback circuit implemented in each section with solenoid valves to automate the system. In addition, we proposed some equipment needed to implement the application. The second one is a software solution in where fuzzy logic has been used as a technique to control the milk production process. The augmented productivity in the factory, minimum downtime, and reduced costs of maintenance are advantages of our solutions.

REFERENCES

[1] L. Zadeh, "Outline of a new approach to the analysis of complex systems and decision processes", IEEE Trans. Syst., Man, Cybern. SMC-3, 1973, pp. 28-44.

[2] P. J. King and E. H. Mamdani, "The application of fuzzy control system to industrial processes", Automatica, vol. 13 (3) 1977, pp. 235-242.

[3] B. G. Krishnan and M. L. McCoy, "Adaptive process control for turning operation using expert systems", International Journal of Industrial and Systems Engineering, vol. 3 (6) 1985, pp. 711-7262.

[4] L. Yang, X. Geng and X. Cao, "A knowledge factor space model on multi-expert systems for oil-gas reservoir protection", International Journal of Industrial and Systems Engineering, (19) (1) 2015, pp. 1-17.

[5] A. H. Marbini, M. Tavana, A. Emrouznejad and S. Saati, "Efficiency measurement in fuzzy additive data envelopment analysis", International Journal of Industrial and Systems Engineering, vol. 10 (1) 2012, pp. 1-20.

[6] S. Chrysostom and R. K. Dwivedi, "A state of the art review of fuzzy approaches used in the failure modes and effects analysis: a call for research", International Journal of Industrial and Systems Engineering, vol. 23 (3) 2016, pp. 351-369.

A Strategic Method for Steering a Photovoltaic Generator

Khyreddine Bouhafna, Mohamed Djamel Mouss, Samia Aitouche, Hanane Zermane
Laboratory of Automation and Manufacturing,
Industrial Engineering Department
University Batna 2, Batna, Algeria
Email: bouhafna_k@hotmail.fr, d_mouss@yahoo.fr, samiaaitouche@yahoo.fr, hananezermane@yahoo.fr

***Abstract*— There are several forms of electricity generation, first, by burning fuels, such as coal, natural gas or oil, which have an effect on the atmosphere, especially increasing greenhouse gases, or, second, from renewable sources, such as wind, hydro and solar, which are clean and renewable sources of energy. Our work focuses on solar sources, especially photovoltaics; we have treated the steering part of photovoltaic generators using artificial intelligence methods, specifically, case-based reasoning. The system we have built generates actions to be applied to the generator based on its current state and reasoning from previous cases recorded in the case base.**

Keywords- photovoltaic system; photovoltaic generator; steering of photovoltaic system; case-based reasonnig; k-means neighbors.

I. INTRODUCTION

Algeria is one of the sunniest countries in the world. Consequently, there are many programs for the installation of huge photovoltaic (PV) stations [17]. In PV systems, we face three important problems: sizing, diagnosis and fault detection, and tracking the maximum power point. These problems need to be addressed before setting up a photovoltaic generator. Our intervention is in the maintenance, as well as detection of faults of the PV generator; it helps regulate the operation of the generator to achieve its objectives. This is achieved by the application we developed to steer the PV generator using a case-based reasoning methodology and intervenes automatically to regulate the effects of an anomaly.

PV generators connected to the grid are usually located in isolated areas where human intervention is late or absent. The objectives of our system are:

- Improve generator productivity by decreasing the defects of the solar panels. This is done by reconfiguring the generator to achieve maximum production of the non-faulty modules.
- Increase the availability of the generator keeping the generator in partial production state when a failure has occurred.
- Increase the life of the system in the case of partial shading of the module that generates the hot spot and automatically isolates the module and invokes the maintenance team when it persists over time.

The rest of the paper is structured as follows. Section 2 concerns the related works. We present the steering functions and its problematics in Section 3. Section 4 is dedicated to the approach of artificial intelligence followed case-based reasoning (CBR). Section 5 presents the objectives and multiple configurations of the proposed steering system. The deployment of the proposed system with the different stages of CBR and the tests of presented cases are discussed in Section 6. Finally, we conclude our work presenting perspectives in Section 7.

II. RELATED WORKS

Research in the supervision and management of PV systems is increasing not only in Algeria but also in the rest of the world. In the photovoltaic field, most researches are focused on dimensioning, diagnosis, fault detection and maximum power point tracking problematic. Hence, several artificial intelligence methods are used such as fuzzy logic, neuronal networks and genetic algorithms to solve these problematics. In this paper, we address another problematic namely, the photovoltaic field steering, which is not directly addressed in other works. So, in the state of the art, we will mention some research works that solve problematics that have an influence on the photovoltaic steering problematic. We start with fault detection using artificial intelligence techniques. Fault detection is a crucial task to increase the reliability, efficiency and safety of photovoltaic systems. The detection and manual removal of faults in photovoltaic systems is very expensive, and, in some cases, impossible, like the photovoltaic systems of satellites. Therefore, automatic fault detection techniques are required [1].

Several methods are used, because of the non-linear nature of the photovoltaic system and some faults are difficult to detect by conventional protection devices. Zhao et al. [2] proposed in their work a model based semi-supervised learning graph for the detection of faults. The proposed model not only detects defects, but also identifies their possible type. In another work, Zhao et al. [3] developed a decision tree model for detecting and classifying photovoltaic field faults. This model analyzes the current-voltage characteristic (I-V) to make detections.

Artificial intelligence techniques are also used for the detection of faults. Zhihua et al. [4] have used neural networks in their work for the detection of faults. At first, the temperature of the module determines the occurrence of defects in a photovoltaic module. Then, the artificial neuron is used to make the diagnosis and define the type of defect. The input parameters of the neuron are: temperature, current, and voltage, while the output is the detection result. Inside of the fault detection, the maximum power point tracking is an important issue in the photovoltaic field. The Maximum Power Point (MPPT) tracking technique is an important requirement in improving the efficiency of power extraction from PV modules. The main goal of all MPPT techniques is to extract the true maximum power of the PV module in any atmospheric condition. However, in the conditions of rapid climate change and partial shading, conventional techniques have not been able to follow the true peak power point. For this reason, artificial intelligence methods have been developed with the ability to search for the true maximum power point with a good convergence speed [5].

Patchara Prakriti et al. [6] have proposed a method of tracking maximum power points using an adaptive fuzzy controller for PV systems connected to the network. From simulation and experimental results, the adaptive blur controller can provide more power than the conventional blur controller. Bahgat et al. [7] presented a maximum power point tracking algorithm for photovoltaic systems using neural networks. According to the authors, the experimental results showed that the photovoltaic plant with MPPT always listens to the maximum power point of the PV module under various operating conditions. The MPPT transmits approximately 97% of the actual maximum power generated by the photovoltaic module.

III. THE STEERING FUNCTIONS AND PROBLEMATICS

A. The steering of production process

The steering is the function of controlling the future and immediate behaviour of the production process according to a given process to achieve the production objectives expressed in terms of quality and productivity [8].

The steering is responsible for carrying out the planned production. It must solve all the problems that are not solved by the forecast level (local loads or constraints). It must also take into account all the manufacturing constraints (quality control, maintenance-related downtime, staff qualification level, etc.), all present at this level, and react to hazards so that the planned production be possible.

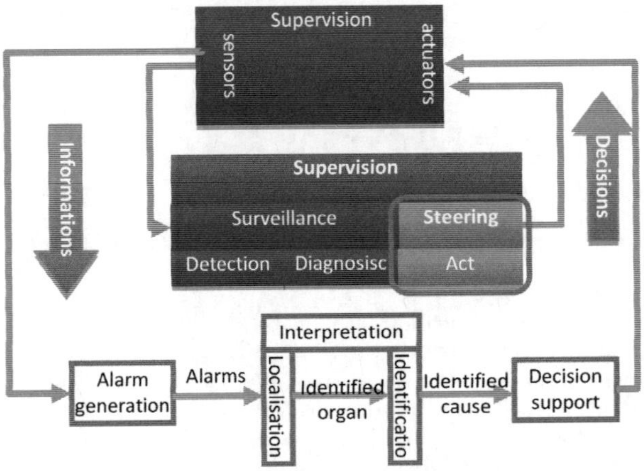

Figure 1. Position of the steering in supervision process [13]

Figure 1 shows the position of steering in the supervision process of production system. It is jointed to action after decision supported by the preliminary steps of surveillance, detection and diagnosis.

We can distinguish three main classes of functions of steering to ensure:

- Communication: with the scheduling function (recovery of forward orders and transmission of order tracking), with the order of the production system (sending orders for launch, control and reception of real-time monitoring), with the other industrial functions (request for intervention, analysis, taking into account urgent orders, transfer availabilities, etc.);
- Data management: concerning products, resources, tasks to be performed;
- Historical and statistical: equipment breakdown statistics, team activity, time spent by batch, by product, etc.

B. The steering problematics

Here, we discuss the problems of operating and analysing steering systems [9].

- **Exploitation**: the problem of operating the steering systems can be seen as a particularization of man-machine cooperation problems. In the field of human-machine cooperation, horizontal cooperation is defined as a means of regulating the human activity of supervision by means of a division of tasks between the operator and a decision-making tool. In vertical cooperation, the tool only offers advice to the operator who remains the final decision maker. The difficulty of operating the steering system lies in the division of tasks between the human operator and the material part of the system. Some authors advocate permanently keeping the human operator in the steering loop by regulating his workload.

- **Analysis:** the analysis of a control system uses, at least in the same way as its design and operation, very complex and highly variable interpretative processes. Based on purely quantitative criteria, the difficulty of the analysis is due to the causal and temporal distances between the implementation of the steering system and the resulting performance. On a more qualitative level, the analysis of the steering system is based on the value it brings to the different actors of the production system: better feedback on everyone's actions, facilitation of monitoring and diagnostic tasks, better organization of the workshop, etc.

IV. CASE-BASED REASONNING

Case Based Reasoning (CBR) is an approach for solving and learning problems. A new problem or case is solved by remembering (recalling) similar cases already pre-analyzed and stored in memory. The solution found is then adapted (reused) to the new problem. The new case is then revised or repaired (by the expert or by the use of the general knowledge of the system). This new case can also be learned from the system (memorization) as a new experience [10][11]. The CBR approach reduces knowledge acquisition efforts. It allows the use of existing data and can adapt to changes in their environment. Figure 2 illustrates the CBR cycle:

- **Retrieve**: Recovery of previously experienced similar cases (e.g., solution-problem-result triples) whose problem is deemed similar.
- **Reuse:** propose a solution to solve the new problem using information and knowledge of the recovered case.
- **Revise:** aims to evaluate the applicability of the proposed solution.
- **Memorize:** Maintaining the new solution once it has been confirmed or validated.

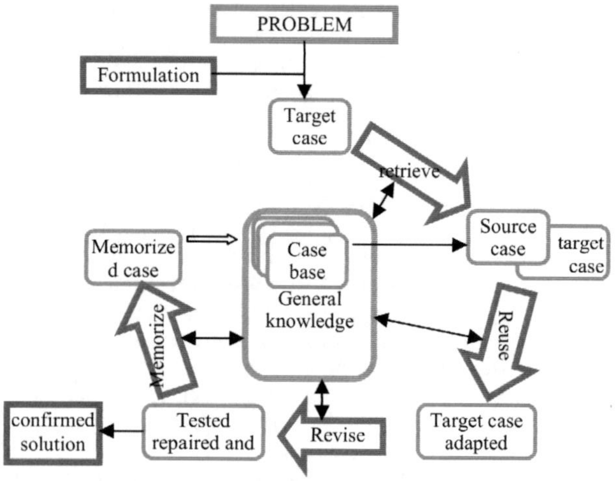

Figure 2. Case-based reasonning process [14]

In many practical applications, the reuse and revision stages are sometimes difficult to distinguish, and many researchers use a single adaptation phase that replaces and combines them. However, fitting into a RAC system is still an open question because it is a complicated process that tries to manipulate case solutions. The cases recorded in the case base have been enriched by general knowledge, which often depends on the domain of the problem [12]. The selection of an appropriate method for each step depends on the problem and requires knowledge in the field of application. In situations where information is incomplete or missing and we want to exploit tolerance for inaccuracy, uncertainty, rough reasoning, and partial soft-truth calculation techniques could provide solutions with traceability, robustness, and low cost.

V. Principles and Multiple Configurations of the Proposed Steering System Using CBR

A. *Architecture of the proposed steering system and case presentation*

Figure 3 illustrates the global architecture of the developed steering system. It contains a formulation of cases to set them as a vector of attributes, a case management, a history management and an automatic steering (the cycle of CBR).

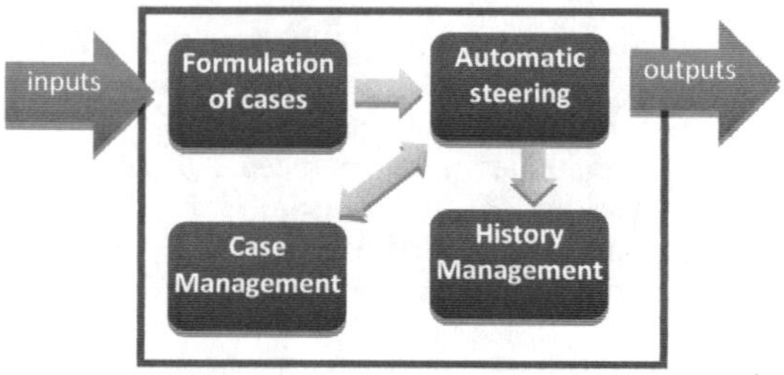

Figure 3. Architecture of the proposed steering system

The case is a state of photovoltaic generator represented by attribute vector to be usable by CBR (Figure 4).

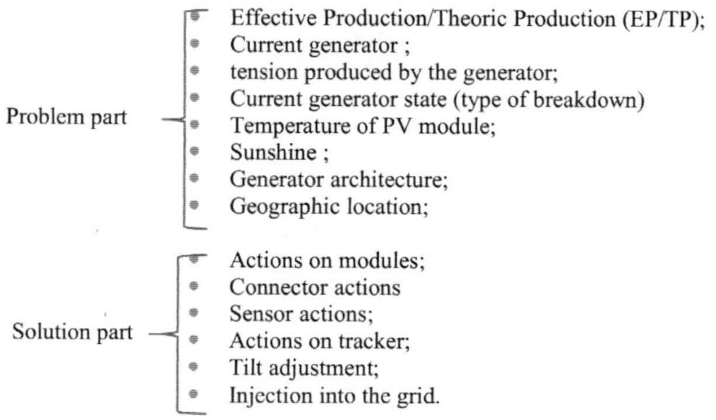

Figure 4. Generator state (target case) attributes

A case is composed of two parts: the problem part and the solution part. The attributes of a case are represented in Figure 4.

B. *Principles of the application of CBR process in the proposed steer system*

Retrieve: Select the most similar cases calculating the distance between the appeared case and the cases of the base cases. We used the types of distances in a developed system and the user has to choose one of them.

- Distance between blocks,

$$d(x,y) = \sum |xi - yi| \quad (1)$$

- Euclidian distance with weights,

$$d = \sqrt[p]{\sum |xi - yi|^p} \quad (2)$$

The first (1) method only measures the distance between 2 cases; however, the second (2) allows us to give importance to attributes that others and exclude some by giving them a 0 weight because in reality not all attributes have the same importance. It is noted that in the second method the sum of the weights must be equal to one (1) [14]. The calculation is done only on the problem part of the ***case.*** The objective of the calculation of the distance is to find the closest cases to the target case (problem), from the base case. We chose the K nearest neighbors method with K=3 to find the 3 closest cases to the target.

Reuse: is the proposal of a solution to solve the new problem by reusing information and knowledge of the three cases found. If the distance is zero (0), the solution is reproduced. If not, an adaptation step is necessary.

Adaptation of the case: The adaptation of the cases consists in giving a coherent solution, one must not find contradictions between the values of the problem part and the solution part. The verification is done using rules of type "if condition then result":

IF <Action on module = Replace and type of failure = Sane>

Then incoherent values

For each attribute of the solution of the nearest case:

- **IF** <the value conflicts with the attributes of the problem part of the target case>
  Then we move to the values of the next case.
- **IF** <all the values of the three cases are in conflict>
  Then the case is recorded in the database of untreated cases.

Revise: It validates the obtained solution, by evaluation with simulation using a model of the generator. After application of the solution:

IF < PE/PT>minimum threshold>

Then the solution is registered in the base.

Otherwise the case is recorded in the database of unprocessed cases.

C. Generator models

Calculation of the generated current: The photovoltaic cells could be presented with one diode or bishop model (Figure 5a, Figure 5b).

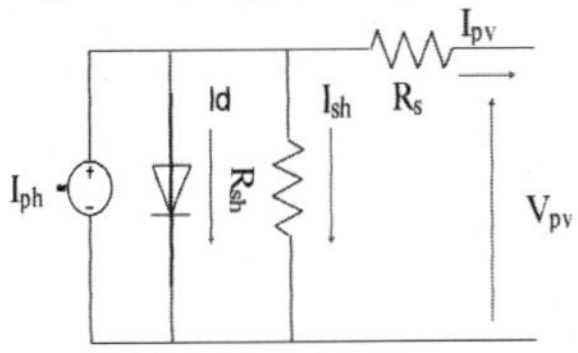

Figure 5a. One diode model [15]

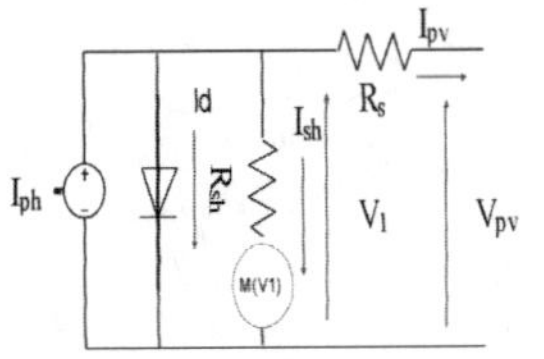

Figure 5b. Bishope model [16]

The bishope model takes the avalanche effect of the cell into consideration by adding to the diode model a nonlinear multiplier in series with the shunt resistor. The user will configure the developed system according to the PV cells used. The electric currents generated are obviously different. These were calculated according to different formulas.

D. Calculation of current and voltage

The current and the voltage of the PV generator are calculated by the formulas (3) and (4) respectively.

- $I_{generator} = N_{string} \times N_{module} \times N_{cell} \times I_{cell}$ (3)
- $V_{generator} = M_{module} \times M_{groupe} \times M_{cell} \times V_{cell}$ (4)

Where

- N_{string}: number of strings in parallel ;
- N_{module}: number of groups of modules in parallel in a string;
- $N_{cellule}$: number of groups of cells in parallel in a module;
- M_{module}: number of modules in series in a string;
- M_{groupe}: number of groups of cells in series in a module;
- $M_{cellule}$: number of cells in series in a cell group;

E. General operation of proposed steering system

Figure 6 presents the proposed generic algorithm of the steering system.

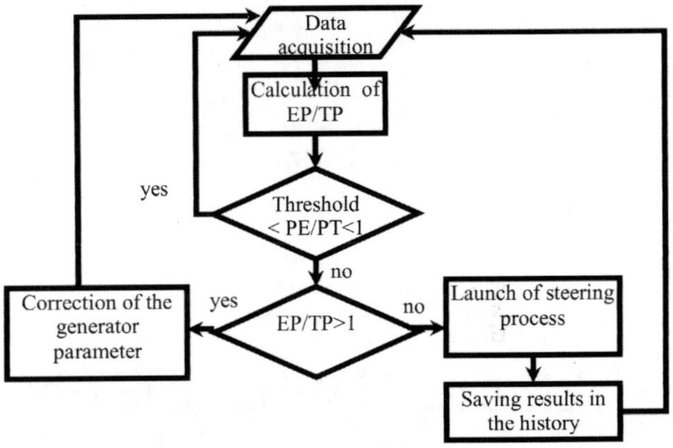

Figure 6. General operation of steering system

The proposed system was developed with LabVIEW (Laboratory Virtual Instrument Engineering Workbench). It is ideal for data acquisition, automation and instrument control. The integrated user interfaces make it easy to use and apply, and, they offer a rapid prototyping.

VI. Deployement of the Proposed Steering System and Discussion

The application is essentially composed of the following modules: system status, system settings, model of the photovoltaic cell, test & simulation and historical. Figure 7 represents the status of the PV system (dashboard) over time displaying parameters graphically (tension, current and other parameters).

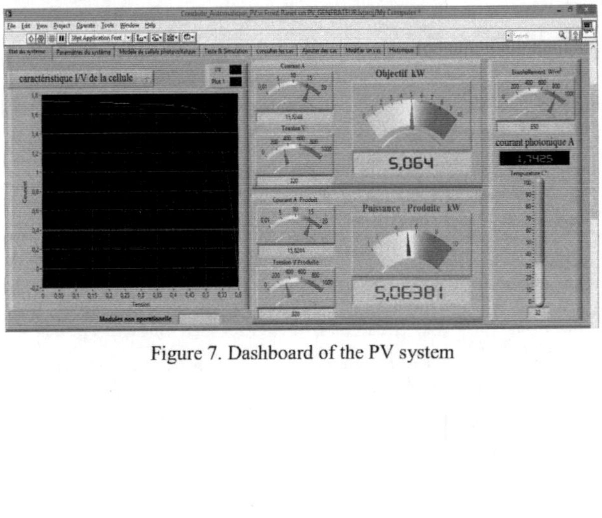

Figure 7. Dashboard of the PV system

Figure 8 is the interface allowing the setting up (model diode or Bishope, type of distance, number of parallel strings, number of serial cells and all the attributes of the target case) of the PV system.

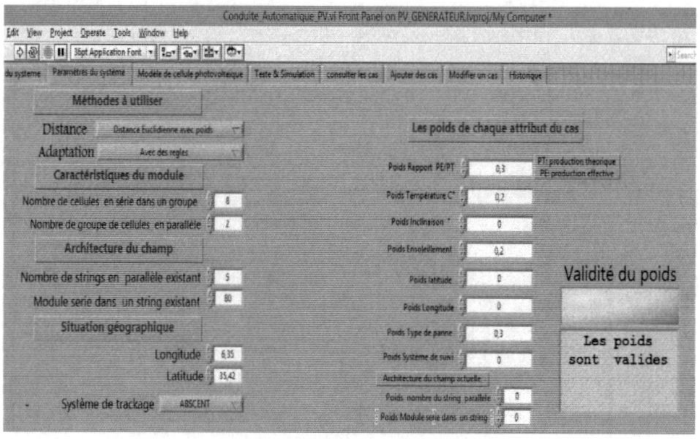

Figure 8. Settings of the PV system

We passed then to the construction of the base case. Table I presents six cases alimenting the base case.

TABLE I. CASES ALIMENTING THE BASE CASE

Attributes	Case 1	Case 2	Case 3	Case 4	Case 5	Case 6
PE/PT report	0.6	0.6	0.6	0.72	0.72	0.72
Temperature	32.00	32.00	32.00	32.00	32.00	32.00
Tilt	23.5	23.5	23.5	23.5	23.56	23.5
Sunshine	650	650	650	650	650	650
Latitude	35.42	35.42	35.42	35.42	35.42	35.42
Longitude	6.35	6.35	6.35	6.35	6.35	6.35
breakdown type	Shady	Disconnected connectivity	Module shorted	Sain	Sain	Sain
Tracking system	Absent	Absent	Absent	Absent	workin g	working
Number of strings in parallel	10	10	10	10	10	10
serial module in a string	80	80	80	80	80	80
Action on Modules	Isolate	no	Replac e	no	no	no
Connector action	no	Maintain	no	no	no	no
Action on Sensors	no	no	no	no	no	no
Action on tracker	no	no	no	no	Setting	Repair
Tilt adjustment	no	no	no	Tilt adjustm ent	no	no
Injection into the grid	Injectio n	Injection	Injectio n	Injectio n	Injecti on	Injectio n

Table II represents the attributes of the case to test in their problem part. The solution part is to find using the simulator of the developped steering system.

TABLE II. CASE TO TEST

Attributes	Case 1	Case 2	Case 3	Case 4
PE/PT report	0.58	0.6	0.65	0.65
Temperature	30,00	32,00	25,00	25
tilt	30	23.5	23.5	23.5
Sunshine	600	650	750	750
Latitude	35.42	35.42	35.42	35.42
Longitude	6.35	6.35	6.35	6.35
breakdown type	shady	Disconnected connectivity	Sain	Sain
Tracking system	Absent	Absent	Absent	working
Number of strings in parallel	10	10	10	10
serial module in a string	80	80	80	80

Table III shows the obtained results as a solution part of the case attributes.

TABLE III. OBTAINED RESULTS

Attributes	TestCase 1	TestCase 2	TestCase 3	TestCase 4
Action on Modules	Isolate	no	no	no
Action on connector	no	Maintain	no	no
Action on sensors	no	no	no	no
Action on tracker	no	no	no	no
Tilt adjustment	no	no	*Set the tilt angle to: 65,259900 °*	no
Injection into the grid	Injection	Injection	Injection	Injection

The results of the tests are acceptable. For the cases TestCase 1 and TestCase 2, the obtained solutions are the optimal ones. The most similar case to TestCase 1 is Case 1, so the solution part of this case is applied. The same is true for TestCase 2, the most similar case is Case 2. The result obtained for TestCase 3 is great. The system finds that the most similar case is Case 4, whose solution is tilt adjustment. The system automatically provides the exact angle of inclination based on the situation information geographical location and the current date.

The adjustment of this anomaly is to enrich the case base with this case by assigning the correct solution to it, or assigning a weight to the attribute "tracking system".

TABLE IV. TEST CASE 4

Attributes	TestCase 4	Case 4
PE/PT report	0.65	0.72
Temperature	25	32,00
Tilt	23.5	23.5
Sunshine	750	650
Latitude	35.42	35.42
Longitude	6.35	6.35
breakdown type	Sain	Sain
Tracking system	working	Absent
Number of strings in parallel	10	10
serial module in a string	80	80
Action on Modules	[illegible]	[illegible]
Connector action	no	[illegible]
Action on Sensors	no	no
Action on tracker	no	no
Tilt adjustment	no	Tilt adjustment
Injection into the grid	Injection	Injection

However, the result of TestCase 4 is not optimal. It can be seen that the PE/PT ratio is less than 0.85 and the solution contains no action. So, we analyse how the system handled this case. We found that the most similar case for TestCase 4 is Case 4, so the system takes its part solution is goes to the adaptation stage of the solution. In the tilt adjustment attribute, the system finds a conflict: "tilt angle setting but the tracker system exists and is running", in which case the system proceeds to the next similar case solution and applies the adaptation rules on it. It finds it to be valid, despite the fact that it is not optimal.

VII. CONCLUSION AND FUTURE WORK

Oil is an exhaustible energy, so renewable energies are those of the future. In our work, we have presented the renewable sources available in Algeria and their exploitation, the methods of artificial intelligence used in the supervision and finally the reasoned steering based on cases. The current exploitation of renewable energies is not extensive, but the program launched for the development of these energies gives importance to these energies, especially photovoltaics. In our work, we have illustrated that photovoltaic solar installations require real-time monitoring of their operation to increase their production and availability. This is done by steering. Our steering system generates the right actions to apply to the generator when its state changes using the case-based reasoning methodology. During this work, we found that the use of case-based reasoning methodology is tricky, especially in the choice of type of case representation and similarity and adaptation calculation methods. The richness of the case base has an important influence on the quality of the solutions obtained. The richer the base, the more appropriate the solutions.

As a perspective, we propose to add to this application a generator fault detection subsystem, an automatic optimal reconfiguration subsystem for better production and a system that allows the exchange of cases between the systems implanted in different sites.

REFERENCES

[1] L. Xue, W. Yanzhi, Z. Di, Ch. Naehyuck and M. Pedram, "Online fault detection and tolerance for photovoltaic energy harvesting Systems", IEEE/ACM International Conference on Computer-Aided Design (ICCAD) 2012, November 5-8, 2012, San Jose, California, USA, pp. 1-6.

[2] Y. Zhao, R. Ball, J. Mosesian, J.F. De Palma and B. Lehman, "Graph-based semi-supervised learning for fault detection and classification in solar photovoltaic arrays", IEEE Energy Conversion Congress and Exposition, September 15–19, 2013, Denver, CO, USA, pp. 1628 - 1634.

[3] Y. Zhao et al., "Decision tree-based fault detection and classification in solar photovoltaic arrays", Applied Power Electronics Conference and Exposition (APEC), 2012, pp. 93-99.

[4] L. Zhihua, W. Yuanzhang, Z Diqing. and W. Chunhua, "An intelligent method for fault diagnosis in photovoltaic array", System Simulation and Scientific Computing Communications in Computer and Information Science, 2012, pp. 10-16.

[5] K. Nur Atharah and T. Chee Wei, "A comprehensive review of maximum power point tracking algorithms for photovoltaic systems", Renewable and Sustainable Energy Reviews 37 pp. 585-598., 2014.

[6] P. Nopporn, P. Suttichai and S. Yosanai, "Maximum power point tracking using adaptive fuzzy logic control for grid-connected photovoltaic system", Renewable Energy, Vol. 30 N° 11, 2005, pp. 1771-1788.

[7] A. Bahgat, N.H. Helwa, G.E. Ahmad and E.T. El Shenawy, "Maximum power point traking controller for PV systems using neural networks", Renewable Energy 2005, pp. 1257–1268.

[8] A. Aberkane, "Centralization of monitoring platforms for automated production chains", University M'hamed Bougara-Boumerdes, Master thesis, 2011.

[9] D. Trentesaux and O. Sénéchal "Steering of manufacturing production systems", Techniques de l'Ingénieur S7598 v1, 2002.

[10] D. Racoceanu, " Contribution to the Monitoring of Production Systems and Using the Techniques of Artificial Intelligence", Ph.D thesis, University of Franche-Comté, France, 2006.

[11] R. Zemouri, "Contribution to the monitoring of production systems using dynamic neural networks: Application to e-maintenance", Ph.D. thesis, University of Franche-Comté, 2003.

[12] Simon C. K. Shiu and Sankar K. Pal, "Foundations of soft case-based reasoning", John Wiley & Sons Hoboken, New Jersey USA, 2004.

[13] B. Ikhlef, " Contribution to the Study of Automatic Industrial Supervision in a SCADA Environment", Master thesis, University M'hamed Bougara, Boumerdes, Algeria, 2009.

[14] M. R. Michael and O. W. Rosina , "Case-Based Reasoning A Textbook", Springer-Verlag Berlin Heidelberg 2013.

[15] K. Helali , "Modeling a photovoltaic cell: comparative study", university of Tizi Ouzou, Algeria, Master thesis, 2012.

[16] B. Lg, "Detecting and Locating Faults for a PV System", University of Grenoble, Ph.D thesis, 2011.

[17] M. Rebhi, M. Sellam, A. Belghachi, and B. Kadri, "Conception and Realization of Sun Tracking System in the South-West of Algeria", Applied Physics Research, Vol. 2, No. 1, 2010.

A Knowledge-based Approach to Enhance the Workforce Skills and Competences within the Industry 4.0

Enrico G. Caldarola*, Gianfranco E. Modoni* and Marco Sacco†
*Institute of Industrial Technologies and Automation
National Research Council, Bari, Italy
Email: {enrico.caldarola, gianfranco.modoni}@itia.cnr.it
†Institute of Industrial Technologies and Automation
National Research Council, Milan, Italy
Email: marco.sacco@itia.cnr.it

***Abstract*—One of the significant challenges of Industry 4.0 is the realization of a more *sustainable manufacturing* along the whole factory life-cycle, which has an impact on three different dimensions: economical, social and environmental. Whereas the economic and environmental dimensions have been widely discussed in many works and progressively integrated in production processes, there is still a shortage of studies aiming at incorporating the social dimension. Consequently, economic planning and policies lack the full acknowledgment of human rights, education, health and gender diversity. With this study, we aim at aligning the technological panorama of Industry 4.0 with the social dimension of sustainable manufacturing, by proposing a semantic model based framework as a reference architecture to enhance social sustainability in manufacturing. Finally, a case study is presented, in which factory environments try to meet workers capabilities and desiderata, by augmenting the quality of life and ensuring people health, at work or in their community during their entire life, while ensuring productivity.**

***Keywords*–Social Sustainable Manufacturing; Industry 4.0; Teaching Factory; Knowledge-Intensive Systems; Cyber-Physical Systems; Semantic Web.**

I. Introduction

In recent years, new trends in manufacturing and automation have embraced *circular economy* models, which emphasize the design and implementation of a new sustainable industry changing at different dimensions: economical, societal and environmental. The concrete realization of this changing tune has been made possible by the adoption of new technological solutions and paradigms coming with the fourth industrial revolution, also known as *Industry 4.0* [1][2]. This latter promotes the computerization of manufacturing grounding on some design principles, such as interconnection, information transparency, decentralized decisions and technical assistance; while the key enabling technologies underpinning it are Internet-of-Things (IoT), Cyber-Physical Systems (CPS) and Smart Factories [3]. One of the main strengths of Industry 4.0 is the creation of intelligent cross-linked modules, holding a great opportunity for realizing sustainable industrial mechanisms on all three dimensions previously mentioned: economic, social and environmental. The value creation in Industry 4.0 can be profitably realized through the adoption of human-centered technologies, which put the human operator (or the knowledge worker) at the center of the innovation process. This vision is in line with the European Commission strategy as reported in [4], where, it is pointed out that, in order for European industry to be competitive and flourishing, it is needed to ensure workforce with the right skills. Indeed, one of the key priorities for the Factories of the Future (FoF) 18-19-20 Work Program [5] is focused on the human factor, addressing in particular the development of competences of the workers in synergy with technological progress. Some of the technological enablers addressing this objective, which have also acknowledged in this work, are: (i) models for individual and collective sense-making, learning and knowledge accumulation; (ii) workers interconnection with machines and processes and developing context-oriented services towards safety practices and decision making. In particular, the work introduced in this paper follows three inspiring paradigms described as follows. Firstly, the *Teaching Factory* concept, which aims to align manufacturing teaching and training to the needs of modern industrial practice. According to this new paradigm, future engineers and knowledge workers (i.e., workers whose main capital is knowledge) "need to be educated with new curricula in order to cope with the increasing industrial requirements of the factories of the future" [6]. Secondly, it exploits the *Visual Approach* concept to manufacturing [7]. In this regard, the efficiency of workers can be enhanced by Augmented Reality/Virtual Reality (AR/VR) systems, such as headmounted displays together with Learnstruments [8] or by using new Information and Communication Technologies (ICTs) for implementing *gamification* in order to support decentralized decision-making. Finally, we have the adoption of *Knowledge-based* systems, which use proper formalisms (semantic-based languages or ontologies) [9] in order to represent the knowledge hidden in the product or production process. All the above paradigms contribute to realize the envisioned concept of Smart Factory, as a thorough Cyber-Physical System allowing safety, wellness and continuous training inside the factory (Figure 1).

Acknowledging the great interest for the human factor in modern factory, this work proposes a multi-layered framework as a leading architecture satisfying the requirements of social sustainability. The framework will be applied to a concrete case study, which demonstrates the use of advanced technologies from the Industry 4.0 panorama in order to create a user-centred factory environment.

The reminder of the paper is structured as follows: Section 2 collects some previous works in defining a conceptual model in Industry 4.0 both from academics and industrial research groups. Section 3 describes the framework highlighting the leading principle that have inspired it. Section 4 presents a

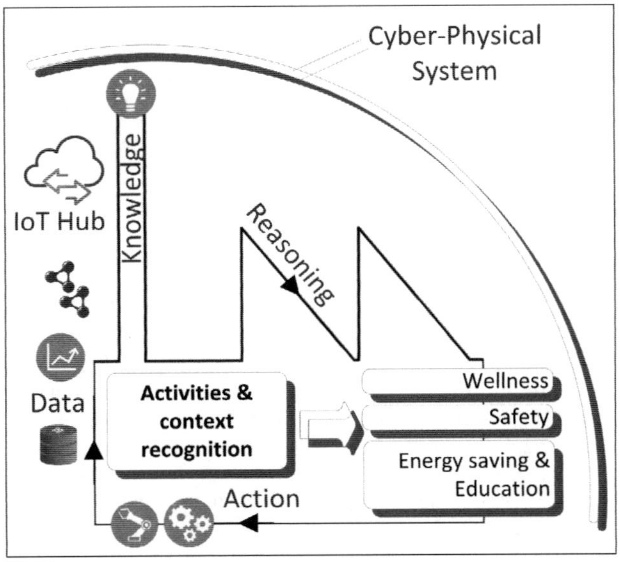

Figure 1. The Smart Factory as a Cyber-Physical system

case study aiming at demonstrating the applicability of the conceptual framework introduced in this work. Finally, the last section summarizes the main findings outlining future research investigations.

II. RELATED WORKS

With the advent of Industry 4.0 and even before, new spreading paradigms, such as *lean manufacturing* and *advanced computer-based manufacturing*, conceptual models or frameworks have been thought in order to clearly highlight the concepts and relationships resulting from the new perspective proposed by the paradigm. Lee et. al. [1] proposes a "5C architecture" for Cyber-Physical Systems in Industry 4.0 manufacturing systems. It is intended to provide a step-by-step guideline for developing and deploying a CPS for manufacturing application. The architecture is layers-based and includes the following levels:

- *Smart connection.* It acquires accurate and reliable data from machines and their components. Data might be directly measured by sensors or obtained from controller or enterprise manufacturing systems such as Enterprise Resources Planning (ERP), Manufacturing Execution Systems (MES), Software Configuration Management (SCM) and Coordinate Measuring Machine (CMM);
- *Data-to-information conversion.* It performs some computational task like multidimensional data correlation, degradation and performance prediction in order to infer information from the data;
- *Cyber.* It acts as central information hub in this architecture by collecting data from all the machines and performing analytics tasks to extract additional information that provide better insight also by taking into consideration historical data coming from machines;
- *Cognition.* It properly presents the acquired knowledge to expert users supporting the correct decision to be taken;
- *Configuration.* It represents the feedback from cyber space to physical space and acts as supervisory control to make machines self-configure and self-adaptive.

Another valuable architectural model is the "Reference Architectural Model Industrie" (RAMI) 4.0 [10]. This model combines the fundamental elements of Industry 4.0 in a three-dimensional layer model including the "Hierarchy Levels" axis, the "Life Cycle & Value Stream" axis and finally the orthogonal vertical axis. The first axis ranges over the different functionalities within factories or facilities and retraces what is provided by the International Electrotechnical Commission (IEC) 62264 document [11]. Such functionalities intersect with the second axis, which represents the life cycle of facilities and products and is based on IEC 62890 [12]. Finally, the vertical axis includes the decomposition of a machine into its properties structured layer by layer: asset, integration, communication, information, functional and business. Within these three axes, all crucial aspects of Industry 4.0 can be mapped, allowing objects such as machines to be classified according to the model, thus providing a common understanding of Industry 4.0 technologies.

The Open Platform Communications Unified Architecture (OPC UA) [13] is the new standard of the OPC Foundation providing interoperability in process automation. It provides a Service-Oriented Architecture (SOA) for industrial applications from factory floor devices to enterprise applications by specifying an abstract set of services mapped to a concrete technology. A communication stack is used on client- and server-side to encode and decode message requests and responses. Also, this architectural model includes a bottom level of data acquisition from heterogeneous data sources, which provide the server implementation with data requested by the client. OPC Ua does not provide Application Program Interfaces (APIs) implementation for client-server communication but a Web service-based implementation that allow heterogeneous clients to communicate with different implementations of server (exploiting Microsoft, Java or C-based technologies).

Among the commercial solutions, which take advantage of a semantic-based approach, it is worth mentioning the Global Real Time Information Processing Solution (GRIPS) [14] developed by Star Group, a software framework that enables intelligent processing capabilities by linking information objects. Specifically, by allowing a geographically distributed and multi-lingual authoring of structured and linked information units, GRIPS supports the creation of product knowledge while enabling semantically linked knowledge management on all business-critical objects. The GRIPS authoring and information processing model distinguishes three layers of information processing: semantic content base layer, publication/document types and structures layer, publishing channels layer. By exploiting the semantic-based enabling technologies, it benefits not only product communication, but also marketing, sales, after sales and the end customer. Moreover, the framework allows enhanced re-use of software components, standardization, cost reduction, quality, sustainability and protection of investments, seamless integration, and so forth.

In [15], the authors proposed a system approach to support sustainability of manufacturing from three perspectives: energy, material, technology. Finally, the use of knowledge-based models for enabling context-awareness in the context

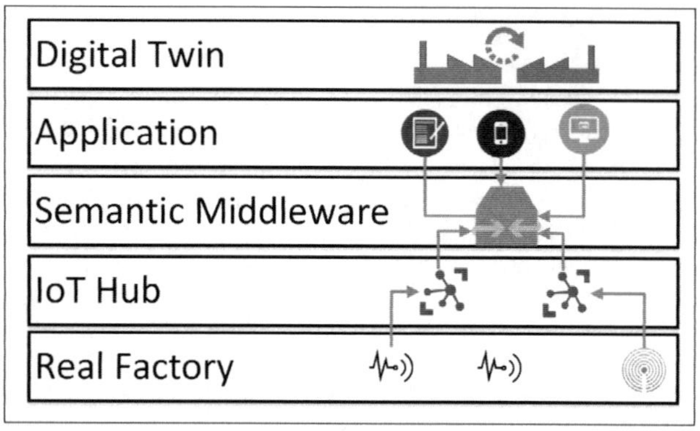

Figure 2. Conceptual framework for the Social User-centered Manufacturing in Industry 4.0

of Smart Home, which can be borrowed in the Smart Factory scenario too, has already been explored and experimented by the authors in [16].

III. THE CONCEPTUAL FRAMEWORK

Figure 2 depicts the layers-based conceptual framework proposed in this work. The leading principles at the base of the framework are: (i) highlight the cutting edge technologies and paradigms belonging to Industry 4.0 in order to meet the social sustainable manufacturing requirements involved in our case study; (ii) separate technologies and solutions according to different layers having in mind the production processes, from the design phase to its realization; (iii) emphasize the *digital synchronization* between the real and digital factory acknowledging the continuous exchange of data and feedback between the factory and its mirror image in the cyberspace.

Starting from the bottom, the *Real Factory* layer represents a unique level of acquisition for data coming from inside or outside the factory. To this level belong data collected from the shop-floor acquired for example through a distributed sensors network (wireless sensors networks) such as in-line inspection and monitoring data, wearable devices, proximity sensors like eBeacon. This layer is also called to operate a preliminary adaptation and integration of data acquired from heterogeneous sources, also just at a syntactical level such as data cleansing and syntactic alignment in order to let them be interoperable and usable by the software tools at the upper levels of the framework.

The *IoT Hub* is conceived as the layer in which the in-depth knowledge of product-process and production systems is elicited from raw data collected at the bottom level. Once elicited, the product-process knowledge can be represented through standard or *de facto* standard languages and technologies so that it can be shared and understood by human and automated agents. The adoption of such formalisms in modelling the information about products, processes and production systems opens several perspectives in managing the complexity of data models used in modern manufacturing scenarios. Furthermore, with the rise of Big Data and Big Data Analytics technologies [17][18], we are witnessing the trend of moving data, applications, or other business components from an organization's on-premises infrastructure to the cloud, or moving them from one cloud service to another. This trend has lead to a new manufacturing paradigm, the *Cloud Manufactruing*, developed from existing advanced manufacturing models and enterprise information technologies under the support of cloud computing, Internet of Things, virtualization and service-oriented technologies, and advanced computing technologies [19].

The *Semantic Middleware* layer at the centre of the framework represents a sort of *gateway* responsible for a systematic integration of data, eventually semantically annotated data [20][21], coming from the enterprise data sources (local databases or legacy database) and from outside (distributed storage or Web of Data). This layer is responsible for: implementing the proper approach to transparently access data from multiple clients, by taking into consideration security, reliability, redundancy and trustability issues, providing reliable mechanisms to publish new data from the upper level applications or by the bottom line and make them available to all interested agents in a real-time or near real-time fashion with respect to changes in critical data. A publisher-subscriber mechanism or an Event Condition Action (ECA) architecture can be used in order to implement such functionality [22]. To this level belong one of the key component used in the scenario described in the next section, i.e., the Digital Factory Model (DFM), which can be conceived as an *omniscient* module able to understand the representation models underlying the whole product life' cycle, the production process and system and the Virtual Individual Model of workers engaged in the production process and their skills.

The *Application* layer embraces different tools used in computerized manufacturing. There exist many Digital Tools that support engineers and designers in different phases of product life-cycle. For example, Computer Aided Design (CAD) software help users in creation, modification, analysis or optimization of a design and are used to increase the productivity of the designer, improve the quality of design, and, importantly, improve communications through documentation. To this level also belong the Virtual Tools, i.e., Augmented Reality Systems (like AR headset and visors), which implement the Visual Approach to production process already described in the introductory section, being one of the solution adopted in the demonstration scenario. Finally, the Smart Tools include all Business Intelligent tools and Analytics [18] used to analyze data and get insight from them to support expert user in the decision making process (e.g., Opinion Mining tools or Information Visualization tools). Proper info-graphics or information visualization tools are necessary to completely transfer acquired knowledge to the users [17] [23].

The highest level of the framework is the *Digital Twin* level. It resembles the Cognition level of the 5C architecture [1], i.e., at this stage proper presentation of the acquired knowledge throughout the lower levels must be provided. Additionally, in this level takes place the digital synchronization: there must be a constant synchronization between the real factory and its replica in the digital world. Such synchronization requires that produced data or acquired by physical sensors spread at the shoop-floor level must be passed to the digital tools, which in turn elaborate them via sophisticate analytics or simulations in order to provide feedback and reactions that impact real-time over the real factory. The Digital Twin is underpinned by representational models about the whole factory. In particular, the demonstration scenario described in the next section rely above three representational models, which formally describe the digital replica of the factory: the *Digital Factory Model*, the *Virtual Individual Model*, and the *Skills Virtual Model*.

IV. USER-CENTRED WORKPLACES: A CASE STUDY

The case study presented here is focused on the production process of wooden furniture, such as sofas, dispensers, chairs and so on. This case study is significant because, on the one hand, the adoption of innovative technologies can improve the whole production process making it more competitive and lean, while, on the other hand, the need for a hand-made production as the most important added value for customers, significantly reduces the freedom of action in terms of processes automation and innovation deployment. Thus, most of the process innovation is user-centred, i.e., it needs to be addressed towards the direct support of human operators activities rather than towards sophisticated machinery.

Typically, human operators involved in this scenario have to deal with two different kinds of issues, which will be further discussed as follows. At first, the operators are not interchangeable in the assembly line, since she/he is formed for (and is in charge of) accomplishing a specific task (e.g., drilling, assembly of parts, cutting, etc.); therefore, *job rotation* is not applicable, and thus, the company has great difficulty in distributing the workload, for example, when it must deal with peaks of requests for a certain product (requiring specific workings) or in the case of unavailability of some resources. Moreover, the lack of a proper job rotation may result frustrating for worker who is forced to perform the same operations all the time. Secondly, the high variety of wooden products along with the mass customization may require an extra effort for workers in order to deal with the rapidly change of work instructions, without the help of technologies. For example, the use of traditional hard copy manuals, instead of technologies based on a Visual Approach, will force the operator to continuously check out the instruction sheets (due to the strong difference among assembling sequences of different products models), and this can lead to a waste of time, which can significantly grow depending on worker experience and on the frequency of production of different models. Conversely, the proper adoption of a Visual Approach supported by technologies, will provide just-in-time information delivering, following the principle of transferring the right information at the right person at the right time.

What we expect from the implementation of user-centred workplaces is: reducing non-value adding activities; reducing mistakes from employees and suppliers; reducing time for employee orientation and training; reducing search time in navigating the facility and locating tools, parts and supplies; reducing unnecessary human motion and transportation of goods; increasing productivity supporting sustainability, mainly from a social perspective. Workers will no longer perform their tasks routinely; instead, they will have to undertake varied and mostly unstructured tasks, depending on the needs of the dynamically changing production process. Teams should/will include flexible and remote ways of working and interacting with the systems as well as with other workers.

As shown in Figure 3, the case study involves different actors and components: the operators, an AR equipment, the Digital Factory Manager (DFM) and the virtual models. It also involves different technological solutions which support such components: an Augmented Reality System, with annex headset or visors like the Oculus Rift, a distributed sensor network, which is spread throughout all machinery and operators, intelligent software robots like *chatbot* able to assist the human operators in accomplishing their tasks, in a high level of abstraction, and finally, representational languages such as ontologies [24], belonging to the Semantic Web technologies panorama [25]. The latter are used for formally representing the knowledge about the whole factory and the involved actors through three virtual models:

- *Digital Factory Model*, which represents the entire production system including the production process and the final product with its parts. It borrows some concepts and idea from the Virtual Factory Data Model introduced in [26];
- *Virtual Individual Model*, which is a formal conceptualization of the operator profile. It includes biographic info (gender, age, language and so on), capabilities and eventually disabilities or impairments, work aspirations and attitudes, training activities and courses the worker has already taken part. This model is based on the Virtual Individual Model provided within the Pegaso project [27] and provides a formally multi-faceted description of the operator within the factory;
- *Skills Virtual Model*, which provides a formal representation of the skills the operator need in order to perform each single phase of the production process and is informed by the knowledge of product and its parts, processes, competencies and operator capabilities.

These formal models need to be properly integrated in order to be used by the DFM, exploiting well-known techniques for ontology integration existing in the literature [20]. Furthermore, related to each model there is an extensional part (the model instance) that need to be persisted through storage technologies such as RDF Stores or TripleStore [22]; One of the key components of the entire case study is the DFM, which can be conceived as an *omniscient* module able to understand the representation models underlying the whole product life' cycle, the production process and system and the Virtual Individual Model of workers engaged in the production process and their skills. With all these information at hand, the DFM is able to infer the right allocation of people to production process phases by ensuring that individuals with proper skills and capabilities (or maybe attitude or desiderata) are engaged in activities that best fit the worker characteristics, this way, realizing the transfer of the right information at the right person at the right time. The synergistic use of these technologies allows the implementation of a close-loop between the real factory and the its digital replica.

With the support of the technologies mentioned above, framed in each layer depicted in Figure 2, it is possible to imagine a demonstration scenario as follows. Once the operator is ready to start her/his work, she/he approaches the workstation and is immediately recognized through proximity sensors like eBeacon. By accessing her/his profile, represented in the VIM (Virtual Individual Model), the system is able to verify if the operator properly fits to do a certain job over a certain machine. Both the Digital Factory Model and the

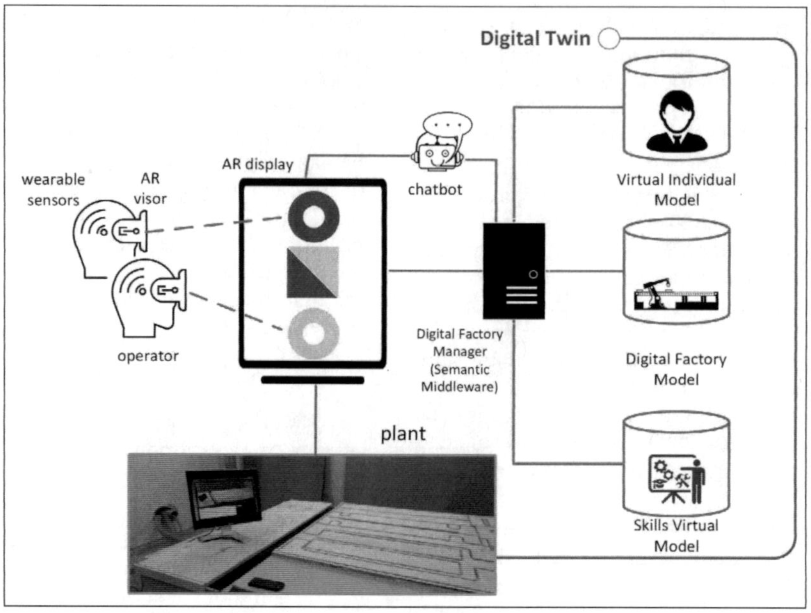

Figure 3. Case study conceptual overview

Skill Virtual Model allow the system to know which skills are needed to use a particular machine, and which machine has to be used in carrying out a specific task for producing a particular item or component of a final product. The operator profile also contains a report of operator performances in accomplishing specific tasks and her/his preferred tasks. The personal record also contains info like impairments, such as, for example, visual or audio deficit, which can be used by the system in order to adjust, for example, the work surface lighting. The operator faces a work plane with all the parts of which the piece is made, but does not know how the different parts should be mounted (or because the operator is not trained or because the piece is new). The operator is guided step-by-step to accomplishing the work by the use of AR equipment, which are constantly connected to a DFM, via wireless networks. The latter constantly informs the operator about the procedures to be followed when accomplishing a certain task. A distributed network of sensor is pervasively used in order to monitor the worker positions with respect to machines and the advancement of her/his work.

In this study, we modeled the skills of the various operators and mapped with the operations to be performed. This way, the AR system is able to display the full piece of work, superimposed on what has so far built by the operator, to provide a clear idea of how to continue the work that is being done. The AR system also displays a preview of the finished piece on the basis of the piece produced so far and on the basis of the drawings in 3D as designed by the CAD. 3D drawings are displayed as a virtual silhouette of the part still to be worked on. The AR display is also provided with a chatbot interface, which allows the user, via a speech recognition system or via a wireless keyboard, to interact with intelligent software robots able to answer the operator questions in a high level of abstraction. The chatbot also acts as an info request router being capable to forward a request to a human operator recognized able to respond according to her/his profile and experiences, as modeled in the Virtual Individual Model. Any updates in the production process or in hardware and software components of machinery can arise the need for a professional upgrade of the operator that is promptly reported by the system, this way ensuring a continuous learning within the factory. The synergistic use of different technological solutions makes the workplace smart, i.e., a sustainable work environment which is attractive for workers, tailored to their specific needs and able to ensure well-being, continuous training and education, by also augmenting overall productivity.

V. CONCLUSIONS

In this work, a conceptual framework for social manufacturing sustainability in the rise of Industry 4.0 has been proposed. The idea of the framework is to put in evidence how the cutting edge technologies under the Industry 4.0 umbrella can support the fundamental principles of social sustainability. In order to demonstrate this, intelligent cross-linked value creation networks have been realized by turning the traditional factory in a Cyber-Physical System, which implements the concept of Teaching Factory and uses knowledge-based systems and a Visual approach to production process. A case study has been presented in order to verge the layered framework introduced on a real case study aligning the needs encountered with the technological solutions belonging to each layer. The paper demonstrates how the framed technologies can help in implementing the user-centred environment within the factory. This is conceived as a smart workplace, which is attractive for workers, tailored to their specific needs and able to ensure well-being, continuous training and education, and sustainability without lessening productivity. Future lines of researches will investigate the adoption of more sophisticated and complete knowledge models of the production process also by applying the proposed framework to other industrial scenario.

References

[1] J. Lee, B. Bagheri, and H.-A. Kao, "A cyber-physical systems architecture for industry 4.0-based manufacturing systems," Manufacturing Letters, vol. 3, 2015, pp. 18–23.

[2] H. Lasi, P. Fettke, H.-G. Kemper, T. Feld, and M. Hoffmann, "Industry 4.0," Business & Information Systems Engineering, vol. 6, no. 4, 2014, pp. 239–242.

[3] M. Hermann, T. Pentek, and B. Otto, "Design principles for industrie 4.0 scenarios," in System Sciences (HICSS), 2016 49th Hawaii International Conference on. IEEE, 2016, pp. 3928–3937.

[4] EC, "Skills for Key Enabling Technologies in Europe," European Commission, Tech. Rep., 0 2016.

[5] EFFRA, "Factories 4.0 and Beyond - Recommendations for the work programme 18-19-20 of the FoF PPP under Horizon 2020," EFFRA. European Factories of the Future Research Association, Tech. Rep., 09 2016.

[6] G. Chryssolouris, D. Mavrikios, and L. Rentzos, "The teaching factory: A manufacturing education paradigm," Procedia CIRP, vol. 57, 2016, pp. 44–48.

[7] H. Hirano, 5 pillars of the visual workplace. CRC Press, 1995.

[8] R. McFarland, C. Reise, A. Postawa, and G. Seliger, "18.9 learnstruments in value creation and learning centered work place design," in Proceedings of the 11th Global Conference on Sustainable Manufacturing - Innovative Solutions, 2013, pp. 624–629.

[9] H. Lin and J. A. Harding, "A manufacturing system engineering ontology model on the semantic web for inter-enterprise collaboration," Computers in Industry, vol. 58, no. 5, 2007, pp. 428–437.

[10] M. Hankel and B. Rexroth, "The reference architectural model industrie 4.0 (rami 4.0)," ZVEI, 2015.

[11] IEC, "Iec 62264-1 enterprise-control system integration–part 1: Models and terminology," Tech. Rep., 2003.

[12] ——, "Iec 62890 life-cycle management for systems and products used in industrial-process measurement, control and automation," Tech. Rep., 2006.

[13] S.-H. Leitner and W. Mahnke, "Opc ua–service-oriented architecture for industrial applications," ABB Corporate Research Center, 2006.

[14] M. Gutknecht, "Introduction to GRIPS," STAR AG, Tech. Rep., 07 2014.

[15] C. Yuan, Q. Zhai, and D. Dornfeld, "A three dimensional system approach for environmentally sustainable manufacturing," CIRP Annals-Manufacturing Technology, vol. 61, no. 1, 2012, pp. 39–42.

[16] M. Sacco, E. G. Caldarola, G. Modoni, and W. Terkaj, "Supporting the design of aal through a sw integration framework: the d4all project," in International Conference on Universal Access in Human-Computer Interaction. Springer, 2014, pp. 75–84.

[17] E. G. Caldarola and A. M. Rinaldi, "Big data visualization tools: A survey - the new paradigms, methodologies and tools for large data sets visualization," in - KomIS,, INSTICC. SciTePress, 2017.

[18] ——, "Big data: A survey - the new paradigms, methodologies and tools," in Proceedings of 4th International Conference on Data Management Technologies and Applications - Volume 1: KomIS, (DATA 2015), INSTICC. SciTePress, 2015, pp. 362–370.

[19] G. Modoni, M. Doukas, W. Terkaj, M. Sacco, and D. Mourtzis, "Enhancing factory data integration through the development of an ontology: from the reference models reuse to the semantic conversion of the legacy models," International Journal of Computer Integrated Manufacturing, vol. 30, no. 10, 2017, pp. 1043–1059.

[20] E. G. Caldarola and A. M. Rinaldi, "A multi-strategy approach for ontology reuse through matching and integration techniques," in Quality Software Through Reuse and Integration. Springer, 2016, pp. 63–90.

[21] G. Modoni, E. G. Caldarola, W. Terkaj, and M. Sacco, "The knowledge reuse in an industrial scenario: A case study," in eKNOW 2015, The Seventh International Conference on Information, Process, and Knowledge Management, 2015, pp. 66–71.

[22] G. E. Modoni, M. Veniero, A. Trombetta, M. Sacco, and S. Clemente, "Semantic based events signaling for aal systems," Journal of Ambient Intelligence and Humanized Computing, 2017, pp. 1–15.

[23] E. G. Caldarola and A. M. Rinaldi, "Improving the visualization of wordnet large lexical database through semantic tag clouds," in Big Data (BigData Congress), 2016 IEEE International Congress on. IEEE, 2016, pp. 34–41.

[24] T. R. Gruber, "A translation approach to portable ontology specifications," Knowledge acquisition, vol. 5, no. 2, 1993, pp. 199–220.

[25] T. Berners-Lee, J. Hendler, O. Lassila et al., "The semantic web," Scientific american, vol. 284, no. 5, 2001, pp. 28–37.

[26] B. Kádár, W. Terkaj, and M. Sacco, "Semantic virtual factory supporting interoperable modelling and evaluation of production systems," CIRP Annals-Manufacturing Technology, vol. 62, no. 1, 2013, pp. 443–446.

[27] A. Sojic, W. Terkaj, G. Contini, and M. Sacco, "Towards a teenager tailored ontology," Ontologies and Data in Life Sciences (odls 2014), 2014, p. 1.

[28] G. Fortino, C. Savaglio, C. E. Palau, J. S. de Puga, M. Ganzha, M. Paprzycki, M. Montesinos, A. Liotta, and M. Llop, "Towards multi-layer interoperability of heterogeneous iot platforms: The inter-iot approach," in Integration, Interconnection, and Interoperability of IoT Systems. Springer, 2018, pp. 199–232.

[29] M. Ganzha, M. Paprzycki, W. Pawłowski, P. Szmeja, and K. Wasielewska, "Semantic interoperability in the internet of things: An overview from the inter-iot perspective," Journal of Network and Computer Applications, vol. 81, 2017, pp. 111–124.

Visualizing the Landscape and Trend of Knowledge Management: 1974 to 2017

Li Zeng, Zili Li, Zhao Zhao
College of Advanced Interdisciplinary Studies
National University of Defense Technology
Changsha, China
crack521@163.com zlli@nudt.edu.cn z_costa@163.com

Yang Li
Institute of Communication
Lumire University Lyon 2
Lyon, France
yanglilyon@gmail.com

Abstract—**A comprehensive assessment of publication data in the Knowledge Management domain was conducted. By using the related literature in the Science Citation Index (SCI) database from 1974 to 2017, a scientometric approach is used to quantitatively evaluate current research landscape and trend. This shows that Knowledge Management is in the growth period with a maturity of 87.22%, a total of 8121 articles covering 113 countries/territories and the top 3 most productive countries are China, USA and England. There are 4556 research institutes engaged in the research field of "Knowledge Management" and the top 3 most productive institutes are Islamic Azad University, Wuhan University of Technology and Harbin Institute of Technology. Research hotspots, such as performance, system, innovation, firm, information technology, strategy, organization and ontology are shown in a keywords clustering mapping. In addition, keywords with the strongest citation burst, such as Expert System, Organizational Memory, Artificial Intelligence, Decision Support, Social Media, Big Data and Total Quality Management demonstrate the trends of this field. The result provides a dynamic view of the evolution of "Knowledge Management" research landscapes, hotspots and trends from various perspectives which may serve as a potential guide for future research.**

Keywords-Knowledge Management; Scientometrics; Mapping of Knowledge Domain.

I. INTRODUCTION

Knowledge Management (KM) is the process of creating, sharing, using and managing the knowledge and information of an organization which has existed for more than 40 years as a research area [1]. KM is widely used in Management [2], Business Information [3], Science [4], Education [5], Engineering [6] and so on.

In the recent years, scholars conducted a comprehensive review of the research in the field of knowledge management. Corso et al. [7] reviewed and described the different streams and approaches emerging in literature on knowledge management in product innovation. Liao [8] surveyed and classified KM technologies using seven categories as follows: KM framework, knowledge-based systems, data mining, information and communication technology, artificial intelligence/expert systems, database technology, and modeling, together with their applications for different research and problem domains. Chen et al. [9] reviewed the development of knowledge management using a literature review and classification of articles from 1995 to 2004. Bjornson et al. [10]'s systematic review identifies empirical studies of knowledge management initiatives in software engineering, and discusses the concepts studied, the major findings, and the research methods used. Gallupe [11] surveyed the landscape of knowledge management system research and provided a framework for research into the development and use of these systems in organizations. Marra et al. [12] debated on the role of knowledge management in supply chain management by reviewing the published literature. Durst et al. [13] reviewed research on knowledge management in small and medium-sized enterprises to identify gaps in the body of knowledge.

In this paper, a scientometric review of the landscape and trend of published knowledge management research is performed by investigating the scientific outputs, geographical distribution and international cooperation, distribution of institutions and journals with the aim to offer another perspective on the development of research in the field of Knowledge Management. Moreover, innovative methods, such as co-citation analysis, keyword semantic clustering and burst detection were applied, which can vividly reveal the landscape and trends from various perspectives.

The rest of the paper is structured as follows. In Section II, we present the data and methods used. Section III contains the results and discussion. WE conclude this work in Section IV.

II. DATA AND METHOD

A. Data Collection

The bibliographic records used for analysis in this paper were collected from Web of Science (WoS) of Clarivate Analytics on November 15, 2017, and specific search strategy is as follows:

Topics = "Knowledge Management*"

Timespan = All years

Databases = SCI-EXPANDED, SSCI, A&HCI, CPCI-S, CPCI-SSH, BKCI-S, BKCI-SSH, ESCI, CCR-EXPANDED, IC.

The query resulted in 8121 bibliographic records. The whole records were then retrieved and downloaded for subsequent analysis.

B. Methods

After data collection, cleaning, conversion, deduplication and other operations, a basic analysis with regard to highly productive countries/territories and institutes, highly cited references and highly cited authors was conducted by Microsoft Excel. H-Index and other metrics were calculated by a Python script, geographic distribution of scholars was mapped by Google Earth according to author affiliations, network analysis of different type entities such as countries/territories, institutes, categories and keywords was conducted by the scientometric software CiteSpace [14] and VOSViewer [15] with the aim to identify the intellectual structure, hotspots and trends of the Knowledge Management research. Semantic clustering of keywords was conducted based on word2vec [16] and burst detection of keywords was conducted by the algorithm proposed by Kleinberg [17].

III. Results and Discussion

A. *Scientific Outputs of Knowledge Management Research*

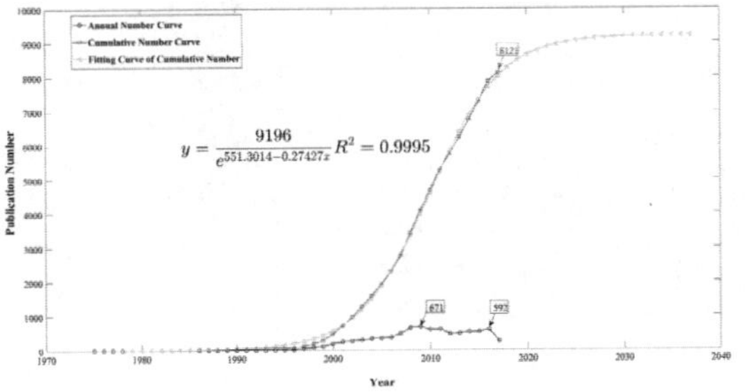

Figure 1. Article Number Curve

Figure 1 shows the number of papers and maturity forecast between 1974 and 2017 in the field of Knowledge Management. The black curve is the annual number of article. The earliest published time is 1974. Henry [18] argued knowledge management as a new concern for public administration. From the curve, we found that a substantial interest in Knowledge Management research did not emerge until 2002, although a few articles related to Knowledge Management were published previously. The highest number of papers arrived at 2009, with 671 articles, accounting for 8.26% of the total number and the average number of articles was 193.4 per year. The red curve is the cumulative number of papers. According to the theory of technology maturity, the cumulative number of documents could be fitted by the Logistic Growth Model [19]. The least squares method for curve fitting is used to get the parameters in the equation, where the blue curve is the result which is described by (1).

$$y = 9196 / (1 + \exp^{551.3014-0.27427x}) \quad (1)$$

Here, x and y denote the year and article number, respectively. According to this, we can divide the development of Knowledge into four stages: infant period (before 2002), growth period (2003-2018), mature period (2019-2024) and stable period (after 2024). According to the above stage division, the research of Knowledge Management in 2017 was in the growth period with a maturity of 87.22%.

B. *Characteristics of Geographic Distribution*

Figure 2 shows the geographic distribution of countries/ territories in the field of Knowledge Management which was generated from author affiliations. One obvious characteristic is that these research institutes are mainly located in Europe, North America, Southeast Asia and Australia. Institutes in Europe are mainly located in the western region containing countries such as Great Britain, France, Germany and Italy. Countries in North America are mainly represented by the US. Institutes in Southeast Asia are mainly located in China (Mainland), South Korea, Taiwan (Territory) and Japan.

Table I lists the top ten most productive countries/ territories in the field of Knowledge Management. Overall, China is the first most productive, but fifth most influential country in this field, with a total number of 1315 papers (1204 independent papers, 111 internationally collaborated papers), 235 institutes and 2755 citations. Its top five most productive institutes are Wuhan University of Technology (54 papers), The Hong Kong Polytechnic University (50 papers), Wuhan University (48 papers), Harbin Institute of Technology (44 papers) and Chinese Academy of Sciences (39 papers), and Chinas H-Index is 30. USA is the second most productive, but the first most influential country in this field, with a total number of 1098 papers (804 independent papers, 294 internationally collaborated papers), 111 institutes and 22073 citations. Its top five most productive institutes are George Washington University (37 papers), IBM Corporation (20 papers), Purdue University (19 papers), Rutgers University (18 papers) and Illinois State University (17 papers), and USA's H-Index is 72. England is the third most productive and also the third most influential country in this filed, with a total number of 581 papers (393 independent papers, 188 internationally collaborated papers), 157 institutes and 6089 citations. Its top five most productive institutes are Loughborough University (55 papers), Coventry University (39 papers), University of Salford (22 papers), Brunel University (21 papers) and University of Sheffield (20 papers), and its H-Index is 38. Other countries/ territories such as Germany, Australia, Taiwan (territory) also make outstanding contributions in this field.

TABLE I. TOP TEN COUNTRIES/ TERRITORIES IN KM

No.	C/T	TP	IP	CP	TC	HI	TI	BC
1	China	1315	1204	111	275	30	235	0.04
2	USA	1098	804	294	22073	72	111	0.29
3	England	581	393	188	6089	38	157	0.13
4	Germany	407	299	108	1888	21	78	0.09
5	Australia	342	230	112	1762	20	124	0.19
6	Taiwan	322	280	42	5206	39	144	0.02
7	Spain	310	215	95	1833	22	111	0.12
8	Malaysia	287	246	41	803	13	180	0.05
9	Italy	212	154	58	910	17	75	0.10
10	Canada	205	121	84	2167	24	69	0.08

No., Rank By TP; C/T, Country/Territory; TP, Total papers; IP, independent papers; CP, Inter-nationally collaborated articles; TC, Total citations counts; HI, H Index; TI, Total Institutes numbers; BC, Betweenness centrality in the Cooperation Networks (CHINA refers to mainland China).

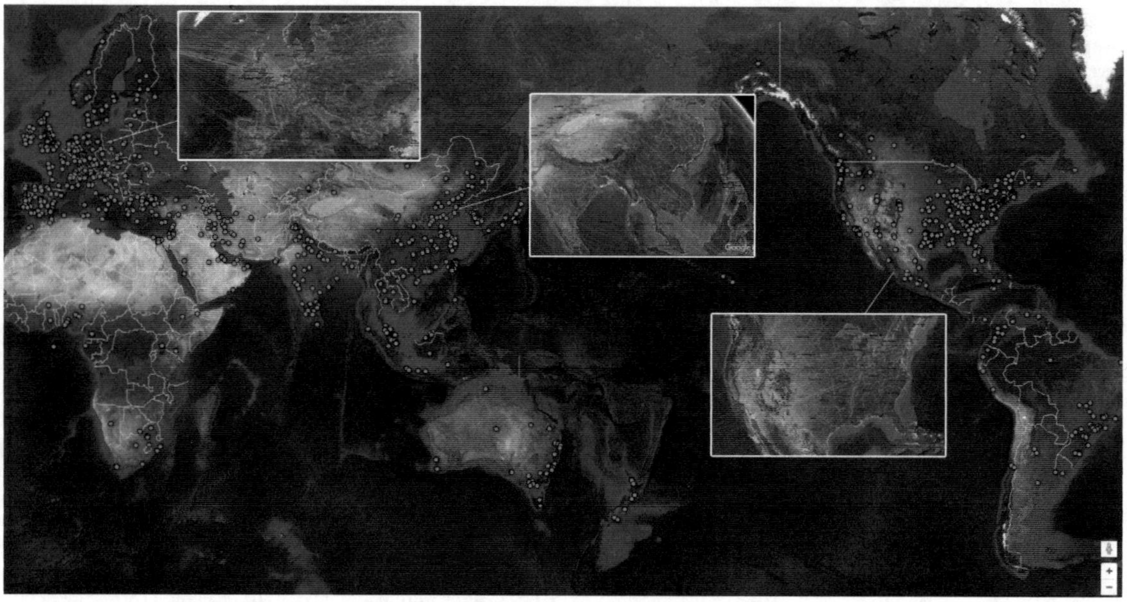

Figure 2. Geographic Distribution of Countries/Territories

C. *International Collaborations*

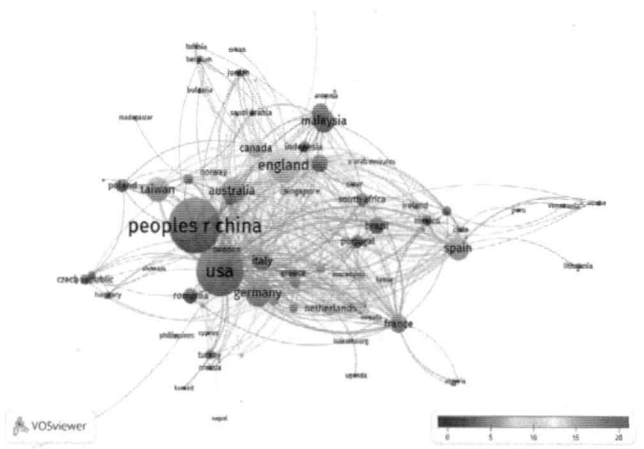

Figure 3. Countries/ Territories Collaboration Network

In order to vividly show the collaboration between countries/ territories, a network was generated by the VOSViewer (Figure 3). The size of the node represents the number of documents, while the color indicates the number of times the node is referenced. In total, there are 113 countries/territories in the field of Knowledge Management. As can be seen, the major contribution of the total output mainly came from three countries, namely, China, USA and England. In order to find the most influential countries in the field, we use the "Burst Detection Algorithm" in CiteSpace to detect the surge in research interest within KM research, and ten countries are found to have citation bursts: USA (119.4374), China (64.0792), Indonesia (29.3474), Germany (24.4142), England (22.4903), Romania (16.0049), India (14.8139), Colombia (14.6504), Poland (13.4845), Australia (12.5315), suggesting that they have abrupt increases of interest in the research of Knowledge Management. Betweenness Centrality metrics provide a computational method for finding pivotal points between different specialties or tipping points in an evolving network [14]. Thus, high betweenness centrality nodes such as USA, Australia, Spain, England indicates that these countries play an important role in this research filed.

D. *Characteristics of Institutes*

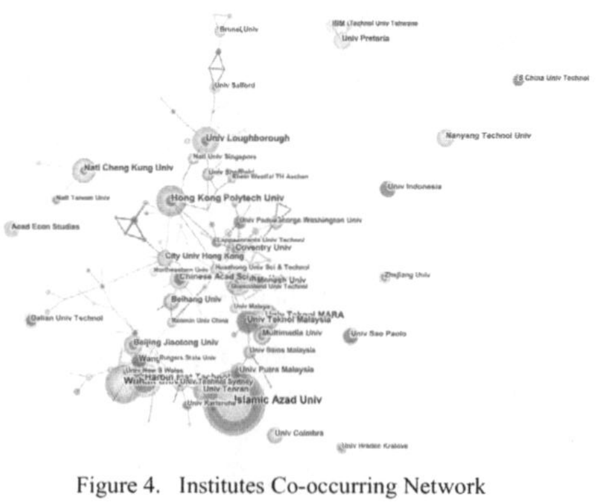

Figure 4. Institutes Co-occurring Network

Overall, a total of 4556 research institutes in the world were engaged in Knowledge Management during the period 1974 to 2017. Figure 4 shows the cooperation network of the institutes. In order to show the core institutions of this field, we filter out the institutions with a small number of publications and get an institute co-occurring network with 256 nodes and 342 links. Obviously, Islamic Azad University takes the first place with a frequency of 75 articles. In second place is Wuhan University of Technology with a frequency of 46 articles. We also notice that China's other institutes, such as Harbin Institute of Technology, The Hong Kong Polytechnic University, Wuhan University and Chinese Academy of Sciences were also on the top of the list. The nodes in the network with red colors are the institutes with strong citation bursts. Obviously, thirteen institutes are found to have citation bursts: Harbin Institute of Technology (11.3197), Wuhan University (10.8479), Universitas Indonesia (10.1611), Islamic Azad University (9.5093), Technological University of Malaysia (8.1657), Dalian University of Technology (7.8935), University of New South Wales (7.5086), University Of Karlsruhe (7.2476), Monash University (7.2389), Multimedia University (7.0823), University of Padua (6.4401), Beijing Jiaotong University (6.1222), Napier University (6.0201). We listed the details in the Table II.

TABLE II. TOP TEN INSTITUTES IN KM

No.	Name	Frequent	Citation Burst	Betweenness	Year
1	Islamic Azad Univ.	75	9.51	0.01	2010
2	Wuhan Univ. Technol.	46	0	0	2006
3	Harbin Inst. Technol.	41	11.32	0	2003
4	Hong Kong Polytech Univ.	39	4.82	0.05	2002
5	Univ Teknol.MARA	34	0	0	2008
6	Univ. Loughborough	34	5.63	0.03	2001
7	Wuhan Univ	32	10.85	0	2007
8	Natl Cheng Kung Univ.	30	4.32	0	2004
9	Univ. Teknol. Malaysia	28	8.17	0.02	2009
10	Coventry Univ.	26	4.68	0.03	2002

E. Journal Distribution and Co-occurring Network

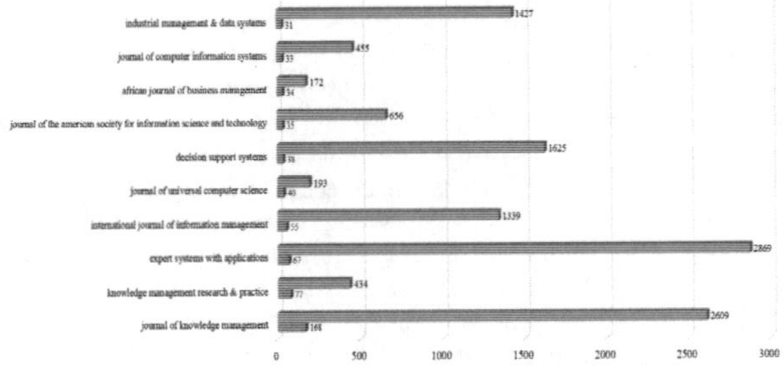

Figure 5. Journal Number Distributions and Citations

The distribution of the Journals in the field of Knowledge Management was displayed in Figure 5. Overall, Journal of Knowledge Management is the most productive one, with a total of 168 papers and 2609 citations, followed by Knowledge Management Research & Practice (77 papers, 434 citations), Expert Systems with Applications (67 papers, 2869 citations), International Journal of Information Management (55 papers, 1399 citations) and so on. We can also conclude that Expert Systems with Applications is the most influential journal, though it has only 67 papers. In order to show the relationship between institutes, a network of co-occurring was generated by VOSViewer and was displayed in Figure 6. Overall, there are 3255 journals in this field and the largest connected component consists of 1710 nodes accounting for a half part of the total nodes, indicating that relationship of journal in this area is getting closer and closer.

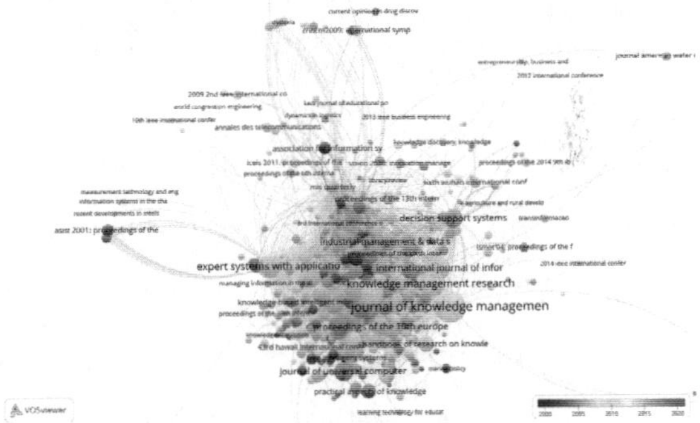

Figure 6. Journal Co-occurring Network

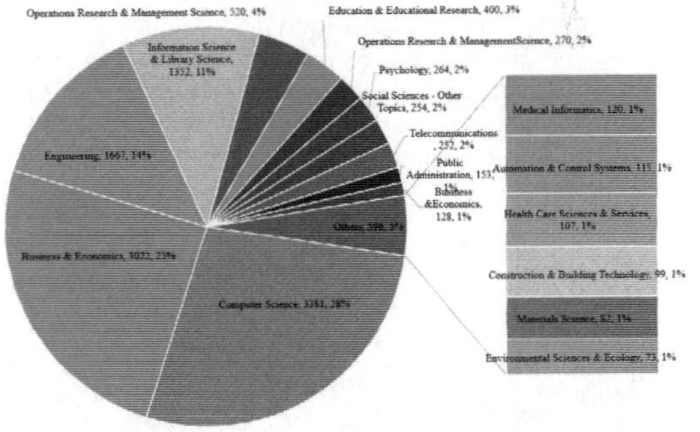

Figure 7. Distribution of Subject Categories

F. Characteristic of Subject Categories

The distribution of the subject categories identified by the Institute for Scientific Information (ISI) was analyzed and the result was displayed in Figure 7. The total of 8121 articles covered 50 ISI identified subject categories in the SCI databases. The annual articles of the top ten productive subject categories were analyzed. The top ten categories

Figure 8. Subject Categories Dual-map

were Computer Science (3381, 28%), Business & Economics (3022, 25%), Engineering (1667, 14%), Information Science & Library Science (1352, 11%), Operations Research & Management Science (520, 4%), Education & Educational Research (400, 3%), Operations Research & Management Science (270, 2%), Psychology (264, 2%), Social Sciences – Other Topics (254, 2%) and Telecommunications (252, 2%).

Figure 8 shows the dual-map overlay of publications in Knowledge Management. Citation links are connected using the z-score. On the left are the source journals, while on the right are the target journals. The two major clusters of source journals are journals in mathematics, systems and mathematical (red), psychology, education, and health journals (blue). We can see that the two major clusters in source journals are cited by the journals in system, computing, computer and the journals in economics, economic, politics which represents the flow of knowledge in this area.

Figure 9. References Co-cited Network

G. Research Hotspots and Emerging Trends of Knowledge

Figure 9 shows the document co-cited network. In order to show the core references in the network, G-Index [20] was used to prune the whole network. The pruned network consists of 803 cited references and 1073 co-citation links. In total, there are 20 co-citation clusters identified in the network. In terms of the average age of a cluster, the oldest ones are Clusters #6 and #17, with 1994 as the average year of publication. The most recent Cluster is #8 and #20, with 2010 as the average year of publication. The average year of publication of Cluster #0, the largest one, is 1998.

TABLE III. TOP FIVE LARGEST CLUSTERS

#	Size	Year	Labels
0	44	1998	administration, organizational capabilities
1	42	2009	information technology, empirical research
2	38	1999	transregional effects, knowledge web
3	35	2005	scientometric research, academics
4	35	2000	virtual groups, information schema

Table III lists the top 5 largest clusters in the network. They all have more than 30 members each. Cluster #0 is the first largest one with the labels administration and organizational capabilities. Cluster #1 is the second largest one with the labels information technology and empirical research. Cluster #2 is the third largest one with the labels transregional effects and knowledge Web. Cluster #3 is the largest one with the labels scientometric research and academics. Cluster #4 is the largest one with the labels virtual groups and information schema.

Table IV presents the top ten articles with high cited counts which can represent the research hotspots of Knowledge Management. Alavi et al. [21] provide several important research issues of knowledge management

TABLE IV. TOP TEN ARTICLES WITH HIGH CITATION COUNTS

No.	Title	Author	Year	Citations
1	Review: Knowledge management and knowledge management systems: Conceptual foundations and research issues	Alavi, M.	2001	2667
2	Knowledge management: An organizational capabilities perspective	Gold, A.H.	2001	1000
3	Successful knowledge management projects	Davenport, T.H.	1998	938
4	Modularity, flexibility, and knowledge management in product and organization design	Sanchez, R.	1996	833
5	A Model of Knowledge Management and the N-Form Corporation	Hedlung, G.	1994	628
6	Knowledge management enablers, processes, and organizational performance: An integrative view and empirical examination	Lee, H.	2003	594
7	Diagnosing cultural barriers to knowledge management	De Long, D.W.	2000	537
8	The state of the notion: Knowledge management in practice	Ruggles, R.	1998	409
9	Knowledge management strategies: Toward a taxonomy	Earl, M.	2001	402
10	From embedded knowledge to embodied knowledge: New product development as knowledge management	Madhavan, R.	1998	393

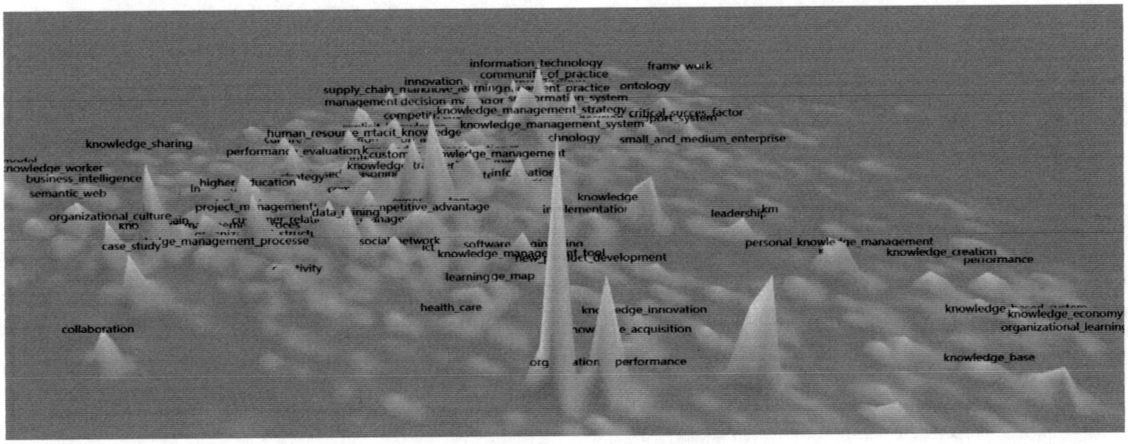

Figure 10. Keyword Co-occurring Network

in different fields with the aim to identifying the important areas for research. Andrew et al. [22] discussed the Knowledge Management from the organizational capabilities perspective through analysis of surveys collected from over 300 senior executives which provide a basis for understanding the competitive predisposition of a firm as it enters a program of knowledge management. Davenport et al. [23] examined the differences and similarities of thirty-one knowledge management projects. Sanchez et al. [24] researched the modularity, flexibility, and knowledge management in product and organization design. Hedlung [25] developed a model of knowledge management and the n-form corporation which was built on the interplay between articulated and tacit knowledge at four different. Lee et al. [26] discussed knowledge management enablers, processes, and organizational performance from an integrative view and empirical examination which can be used as a stepping stone for further empirical research and can help formulate robust strategies that involve tradeoffs between knowledge management enablers. Long et al. [27] diagnosed cultural barriers to knowledge management and concluded four perspectives. Ruggles [28] discussed the state of the notion about Knowledge Management in practice. Earl [29] drew on primary and secondary data to propose a taxonomy of strategies, or "schools" for knowledge management with the aim to guide executives on choice to Initiate KM Projects. Madhavan et al. [30] used the notions of tacit knowledge and distributed cognition as a basis to elaborate that the T-shaped skills, shared mental models, and new product development (NPD) routines of team members, as well as the A-shaped skills of the team leader, are key design variables when creating NPD teams.

In order to find the research landscape about Knowledge Management in detail, a keyword clustering and visualization method based on word2vec [16] was used, and Figure 10 shows the result of such method. Each peak in the figure represents a keyword or topic in the field. The distance between peaks is determined by the semantic similarity between them, and the height of the peaks indicates the importance of the keywords which can be calculated by indicators such as frequency, betweenness centrality and so on. Here, the frequency was chosen as the basic indicator. From the figure, we can clearly conclude that keywords such as performance, system, innovation, firm, information technology, knowledge management system, strategy, organization, ontology are the research hotspots in this fields. Figure 11 shows the temporal graph of burst keywords detected by CiteSpace, which can be seen as the research front of knowledge management research. According to the order of this emergence of the research front, they are Expert Systems (1975), Organizatorial Memory (1999), Artificial Intelligence（2000）, Decision Support (2001) and the latest research fronts are Social Media, Big Data and Total Quality Management.

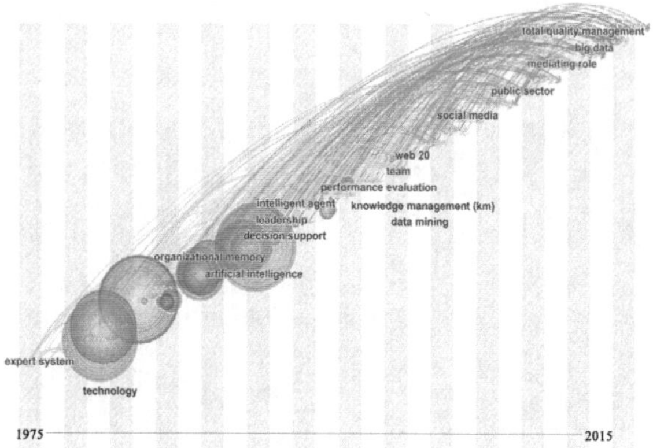

Figure 11. Temporal Graph of Research Fronts in KM

IV. CONCLUSION

This paper presents a comprehensive assessment of publication data in the Knowledge Management domain. A scientometric method was used to quantitatively assess current landscape, research hotspots and trends on Knowledge Management, using the related literature in the Science Citation Index (SCI) database from 1974 to 2017. References about Knowledge Management were concentrated on the analysis of scientific outputs, geographic distribution, institutions, journals and subject categories. Moreover, innovative methods such as co-citation analysis, keyword semantic clustering and burst detection were applied, which can vividly reveal the landscape and trends from various perspectives.

REFERENCES

[1] J. Girard and J. A. Girard, "Defining knowledge management: Toward an applied compendium," Online Journal of Applied Knowledge Management,vol.3,no.1, 2015,p.1.

[2] I. Nonaka and G. V. Krogh, "Perspectivetacit knowledge and knowledge conversion: Controversy and advancement in organizational knowledge creation theory," Organization Science, vol. 20, no. 3, 2009, pp. 635–652.

[3] I. Nonaka, "The knowledge-creating company." Harvard Business Review,vol. 69, no. 6, 1991, pp. 96–104.

[4] O. B. Onyancha and D. N. Ocholla, "Conceptualising'knowledge management'in the context of library and information science using the core/periphery model," South African Journal of Information Management,vol. 11, no. 4, 2009, pp. 1–15.

[5] L. A. Petrides and T. R. Nodine, "Knowledge management in education: Defining the landscape," ERIC, 2003,p.4.

[6] I. Rus and M. Lindvall, "Knowledge management in software engineering," IEEE software, vol. 19, no. 3, 2002, p. 26.

[7] M. Corso, A. Martini, E. Paolucci, and L. Pellegrini, "Knowledge management in product innovation: an interpretative review," International Journal of Management Reviews, vol. 3, no. 4, 2001, pp. 341–352.

[8] S.-H. Liao, "Knowledge management technologies and applicationsliterature review from 1995 to 2002," Expert systems with applications, vol. 25, no. 2, 2003, pp. 155–164.

[9] M.-Y. Chen and A.-P. Chen, "Knowledge management performance evaluation: a decade review from 1995 to 2004," Journal of Information Science, vol. 32, no. 1, 2006, pp. 17–38.

[10] F. O. Bjørnson and T. Dingsøyr, "Knowledge management in software engineering: A systematic review of studied concepts, findings and research methods used," Information and Software Technology, vol. 50,no. 11, 2008, pp. 1055–1068.

[11] B. Gallupe, "Knowledge management systems: surveying the landscape,"International Journal of Management Reviews, vol. 3, no. 1,2001, pp. 61–77.

[12] M. Marra, W. Ho, and J. S. Edwards, "Supply chain knowledge management: A literature review," Expert systems with applications,vol. 39, no. 5, 2012, pp. 6103–6110.

[13] S. Durst and I. Runar Edvardsson, "Knowledge management in smes:a literature review," Journal of Knowledge Management, vol. 16, no. 6,2012, pp. 879–903.

[14] C. Chen, "Citespace ii: Detecting and visualizing emerging trends and transient patterns in scientific literature," Journal of the Association for Information Science and Technology, vol. 57, no. 3, 2006, pp. 359–377.

[15] N. J. Van Eck and L. Waltman, "Vosviewer: A computer program for bibliometric mapping," Social Science Electronic Publishing, vol. 84,no. 2, 2009, pp. 523–538.

[16] T. Mikolov, I. Sutskever, K. Chen, G. S. Corrado, and J. Dean,"Distributed representations of words and phrases and their compositionality,"in Advances in neural information processing systems, 2013,pp. 3111–3119.

[17] J. Kleinberg, "Bursty and hierarchical structure in streams," Data Mining and Knowledge Discovery, vol. 7, no. 4, 2003, pp. 373–397.

[18] N. L. Henry, "Knowledge management: a new concern for public administration," Public Administration Review, 1974, pp. 189–196.

[19] D. Rogosa, D. Brandt, and M. Zimowski, "A growth curve approach to the measurement of change." Psychological bulletin, vol. 92, no. 3,1982, p. 726.

[20] L. Egghe, "Theory and practice of the g-index," Scientometrics, vol. 69,no. 1, 2006, pp. 131–152.

[21] M. Alavi and D. E. Leidner, "Knowledge management and knowledge management systems: Conceptual foundations and research issues,"MIS quarterly, 2001, pp. 107–136.

[22] A. H. Gold and A. H. S. Arvind Malhotra, "Knowledge management:An organizational capabilities perspective," Journal of management information systems, vol. 18, no. 1, 2001, pp. 185–214.

[23] T. H. Davenport, D. W. De Long, and M. C. Beers, "Successful knowledge management projects," Sloan management review, vol. 39,no. 2, 1998, p. 43.

[24] R. Sanchez and J. T. Mahoney, "Modularity, flexibility, and knowledge management in product and organization design,"

Strategic management journal, vol. 17, no. S2, 1996, pp. 63–76.

[25] G. Hedlund, "A model of knowledge management and the n-form corporation," Strategic management journal, vol. 15, no. S2, 1994, pp.73–90.

[26] H. Lee and B. Choi, "Knowledge management enablers, processes, and organizational performance: An integrative view and empirical examination," Journal of management information systems, vol. 20, no. 1, 2003, pp. 179–228.

[27] W. David and L. Fahey, "Diagnosing cultural barriers to knowledge management," The Academy of management executive, vol. 14, no. 4, 2000, pp. 113–127.

[28] R. Ruggles, "The state of the notion: knowledge management in practice," California management review, vol. 40, no. 3, 1998, pp. 80–89.

[29] M. Earl, "Knowledge management strategies: Toward a taxonomy,"Journal of management information systems, vol. 18, no. 1, 2001, pp.215–233.

[30] Madhavan, Ravindranath, and R. Grover. "From Embedded Knowledge to Embodied Knowledge: New Product Development as Knowledge Management." Journal of Marketing vol. 62, no. 4, 1998, pp.1-12.

Towards an Integrated Knowledge Management System for Small and Medium-sized Enterprises in the Field of Assembly System Engineering

Rainer Müller, Matthias Vette-Steinkamp, Leenhard Hörauf, Christoph Speicher, Johannes Obele
Group of Assembly Systems and Automation Technology
Centre for Mechatronics and Automation gGmbH (ZeMA)
Saarbrücken, Germany
email: {rainer.mueller, matthias.vette, leenhard.hoerauf, christoph.speicher, j.obele}@zema.de

***Abstract*—The development of assembly systems requires deep knowledge about assembly processes and process technologies as well as profound knowledge about the product to be assembled. A method supporting communication and knowledge management during assembly system development and manufacturing will be described in this paper. The method is designed to meet the needs of small and medium-sized enterprises (SME) and consists of several modules. One of the modules visualizes the product and the assembly line in order to gain a common understanding of the system. By adding metadata to files, the assembly line manufacturer's staff can quickly access data from completed projects using semantic searches. The communication module ensures an information exchange without changes between different media formats amongst all parties during assembly line development. All modules will be put together in a web-based software application to enable multiuser access and collaborative work. The interaction of the modules allows transparent communication, as well as the linking of data and elements of knowledge throughout the entire assembly system development process.**

Keywords-assembly system; collaborative engineering; knowledge management; information sharing.

I. INTRODUCTION

The demand of consumers for individual and innovative products has been continuously increasing. New, more complex products and new model generations are demanded by market in ever-shorter intervals [1]. This leads to an increased number of variants and higher complexity along the entire value chain and its components, like special machinery and assembly systems (see Figure 1), as a subcategory of special machinery.

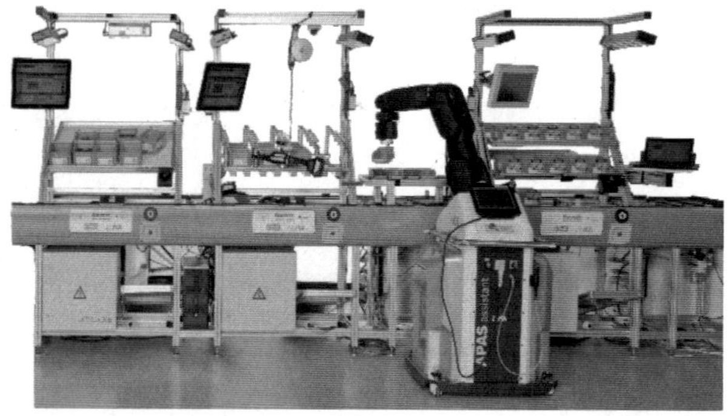

Figure 1. Assembly system with manual and human robot collaboration workstations.

The development of special machinery requires high planning efforts, as each machine is designed individually for the product and the task to be performed. Therefore, assembly systems are often built only once. These small lot sizes are complicating a standardization of design and construction [2].

Assembly system development poses a challenge to knowledge management. Persons involved in the process of assembly system development require a deep knowledge on the product to be produced as well as on the assembly system and its production processes and production resources. Given restrictions like structural conditions, the legal framework and others have also to be taken into account. Changing one element in the system is potentially affecting other system elements. For that reason, assembly system design is a recursive process, integrating the product, the production processes, the production resources and given restrictions (see Figure 2).

Almost each assembly system is a new project for the manufacturer. Correspondingly, project folders for each project are created on the servers. If many assembly systems already have been built in a company, then the number of folders and data is difficult to survey for an individual person. Particularly new employees spend a lot of time searching for design data of already created concepts. If a previously created concept or a drawn part could be used in another project, the employee has to know in which project folder the required file is stored or he/she searches extensively for it. New employees do not have detailed knowledge about past projects, the challenges, built in parts, and so on. Therefore, these employees do not have the opportunity to search for specific concepts. Especially since file names are not always meaningful. However, due to their lack of experience, new employees need more and structured information about completed projects, to prevent a re-development of already existing concepts.

Although the number of features of an assembly system increased over the last years, customers of special machinery are demanding ever shorter delivery times [3] because the

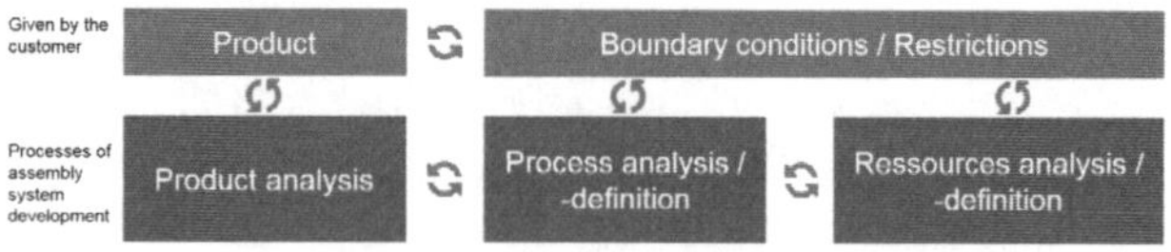

Figure 2. Process elements of assembly system design.

time-to-market for products with short product life cycles is decisive for the market success of the product. In order to keep the time-to-market as short as possible, special machinery is ordered at an early stage of product development. With completion of the product development, the machine shall be available for production [4].

On the one hand, simultaneous development of the product and the special machinery offers potential for improving quality, reducing costs and reducing the time to market [5][6]; on the other hand, there are also disadvantages associated with simultaneous development. In the course of product development, there is a large number of changes in product design. Some of these design changes necessitate a design change of the special machinery. Another disadvantage is the increased coordination effort for the communication of product design changes and the resulting impact on the system, on costs and on the schedule [4].

To guarantee a uniform level of knowledge amongst all team members, all relevant changes to the product have be communicated quickly and comprehensibly. This requires a frequent exchange of data and knowledge between the project partners. As schematically shown in Figure 3, there is a multitude of information flows amongst the project partners. The provision of the latest product data from the customer to the system manufacturer is often not immediately carried out after a change was made.

After receiving information about product changes, the product manager coordinates the incoming requests and assigns tasks to persons concerned. This procedure leads to long information transfer times and binds personnel capacity.

For a successful simultaneous product and assembly system development process, a common understanding of the product as well as of the assembly system, concerted actions and sharing of information between the right people at the right time is crucial [7]. In direct communication at meetings or telephone conferences, communication is hampered by a lack of common understanding of the

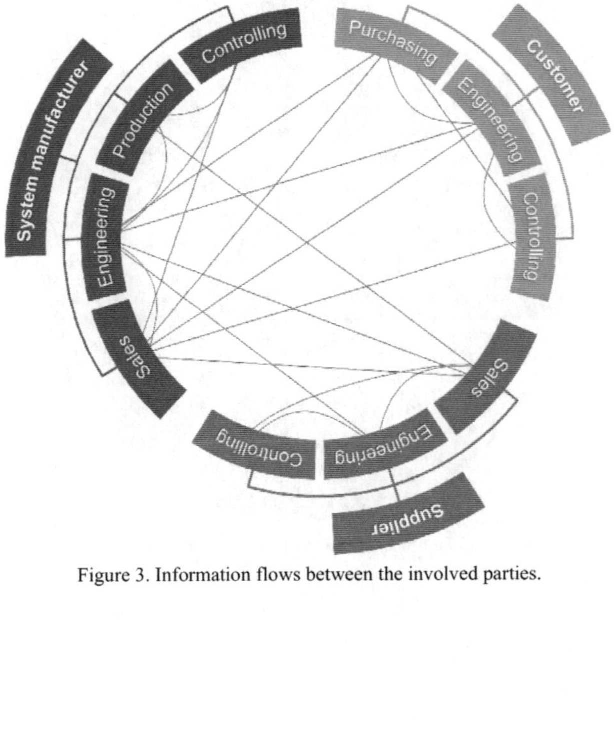

Figure 3. Information flows between the involved parties.

product, the processes and resources and their interdependencies. Especially people without profound technical knowledge have difficulties understanding the structure and relationships of the interconnected system elements. Even for experts, communication is susceptible to errors since terms for the same component differ from company to company.

Inefficient communication between the project partners and suboptimal knowledge management within the company leads to unnecessary work. For companies, efficient communication and processing of information is vital, as the available personnel capacity is scarce and expensive due to a shortage of skilled workers [8][9]. Another reason for the need of an efficient knowledge management is the competition between the companies. Thus, efficient order processing and a shorter delivery time compared to the competitors can generate a competitive advantage. Because of this, a concept that allows simple, transparent and media-break-free communication amongst all parties as well as an efficient knowledge management for small and medium-sized companies is presented.

The key contributions of this work are the following: (i) schematic visualization of the assembly system to support better understanding; (ii) semantic description of assembly system elements and associated files beneficial to ease the reuse of available knowledge; (iii) improved collaboration through communication and annotation tools.

The paper is structured as follows: In Section II the state of the art of the key subjects is shown. Section III introduces the methodology and its elements. Section IV concludes the paper and gives a prospect on future works.

II. State of the Art

Design and construction of assembly systems involve a holistic consideration of several research areas. The analysis of the literature focuses on the three main topics: assembly system design, simultaneous/collaborative engineering and knowledge management. Due to the wide scope of each subject area, the state of the art is presented separately for each subject area.

A. Assembly System Design

There are different models, procedures and methodologies of the assembly system design process. The product is the starting point for the planning method proposed by Müller [10]. A process chain is derived from structure of the product, the geometric characteristics of its parts and their type of connection. With knowledge about the product and the necessary processes for product assembly, suitable production resources will be determined. The dependencies between product, process and production resources are also taken into account in the process of assembly system design [10]. This concept is taken up by Eilers [11] and extended by a methodology for designing multi-variant production lines. Kluge [12] focuses on the capabilities of production resources, the consideration of different quantity scenarios and their influence on the assembly system. Konold and Reger [13] divide the process of assembly system design into the five phases: problem definition, rough design, detailed design, realization and production start-up. A review of the outcomes at the end of each phase should protect against misplanning and malinvestments. In literature, further methods for assembly system design can be found, differing in procedure and focus [14]-[17]. The examined methods focusing on assembly system design, the topics cooperation and knowledge management are only considered marginally.

B. Simultaneous, concurrent and collaborative Engineering

Product development as well as assembly system development takes place in teams with people from different disciplines. This collaboration has been explored for several decades, over time this research has been dubbed differently. Therefore, the terms simultaneous engineering and concurrent engineering are synonyms. The term collaborative engineering is intended to clarify the integration of different subject areas and engineering disciplines [18]. A clear demarcation of the terms is not possible because each author has another focus. Thus, there are many overlaps, since the basic elements of concurrent engineering, parallel workflows, development teams, early integration of all parties [19], for collaborative engineering also applies [20][21]. In the following, for simplification and due to its broader scope, only the term collaborative engineering is used.

In literature, a multitude of methods and concepts for collaborative engineering is presented [5][21]-[24]. Kamrani [21] introduces seven principles for a collaborative development of a product and names the faculties of a collaborative team. He also emphasizes the importance of knowledge management and communication in a collaborative engineering team. The presented communication tool allows the exchange of files, direct communication between the involved parties is not intended. Mas et al. [25][26] addresses the importance of communication, he notes that even in big companies, over the wall communication is practiced. In order to solve this problem, he proposes to expand the digital mockup of a product by production equipment so that a common visualization of the product and production equipment is possible. Several tools are available on the market, supporting collaborative engineering and teamwork [27]. Wognum [18] notes that despite the variety of tools and methods that promise to support collaborative engineering, these systems are not sufficiently developed to cover all the needs. In particular, classical product lifecycle management systems (PLM) do not meet the requirements of collaborative engineering [25].

C. Knowledge Management

The term knowledge management summarizes the ability to identify, store and retrieve knowledge. For a successful knowledge management system in companies there has to be understood which information and knowledge is important for the company, which goals are pursued and which challenges have to be solved [28]. Amongst others, the most important challenges for SME is the rapid integration of new employees, the use of existing knowledge, the transfer of knowledge across projects, as well as a consistent documentation over the whole product lifecycle [29]. Anderl [30] identifies documents that are relevant to each phase of the product lifecycle and highlights the need for cross-disciplinary knowledge sharing. Another important success factor for companies is to empower the employees to access the existing knowledge of the company [31]. Different knowledge management systems are established in companies. Products like Wikis, document management tools, blogs, groupware systems, forums, etc. are used for knowledge management [32]-[34]. Depending on the used system, the access to certain information is difficult because of missing possibilities to cross-link information stored in different systems [3]. In particular, systems, tools and methodologies for knowledge management, fitting to the needs of SME are poorly understood [35].

III. METHOD

The deep process analysis showed the major issues during assembly system development. Based on these results, a method was developed, which meets the special requirements for a simultaneous development process of a product and an assembly system. The focus of the developed method is to support the design of assembly systems, to improve information exchange and communication as well as knowledge management. The functions and modules resulting from the defined focus are shown in Figure 4.

The developed method has to be transferred in a software application that supports all parties in the structured development of assembly systems. The software application has a modular structure, so the functional scope can be expanded with new modules. Due to the special demands of assembly system manufactures, the software will be customized to their needs.

In-house developments and Open Source software modules offer comprehensive possibilities for adapting

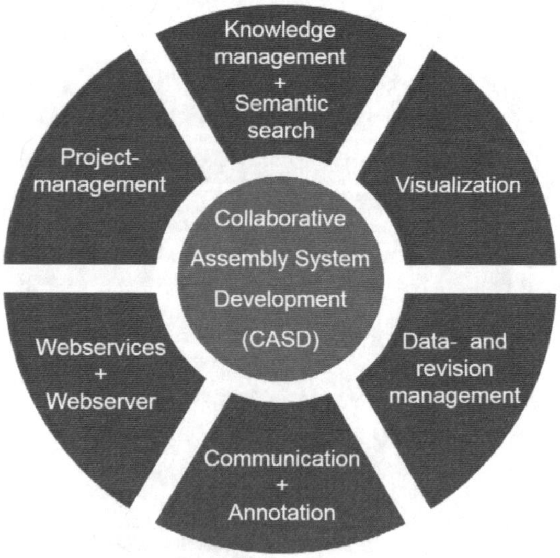

Figure 4. Modules and functions of the methodology for assisted assembly system development.

functions to the given requirements. The use of software without license costs helps to make the software attractive for SME also from a financial point of view. In the following the most important functions and modules of the Collaborative Assembly System Development (CASD) tool are described.

A. *Knowledge Management and Semantic Search*

The knowledge management module offers different tools. The most basic tool is the possibility to search file contents and to have the search results displayed. However, this method cannot be applied to files with content that is not textually searchable (e.g., images, CAD data, sketches, etc.). Therefore, metadata can be attached to describe the content. This metadata can be interpreted and searched by a computer as well as a human. Further information about the file can be written to this metadata. For example, there could be a link to the operating instructions or to the supplier's homepage in case of purchased parts.

A tag is a special variant of metadata, which describes the file content with keywords [36]. Semantic searches can be performed since metadata is attached to the files. The result of a semantic search shows not only results, containing the search term but also a context sensitive results are displayed [37]. For example, one wants to grab round rods with a diameter of 40 mm, one can search for files which are marked with the tags gripper jaw, round, rod, 40 mm. This allows easy access to files and knowledge that has been developed in previous projects.

Furthermore, existing knowledge can be enhanced by deploying queries analyzing the data, metadata, semantics and links. With this method, also new employees are able to get access to knowledge, which is already available on the servers. The description of the file contents with metadata enables the computer to find files with similar content. If the user searches for a concept or a drawing in order to adopt it to the current project, this function can be used to show files with similar metadata to the user. This helps to accelerate the process of familiarization as well as to increase the reuse rate of already available concepts and design data.

B. *Visualization*

In order to create a common understanding of the product, the processes, the resources and their interdependencies and dependencies, the assembly system is represented schematically by means of symbols (see Figure 5). Each part and subassembly of the product is represented by a symbol. In the first step, symbols of the product are positioned and connected with edges in accordance to the assembly sequence. In the next step, the assembly processes are defined and drawn into the schema. Processes are connected to the visualization of the assembly sequence, in order to show the match between the parts and the respective assembly processes. Finally, the production resources are defined, drawn in the visualization and connected with the processes. At the end, the whole system is visualized. The graph is showing all connections between the parts of the product, the assembly processes and the

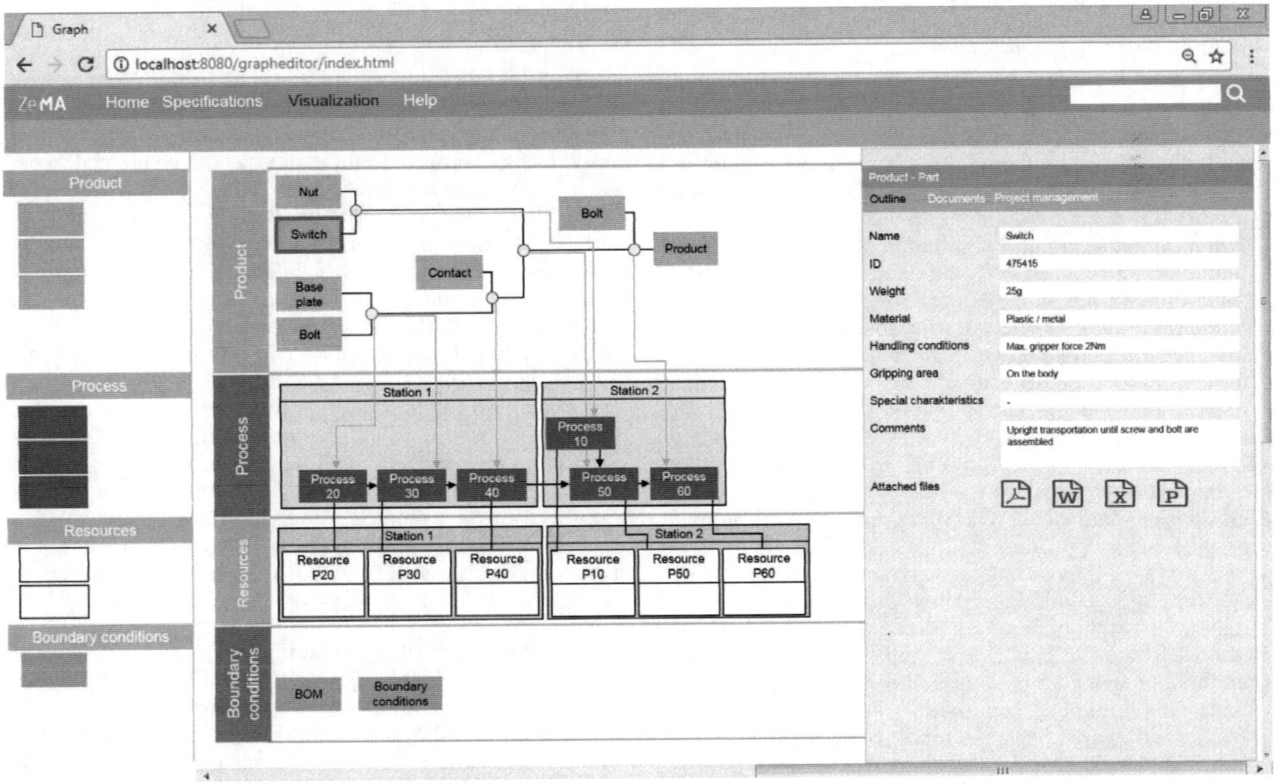

Figure 5. User interface of the visualization tool.

production resources. This graph can be used for further analysis and automatic optimization of the system.

Another result of the visualization is the uniform understanding of the product, processes and resources as well as the constraints for all parties involved. This contributes to an improvement in communication because a scheme of the assembly system is present to all parties and the named symbols allowing a precise communication. Influences on the assembly system design and the parts of the system, resulting from product changes, can be shown quickly and vividly to the customer.

Depending on the real world element, which is represented by a symbol, different input forms are available. For example, the parameters for a bolted connection can be entered in the input form that belongs to the process symbol bolting process. Furthermore, documents (e.g., operating instructions, CAD data, CE declarations of built-in products, etc.), annotations, process characteristics, etc. can be stored and assigned to the symbol using the input forms. The metadata collected in this way can also be used for semantic search.

By collecting all the information belonging to the object in one place, the user has the opportunity to get all important information about a specific object quickly and without any search effort. In addition, data entered in the input forms as well as the graph with its connections between the symbols is a further input to the knowledge management system. The knowledge about the connections of the symbols combined with the knowledge from the input forms can be used to check the validity of the system automatically.

C. Communication and Annotation

Assembly system development requires numerous documents. Among these documents, the specification sheet takes on a prominent role, since the system requirements and specifications are described from the customer's point of view with this individual document. The specification sheet is the basis for the creation of an assembly system, the assembly system manufacturer has to work on it intense. Different departments are working on the specification sheet simultaneously. Thus, at the assembly system manufacturer's site several copies of the specifications are edited. This means that ideas, solution concepts and knowledge are not transferred to other departments.

The annotation module provides the framework for working together on one single specification. Comments and information can be added to the digital version of the specification and are therefore visible to all authorized users. Annotations are individual-related, depending on the group a person belongs to, reading and writing of annotations is possible or not. Internal annotations are for example only visible for employees of the system manufacturer.

These annotations are connected to the correlating symbols in the visualization of the assembly system. Therefore, a quick switch between the specification and the visualization is possible. This helps during process definition as well as in the case of changes in the specifications.

The method allows the integration of several persons with different tasks in the project as well as non-project experts to solve problems even if they work with a time shift. In addition, forums offer the opportunity for transparent and open communication. Persons in charge kept up to date about the current development and discussions by a RSS feed. The communication module enables an easier more transparent and quick exchange of data and information, leading to a better collaboration of the parties and better project results.

D. Data Management and Revision Management

During assembly system development, many files are created and changed over time. This is especially common with CAD design data. In order to work on the right files, for project participants it is essential to recognize the latest version of a file. In particular, this is important when multiple people are working on one file. The file management is supported by a document management system, which is adapted for the specific requirements of the collaborative assembly system development process. This tool offers the opportunity for revision management and the attachment of metadata to the files. Documents can be identified via a unique identification number. This helps to connect the documents to a symbol in the visualization and supports therefore a speedier access on the document. Data access management is integrated in the document management system. Every user is assigned to one or more user groups. For each folder with all its documents or if necessary for each document the rights (read, write, delete) are defined for each user group. This avoids unauthorized access to sensitive information like cost calculations.

E. Project Management

The visualization offers also a feature for project management tasks. Data that is recorded with the input forms can also be used for project management. For instance start and end dates for the execution of tasks can be defined. After the user confirms the start or completion of a task, the color of the task changes. An automatically generated gant chart can be used to create an overview of the tasks to be performed and used for scheduling. Work orders with a detailed description of the task can be assigned to a person and followed up. The project manager gets an outline of pending, started and completed work orders. With this information he/she can track the time course of the project. The knowledge of how the system elements are connected with each other, enables the project manager to identify persons to be informed about a specific product change. If the company has already installed a project management software, all the recorded information can be exported to JSON file. This file can converted into the data format of the available project management software and imported then.

F. Web Services and Web Server

The backbone of the platform is a web server that manages the users' requests and assembles the individual software modules into one application. A web based software design allows the use of Open Source web tools, which are made for social media and web communication. In order to keep the organizational efforts, for the management of the personalized access to the system, little there will be a user management with predefined user groups. The web-based concept allows to run the system on premise as well as in a cloud, depending on the strategy and the IT infrastructure of the company.

IV. CONCLUSION

In this article, the need for a holistic treatment of knowledge management and communication during product and assembly system development is shown. From the findings of the deep analysis of processes, communication and knowledge management during assembly system development, the requirements and modules for the method could be derived. Through the visualization of the assembly system by a schematic representation a common understanding of the system is created. The graph which is created in the visualization tool shows the connections of product parts, processes and production resources and allows a direct identification of affected persons, processes and resources in case of product changes.

Easy access to already existing data can be achieved with the knowledge management module and its ability to perform semantic searches. Thereby, the training period for new employees can be reduced. By linking information and files using metadata, contents of files like CAD-drawings or images are getting accessible to the user and the computer.

Transparent communication helps to keep every team member on the same level of knowledge and thus better teamwork is supported. The project manager is able to follow up the progress of the project by using the project management module.

Modules as the visualization tool, the project management tool and the web server have already been implemented. As the project progresses, the graph analyzing software as well as the document management software will be connected to the visualization tool by a bidirectional interface. Since graph analysis as well as document management software is available on the market, we will revert to an already implemented and tested product. Finally, the method and the software will be tested with different user groups.

Overall, a method for communication and knowledge management, which meets the needs of assembly system manufacturers and their clients, was developed and briefly presented.

ACKNOWLEDGMENT

This paper was written in the framework of the research project NeWiP, which is funded by the Federal Ministry of Education and Research (BMBF) and supervised by the lead partner PTKA-Karlsruhe Institute of Technology under the funding code 02P14B203.

REFERENCES

[1] R. Müller, J. Eilers, L. Hermanns, and R. Gerdes, „Model-supported buildability check during assembly planing, increasing planing accurancy for the integration of variants," in „wt Werkstattstechnik online," vol. 9, pp. 253-260, May 2017.

[2] S. Poeschl, F. Wirth, and T. Bauernhansl, „Situation-based Methodology for Planning the Commissioning of Special Machinery using Bayesian Networks," in "Factories of the Future in the digital environment - Proceedings of the 49th CIRP Conference on Manufacturing Systems," vol. 57, pp. 247-252, ISSN: 2212-8271, 2016.

[3] U. Sendler, „Boundless industry 4.0," Springer Vieweg, Berlin Heidelberg, vol. 1, pp. 213, ISBN: 9783662482780, 2016.

[4] R. Müller et al., „Communication during assembly system development, platform to support the communication between costumer and assembly system manufacturer," in „wt Werkstattstechnik online," vol. 9, pp. 647-651, Okt. 2017.

[5] W. Eversheim, W. Bochtler, and L. Laufenberg, „Simultaneous Engineering – Industry experience for the industry," Springer, Berlin, vol. 1, pp. 15, ISBN: 9783642789182, 1995.

[6] M. Weck, W. Eversheim, and W. König, „ Production Engineering: The Competitve Edge," Butterworth Heinemann, vol. 1, pp. 65, ISBN: 9781483102122, 1991.

[7] D. Dixius, „Simultaneous project organization: A guideline for project work in simultaneous engineering," Springer, Berlin Heidelberg, vol. 1, pp. 177, ISBN: 9783642589768, 1998.

[8] PricewaterhouseCoopers GmbH, „Utilization on the limit: skilled workers in mechanical engineering are becoming scarce," Available rom: https://www.pwc.de/de/pressemitteilungen/2017/auslastung-am-limit-fachkraefte-im-maschinenbau-werden-knapp.html, Retrieved: February, 2018.

[9] K. Suder et al., „Competitive factor professionals, Strategies for Germany's companies," McKinsey Deutschland, pp. 39, 2011.

[10] J. Feldhusen et al., „Pahl/Beitz Design theory methods and application of successful product development," Springer Vieweg, vol. 8, pp. 702-725, ISBN: 9783642295690, 2013.

[11] J. Eilers, „Methodology for planning scalable and reconfigurable assembly systems," Apprimus, ISBN: 9783863592950, 2014.

[12] S. Kluge, " Methodology for the ability-based planning of modular assembly systems," Jost-Jetter, ISBN: 9783939890812, 2011.

[13] P. Konold and H. Reger, „Practice of assembly technology Product design, planning, system design," Springer-Vieweg, pp. 32-75, ISBN: 9783663016090, 2003.

[14] B. Lotter and H. Wiendahl, „Assembly in industrial production: A manual for the practice," Springer-Vieweg, ISBN: 9783642290619, 2012.

[15] H. Bullinger, D. Ammer, K. Dungs, U. Seidel, and B. Weller, „Systematic assembly planning," Carl Hanser, ISBN: 3446146067, 1986.

[16] B. Rekiek and A. Delchambre, „Assembly Line Design: The Balancing of Mixed-Model Hybrid Assembly Lines with Genetic Algorithms," Springer, ISBN: 9781846281143, 2006.

[17] N. Thomopoulos, "Assembly Line Planning and Control," Springer, ISBN 9783319013992, 2014.

[18] N. Wognum and J. Trienekens, "The System of Concurrent Engineering," in "Concurrent Engineering in the 21st Century Foundations, Developments and Challenges," Springer, vol. 1, pp. 21-50, ISBN: 9783319137766, 2015.

[19] X. Koufteros, M. Vonderembse, and W. Doll, „Concurrent engineering and its consequences," in "Journal of Operations Management," vol. 19, pp. 97–115, ISSN: 0272-6963, 2001.

[20] S. Willaerta, R. de Graafb, and S. Minderhoudc, „Collaborative engineering: A case study of Concurrent Engineering in a wider context," in "Journal of Engineering

and Technology Management," Elsevier, vol. 15, pp. 87-109, ISSN: 0923-4748, 1998.

[21] K. Kamrani, "Collaborative Design Approach in Product Design and Development," in "Collaborative Engineering Theory and Practice," Springer, vol. 1, pp. 1-18, ISBN: 9780387473215, 2008.

[22] J. Leimeister, "Collaboration Engineering: Systematically develop and execute IT-supported collaboration processes," Springer Gabler, vol. 1, ISBN: 9783642208911, 2014.

[23] J. Krottmaier, " Simultaneous Engineering Guide: Short Development times Low Costs High Quality," Springer, vol. 1, ISBN: 9783642793813, 1995.

[24] H. Bullinger and J. Warschat, „Concurrent Simultaneous Engineering Systems: The Way to Successful Product Development," Springer Science & Business Media, vol. 1, ISBN: 9781447114772, 1995.

[25] F. Mas, J. Menéndez et al., "Design Within Complex Environments: Collaborative Engineering in the Aerospace Industry," in "Information System Development, Improving Enterprise Communication," Springer, vol. 1, pp. 197 - 205, ISBN: 9783319072159, 2014.

[26] F. Mas, J. Menéndez, and M. Oliva, J. Rios, "Collaborative Engineering: an Airbus case study," at "Procedia Engineering, The Manufacturing Engineering Society International Conference, MESIC 2013" vol. 63, pp. 336 – 345, ISSN: 1877-7058, 2013.

[27] R. Damgrave and D. Lutters, "Multi-user Collaborative Design Tools for Use in Product Development," in "Global Product Development Proceedings of the 20th CIRP Design Conference," Springer vol. 20, pp.227-236, ISBN: 9783642159732, 2011.

[28] D. Olson, "Descriptive Data Mining," Springer, vol.1, pp.1-7, ISBN: 9789811033407, 2017.

[29] R. Orth, S. Voigt, and I. Kohl, " Practice Guide Knowledge Management, Implement Process-Based Knowledge Management Using the ProWis Approach," Fraunhofer, vol. 1, pp. 7, ISBN: 9783839603062, 2011.

[30] R. Anderl and R. Deger, „The role of consistent documentation of mechatronic products as a success factor for quality and customer satisfaction," research study, Technische Universität Darmstadt, pp. 27, 2008.

[31] H. Kohl, K. Mertins, and H. Seidel „Knowledge Management in SMEs: Basics - Solutions - Practical Examples," Springer, vol. 1, pp. 9-18, ISBN: 9783662492208, 2016.

[32] F. Kramer et al., " Computer-Supported Knowledge Management in SME -A Combined Qualitative Analysis-," in "Proceedings of the 50th Hawaii International Conference on System Sciences," pp. 4567-4576, ISBN: 9780998133102, 2017.

[33] P. Hentsch, " Development of assembly systems for varied precision engineering products," pp. 119-122, 2014.

[34] R. Cerchione and E. Esposito, "Using knowledge management systems: A taxonomy of SME strategies," in "International Journal of Information Management," vol. 37, pp. 1551-1562, 2017.

[35] I. Ul Haq et al., "Product to process lifecycle management in assembly automation systems," in "Proceedings of the 7th CIRP International Conference on Digital Enterprise Technology," pp. 1-11, 2011.

[36] H. Tipton, M. Krause, "Information Security Management Handbook," Auerbach Publications, vol. 5, pp. 1094, ISBN: 9780203325438, 2003.

[37] G. Bruno, "Product Knowledge Management in Small Manufacturing Enterprises," in "Knowledge Management Initiatives and Strategies in Small and Medium Enterprises," IGI Global, vol. 1, pp. 157-180, ISBN: 9781522516439, 2016.

The Digital Diamond Framework: An Enterprise Architecture Framework for the Digital Age

Roy Oberhauser
Computer Science Dept.
Aalen University
Aalen, Germany
email: roy.oberhauser@hs-aalen.de

Abstract—**Enterprise architecture (EA) frameworks of the past have attempted to support the cohesive and comprehensive modeling and documentation of the enterprise, often with a focus on business and information technology (IT). However, the digitalization of enterprises and the complexity of IT have outgrown these matrix box-like frameworks. This paper proposes a digital, holistic, and sustainable EA framework, called the Digital Diamond Framework, to support digitized enterprises in aligning the real EA state with the desired state.**

Keywords- enterprise architecture frameworks; enterprise architecture; enterprise modeling; business architecture; digitalization.

I. INTRODUCTION

Enterprise Architecture (EA) is concerned with comprehensively modeling and documenting the structure and behavior of the business and IT infrastructure of an enterprise in a cohesive way as a set of artifacts in order to communicate, implement change, and develop insights in support of strategic business planning and management science. Historically, EA emerged from a necessity to document information systems for management stakeholders. One of the most well-known EA Frameworks (EAF) is the Zachman Framework, first publicized in 1987 [1]. While one might think that after 30 years the EA area must be mature, Gartner's 2017 Hype Cycle for Enterprise Architecture [2] shows EA and EA Tools within the slope of Enlightenment - not yet in the Plateau of Productivity, and EAFs are in the Trough of Disillusionment.

Currently, enterprises face multiple contemporaneous challenges: 1) A major digital transformation [3] of their industry. While the digitalization rate (digital score) may vary across industries and economies, it is nevertheless impacting business strategies and necessarily EA. As big data, data analytics, business intelligence, and machine learning make inroads into enterprises, improved decision-making capabilities at all levels and across organizational entities empowers employees with new insights and assistance and additional automation. 2) Agility is restructuring internal people-centric enterprise management, processes, and projects to continuously flexible and responsive business forms, accelerating product and service delivery and improving efficiency (e.g., Scrum, DevOps, BizDevOps). 3) Service-networked and mobile software: the IT landscape is rapidly changing from large, siloed, hierarchical, and static deployments to cloud-centric, networked, and containerized micro functionality deployments. Software/data functionality becomes easily reusable and accessible via standard protocols and formats independent of programming language or platform. Its scale can be seen in various "death star"-like microservice network landscape visualizations (see Figure 1)

Figure 1. Visualization of microservices at Amazon [4].

In lieu of these major trends, the reality that EA is attempting to comprehensively model, document, and change has become much more complex than in previous decades. The era of siloed functional teams and applications is fading, and a highly networked and integrated digitized era has begun. This challenges currently available EAFs, which were mostly developed before these trends swept into enterprises and typically rely on a simplified box-and-matrix paradigm.

In 2007, Ivar Jacobson reckoned 90% of the EA initiatives he was aware of had not resulted in anything useful, giving big gaps vs. seamless relationships as a primary reason [5]. A 2008 study showed two-thirds of EA projects failing to improve IT and business alignment [6], with the most frequent explanation being that connecting EA to business elements was difficult in practice. Hence, the EA frameworks of the past with their associated paradigms and their models cannot continuously reflect the dynamic enterprise realities, thus they are illusionary, ineffective, inefficient, and no longer viable.

To enable more responsive and agile enterprises with better alignment of business plans and initiatives with the actual enterprise state while addressing the EA needs of digitized enterprises for structure, order, modeling, and documentation, this paper contributes a digitized, holistic, hyper-model EA conceptual framework called the Digital Diamond Enterprise Framework (D^2F), providing a sustainable EA framework for a digital EA future.

Section 2 discusses background material on EA. Section 3 describes the D^2F, which is followed by a conclusion in Section 4.

II. Enterprise Architecture Background

EA comprises the structural and behavioral aspects needed for the enterprise to function and their adaptation to align with a vision. It thus covers business (including people), information (data), and technology (IT, hardware and software). EA has been compared to city planning [7], designing in the face of many unknowns.

A. EA Frameworks (EAFs)

EAFs offer structure, associated terminology, and at times processes for EA-related work. Zachman's EAF [1] utilizes a matrix paradigm and has changed over the years, using rows (layers) to address highest level business, then logical to the most detailed technical levels, and columns for the 5W's and H (who, what, where, when, why, how). Many of these EAFs have common ancestors and historical influences. The Open Group Architecture Framework (TOGAF) [8] was first publicized in 1995 and provides a methodology for EA and a boxed architecture. The National Institute of Standards and Technology (NIST) EA Model is a five-layered reference model stemming from the 1980s and formed the basis for the Federal Enterprise Architecture Framework (FEAF) [9]. The Generic Enterprise Reference Architecture and Method (GERAM) [10] is a generalized EAF from the 1990s and focuses on enterprise integration and business process engineering. Most EAFs use a 2D box or 3D cube paradigm in attempting to deal with the inherent complexity.

B. Enterprise Modeling

Modeling abstracts and simplifies an area of interest while maintaining certain its essential characteristics. So, reality is more complex than our models. We model in order to reason or understand within our cognitive limitations and to convey insights to others. Different domains and enterprises have different weightings and expectations as to what and how much, if any, modeling and its associated overhead should occur. The modeling spectrum can span from nothing for small organizations to modeling everything, but usually it is in the area between (see Figure 2). Something is inherently absent and models are imperfect, and manual adjustments may be necessary if the reality changes.

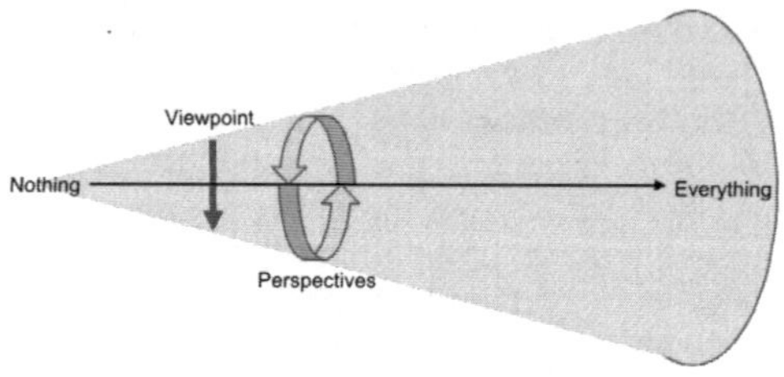

Figure 2. Modeling spectrum.

An international standard for enterprise modelling (EM) and enterprise integration is ISO 19439:2006, which based on GERAM and Computer Integrated Manufacturing Open System Architecture (CIMOSA). It uses a cube paradigm with model phase, model view, and genericity on each axis. As to business modeling, Meertens et al. [11] argue that there is hardly any agreement or standardization in the area as yet.

The reality is enterprise models for dynamic enterprises can become extremely complex and perhaps difficult to maintain, as illustrated in Figure 3 with a CHOOSE semantic meta-model [12] for an SME (small-to-medium enterprise).

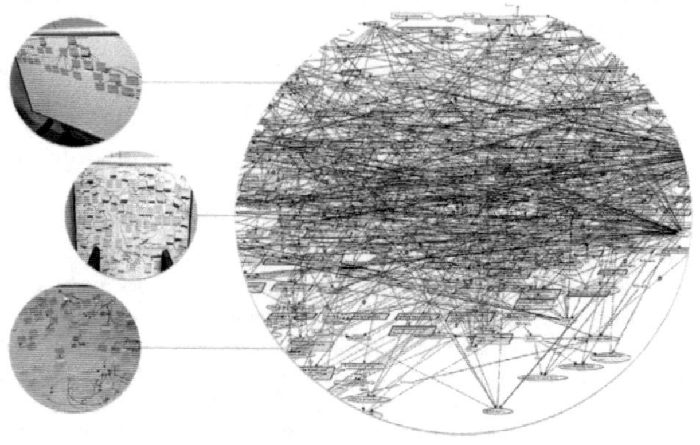

Figure 3. A example CHOOSE enterprise model for an SME, from [12].

C. Related Standards

Related standards in the EA area are ISO/IEC 38500:2008, which deals with corporate governance of information technology. ISO/IEC/IEEE 42010 Systems and software engineering — Architecture description deals with describing system and software architectures. ISACA's COBIT (Control Objectives for Information and Related Technologies) is a good-practice framework for IT management and governance.

D. Summary

John Zachman admitted in 2004 [13] "if you ask who is successfully implementing the whole framework, the answer is nobody that we know of yet." Gartner's 2011 global EA survey showed more than 60 EA frameworks in use, with the most popular being blended followed by homemade [14]. This indicates that none of the current EAFs suffice for enterprise needs, and many were not designed for the new digital enterprise era and lack the ability to leverage its capabilities.

The EAFs and methods mentioned above typically use some layer-and-column matrix and most aspects related to models and views land in a box. This the clean-box paradigm (or syndrome depending on your view). Everything appears nicely modeled, complete, consistent, traceable, and semantically precise. But this apparent harmony is an illusion, the grey areas that cross boundaries or are cross-cutting concerns are not explicitly dealt with. The above EAFs currently lack an integrated digitalized and data-centric concept. They fail to provide real-time dynamic updates and thus reflect stale or inaccurate data. They also require additional manual labor to maintain independent artifact consistency with changing reality or to monitor and detect inconsistencies when they occur since they have independent data sources that are not automatically synchronized.

A new sustainable "out-of-the-box" paradigm for a new era that can deal with digitalization, ambiguity, further IT complexity, and additional automation is needed.

III. The Digital Diamond EA Framework

In the following, the key areas, activities, principles, integrative facets (potentially applicable when applying D^{2}F), maturity levels, and roadmap to D^{2}F are portrayed.

A. D^{2}F Key Areas

Key Areas cluster related facets (concepts or elements) and provide a focus for human thought. In contrast to boxes/levels, here boundaries are intentionally absent, reflecting the lack of boundaries in the digital world, wherein facets can relate to multiple areas. Mind maps can be seen as a useful analogy. Figure 4 shows key areas involved in D^{2}F, with cross-cutting areas shown angled on the left and right:

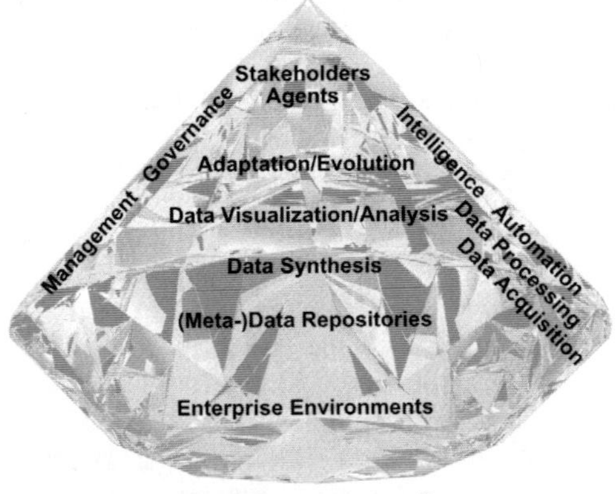

Figure 4. Key areas D^{2}F.

1) Enterprise Environments: comprises all actual human, business, infrastructural, and IT operational objects.

2) (Meta-)Data Repositories: includes all (meta-)data concept repositories in the enterprise from a logical standpoint, reflecting *Enterprise Environments* in a data-centric way in support of higher level data-centric analyses. While such repositories also reside in an *Enterprise Environment*, the focus is support for data acquisition, data processing, and other data-centric higher-level activities.

3) Data Acquisition: involves collecting data and meta-data into *Data Repositories* and making these accessible.

4) Data Processing: includes characterizing, filtering, preparing (e.g., deriving), transforming (e.g., between formats, sorting), and cleansing data, the outputs of which are also stored in *Data Repositories* and hence available to other areas (e.g., automation, synthesis, analysis).

5) Data Synthesis: involves aggregating, clustering, and correlating related or unrelated enterprise data, e.g., for digital key performance indicators (KPIs), dashboards, model conformance, etc. While this area overlaps the previous one, its focus is on determining and structuring aggregates.

6) Data Visualization/Data Analysis: provides data-centric analysis and visualization of data, models, and other EA artefacts for understanding, exploration, and insights.

7) Adaptation/Evolution: includes taking action, responding to issues or concerns, stimulating or commissioning adaptive changes to fix or optimize the enterprise, and creating new initiatives and capabilities that let the enterprise evolve to a new state.

8) Stakeholders/Agents: stakeholders can be viewed as anyone with an interest in the enterprise, and they may have conflicting and overlapping interests and (informational) needs. Agents (human or software) are able to directly effect changes within the enterprise.

9) Automation and Intelligence: automation will increasingly support digital enterprise processes and will leverage data to improve efficiency and effectiveness and is thus explicitly considered. Beyond automation, intelligence utilizes data analysis and machines learning capabilities to assist humans in forming decisions or, via intelligent software agents, directly supporting autonomic decisions in given areas. For instance, automatic real-time adjustment of business product prices based on market movements or IT forecasting of required cloud infrastructure capacities.

10) Management and Governance: involves managing and directing enterprise resources to reach enterprise goals as well as the enterprise governance including controlling, compliance, and assessments at various enterprise levels .

Note that *Key Areas* can overlap (a data or meta-data repository will likely reside in an enterprise environment) and thus may appear redundant or inconsistent, yet this is not problematic and one strength of the D^{2}F paradigm. *Key Areas* may be tailored for a specific enterprise. A prerequisite to a complete implementation of D^{2}F presumes digitalization of EA-relevant areas for any given enterprise. As to scaling, the concept of a connected *D^{2}F Chain (Diamond Necklace)* can be considered for applying D^{2}F within various entities (e.g., divisions) but tied into a larger enterprise organization.

B. D^{2}F Key Principles and Qualities

Key principles and resulting qualities of D^{2}F include:

1) Digitized (digital and networked): data and artifacts are acquired or transformed into a digital and network-accessible form, open and transparent within the enterprise (to the degree feasible from a security standpoint), and preferably retained in some version-controlled repository (database or configuration-management database (CMDB) such as git). Internet-of-Everything and concepts such as digital twins can be used for physical entities to mimic real properties. Standards for data formats and interface access are considered for the enterprise.

2) Meta (self-describing): all (data) elements including artefacts, entities, services, etc. should, as far as feasible, provide (its own) metadata (properties and semantic meaning) that can be integrated in metadata repositories (e.g., federated CMDBs) or searched via metadata networks (e.g., LinkedData), and which can be utilized by data processing and data synthesis. Various technologies such as semantic data graphs, RESTful services, JSON-LD, etc. can be used.

3) Linked: Related networked data and meta-data are (semantically) linked in such a way that related data to some element or concept can be discovered and accessed.

4) Dynamicity: In an adapting and evolving digital enterprise, all artefacts and enterprise elements (or the digital twins thereof) as well as their relationships are assumed to be dynamic, and configurations are used to "snapshot" a set of element states that can be used in some analysis or communication. Models can be based on functions that transition from simulated to real data rather than static structures detached from external values.

5) Holistic: bottom-up and top-down deep integration of applicable enterprise facets, such that various concepts (e.g., business models, business strategies, policies, architectures) can be tied to various related artefacts, models, operational data, and actual enterprise entities and thus be holistically analyzed across various factors.

6) Hyper-models: embraces many coexistent and co-evolving intertwined models (domain, business, process, software, IT architectures, context), perspectives, viewpoints, and views (not necessarily consistent) supported by data processing. Manual modeling is waning, and automation will also affect modeling, thus we must adapt our tooling and methods towards sustainable integrative modeling. Humans desire simplicity and computers can better deal with complexity and massive data volume, thus a symbiotic relationship should be pursued.

7) Actuality processing (real/continuous/resilient/fuzzy): ongoing data acquisition and processing should be able to continuously access and adjust the data picture to the real live enterprise truth. To have resilient processing (vs. expecting consistency or exact values), data processing should embrace data ranges and the inconsistencies that will occur between data, models (inter- and intra-), reality, etc., and develop (automated) strategies and methods for detecting and working with exceptions, ranges, and thresholds and escalating more serious issues. That may include automated discrepancy monitoring and analysis and criticality weightings based on thresholds, risks, and potential impacts. While data cleansing can remove some of the dirt, rather expect issues to occur and have measures and thresholds in place to detect and govern these and processing that can work with ambiguity such as semantic imprecision.

8) Analytics: data forms the basis for EA decisions. Data-centric processing and analysis capabilities are available for the present, past, and planned enterprise states to determine alignment to expectations. Digital KPIs, dashboards, reports, and visual data analytics enable investigation and exploration of EA-related views, perspectives, viewpoints, and any other factor of interest (X-Factors) to contribute to understanding and insights on various EA factors.

9) Actionable: data is leveraged to support decisions and governance, enabling responsive and predictive adaptation and evolution of the enterprise to a better state.

10) Automation/Intelligence: Data is leveraged for automation to reduce sources of error and improve effectiveness and efficiency. For example, business process management systems and business and IT rules can be utilized. Intelligence via data-centric machine learning is integrated where possible to improve, support, or automate (human and software agent) decision making.

11) Traceability and Logging: mistakes will happen, and people and enterprises can learn from mistakes. To embrace this fact, changes to data, elements, artefacts, and all actions with their associated agents are tracked (and versioned if appropriate), logged, and traced in order to be able to investigate and resolve potential issues that might arise.

C. D^2F Key Activities

Various (ongoing) human and IT activities are involved to apply and maintain D^2F. We use the term activities instead of processes, as processes have a clearly-defined goal and workflow and can be documented with specified artifacts, whereas activities can be agile and integrated where and when needed in whatever agile method is currently being used and done in any order deemed appropriate. They can be recurring and continuous to maintain D^2F capabilities. As shown in Figure 5, key D^2F activities include:

1) Data Acquisition: ensures necessary and desired (meta-)data is collected, characterized, and accessible.

2) Data Processing: ensures data is cleansed, filtered, prepared, and transformed into expected (standard) formats.

3) Data Synthesis: aggregates and correlates data from various repositories for a specific purpose, such as providing data needed for a certain viewpoint or dashboard.

Figure 5. Digital Diamond Framework (D^2F) activities.

4) Data Analysis, Visualization, & Exploration: involves agents (human or software) exploring, forming questions or hypotheses, utilizing various data and visualization analysis techniques from certain perspectives and viewpoints to address the concerns of various stakeholders, developing solutions, detecting opportunities and develop insights.

5) Adapting & Evolving: directing and commissioning change, usually involving the previous activity (4), be it adjustments to align or to evolve the enterprise, its EA, or its supporting infrastructure. It may utilize effectors available in the enterprise environments and/or human efforts via initiating projects or enacting processes.

6) Modeling & Configuring: involves creating and maintaining (hyper) business, operational, architectural, product and other models (which can be logical in nature) and provide some simplification of some structure of interest and associated properties. These can be for a pre-development, development, or operational stage. While maintaining models is burdensome, incorrect models are worse, thus the basis for models should be tied into current enterprise data. Configuring involves (re)arranging enterprise elements in various ways to optimize certain desired properties.

7) Testing & Simulating: involves testing and/or simulating hypotheses and models with potential real or generated data on virtual or real staged or production elements. The goal is to develop an improved basis for decisions affecting elements of the EA, and might include concepts such as a delivery pipeline. These activities become more important as the systems increase in complexity. Without the data from these activities, decision making at the higher levels can be hampered.

8) Management & Governance: includes setting the vision and goals for the enterprise, perceiving and acting on opportunities and risk, planning, organizing, directing, and managing enterprise resources, making decisions, performing assessments, determining compliance with policies and alignment with expectations, supporting the development and application of strategies, best practices, policies, and guidelines, and making this information available to the enterprise. It is both top-down and bottom-up in its approach. It includes a feedback loop for continuous improvement or adjustment, enabling the enterprise to learn from mistakes and to optimize its future state. It ensures that logging and traceability of the data used for decisions, the decisions made, and the resulting actions are accessible.

9) Intelligence & Automation: involves developing, maintaining, and optimizing automation processes in the enterprise, including EA analysis activity. Activity to support intelligence builds on automation and includes decision assistance for humans and software agents.

D. D²F Enterprise Facets

Any enterprise concept or element can be a facet. To provide further detail on which enterprise facets might be of interest for an enterprise when using D²F, Figure 6 clusters facets near *Key Areas*. Its intent is not to portray every possible facet, or by neglect thereof or apparent inconsistency to negate the entire approach. Rather, it shows that grey or inconsistent areas with which matrix approaches struggle are not as problematic with D²F, since it embraces these types of relations. A short explanation of selected facets follows:

Enterprise Environments can involve a *Business* in a *Market* with *Customers*, involving *Projects*, *Processes* (business, development, agile, IT Infrastructure Library), *Products*, and *Services* (business, IT) together with *Actors* organized in *Teams* utilizing *Infrastructure*, *IT* (cloud, microservices, mobile), *Resources*, *Tools*, and *Technologies*. *Entities* can be organizational units or any other enterprise element not already covered by other facets. *Sensors* permit data about changes in the enterprise state to be acquired, while *Effectors* permit desired changes to be applied. *IT Rules* and *Biz* (Business) *Rules* support automation or escalation.

Figure 6. Illustrative enterprise facets when applying D²F.

(Meta-)Data Repositories includes data and metadata about *Projects*, *Processes*, *Products*, and *Services* as well as *Planning Data* and *Ops* (Operational) *Data*. *CMDBs* provide data and metadata about the *IT* landscape, *X-Assets* are repositories for data and metadata about other enterprise assets (e.g., program code). *Knowledge* repositories may be used. Archives provide historical data. *Digital Twins* provide a digital representation of real enterprise elements not covered by the above. *X-Architectures* stands for any (enterprise, business, software, IT) architecture, describing the goals and representation of some structure and its properties and involving principles, rules, abstractions, and views. *Models* (conceptual, mathematical, business, data, etc.) are a partial representation of some reality.

Data Synthesis, *Data Visualization*, and *Data Analysis* can be used to develop Insights and can include *digiKPIs* (digital KPIs), *Dashboards*, and *Reports*. *Perspectives* address a particular quality property and have an implicit goal or intention. *Views* (partially) address some concern. *Viewpoints* are a class of views to address associated concerns. *X-Factors* can be qualities, capabilities, properties, aspects, etc. otherwise not addressed by the above.

Adaptation/Evolution includes *Decisions* and *Actions* to respond to disruptions, support change such as enterprise element lifecycle adjustments (acquire, prepare, operate, maintain, retire) as well as discovering and utilizing Innovations and instigating digital transformation initiatives.

Stakeholders/Agents are driven by some *Motivation*, have *Knowledge*, *Values* (what they hold to be good), and *Beliefs* (what they hold to be true), develop *Ideas*, and have future-oriented *Goals* and present-oriented *Intentions* with

Expectations and *Concerns* they would like addressed, including a (common) *Vision* (future desired state) for the enterprise and some *Mission* (purpose) it intends to fulfill.

Automation involves *Processes.* In an intelligent enterprise, *Autonomically-Capable Processes* (ACPs) [15] will increasingly be desired and expected. These ACPs can be completely autonomic, involve human interaction, or assist human operators in some fashion. These intelligent ACPs are much more complex than normal business processes.

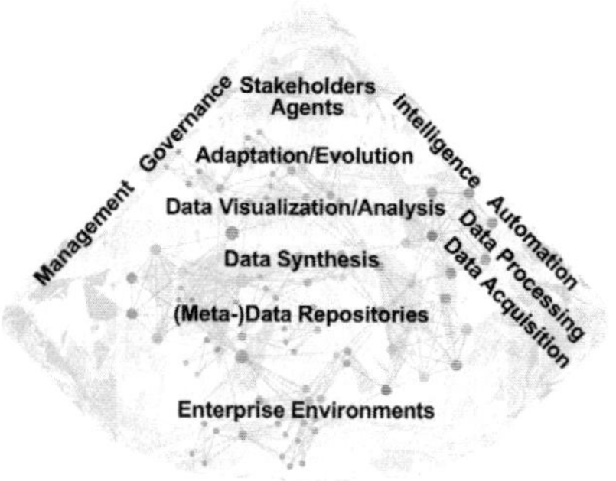

Figure 7. Colored graph showing possible linked facet instantiations.

The random colored node graph superimposed in Figure 7 conceptually illustrates how facet instantiations (data) across various areas could be linked via graph relations to provide various insights addressing stakeholder concerns.

E. D²F Maturity Levels

Because D²F is a digital EAF, to achieve and apply all D²F principles across all levels of any existing large enterprise will require a transformation and enterprises will be in different states of transformation. The following Maturity Levels shown in Table I can be helpful to guide and ensure that requisite capabilities are addressed before focusing on higher level capabilities. Each level subsumes the one below.

TABLE I. D²F MATURITY LEVELS

Level	Label	D²F Qualities	Data Perspective
0	Arbitrary	-	-
1	Digitized	Digitized Meta	Data Acquisition
2	Linked	Dynamicity Linked	Data Processing
3	Analytical	Hyper-models Analytics Actuality processing	Data Synthesis Data Analysis Data Visualization
4	Adaptive	Holistic Actionable Traceability/Logging	Effectors
5	Autonomic /Intelligent	Automation Intelligence	Automation Intelligence

F. D²F Roadmap

Each enterprise and its IT infrastructure are unique. The digital nature of D²F requires access to (semantically annotated) data repositories and software functionality. Various methods and best practices related to enterprise application integration (EAI), EA and other IT tools, protocol standards and formats (JSON/REST), and data visualization techniques can be leveraged to realize D²F in an enterprise.

IV. CONCLUSION

A sustainable EAF is needed that can embrace the digitized enterprise era. This paper described the Digital Diamond Framework (D²F) to support digitized enterprises with the structure, order, modeling, documentation, and analysis needs to enable more responsive and agile enterprises with better alignment of business plans and initiatives with the actual enterprise state. Key areas, principles, activities, facets, and maturity levels were elucidated.

While D²F can be applied at a high-level, as the framework is digital-centric, any concrete application in an enterprise requires concrete and integrated EA tooling utilizing the standards and formats available to that enterprise. Future work includes applying D²F in case studies in various organizations.

REFERENCES

[1] J. Zachman, "A framework for information systems architecture." IBM Systems Journal, 26(3), pp. 276-292, 1987.

[2] M. Blosch and B. Burton, "Hype Cycle for Enterprise Architecture, 2017," Gartner, 2017.

[3] M. Muro, S. Liu, J. Whiton, and S. Kulkarni, *Digitalization and the American Workforce.* Brookings Institution Metropolitan Policy Program, 2017. [Online]. Available from: https://www.brookings.edu/wp-content/uploads/2017/11/mpp_2017nov15_digitalization_full_report.pdf 2018.01.27

[4] C. Munns, *I Love APIs 2015: Microservices at Amazon.* [Online]. Available from: https://www.slideshare.net/apigee/i-love-apis-2015-microservices-at-amazon-54487258 2018.01.27

[5] I. Jacobson, *EA Failed Big Way!* [Online]. Available from: http://blog.ivarjacobson.com/ 2018.01.27

[6] S. Roeleven, *Why Two Thirds of Enterprise Architecture Projects Fail.* ARIS, 2011. [Online]. Available from: https://www.computerworld.com.au/whitepaper/370709/why-two-thirds-of-enterprise-architecture-projects-fail/ 2018.01.27

[7] R. Nolan and D. Mulryan, "Undertaking an Architecture Program," Stage by Stage, 7(2), pp.63- 64, 1987.

[8] The Open Group, "TOGAF Version 9.1," Van Haren Publishing, 2011.

[9] Chief Information Officers Council: Federal Enterprise Architecture Framework Version 1.1.

[10] IFAC-IFIP Task Force, "GERAM - Generalized enterprise reference architecture and methodology, version 1.6.3," 1999.

[11] L. Meertens, M. Iacob, and L. Nieuwenhuis, "Developing the business modelling method," In: First Int'l Symp. Bus. Model. & Softw. Design, BMSD 2011, SciTePress, pp. 88-95, 2011.

[12] M. Bernaert, G. Poels, M. Snoeck, and M. De Backer, "CHOOSE: Towards a metamodel for enterprise architecture in small and medium-sized enterprises," Information systems frontiers, 18(4), pp. 781-818, 2016.

[13] D. Ruby, *Erecting the Framework, Part III.* 2004-03-18 Interview with John Zachman. [Online]. Available from http://archive.visualstudiomagazine.com/ea/magazine/spring/online/druby3/default_pf.aspx 2018.01.27

[14] Gartner, "Gartner's 2011 Global Enterprise Architecture Survey: EA Frameworks Are Still Homemade and Hybrid," Gartner, 2012.

[15] R. Oberhauser and G. Grambow, "Towards Autonomically-Capable Processes: A Vision and Potentially Supportive Methods." In Adv. in Intell. Process-Aware Information Systems: Concepts, Methods, and Technologies. Springer, 2017, pp. 79-125.

A Governance Framework for (Semi) Automated Decision-Making

Koen Smit
Digital Smart Services
HU University of Applied Sciences Utrecht
Utrecht, the Netherlands
Koen.smit@hu.nl

Martijn Zoet
Optimizing Knowledge-Intensive Business Processes
Zuyd University of Applied Sciences
Sittard, the Netherlands
Martijn.zoet@zuyd.nl

Abstract—**Proper decision-making is one of the most important capabilities of an organization. Therefore, it is important to have a clear understanding and overview of the decisions an organization makes. A means to design and specify decisions is the Decision Model and Notation (DMN) standard published by the Object Management Group in 2015. In this standard, it is possible to specify how a decision should be taken but lacks elements to specify the actors that fulfill different roles in the decision-making process. Additionally, DMN does not take into account the autonomy of machines. In this paper, a framework is proposed and demonstrated that takes into account different roles in the decision-making process, and also includes the extent of the autonomy when machines are involved in the decision-making processes. Based on the model presented, we identify several directions for future research, including more rigorous validation of the proposed model to ensure the model is applicable in most, if not all, contexts.**

Keywords - Decision-Making; DMN; RAPID; Autonomy.

I. INTRODUCTION

In September 2015, the Object Management Group (OMG) released a new standard for modelling decisions and underlying business logic, DMN [1]. In line with the DMN standard, a decision is defined as: "*A conclusion that a business arrives at through business logic and which the business is interested in managing.*" [2]. Furthermore, business logic is defined as: "*a collection of business rules, business decision tables, or executable analytic models to make individual decisions.*" [1].

Proper decision-making is one of the most important capabilities of an organization [3]. In the previous decades, decision making was a capability only executed by human actors. However, given the technical developments in computer hard- and software, the possibilities to automate decision-making have increased. Examples of techniques applied during automated decision making are business rules systems, expert systems, and neural networks [4]. To achieve proper decision-making, organizations must design and specify their decisions and decision-making processes. One aspect that influences the specification of the decision and the decision-making process is the level of automated decision-making. Machines can execute decisions only when the decision and the underlying business logic is specified formally [5]. Furthermore, when organizations choose to specify their decisions and decision-making processes, the level of detail is of importance. This is based, amongst others, on the type of decision and the actor that executes the decision. For example, a strategic decision needs to be specified on a different level of detail compared to an operational decision and therefore needs a different type of specification and a different decision-making process.

While DMN is mainly applied to express operational decisions that will be automated, it can also be used for manual decision-making. However, the current DMN standard lacks a formal concept to specify a governance structure for each decision. In this context, a governance structure is defined to express the roles and responsibilities relevant to a decision and the underlying decision-making process. This becomes important when a decision is executed by instantiating a decision-making process that features both human and machine actors. Research on specifying a proper governance structure for decision-making already concluded that assigning clear roles and responsibilities are the most important steps in the design and specification of decisions and result in better coordination and quicker response times [3][6].

Another aspect of designing and specifying decisions and decision-making is the use of machine actors instead of human actors. Assigning machine actors to parts of the decision-making process requires organizations to evaluate the autonomy of the machine. Machine autonomy refers to the system's capability to carry out its own tasks and making decisions [7]. As Parasuraman, Sheridan and Wickens [8] stated in their work, the question now is: "*which system functions should be automated, and to what extent?*" For example, when possible, do we want to let a machine decide whether a person should or shouldn't be admitted to enter a given country, based on the premise that the machine is more accurate compared to a human actor in determining the eligibility of a person.

One reason why it is essential to include proper governance structure when designing and specifying decisions and decision-making processes is the increasingly stricter laws and regulations on digital privacy and data regulation, i.e., the Health Insurance Portability and Accountability Act (title II) and the General Data Protection Regulation [9]. Such laws and regulations can prohibit the use of machine actors in decision-making, and when it allows organizations to include them, specifies exactly what is allowed and what is not allowed. For example, how exactly personal data is processed, and which roles have access to it. Thus, to design compliant decisions and decision-making, an organization must be able to define exactly what actors are responsible for, and, when a machine is made responsible, how autonomously it will operate.

In literature, studies are conducted that resulted in a model to define, for example, the autonomy of a machine in decision-making [8][10][11]. Moreover, studies are conducted that specify the roles that are used to design decision-making processes between stakeholders [3][12]. However, to the knowledge of the authors, no studies exist that combine both.

Therefore, in this paper, a model is proposed that includes the roles and responsibilities aspect, taking into account human-machine interaction, while also including the autonomy level of a machine as part of the human-machine interaction in decision-making. To be able to do so, the following research question is addressed: "*How can a governance structure be designed to explicate the decision-making process?*"

The remainder of this paper is organized as follows. First, a literature overview is presented in section two in which the existing models that define the possible interaction between a human and a machine are explored and compared. This is followed by the construction of the model in section three. Next, in section four, the case to demonstrate and validate the model is described, which is followed by the actual demonstration of the model. Lastly, the conclusions are drawn and we propose directions for future research in section five.

II. Background and Related Work

The DMN standard consists of two levels: the Decision Requirements Level (DRD) and the Decision Logic Level (DLL). The DRD level consists of four concepts that are used to capture essential information with regards to decisions: 1) the decision, 2) business knowledge, which represents the collection of business logic required to execute the decision, 3) input data, and 4) a knowledge source, which enforces how the decision should be taken by influencing the underlying business logic, see Figure 1. The contents of the DLL level are represented by the business knowledge container in the DRD level. In the current version of DMN, two standard languages are suggested for expressing business logic, Friendly Enough Expression Language (FEEL) and Simple Expression Language (S-FEEL) [1]. However, it also allows the use of other, more adopted languages like JavaScript, Groovy, and Python [1]. Still, the language selected to represent the decision logic does not influence the decision requirements level. Analysis of the DMN standard reveals that no formal elements exist to specify roles in the decision-making process. To add to the DMN standard, roles and responsibilities should be taken into account.

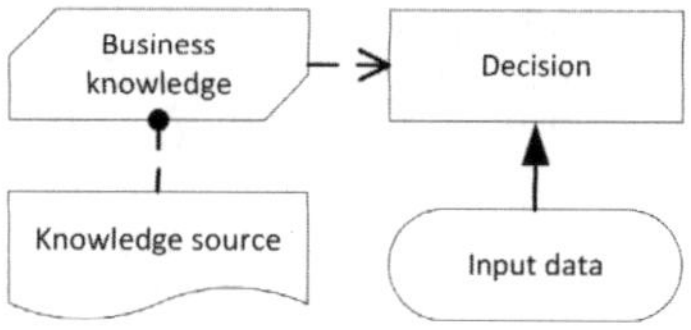

Figure 1. DRD-level elements

A. Roles and responsibilities in decision-making

In the current body of knowledge, frameworks that define roles and responsibilities in decision-making processes exist. These studies focus on different perspectives in the decision-making process. For example, there are studies that focus on the influences of decision-making roles, i.e., family/collegial pressure and gender or cultural preferences [13][14]. In addition, there are also studies that focus on specific application areas for decision-making, i.e., transportation, medical, financial and governance [15][16]. For example, in a patient-doctor context where a treatment has to be decided, multiple roles are relevant, i.e., the patient, different medical specialists, the doctor, a nurse, and in some cases family members of the patient [16].

However, as the scope of this paper lies on the creation of a framework which can be applied to define the governance structure of any decision, a more generic set of roles and responsibilities is required.

The work of Rogers and Blenko [3] features a generic model named RAPID, which presents five different roles that are applied during the decision-making process. However, one limitation in the original study is the focus on decisions that are only executed by human actors. To ground our framework construction, a detailed description of the RAPID framework is provided here.

RAPID focuses on assigning a set of specific roles with regards to a decision. This framework is characterized by a simple, yet grounded in practice approach and consists of five different roles and underlying responsibilities that are related to a decision. The first role is ***Recommend***, which is responsible for making a proposal and gathering input for decision-making. This role communicates with the input role to ensure their viewpoints are embedded in the recommendation. The second role is ***Agree***, which is responsible for evaluating a proposal provided by the recommender. This role has veto power over the recommendation. When this role declines a recommendation, a modified proposal has to be made. The third role is ***Input***, which is responsible for providing input (data) to make the decision and are typically consulted on the decision. The opinion of this role is non-binding, but should be taken into account to ensure the decision does not falter during its execution. The fourth role is Decide, which is responsible as the formal decision maker and is accountable for the decision and its results. This role has the most authority compared to the other roles as it is able to resolve the decision-making between the previous roles by making the actual decision. By doing so, this role has the power to commit an organization to action based on decision-making. Lastly, the fifth role stands for Perform, which is responsible for executing the actual decision in the organization after it is decided by the previous role.

Based on RAPID, Taylor [12], in a professional article, adapted the RAPID model but made a distinction between a human and a machine for decision-making processes in which he stresses that the action component can be different between these two. For example, when a decision must be executed in an organization, human actors perform the actual decision and also handle possible exceptions. When a machine executes decisions, exceptions are filtered out and send to human actors for further examination. Another significant difference between a human and a machine actor is the explicitness of business rules that a machine must be able to execute, and therefore must be maintained adequately versus the implicit knowledge for the decision-making utilized by human actors in the actual decision-making process.

B. Autonomy level of stakeholders in human-machine interaction

Machine autonomy broadly refers to a machine's capability to carry out its own processes and tasks, along with the decision-making needed to do so [7].

With regards to machine autonomy, also referred to as robot autonomy or computer autonomy, many authors added a framework to the body of knowledge that define autonomy levels. Both general and context-specific frameworks for levels of autonomy (LOA) exist, while some define very detailed levels of autonomy, others utilize autonomy as a concept without exactly defining the spectrum of autonomy [17]. In this paper, the focus is on generic LOA frameworks. Regarding generic LOA frameworks, the work of Sheridan and Verplanck [18] and later Parasuraman, Sheridan and Wickers [8] defined ten levels of autonomy for decision-making with automation (i.e., machines/computers), also abbreviated to LOADAS. Their classification ranks from full human decisions and actions (level 1) until full autonomy without interaction with humans (level 10) and takes into account several variants with alternatives. For example, veto voting by human actors and the level of interaction between a machine and human actor. This LOA framework is, to the knowledge of the authors, the most popular work as it is cited numerous times and used in the construction of many other theoretical and practical constructs. However, the ten LOA levels described in the work of Parasuraman, Sheridan and Wickers [8] are too much prone to interpretation, which can be concluded by how the different authors of subsequent LOA frameworks and related work described this framework. For example, the work of Endsley and Kaber [19] describes that the first of ten levels is not fully manual as it is handed over to the machine to execute it. This is in contrast with the interpretation and description by Miller and Parasuraman [20], which describes that a human actor is responsible for everything in the decision-making process, including the execution of the decision. A second example of an interpretation that is not specific enough with regards to this framework is the notion of levels one and two in the work of Beer, Fisk and Rogers [7], which state that these two levels are exactly the same. This would mean that the model contains a redundant level.

Endsley and Kaber [10] defined in their work ten categories of the level of automation along with definitions for the level of autonomy for each category, based on earlier work by Endsley [19]. However, the ten levels, which are all activity focused, are grounded by five levels of autonomy defined by Endsley [19], which are: 1) manual support, 2) decision support, 3) consensual AI, 4) monitored AI, and 5) full automation. This framework's strength is its simplistic approach to autonomy, which is also its drawback. Compared to the framework of Parasuraman, Sheridan and Wickers [8], this framework lacks proper detail with regards to the possibilities a machine nowadays has. For example, based on the five levels of autonomy it is based on, it is unclear how recommendations are provided and how the human actor is informed about executing the actual decision or the result of the decision after execution by a machine.

A third generic framework is the Autonomy Levels For Unmanned Systems (ALFUS) [11]. This framework includes increasingly complex environments in which a machine makes decisions and executes actions. The LOA levels included in ALFUS, range from zero (remote control) to ten (full intelligent autonomy). At the lowest LOA, there is 100% interaction between a human and machine actor, while at the 10th LOA, almost no interaction between a human and machine actor is present. While ALFUS describes in more detail the amount of interaction between human and machine actors, the composition of this interaction is left implicit as it requires the ALFUS generic framework to be instantiated into program specific ALFUS frameworks [11].

The currently available frameworks very accurately describe what levels of autonomy could be taken into account and how the interaction is possible between human and machine actors. However, as pointed out earlier, the existing frameworks lack the exact separation of tasks and responsibilities in complex human-machine interaction environments. Therefore, in the next section, a model is proposed that combines both the roles relevant for decision making with the different levels of autonomy possible for machines in human-machine interaction to overcome this gap.

III. GOVERNANCE FRAMEWORK CONSTRUCTION

For the construction of our framework that fills the gaps identified in the previous section, two perspectives have to be merged: detailed decision-making roles and detailed LOA's. Regarding the decision-making roles, the RAPID framework [3] is adopted due to its generic nature, thus is applicable in all contexts. Then, with regards to autonomy, the LOADAS framework [8] has been adopted due to the fact that it is utilized by many newer autonomy frameworks. However, the low level of detail and different interpretations of this framework and those that preceded LOADAS were already considered a drawback for the design and specification of decisions and decision-making as discussed in the previous section. Therefore, these models have been analyzed to identify Situational Factors (SFs) that need to be taken into account for the construction of the governance framework. By doing so, the governance framework adopts all essential constructs from related work on the subject of autonomy. Analysis of the models resulted in four SF's. The four SFs identified from the literature are: 1) type of actor, 2) alternatives, 3) veto and 4) inform.

The first SF is the type of actor, see for example "*The **computer** informs the human only if asked*" [8]. Simply stated, when decision-making is defined, a choice has to be made whether this should be performed by a human actor only (variant one), a combination of a human and a machine actor (variant two) or solely by a machine (variant three). The second SF concerns the alternatives and the number of alternatives that are provided by a machine actor to the human actor, see for example "*The computer narrows the selection down to a few* ***alternatives***" [8]. This SF comprises three possible variants. The machine actor could provide a full list of possible alternatives to the human actor, offering no filtering or selection at all (variant one). In the second variant, the machine actor could provide a selected set of alternatives for evaluation by a human actor. This means that the machine actor already filtered out one or more alternatives. The amount of alternatives in this variant depends on the context of the decision-making, and therefore is not fixed compared to the first and third variant. Lastly, the machine actor could provide one alternative to the human actor, which means that the machine actor performs the complete selection for the human actor, which only has to decide whether to execute the provided alternative or not (variant three). The third SF is veto, which encompasses the time a human actor is provided by the machine actor to activate a veto over the decision-making by the machine actor, see for example "*Allows the human a restricted time to* ***veto****...*" [8]. The amount of time provided by the machine actor to veto depends on the context of the decision-making, which results in two possible variants, decision-making including a veto possibility regardless of the time specified to do so (variant one) or decision-making without the possibility to veto (variant two). The fourth SF comprises the interaction between the human and machine actor regarding the output of the decision-making, see for example "***Informs*** *the human only if the computer decides to*" [8]. This interaction could entail four possible variants. The first variant requires the machine actor to always inform the human actor with the result of the decision-making by the machine actor. The second variant requires the human actor to file a request for information about the decision-making by the machine actor. The third variant leaves the responsibility to inform the human actor about the decision-making in the hands of the machine actor, which has to decide whether it is necessary. For example, this could be determined by the machine actor based on pre-programmed or self-learned exceptions. The fourth variant is a fully autonomous state regarding decision-making by the machine actor, ignoring the human actor.

Combining the RAPID roles and the four identified SFs a framework is created that supports the detailed design of a governance structure, see Figure 3. In the governance framework, each role involved (five in total) is characterized by four SFs in the decision-making process and should be specified accordingly.

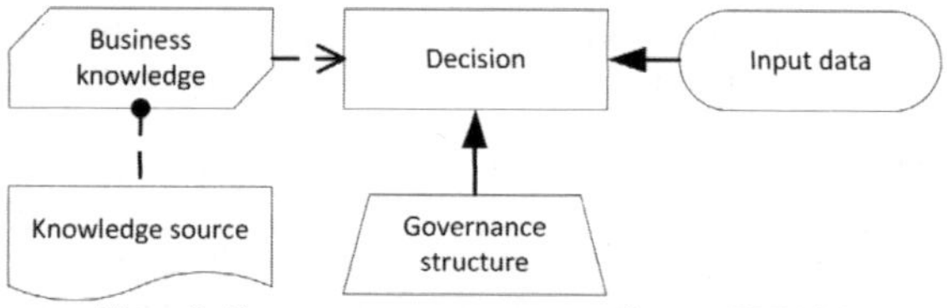

Figure 2. Governance structure to complement DMN 1.1

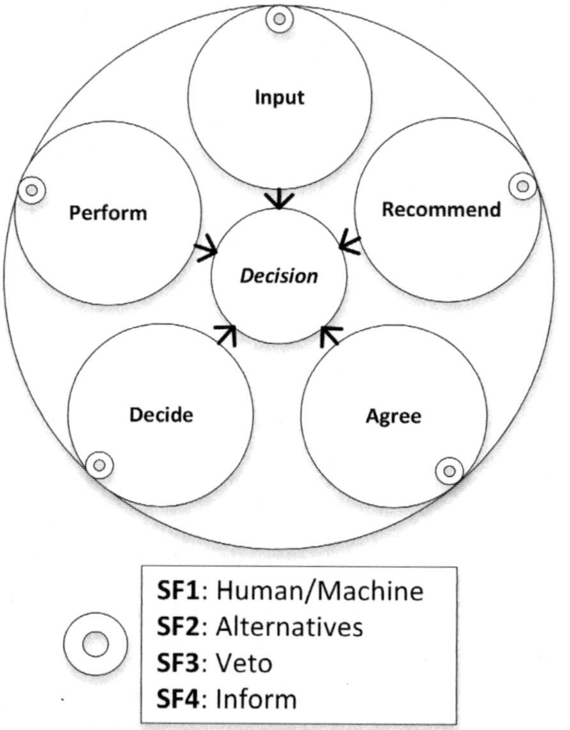

Figure 3. Governance Framework for Decision-making

Based on Figure 3, a governance structure for each decision can be taken into account. Therefore, an additional element to enrich the current DMN standard is proposed, see Figure 2.

IV. CASE DESCRIPTION & APPLICATION

The hypothesized application of the model is demonstrated using a scenario with three variants. The first two variants are based on case study data, while the third variant is based upon a real-world situation, but is not an exact real-life organizational interpretation of it (simulation). First, the scenario is described after which the application of the model is demonstrated using the scenario.

A. Description of scenario

The scenario used to demonstrate the model embodies a governmental institution that is responsible for providing digital services to apply for child benefits, see Figure 4. In this scenario, civilians need to provide information for the governmental institution to be assessed whether the household is eligible to receive child benefits, and when this is the case, the amount of the child benefits and for what period the child benefits can be received. In this scenario, a citizen applies for child benefits.

B. Application of the model

The application of the model is demonstrated using three variants of the scenario. Each of the variants is characterized by a different composition of roles and corresponding SFs.

In the context of this demonstration, three steps are required before the model can be demonstrated: 1) the decision has to be modelled in DMN. In this context, this means that the DRD for this particular decision has to be established (the decision, its input data, its ruleset and relevant sources), see Fig 1. 2) The governance structure element has to be added to the DRD, connected to the appropriate decision, see Figure 2. Lastly, 3). The roles and SFs need to be specified. An example template to do so is presented in Table 1.

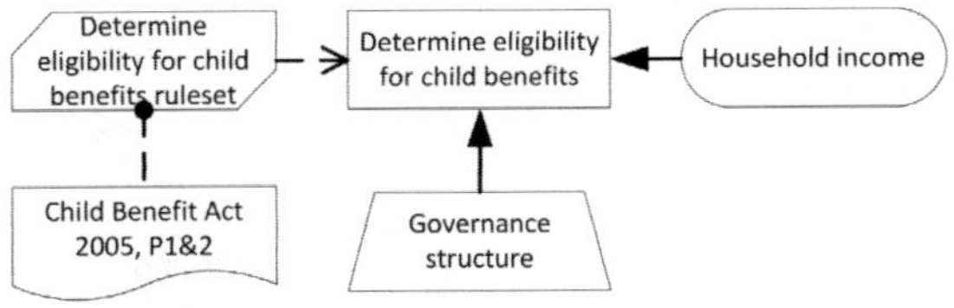

Figure 4. DRD for determining eligibility for child benefits

To demonstrate the usefulness of this template, the governance structure for the scenario in this demonstration is also specified in Table 1. For each variant, the design is changed and depicted in a new table.

Variant 1: Manual human decision-making

TABLE 1. GOVERNANCE STRUCTURE FOR VARIANT ONE

	SF1: Human/ Machine	SF2: Alter-natives	SF3: Veto	SF4: Inform
Input	Human (applicant)	N.A.	N.A.	Always
Recommend	Human (template)	N.A.	N.A.	Never
Agree	Human (manager)	N.A.	N.A.	Never
Decide	Human (employee)	N.A.	N.A.	Always
Perform	Human (employee)	N.A.	N.A.	Always

In the first variant, the applicant fills in a paper template and delivers it to the governmental counter (**Input**). Then, the governmental employee assesses the situation by analyzing the information in the template (**Recommend**) and decides for which benefits the household is eligible (**Decide**) based on a discussion about the case with the manager (**Agree**). In practice, it can be the case that one actor fulfills multiple decision-making roles. When the decision is made, the governmental employee enters the outcome into the governmental system (**Perform**). This allows the applicant to, on a monthly basis, pick up the appointed benefits at the governmental counter. Lastly, the applicant is informed by letter regarding the outcome of the decision and is able to make an appeal within two weeks.

The template used contains information about the different benefits available and thus guides the decision-making for both the input and decide roles.

Variant 2: Machine-supported decision-making

TABLE 2. GOVERNANCE STRUCTURE FOR VARIANT TWO

	SF1: Human/ Machine	SF2: Alter-natives	SF3: Veto	SF4: Inform
Input	Human (applicant)	N.A.	None	Always
Recommend	Machine (system)	One	None	Always
Agree	Human (manager)	N.A.	N.A.	Always
Decide	Human (employee)	N.A.	N.A.	Never
Perform	Machine (system)	N.A.	None	On request

In this variant, the applicant fills in an application template and uploads it to the online governmental portal (**Input**). Then, the government employee receives a notification of the system, which also provides a suggestion (**Recommend**) with regards to the eligibility of the application. The governmental employee decides (**Decide**) based on a discussion about the case with the manager (**Agree**), taking into account the suggestion of the system. Next, the system notifies the applicant and transfers the benefits automatically once a month (**Perform**).

In this variant, the machine generates a suggestion and is provided with the result of the decision as it needs to apply machine-learning to increase and maintain the accuracy of suggestions.

Variant 3: Autonomous decision-making

TABLE 3. GOVERNANCE STRUCTURE FOR VARIANT THREE

	SF1: Human/ Machine	SF2: Alter-natives	SF3: Veto	SF4: Inform
Input	Machine (system)	None	None	Always
Recommend	Machine (system)	None	None	Never
Agree	Human (citizen)	None	30d	Always
Decide	Machine (system)	None	None	On request
Perform	Machine (system)	None	None	Always

In this variant, the citizen's data (all digitally available) is evaluated on a yearly basis by a machine to determine the eligibility for benefits (**Input**). Based on this, the citizen is informed about the pre-filled applications and is able to veto the data in the pre-filled applications or veto the eligibility in general. For this example, the time to veto is one month (**Agree**). When no veto is cast by the citizen, the system decides to process the relevant benefits (**Recommend &**

Decide) and the benefits are automatically transferred once a month (**Perform**).

In the last variant, the citizen is informed about his/her pre-filled and analyzed data on top of the actual confirmation after the benefits are approved after no veto has been cast by the citizen.

The tree variants described provide an overview of a decision-making process, the role distribution between humans and machines, the autonomy of the machine, and SF's that have to be taken into account. The framework can also be applied to guide the creation of a roadmap, as it shows how decision-making processes can be further automated and plan accordingly.

V. Discussion and Conclusion

Since the DMN standard is getting more commonly utilized in practice, more decisions are being modelled explicitly for documentation or automation. However, the current DMN standard does not take into account roles and autonomy regarding decisions and the underlying decision-making process. In this paper, a governance structure framework is being proposed to complement the design and specification of decisions in the DMN standard. To do so, the theoretical constructs of decision-making roles (RAPID) and autonomy levels together with four SFs (LOADAS) are combined. The proposed governance structure framework has been demonstrated using a scenario based on three variants. For each variant, the roles, responsibilities and SF's (human-machine, alternatives, veto and inform) are different. These variants demonstrate that various choices in decision-making processes lead to design considerations that should be taken into account. For example, when machines autonomously decide on what benefits are relevant, what is the best method of informing humans in a specific context, or the appropriate timeframe applicable to veto a decision by a human, in a specific context?

The suggested framework has its limitations. The framework is a suggested solution derived from the existing knowledge base in the area of decision management, decision-making and machine autonomy, and thereby the result of a 'generate design alternative' phase [21]. However, we believe that the proposed framework reached a level of maturity such that it can enter a detailed validation phase. In a planned study, a collection of cases will be used to further validate the framework and to further demonstrate its practical usefulness.

References

[1] Object Management Group, "Decision Model And Notation (DMN), Version 1.1," 2016.

[2] OMG, "ArchiMate® 3.0 Specification," 2016.

[3] P. Rogers and M. Blenko, "Who has the D?," *Harv. Bus. Rev.*, vol. 84, no. 1, pp. 52–61, 2006.

[4] M. Zoet, *Methods and Concepts for Business Rules Management*, 1st ed. Utrecht: Hogeschool Utrecht, 2014.

[5] B. Hnatkowska and J. M. Alvarez-Rodriguez, "Business Rule Patterns Catalog for Structural Business Rules," in *Software Engineering: Challenges and Solutions*, 1st ed., Springer International Publishing, 2017, pp. 3–16.

[6] M. W. Blenko, M. C. Mankins, and P. Rogers, "The Decision-Driven Organization," *Harv. Bus. Rev.*, vol. 88, no. 6, pp. 54–62, Jun. 2010.

[7] J. Beer, A. D. Fisk, and W. A. Rogers, "Toward a framework for levels of robot autonomy in human-robot interaction," *J. Human-Robot Interact.*, vol. 3, no. 2, p. 74, 2014.

[8] R. Parasuraman, T. B. Sheridan, and C. D. Wickens, "A model for types and levels of human interaction with automation," *IEEE Trans. Syst. man, Cybern. A Syst. Humans*, vol. 30, no. 3, pp. 286–297, 2000.

[9] European Commission, "Protection of personal data - GDPR," 2017. [Online]. Available: http://ec.europa.eu/justice/data-protection/. [Retrieved: 03-Feb-2018].

[10] M. R. Endsley and D. B. Kaber, "Level of automation effects on performance, situation awareness and workload in a dynamic control task," *Ergonomics*, vol. 42, no. 3, pp. 462–492, 1999.

[11] H. M. Huang, K. Pavek, B. Novak, J. Albus, and E. Messin, "A framework for autonomy levels for unmanned systems (ALFUS)," in *Proceedings of the AUVSI's Unmanned Systems North America*, 2005, pp. 849–863.

[12] J. Taylor, "Who has the 'D' when the 'D' is automated?," 2007. [Online]. Available: http://www.beyeblogs.com/edmblog/archive/2007/02/who_has_the_d_w_2.php. [Retrieved: 03-Feb-2018].

[13] B. W. Husted and D. B. Allen, "Toward a model of cross-cultural business ethics: The impact of individualism and collectivism on the ethical decision-making process," *J. Bus. Ethics*, vol. 82, no. 2, pp. 293–305, 2008.

[14] A. Ho, "Relational autonomy or undue pressure? Family's role in medical decision-making," *Scand. J. Caring Sci.*, vol. 22, no. 1, pp. 128–135, 2008.

[15] P. S. Scherrer, "Directors' responsibilities and participation in the strategic decision-making process," *Corp. Gov. Int. J. Bus. Soc.*, vol. 3, no. 1, pp. 86–90, 2003.

[16] C. Charles, A. Gafni, and T. Whelan, "Decision-making in the physician-patient encounter: revisiting the shared treatment decision-making model," *Soc. Sci. Med.*, vol. 49, no. 5, pp. 651–661, 1999.

[17] C. Bartneck and J. Forlizzi, "A design-centred framework for social human-robot interaction," in *Proceedings of the 13th IEEE International Workshop on Robot and Human Interactive Communication*, 2004, pp. 591–594.

[18] T. B. Sheridan and W. Verplank, "Human and Computer Control of Undersea Teleoperators," Cambridge, MA, 1978.

[19] M. R. Endsley, "The application of human factors to the development of expert systems for advanced cockpits.," in *Proceedings of the Human Factors Society Annual Meeting*, 1987, pp. 1388–1392.

[20] C. A. Miller and R. Parasuraman, "Designing for flexible interaction between humans and automation: Delegation interfaces for supervisory control," *Hum. Factors*, vol. 49, no. 1, pp. 57–75, 2007.

[21] A. R. Hevner, S. T. March, J. Park, and S. Ram, "Design Science in Information Systems Research," *MISQ.*, vol. 28, no. 1, pp. 75–105, 2004.

Solving Problems by Implementing a Business Rules Management System

A case study towards identifying design problems in Business Rules Management Systems

Sam Leewis
Digital Smart Services
HU University of Applied Sciences Utrecht
Utrecht, The Netherlands
sam.leewis@hu.nl

Koen Smit
Digital Smart Services
HU University of Applied Sciences Utrecht
Utrecht, The Netherlands
koen.smit@hu.nl

Martijn Zoet
Optimizing Knowledge-Intensive Business Processes
Zuyd University of Applied Sciences
Sittard, The Netherlands
martijn.zoet@zuyd.nl

Matthijs Berkhout
Digital Smart Services
HU University of Applied Sciences Utrecht
Utrecht, The Netherlands
matthijs.berkhout@hu.nl

Abstract— **During the timespan of the implementation of a system, the why and what against the actual state of the system can change. This difference is referred to as the design problem. Currently, no design problems are identified in Business Rules Management (BRM) and Business Rules Management System (BRMS) literature. To solve problems with a BRMS implementation it is important that the problems solved by this implementation are known, which is not the case. A case study approach is utilized containing two phases of data collection. Phase one consisted of multiple expert interviews focused on creating a set of design problems utilizing existing literature on BRMS design problems. Then, in phase two, the set of design problems were proposed to a selection of thirteen organizations, which indicated if the design problems occurred in a BRMS implementation. This resulted in a set of 24 design problems. The identification of design problems contributes to future research in evaluating BRMS's. Furthermore, the identification of design problems is a contribution towards situational artifact construction in the field of BRM.**

Keywords-Business Rules; Business Rules Management; Business Rules Management System; Design Problems.

I. INTRODUCTION

Organizations aim for a shorter time to market and lowering the cost of developing and maintaining any information systems to support their operations. Business Rules Management (BRM) technologies play an important role in organizations daily operations [1]–[3]. BRM is defined as: "*a systematic, and controlled approach to get a grip on business decisions and business logic to support the Elicitation, Design, Specification, Verification, Validation, Deployment, Execution, Governance, and Monitoring of both business decisions and business logic.*"[4]. Organizations have or could implement a system to support BRM. This is known as a Business Rules Management System (BRMS), which is defined as: "*a set of software components for the Elicitation, Design, Specification, Verification, Validation, Deployment, Execution, Monitoring, and Governance of business rules*"[5].

An increasing amount of BRMS implementations are executed nowadays, of which many are characterized by complications. The fundamental principle of creating and implementing an artifact is that having an understanding of a design problem and its solution (the capabilities of a BRMS [5]) are acquired in the building and application of an artifact (the BRMS) [6]. Therefore, the problem arises that no design problems are identified in the BRM research field. Compared to neighboring research fields, for example, Business Process Management [7], Software Product Management [8] and Enterprise Architecture [9], were the design problems are identified in detail. To explore the design problems related to BRM, an answer is required on the following research question: *Which design problems can be identified regarding the implementation of a Business Rules Management System?*

The goal of this study is to identify design problems which can be solved by implementing a BRMS. The identification of design problems creates a possibility for organizations to better clarify what problems they have and thereby what solution (e.g., a BRMS) is needed to solve these problems. The identification of design problems can be utilized for situational artifact construction. This technique requires the identification of design problems and uses these design problems to create BRMS instantiations for organizations with different specifics [10][11], for example, government agencies or insurance companies.

The structure of the paper is as follows: First, the context of this study, i.e., business rules, BRM, BRMS, and design problems are addressed. Second, the research method used to identify design problems which are solved by implementing a BRMS are discussed. Next, the data collection and analysis of this research regarding case study research is explained. Subsequently, the results which led to the set of design problems are elaborated. Finally, the conclusions that can be drawn from the results of this research, together with a critical view on the limitations of this research and possible future research possibilities are discussed.

II. RELATED WORK

Business rules describe the state of affairs of what the business demands [3] and the use in business and technology models [12]. A business rule is defined as: "*a statement that defines or constrains some aspect of the business intending to assert business structure or to control the behavior of the business*" [3]. For organizations to be in control of their business rules, an approach is utilized, which is known as BRM. BRM is an approach which contributes to the improved productivity or effectiveness of a Business Rules Management System. Each capability of the BRMS has its own goals and aims to increase the effectiveness and productivity of the BRM activities. The benefits of implementing a BRMS can be translated into design problems. For example, a BRMS is implemented to solve Elicitation productivity problems). In current BRM literature, benefits and advantages of using a BRMS are described in the work of [1]–[3], [13]–[16].

Design problems occurring in organizations are generally defined as "*the differences between a goal state and the current state of a system*" [6].

In the context of this study, this would mean that the current state is not having a BRMS implemented, and the goal state, an implemented BRMS. A specific configuration of the capabilities of a BRMS solve specific problems, the design problems, as demonstrated in Figure 1.

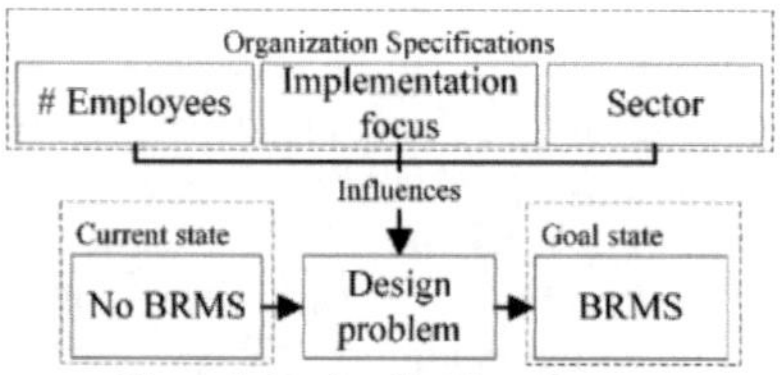

Figure 1. Design Problem Context

Research field maturity can be classified as nascent, intermediate and mature [17]. At the moment, the state of the BRM research field is nascent [16]. Therefore, research from neighboring fields on the identification of design problems is taken into consideration [7]–[9].

III. RESEARCH METHOD

The goal of this research is to identify design problems which occur when organizations implement a BRMS. To reach this goal, design problems which are encountered when implementing a BRMS should be identified. Therefore, a qualitative research approach is the most appropriate research methodology. Case study research is selected so the researchers could gather design problems in a specific context. This all leads towards the explorative nature of the case studies. The organizations included in the case study are distributed over the financial and public sector in the Netherlands. The researchers believe that the organizations from the public and financial sector are representative towards recognizing design problems in BRMS implementations because of their extensive experience with rules, laws, regulations, and compliance. This research includes a holistic case study approach [18], consisting of several reasons of why an organization should implement a BRMS (context), thirteen organizations which implemented a BRMS within the context (cases), and the BRMS design problems (unit of analysis). The data collection consisted of two phases. Phase one is characterized by a combination of first degree and third-degree data collection techniques [19]. The third-degree data collection focused on gathering existing literature on design problems which occur when organizations implement a BRMS. The literature is mainly used to show the existence of benefits and advantages of using a BRMS. The first-degree data collection focused on experts validating the completeness of the set of design problems through expert interviews. Phase two is characterized as a first-degree data collection technique using expert interviews to state which design problem occurred during their BRMS implementation [19].

IV. DATA COLLECTION AND ANALYSIS

Phase one data collection was completed in November 2016. The literature study was focused on identifying the existence of benefits and advantages of implementing a BRMS. The studied literature was used as an indication of the existence of advantages and benefits of which occur when utilizing a BRMS (as shown in Figure 2).

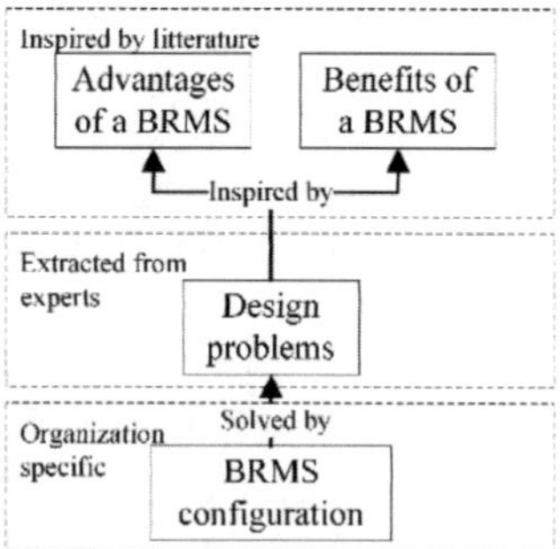

Figure 2. Collection Of Design Problems

These were translated into a set of 24 design problems. The 24 design problems were validated through expert interviews. These expert interviews focused on validating the existence of the design problems and the completeness of the set of design problems derived from literature. Four expert interviews were conducted with an average duration of one hour. Each design problem was proposed to experts and input was asked about whether these were relevant in practice and if the design problem was complete enough to describe the spectrum of design problems that can be solved by implementing a BRMS. The four experts had the following backgrounds: expert 1: a professor with eight years of practical and research experience in the field of BRM and BRMS; expert 2: a lecturer and PhD-candidate with five years of practical and research experience in the field of BRM and

BRMS; expert 3: a Master student with four years of practical and research experience on BRMS capabilities, and expert 4: a BRM and BRMS practitioner with 21 years of experience on multiple BRM and BRMS implementations.

Phase two data collection is completed during a period of four months, between January 2017 and April 2017, through a case study at 13 organizations. The organizations requested that their data is handled anonymously. Therefore, ID's are added ranging from 1 to 13. Participants of this research are selected based on their knowledge towards the studied phenomenon, which are: the group of individuals, organizations, information technology, or community [20]. Translated to this research, the studied phenomenon is represented by organizations and individuals within these specific organizations which deal or that dealt with the implementation of a BRMS. Therefore, are knowledgeable on *why* and *how* a BRMS is implemented. The organizations included in this case study are distributed over the Dutch financial and public sector. These two sectors are selected due to the fact that these organizations have many products and services that are (semi) digitally handled in combination with high numbers of applications. This ensures that large parts of their products and services use business rules. To characterize the 13 organizations, certain situational factors are identified at each organization to create an overview as shown in Table I. The 24 design problems (from phase 1) were proposed, separately, to the participants, thereby creating a list of the occurrences of the known 24 design problems at the thirteen organizations.

TABLE I. CASE STUDY ORGANIZATIONS

Case ID:	Sector:	Employees:	Implementation focus:
1	Public	2001 - 5000	Organization-wide
2	Public	2001 - 5000	Organization-wide
3	Public	>5000	Application focused
4	Public	2001 - 5000	Organization-wide
5	Financial	2001 - 5000	Application focused
6	Financial	2001 - 5000	Line of business focused
7	Financial	501 - 1000	Line of business focused
8	Financial	251 - 500	Line of business focused
9	Financial	>5000	Organization-wide
10	Public	251 - 500	Application focused
11	Public	>5000	Line of business focused
12	Financial	501 - 1000	Organization-wide
13	Public	2001 - 5000	Organization-wide

The employee range of the organizations is identified as a situational factor. These employee ranges could influence different implementation setups. For example, Organization 1, with 2001 - 5000 employees possibly need a different configuration of BRMS capabilities compared to Organization 10 with 251 - 500 employees. The employee ranges are adopted from previously conducted research where design problems are also a topic of research [10][11]. Three main implementation scopes can be identified, which are: Application focused, Line of Business focused and Organization-wide. The work of Nelson et al., [21] demonstrated the scoping from narrow (single application focused) and expanded to Line of Business focused and eventually to Organization-wide. The implementation focus intends to characterize the aim of each separate type of implementation.

V. RESULTS

Phase one and phase two of the data collection resulted in a set of 24 design problems and are validated (on occurrence) by thirteen organizations. The organizations were asked if they recognized one of the design problems as a design problem in their BRMS implementations. The 24 design problems are listed in Table II.

TABLE II. DESIGN PROBLEMS

Design problem #:	Design problem name:
1	Increase Elicitation productivity
2	Increase Elicitation effectiveness
3	Construct library of decisions
4	Ensure artifact relationship insight
5	Reduce Design effort
6	Shortening the Design phase
7	Increase Design productivity
8	Increase Design effectiveness
9	Support experts mobilization
10	Mapping of business rules
11	Improve Validation and Verification quality
12	Ensure automated Verification
13	Reduce Verification effort
14	Increase Verification productivity
15	Increase Verification effectiveness
16	Ensure automated test cases generation
17	Ensure automated Validation testing
18	Perform impact analysis
19	Create validated and accessible business rules
20	Reduce testing for implementation independent and dependent models
21	Reduce Validation effort
22	Ensure working with implementation independent business rules to export models
23	Simplify models into code
24	Separate 'know' and 'flow'

The occurrence of the 24 design problems (DP#) during the BRMS implementations at the 13 organizations is questioned, and this resulted in an occurrence percentage for each design problem together with a description, as shown down below. Most of the design problems affect a BRM capability (Elicitation, Design, Specification, Verification, Validation,

Deployment, Execution, Monitoring, and Governance). These BRM capabilities are explained, in detail, in the work of Smit and Zoet [5].

Design problem 1: Increase Elicitation productivity

DP1 requires a specific configuration of a BRMS to increase the productivity of the Elicitation capability. For example, an implemented BRMS facilitates employees working on Elicitation with the possibility of supporting the comparison of different elicitation sources. 46.15% of the organizations identified this as a known design problem.

Design problem 2: Increase Elicitation effectiveness

DP2 requires a BRMS configuration to increase the effectiveness of the Elicitation capability. For example, an implemented BRMS facilitates the stakeholders of Elicitation with the possibility of automatizing annotations of sources. 76.92% of the organizations identified this as a design problem in their context.

Design problem 3: Construct library of decisions

DP3 requires a BRMS configuration to solve the problem of constructing a library of decisions. For example, an implemented BRMS supports the creation of a library of decisions on one central location. 61.54% of the organizations identified this as a design problem in their context.

Design problem 4: Ensure artifact relationship insight

DP4 requires a BRMS configuration to give insight into relationships between artifacts. For example, an implemented BRMS provides the stakeholders with an estimation of the impact of a to be made term change. 76.92% of the organizations identified this as a design problem in their context.

Design problem 5: Reduce Design effort

DP5 requires a BRMS configuration to reduce the effort needed in the Design capability, specific for the requirements and specifications. For example, an implemented BRMS creates the possibility for the stakeholders of Design to support them by selecting the right rule base automatically. 69.23% of the organizations identified this as a design problem in their context.

Design problem 6: Shortening the Design phase

DP6 requires a BRMS configuration to shorten the Design phase of BRM. For example, an implemented BRMS enables the reuse of decision structures or decisions. 69.23% of the organizations identified this as a design problem in their context.

Design problem 7: Increase Design productivity

DP7 requires a BRMS configuration to increase the productivity of the Design capability. For example, an implemented BRMS reuses patterns by filtering the rule base elements on features, such as type, status, version, and validity. 76.92% of the organizations identified this as a design problem in their context.

Design problem 8: Increase Design effectiveness

DP8 requires a BRMS configuration increase the effectiveness of the Design capability. For example, an implemented BRMS facilitates the stakeholders of Design with the possibility of automatizing the creation of diagrams. 92.31% of the organizations identified this as a design problem in their context.

Design problem 9: Support experts mobilization

DP9 requires a BRMS configuration to support the mobilization of experts involved in the BRM process. For example, an implemented BRMS supports printing reports in a specific format to be used by the involved experts. 69.23% of the organizations identified this as a design problem in their context.

Design problem 10: Mapping of business rules

DP10 requires a BRMS configuration to facilitate the mapping of business rules. For example, an implemented BRMS creates the possibility to link decisions by modeling them together visually. 76.92% of the organizations identified this as a design problem in their context.

Design problem 11: Ensure Validation and Verification quality

DP11 requires a BRMS configuration to ensure the quality assurance of the Validation and Verification capabilities. For example, an implemented BRMS ensures the securing of the quality of Validation and Verification by generating a report. 84.62% of the organizations identified this as a design problem in their context.

Design problem 12: Ensure automated Verification

DP12 requires a BRMS configuration to ensure the automated Verification of business rules. For example, an implemented BRMS ensures automated Verification of redundancy and lexical errors. 61.54% of the organizations identified this as a design problem in their context.

Design problem 13: Reduce Verification effort

DP13 requires a BRMS configuration to reduce the effort needed in the Verification capability. For example, an implemented BRMS creates the possibility for the stakeholders of Verification to suggest repair options. 46.15% of the organizations identified this as a design problem in their context.

Design problem 14: Increase Verification productivity

DP14 requires a BRMS configuration to increase the productivity of the Verification capability. For example, an implemented BRMS facilitates the stakeholders of

Verification by filtering and sorting reports to execute a specific check. 53.85% of the organizations identified this as a design problem in their context.

Design problem 15: Increase Verification effectiveness

DP15 requires a BRMS configuration to increase the effectiveness of the Verification capability. For example, an implemented BRMS facilitates the stakeholders of Verification by displaying the conclusions of other colleagues to check for inconsistencies. 61.54% of the organizations identified this as a design problem in their context.

Design problem 16: Ensure automated test cases generation

DP16 requires a BRMS configuration to create the possibility for the generation of automated test cases in the Validation capability. For example, based on fact types and fact values within the context of scenarios, a number of combinations are tested. 46.15% of the organizations identified this as a design problem in their context.

Design problem 17: Ensure automated Validation testing

DP17 requires a BRMS configuration to perform automated testing in the Validation capability. For example, an implemented BRMS supports the creation of generated test cases to be used for the automated Validation testing. 46.15% of the organizations identified this as a design problem in their context.

Design problem 18: Perform impact analysis

DP18 requires a BRMS configuration to give insight which artifacts are hit when a change is performed. For example, an implemented BRMS gives an overview of the impact of a law change which affects related terms. 69.23% of the organizations identified this as a design problem in their context.

Design problem 19: Create validated and accessible business rules

DP19 requires a BRMS configuration to provide validated and accessible business rules. For example, an implemented BRMS implementation generates a validation report. 84.62% of the organizations identified this as a design problem in their context.

Design problem 20: Reduce testing for implementation independent and dependent models

DP 20 requires a BRMS configuration to reduce the testing of implementation independent models (models not specified to a specific context) and implementation-dependent models (models specified to a specific context). 30.77% of the organizations identified this as a design problem in their context.

Design problem 21: Reduce Validation effort

DP21 requires a BRMS configuration to reduce the effort needed in the Validation capability. For example, an implemented BRMS automatically determines the input and output variables when testing. 53.85% of the organizations identified this as a design problem in their context.

Design problem 22: Ensure working with implementation independent business rules to export models

DP22 requires a BRMS configuration to ensures for implementation independent business rules to export models. For example, an implemented BRMS ensures implementation independent business rules to export models (e.g., Decision Modeling Notation (DMN)). 38.46% of the organizations identified this as a design problem in their context.

Design problem 23: Simplify models into code

DP23 requires a BRMS implementation to simplify converting from models to code. For example, DMN into java code. 61.54% of the organizations identified this as a design problem in their context.

Design problem 24: Separate 'know' and 'flow'

DP24 requires a BRMS configuration to separate the implementation of the 'know' and the 'flow'. For example, an implemented BRMS separates the business logic, business rules, concepts and relations from the business process. 69.23% of the organizations identified this as a design problem in their context.

VI. DISCUSSION AND CONCLUSIONS

The goal of this research is to identify BRMS design problems. To achieve this, the following research question is answered: *''Which design problems can be identified regarding the implementation of a Business Rules Management System?''* In order to identify BRMS design problems, the researchers utilized a case study approach and conducted two phases of data collection. Phase one, aimed at existing literature on advantages and benefits of a BRMS and experts validating the completeness and relatability of the gathered design problems. Phase two focused on validating the set of design problems at thirteen organizations with BRMS implementations. From a research perspective, this research provides a basis upon which future identification of design problems in the field of BRM of related fields can be built. Furthermore, the identification of design problems is a key element for conducting situational artifact construction, due to the fact that situational artifacts are created to solve specific problems, design problems [10]. Therefore, this research contributes towards future situational artifact construction in the BRM domain. From a practical point of view, organizations could benefit from the identified design problems because it provides them with explicit design problems which can be solved by implementing a BRMS. Additionally, organizations can compare problems by using the set of design problems as a reference to their own design problems. Furthermore, the results of this study are used to create a substantiated business case.

Several limitations may affect the results of this research. The first limitation is the sampling technique. The case only existed of organizations drawn from the public and financial sector. We believe that the organizations from the public and financial sector are representative towards recognizing design problems in BRMS implementations. Further increasing the sample including industries other than public and financial organizations is required. The second limitation is that of the lack of any nominal comparison. Additional nominal comparison could be conducted to indicate the importance of identified elements, which design problem affects the implementation of a BRMS [22]. Being that a design problem is a problem (1) or not a problem (0), compared to that of situational factors [16] where there the organizations cannot select their situational factors.

Following these limitations, we believe that future research should incorporate organizations from other industries, to compare occurrences of design problems between sectors. Furthermore, the next recommended step would be using this set of design problems in the context of situational artifact construction in the BRM domain.

REFERENCES

[1] I. Graham, *Business rules management and service oriented architecture a pattern language*, 1st ed. Hoboken, NJ: John Wiley & Sons, 2007.

[2] J. Boyer and H. Mili, *Agile business rule development*. Berlin, Heidelberg: Springer, 2011.

[3] T. Morgan, *Business Rules and Information Systems : Aligning IT with Business Goals*. Boston, MA: Addison-Wesley, 2002.

[4] K. Smit, M. Zoet, and M. Berkhout, "Functional Requirements for Business Rules Management Systems," *Twenty-third Am. Conf. Inf. Syst.*, pp. 1–10, 2017.

[5] K. Smit and M. Zoet, "Management control system for business rules management," *Int. J. Adv. Syst. Meas.*, vol. 9, no. 3, pp. 210–219, 2016.

[6] A. R. Hevner, S. T. March, J. Park, and S. Ram, "Design Science in Information Systems Research," *MIS Q.*, vol. 1, no. 28, pp. 75–105, 2004.

[7] T. Bucher and R. Winter, "Taxonomy of business process management approaches," in *Handbook on Business Process Management*, New York, NY: Springer, 2010, pp. 93–114.

[8] W. Bekkers, I. van de Weerd, S. Brinkkemper, and A. Mahieu, "The Influence of Situational Factors in Software Product Management: An Empirical Study," in *2008 Second International Workshop on Software Product Management*, 2008, no. 21, pp. 43–50.

[9] S. Aier, C. Riege, and R. Winter, "Classification of enterprise architecture scenarios – an exploratory analysis," *Enterp. Model. Inf. Syst. Archit.*, vol. 3, no. 1, pp. 14–23, 2008.

[10] R. Winter, "Problem analysis for situational artefact construction in information systems," in *Emerging themes in information systems and organization studies*, Berlin: Springer, 2011, pp. 97–113.

[11] R. Winter, "Design Solution Analysis for the Construction of Situational Design Methods," in *Engineering Methods in the Service-Oriented Context*, Berlin: Springer, 2011, pp. 19–33.

[12] Business Rules Group, "The Business Rules Manifesto," 2003.

[13] C. J. Date, *What not how: The business rules approach to application development*, 1st ed. Boston, MA: Addison-Wesley, 2000.

[14] R. G. Ross, *Principles of the business rule approach*, 1st ed. Boston, MA: Addison-Wesley Professional, 2003.

[15] B. Von Halle, *Business Rules Applied — Business Better Systems Using the Business Rules Approach*. New York, NY: John Wiley & Sons, 2002.

[16] M. Zoet, *Methods and Concepts for Business Rules Management*. Utrecht: Hogeschool Utrecht, 2014.

[17] A. C. Edmondson and S. E. Mcmanus, "Methodological Fit in Management Field Research," *Acad. Manag. Rev.*, vol. 32, no. 4, pp. 1155–1179, 2007.

[18] R. K. Yin, *Case Study Research: Design and Methods, 5th edition*, 5th ed. London: SAGE Publications Ltd., 2013.

[19] P. Runeson and M. Höst, "Guidelines for conducting and reporting case study research in software engineering," *Empir. Softw. Eng.*, vol. 14, no. 2, pp. 131–164, 2009.

[20] A. Strauss and J. Corbin, *Basics of Qualitative Research: Techniques and Procedures for Developing Grounded Theory*, 3rd ed., vol. 3. Thousand Oaks, CA: SAGE Publications Ltd., 2015.

[21] M. L. Nelson, J. Peterson, R. L. Rariden, and R. Sen, "Transitioning to a business rule management service model: Case studies from the property and casualty insurance industry," *Inf. Manag.*, vol. 47, no. 1, pp. 30–41, 2010.

[22] J. Mahoney, "Nominal, Ordinal, and Narrative Appraisal in Macrocausal Analysis," *Am. J. Sociol.*, vol. 104, no. 4, pp. 1154–1196, 1999.

A Tool for Analyzing Business Rules Management Solution Implementations

Sam Leewis
Digital Smart Services
HU University of Applied Sciences Utrecht
Utrecht, The Netherlands
sam.leewis@hu.nl

Koen Smit
Digital Smart Services
HU University of Applied Sciences Utrecht
Utrecht, The Netherlands
koen.smit@hu.nl

Martijn Zoet
Optimizing Knowledge-Intensive Business Processes
Zuyd University of Applied Sciences
Sittard, The Netherlands
martijn.zoet@zuyd.nl

***Abstract*— Evaluating an (implemented) Business Rules Management Solution (BRMS) is not a frequently conducted process within organizations. A tool is needed, which supports this process and supports future BRMS implementations. A literature study is conducted on the relevant building blocks of a BRMS. The results are validated through qualitative expert interviews. This resulted in the BRMS analysis tool that can be utilized to structure the analysis for one or multiple BRMS implementations. Next, the BRMS analysis tool is applied at 13 organizations that implemented a BRMS. The BRMS analysis tool provides the BRMS implementation stakeholders with a tool that structures, in a systematic and controlled way, that is capable to analyze a BRMS implementation for one or multiple organizations. This research contributes to structured and managed information which is important for better business and IT alignment. Furthermore, structured and managed information contributes towards the easier creation of a business case.**

Keywords-Business Rules Management; Business Rules Management Solution; Implementation; Analysis tool

I. INTRODUCTION

The increasing number of business rules, the pace at which the business rules change, the different types of business rules, the necessity to execute business rules consistently and being transparent towards external stakeholders produce many challenges for organizations [1][2]. A business rule is defined as ''*a statement that defines or constrains some aspect of the business. It is intended to assert business structure or to control or influence the behavior of the business.*'' [3]. A systematic and controlled approach is required to get a grip on these business rules, which is known as Business Rules Management (BRM) [4]–[6]. BRM is defined as "*a systematic, and controlled approach to get a grip on business decisions and business logic to support the Elicitation, Design, Specification, Verification, Validation, Deployment, Execution, Governance, and Monitoring of both business decisions and business logic.*"[7]. The solution supporting implementing this method in a practical context is known as a Business Rules Management Solution (BRMS). A BRMS is a configuration of capabilities which supports the Elicitation, Design, Specification, Verification, Validation, Deployment, Execution, Monitoring, and Governance of business rules. Both the BRM System and BRMS support Business Rules Management as a method. A distinction is needed between a BRM System and a BRMS. A BRM System is ''*a set of software components for the Elicitation, Design, Specification, Verification, Validation, Deployment, Execution, Monitoring, and Governance of business rules*''[5]. The BRMS contains the BRM System as a whole together with the utilization of the capabilities (e.g., the processes, data models).

BRMS research is part of the IS research field. In the IS field it is not a habit to publish work on questionnaires or surveys, contrary to the alpha sciences where this is usually the case [8]–[10]. Publishing created and validated questionnaires shows a level of transparency and can thereby be utilized by other researchers for future research. Furthermore, the field of BRM lacks research focused on the organizational implementation of a BRMS and is more focused on the technical aspects of a BRMS implementation [1][11]. This research contributes to the knowledge on the organizational implementation of a BRMS by providing a tool that creates the possibility to structure, in a systematic and controlled way, the analysis of a BRMS implementation. The existing research focused on BRM maturity models is relatable towards BRMS implementations [11]–[13]. Therefore, it is not possible to structure data focused on analyzing a BRMS implementation. To utilize such data, it needs to be structured into information [14]. The BRMS analysis tool provides that structure. A BRMS implementation is more than only data and information; knowledge is an important element as well. Davenport and Prusak [15] state that: ''*Knowledge can and should be evaluated by the decisions or actions to which it leads*''. This research provides organizations with a tool that structures the data collection process on how to have the most optimal configuration of a BRMS for an organization with different specifications. The business rules and the Business Rules Management definition define ''structure'' as an important element when dealing with data and information, which is also supported by Davenport and Prusak's work on data and information [14]. The BRMS analysis tool provides ''*structure*'' in a ''*systematic*'' and ''*controlled*'' way when analyzing a BRMS implementation for one or multiple organizations.

Furthermore, the BRMS analysis tool provides organizations with the option to get to know more about the current or completed BRMS implementation, which can lead to the improvement of the current or possible future implementations.

Multiple problems exist in the BRM research field: 1) no structure in the data collection process on how to have the most optimal configuration of a BRM Solution for an organization given their characteristics, 2) no possibility exists to get to know more about the current or completed BRMS implementation, and 3) no tool exists which supports the gathering of cases used in situational artefact construction in the BRM field. The situational artifact construction technique requires an input of different situations for the creation of a situational artifact [16].

The remainder of the paper is structured as follows: First, the research methods that were utilized to create the BRMS analysis tool are discussed. Second, this is followed by the construction of the BRMS analysis tool, which was the result of a literature study. Subsequently, the BRMS analysis tool is validated through expert interviews and by utilizing the BRMS analysis tool on 13 organizations, distributed over the Dutch public and Dutch financial sector. Lastly, the conclusions are provided that can be drawn from the results, together with a critical view towards the used research methods and the results of this study followed by possible future research directions.

II. RESEARCH METHOD

In this research, structured interviews are utilized to gather BRMS implementation cases, focused on the specific configuration of the BRMS elements (the *what?*) and specific problems that the implementation of BRMS should solve (the *why?*). The BRMS analysis tool is constructed with the use a literature review, containing relevant building blocks of a BRMS and its implementation (building blocks are elements of which a BRMS consists of). The questionnaire is validated through expert interviews with experts from the BRM community. The experts are chosen on their experience and knowledge in the field of BRM and BRMS. The experts consisted of a professor lecturing and performing research in the field of BRM and BRMS (expert 1), a lecturer and PhD with practical and research experience in the field of BRM and BRMS (expert 2), and a master-student with 3 years of practical and research experience on BRMS capabilities (expert 3). All the interviews were conducted in a controlled environment and each interview had a length of around 90 minutes.

III. THE BRMS ANALYSIS TOOL CONSTRUCTION

The BRMS analysis tool [17] consists of the building blocks of a BRMS containing questions related to that specific building block. The following subsections contain literature supporting the construction BRMS building blocks. The upcoming subsections are referring to questions in the BRMS analysis tool by ''Q#''.

A. Organizational characteristics

The organization information section retrieves specific organizational characteristics and are identified as situational factors. These questions are focused on retrieving the sector, the number of employees, and the scope of the BRMS implementation of the organization. Q2 retrieves the number of employees of the organization at which the implementation is conducted. These number of employees could influence different implementation setups. Example: Organization A with <50 employees possibly needs a different setup of BRMS capabilities than Organization B with >5000 employees. The employee numbers are adopted from previous questionnaires conducted in comparable studies in other research fields [6][16]. Q3 intends to retrieve the organizational scope at which the BRMS implementation is conducted. Three main organizations scopes can be identified, which are: Application focused, Line of Business focused and Organization-wide. This is supported by the work of Nelson et al. [11], which showed the scoping from narrow (single application focused) and expanded to Line of Business focused and eventually to Organization-wide. This question intends to retrieve data about what the scope was of the BRMS implementation conducted by the organization.

B. Characterization of Business Rules Management

The characterization of BRM section (Q4) defines how and why organizations are using BRM and a BRMS. In other words, the benefits or advantages of a BRMS [1]–[3], [18], [19]. Similar questionnaires in other research fields also propose a characterization section and therefore, for this tool, this is also adopted [6][16].

C. Business Rules Management Solution Building Blocks

This section will contain the building blocks of a BRMS. Each building block correlates with one of the nine BRM capabilities, which are addressed in detail in the work of Smit and Zoet [5], and Zoet and Versendaal [6]. Each building block has a specific set of questions which are unique to each building block and thereby creating possible different BRMS configurations.

Elicitation

The elicitation capability determines the knowledge, which realizes the value proposition of the business rules. This knowledge needs to be captured from various sources including, but not limited to, laws and regulations. The second goal of the elicitation capability is to conduct an impact analysis. This is only performed when a business rule architecture is already in place [5], [20].

Q6 extracts what sources are used for the elicitation capability at a specific organization. For example, Subject-Experts (people), existing organization regulations and guidelines (documents), existing database data, or a combination of the previously mentioned examples. Besides extracting what sources are used during elicitation retrieving if these sources are actually stored for possible future use is covered in Q7.

Q7 is focused on retrieving if this capability is actually used as it was intended to be used. The possibility exists that only data is extracted and nothing is done with the sources that are used for extracting data. Extra effort is needed when new business rules should be created because of the change in laws or regulations. The stored sources can be used for the type of analysis retrieved in Q8.

Q8 measures which type of analysis (source analysis and scenario analysis) is applied in the elicitation capability. Source analysis compares sources (e.g., parliament documents versus organization regulations) with each other, determines where the source is from and whether the source is reliable or not [20]. Scenario analysis is the development and comparison of possible business scenarios [20], [21]. A combination of both source and scenario analysis is also a possibility, also known as a hybrid.

Originally, impact analysis should be performed in the design capability. Nonetheless, the BRM experts state that, in practice, this is also performed in the elicitation capability (Q9). Impact analysis is conducted when there already is a business rule architecture in place [5], [20].

Design

The output of the design capability is the business rule architecture and contains a combination of context designs and derivation structures [5], [20].

Q10 is focused on retrieving if the 5 V's (value, velocity, volume, variety, and veracity) are taken into account when implementing the design capability. The Big Data five V's [22] are adopted and altered to the field of BRM. The BRM 5 V's depict the value, velocity, volume, variety, and veracity of a decision. Besides these five dimensions concerning decisions, good decision-making also depends on the assignment of specific and clear roles.

Rogers and Blenko [23] created the RAPID model to clarify the decision-making process (Q11). RAPID stands for Recommend, Agree, Perform, Input and Decide. Recommend, people carrying this role are responsible for gathering input, and proving the correct data to ensure a sensible decision in a correct and timely order. Agree, people in this role have the responsibility to state if the recommendation is good or not, respond with yes or no or, in other words, the so-called right to veto the recommendation. Perform, someone or multiple people have the responsibility of executing the decision, once the decision is made. Input, the role of input is consulted on the decision. Decision, the person in the deciding role is the formal decision maker.

Same as in the elicitation capability, Q12 is focused on retrieving if an impact analysis is conducted when there already is a business rule architecture in place. The impact analysis provides the organization with an overview of which artifacts within a business rules architecture are hit when a change or the addition of a new artifact occurs.

Specification

The specification capability specifies the content of each separate context design. [5], [20]. Specifying business rules in models is based on the idea that humans should not use a programming language to write code, but instead, should create models from which code is generated [24]. In this case (Q13), the business rules (and the underlying elements of the business rule) are specified with the use of models. An example of such a modeling language is the Decision Model and Notation (DMN) [25]. Specifying business rules in text is based on the premise that business rules are specified with the use of different types of languages. Any form of language ranges from programming code to natural language. In this case, the business rules are specified in any form of text. Examples of this are the Dutch language and Semantics of Business Vocabulary and Business Rules (SVBR) [26]. The language retrieved in Q13 is implemented in the rule engine. Q14 is focused on retrieving if the language used in the specification capability is implemented in the rules engine without any influence of a person, thereby ensuring that the language used in the capability only has one meaning. Therefore, being unambiguous.

Verification

The verification capability checks for semantic and syntax errors in the created business rule architecture [5], [27].

Semantic and syntax errors need to be detected to prevent future problems in the business rule architecture. This is supported by the IT Controls Automation Strategy of Tarantino [28] which shows in what degree the control system is automated. The IT Controls Automation Strategy is adopted by Smit, Zoet, and Versendaal [27] for the BRM field and therefore used in Q15 and measures the degree of automation of the verification capability. The matrix consists of four archetypes 1) manual - detection, 2) automatic - detection, 3) manual - prevention, and 4) automatic - prevention of verification errors in business decisions and business logic. Manual - detection is the element where employees manually check for possible errors and report back to the author of the business logic if any errors were found. Automatic - detection is the element that is defined as a system that checks the business logic after its creation and reports back in the form of a list of identified errors. Manual - prevention is the element that employees are always authoring business logic together with the author and manually intervene when an error is made, enforcing the business logic author to correct the error. Automatic - prevention is the element which is applied by the system, suggesting or enforcing certain behavior regarding the authoring of business logic to prevent errors.

Validation

The validation capability checks the value proposition for possible errors in its intended behavior [5], [27].

Q16 is focused on retrieving what type of validation (peer review, scenario validation, and source validation) is used in a certain BRMS configuration. Peer review is the validation of work by colleagues of similar expertise and competence to the authors of the work. In the case of peer review, a colleague (peer) checks if the artifacts are similar to its sources. When errors are identified that artifact is rejected and the capability cycle (elicitation, design, specification, and verification) starts from the beginning [27], the sequence depends on the identified error. Scenario validation is a validation method that uses hypothetical stories to support the tester through a test system or complex system. In the case of a BRMS, scenario validation makes use of all possible business scenarios. Source validation validates with the use of actual sources (laws and regulations) [27]. The types of validation are controlling on a specific set of quality attributes, different in each BRMS implementation, which are retrieved in Q17.

Q17 is focused on retrieving whether the validation capability controls with the following quality attributes in mind [29]: traceability, completeness, accuracy, and usability. Traceability is the ability to provide an audit trail of access to the business rule and of any changes made to the business rule. Traceability provides organizations with the ability to verify history, location, or the application of a business rule by means of documented identification. Completeness indicates which data (element) need to be registered regarding the objects within the process. Accuracy indicates the degree to which the stored data reflects the reality concerning an object, thereby describing the closeness of a measurement to the true value. Usability indicates the ease of use and learnability of the business rule. These four quality attributes are selected because of the relevance in the BRM field [19].

Deployment

The deployment capability transforms implementation-independent business rules to implementation-dependent executable business rules. The stakeholders of this capability can be both human and a system [1]. During that data collection phase no specific questions where identified for the deployment capability.

Execution

The execution capability processes and executes the Implementation-dependent rules that were transformed in the deployment capability. The realization of the added value is conducted by executing the business rules by (a combination of) information system or human actors [1].

Q18 is focused on retrieving if the principle of gaming is taken into consideration. Gaming gives the user of the system the possibility to generate any desired result by trial and error [30]. For example, a user working with a BRMS in the governmental sector needs a custom solution for a citizen, in this case, the result is more important than the way it is executed. Therefore, the user is ''gaming the system'' to generate the desired result. Gaming also has a negative side because the possibility exists that the user of the system is doing this for all the wrong reasons. Besides the possibility of ''gaming the system'' the execution capability can be configured to store input data, output data, and executed rules.

Q19 retrieves what specific data is stored during the execution. Stored data can be categorized in input data, output data, and executed rules. Input data is the data that is required to execute the business rules. Output data is the stored data and the outcome of the executed business rules.

Monitoring

The monitoring capability monitors the execution of the value proposition and the full range of activities part of the BRM capabilities that realize the value proposition [1].

Q20 is focused on retrieving what is being evaluated in the monitoring capability. The BRM Key Performance Indicators are adopted from the work of Smit and Zoet [5] to measure what is being evaluated in the monitoring capability. The unit of measurement used in the question is the frequency of the evaluation of the KPI's. For example, evaluation of the KPI's could be applied on a daily, monthly or yearly basis or a combination of such frequencies. The possibility exists that there are differences in the frequency of evaluation between sectors. The existing set of KPI's is limited because of the small sample size and the industry where it was focused on (public). The authors of the earlier mentioned work state that the government institutions are representative towards organizations implementing BRMS [5].

Governance

The governance capability contains three sub-capabilities: version management, validity management, and traceability management [3], [5].

Q23 is focused on retrieving which sub-capabilities (version management, validity management, and traceability management) of the governance capability are implemented during the BRMS implementation. The purpose of the version management capability is capturing and keeping track of elements which are created or modified in the other eight capabilities. The purpose of validity management is to create the possibility to provide a specific version of a value proposition at any given moment of time. The purpose of the traceability capability is to ensure the possibility to trace created elements to their corresponding laws and regulations. Furthermore, the traceability capability creates a foundation for impact analysis when, for example, new laws are needed to be processed into value propositions. Alternatively, a combination of the options mentioned above.

D. Leader of the capability

The business rules task/service model from [11] identifies three areas within a firm relevant when dealing with the responsibility of working with a BRMS: IT, Business and a Central IT/Business group. Q24 focusses on retrieving which area has the responsibility of a specific capability. The model provides high-level services, and functions focused on a BRMS as a whole. Focusing more on the capabilities of a BRMS, different responsibilities of capabilities connect with different areas. Often the technical-oriented capabilities of a BRMS are more IT related and management-oriented capabilities are more related to the Business.

E. Autonomy

Coming into the era of computer automatization, the possibilities are growing where computers take over some tasks or whole processes from humans [31]. The same is possible with some of the capabilities of a BRMS. Therefore, the question is asked what the level of autonomy of the machine within the confines of the implemented capability runs. Measuring the degree of autonomy can be performed with ten degrees of autonomy [31]. Q25 is focused on retrieving on what degree of autonomy the machine within the confines of the capability runs. The degree of autonomy ranges from level 1, the computer does not help, and humans must do everything, to level 10, the computer takes a decision independently without any intervention from humans.

IV. BRMS ANALYSIS TOOL VALIDATION

Validation is required to ensure the correctness of the created BRMS analysis tool. A selection is made from experts from the BRM community. The group of experts existed of a professor conducting research focused on utilizing BRM, a Ph.D. student conducting research in the BRM domain, and a master student with research and practical experience in the BRM domain. The interviews were focused on the completeness and the relatability to practice of the concepts, themes, and questions. All the elements of the questionnaire were discussed and validated on completeness and relatability in practice. The experts gave examples of what should be included in a questionnaire on implementing BRMSs. This resulted in comparable structure and content as compared to the BRMS analysis tool created out of literature. Elements adopted from comparable questionnaires which handle the same problem in a different research field were not mentioned during the expert interview. Nonetheless, these elements were still included in the BRMS analysis tool for the sole reason that previous work, conducted in this field, has proven useful [16], [32].

To further validate the BRMS analysis tool, a pilot test is conducted where the BRMS analysis tool is implemented at 13 organizations. This BRMS analysis tool aims at experts with experience in implementing BRMS. The groups consist of members distributed over a wide range organizations, mostly from the public and finance sector. An interview approach is used for the implementation of the BRMS analysis tool [33]. The data is gathered from different organizations distributed over the financial (n=6) and public sector (n=7). Employee ranges included 251 – 500 (n=2), 501 – 1000 (n=2), 2001 – 5000 (n=6), and >5000 (n=3). The implementation focus added an additional characterization of the BRMS implementation cases. The implementation focusses are divided into Application focus (n=3), Line of business-focused (n=4), and Organization-wide (n=6).

V. DISCUSSION AND CONCLUSIONS

The goal of this research is to create a tool that structures, in a systematic and controlled way, the data collection process on how to have the most optimal configuration of a BRMS for an organization with different specifications. Furthermore, the BRMS analysis tool provides organizations with the option to get to know more about the current or completed BRMS implementation. This can lead to the improvement of the current or possible future implementations. The BRMS analysis tool included important BRMS building blocks gathered from literature and expert opinion. The BRMS analysis tool is validated through expert interviews and implemented using a sample of 13 organizations distributed over the Dutch public and financial sector.

From a research point of view, this study provides a fundament for situational artifact construction in the BRM field and related fields. Gathering different implementations to eventually create a situational artifact is deemed as an important phase in situational artifact construction [16]. Furthermore, this study brings the building blocks of a BRMS implementation together in a BRMS analysis tool. From a practical perspective, this study provides organizations with a tool that structures, in a systematic and controlled way, the data collection process on different BRMS configurations an organization with different specifications.

Several limitations may affect the results of this study. The first limitation is the sample of the validation of the BRMS analysis tool. This sample is limited to three experts and to state with confidence that the elements included in the BRMS analysis tool are the only needed elements in such a technique, more experts need to be included for the validation of the BRMS analysis tool. The second limitation is that of the implementation of the BRMS analysis tool. The implementation is limited to only 13 organizations distributed over the public and financial sector. We believe that the public and financial organizations are representable towards other organizations, although additional organizations from other industries are recommended to increase the representability of the sample. Furthermore, the addition of new possible technologies could affect the completeness of the BRMS analysis tool, and continuous research is needed on the validity and relevance of the elements of the BRMS analysis tool.

REFERENCES

[1] J. Boyer and H. Mili, *Agile business rule*

development. Berlin, Heidelberg: Springer, 2011.

[2] I. Graham, *Business rules management and service oriented architecture a pattern language*, 1st ed. Hoboken, NJ: John Wiley & Sons, 2007.

[3] T. Morgan, *Business Rules and Information Systems : Aligning IT with Business Goals*. Boston, MA: Addison-Wesley, 2002.

[4] M. W. Blenko, M. C. Mankins, and P. Rogers, "The Decision-Driven Organization," *Harv. Bus. Rev.*, no. june, p. 10, 2010.

[5] K. Smit and M. Zoet, "Management control system for business rules management," *Int. J. Adv. Syst. Meas.*, vol. 9, no. 3, pp. 210–219, 2016.

[6] M. Zoet and J. Versendaal, "Business Rules Management Solutions Problem Space: Situational Factors," in *Pacific Asia Conference on Information Systems 2013 (PACIS)*, 2013, p. 247.

[7] K. Smit, M. Zoet, and M. Berkhout, "Functional Requirements for Business Rules Management Systems," *Twenty-third Am. Conf. Inf. Syst.*, pp. 1–10, 2017.

[8] P. J. Cooper, M. J. Taylor, Z. Cooper, and C. G. Fairburn, "The Development and Validation of the Body Shape Questionnaire The Development and Validation of the Body Shape Questionnaire," *Int. J. Eat. Disord.*, vol. 6, no. 4, pp. 485–494, 1987.

[9] L. R. Derogatis, K. Rickels, and a F. Rock, "The SCL-90 and the MMPI: a step in the validation of a new self-report scale.," *Br. J. Psychiatry*, vol. 128, pp. 280–289, 1976.

[10] T. J. Meyer, M. L. Miller, R. L. Metzger, and T. D. Borkovec, "Development and validation of the penn state worry questionnaire," *Behav. Res. Ther.*, vol. 28, no. 6, pp. 487–495, 1990.

[11] M. L. Nelson, J. Peterson, R. L. Rariden, and R. Sen, "Transitioning to a business rule management service model: Case studies from the property and casualty insurance industry," *Inf. Manag.*, vol. 47, no. 1, pp. 30–41, 2010.

[12] B. Von Halle and L. Goldberg, *The Business Rule Revolution*. Silicon Valley: Happy About, 2006.

[13] B. Von Halle and L. Goldberg, *The Decision Model: A business logic framework linking business and technology*. New York, NY: Taylor and Francis Group, LLC, 2009.

[14] T. Davenport and L. Prusak, *Working Knowledge*, 2nd ed. Brighton, MA: Harvard Business Review Press, 2000.

[15] T. Davenport and L. Prusak, "Working Knowledge How Organization Manage What They Know," *Harvard Bus. Sch. Press*, no. January 1998, p. 15, 1998.

[16] R. Winter, "Problem analysis for situational artefact construction in information systems," in *Emerging themes in information systems and organization studies*, Berlin: Springer, 2011, pp. 97–113.

[17] S. Leewis, K. Smit, M. Zoet, and M. Berkhout, "BRMS analysis tool," 2017. [Online]. Available: https://goo.gl/f9ems3.

[18] B. Von Halle, *Business Rules Applied — Business Better Systems Using the Business Rules Approach*. New York, NY: John Wiley & Sons, 2002.

[19] M. Zoet, *Methods and Concepts for Business Rules Management*. Utrecht: Hogeschool Utrecht, 2014.

[20] K. Smit, M. Zoet, and J. Versendaal, "Identifying Challenges In BRM Implementations Regarding The Elicitation, Design And Specification Capabilities At Governmental Institutions," in *Twenty-Fifth European Conference on Information Systems (ECIS)*, 2017, p. 14.

[21] D. A. Aaker, *Strategic market management*. Hoboken, NJ: John Wiley & Sons, 2008.

[22] A. McAfee and E. Brynjolfsson, "Big Data. The management revolution," *Harvard Buiness Rev.*, vol. 90, no. 10, pp. 61–68, 2012.

[23] P. Rogers and M. Blenko, "Who Has the D?," *Harv. Bus. Rev.*, vol. 84, no. 1, pp. 52–61, 2006.

[24] L. Bass, P. Clements, and R. Kazman, *Software architecture in practice*, 3rd ed. Boston, MA: Addison-Wesley, 2012.

[25] Object Management Group, "Decision Model and Notation," 2014.

[26] Object Management Group, "Semantics of Business Vocabulary and Business Rules," 2013.

[27] K. Smit, M. Zoet, and J. Versendaal, "Identifying challenges in BRM implementations regarding the verification and validation," in *Twenty First Pacific Asia Conference on Information Systems*, 2017, p. 4.

[28] A. Tarantino, *Governance, risk, and compliance handbook: technology, finance, environmental, and international guidance and best practices*. Hoboken, NJ: John Wiley & Sons, 2008.

[29] A. Rula, A. Maurino, and C. Batini, *Data and Information Quality: Dimensions, Principles and Techniques*, 1st ed. New York, NY: Springer, 2016.

[30] G. Bevan and C. Hood, "What's measured is what matters: Targets and gaming in the English public health care system," *Public Adm.*, vol. 84, no. 3, pp. 517–538, 2006.

[31] R. Parasuraman, T. B. Sheridan, and C. D. Wickens, "A model for types and levels of human interaction with automation.," *IEEE Trans. Syst. Man. Cybern. A Syst. Hum.*, vol. 30, no. 3, pp. 286–297, 2000.

[32] T. Bucher and R. Winter, "Taxonomy of business process management approaches," in *Handbook on Business Process Management*, New York, NY: Springer, 2010, pp. 93–114.

[33] P. R. Newsted, S. L. Huff, and M. C. Munro, "Survey Instruments in Information Systems," *MIS Q.*, vol. 22, no. 4, p. 553, 1998.

A New Explorative Model to Assess the Financial Credit Risk Assessment

Eric Mantelaers
Optimizing Knowledge-Intensive Business Processes
Zuyd University of Applied Sciences
Sittard, the Netherlands
eric.mantelaers@zuyd.nl

Martijn Zoet
Optimizing Knowledge-Intensive Business Processes
Zuyd University of Applied Sciences
Sittard, the Netherlands
martijn.zoet@zuyd.n

***Abstract*—In recent years, Financial Credit Risk Assessment (FCRA) has become an increasingly important issue within the financial industry. Therefore, the search for features that can predict the credit risk of an organization has increased. Using multiple statistical techniques, a variance of features has been proposed. Applying a structured literature review, 238 papers have been selected. From the selected papers, 700 features have been identified. The features have been analyzed with respect to the type of feature, the information sources needed and the type of organization that applies the features. Based on the results of the analysis, the features have been plotted in the FCRA Model. The results show that most features focus on hard information from a transactional source, based on official information with a high latency. The main contribution of this paper is the FCRA Model combined with the plotted results, indicating multiple questions for further research.**

Keywords-Financial Credit Risk Assessment; Business Failure Prediction; Credit Risk Features; DMN Requirements Diagrams (DRD).

I. INTRODUCTION

Within the field of the Financial Credit Risk Assessment (FCRA) there are two main areas of interest. Credit rating (or scoring) is used to solve the problem to label companies as bad/good credit or bankrupt/healthy. Credit rating is used not only internally for screening borrowers, pricing loans and managing credit risk thereafter, but also externally for calibrating regulatory capital requirements [1]. Bankruptcy (failure) prediction (or business failure prediction or going concern assessment) is intended to predict the probability that the company may belong to a high-risk group or may become bankrupt during the following year(s). Both of them are strongly related and solved in a similar way, namely as a binary classification task. In this paper, both categories of problems are collectively called Financial Credit Risk Assessment, which is a business decision-making problem that is relevant for creditors, auditors, senior management, bankers and other stakeholders.

Financial Credit Risk Assessment is a domain which has been studied for many decades. According to Balcaen and Ooghe [2], there are four main areas with reference to Financial Credit Risk Assessment: (1) Classical paradigm (arbitrary definition of failure, non-stationarity and data instability, sampling selectivity), (2) Neglect of the time dimension of failure (use of one single observation, fixed score output/concept of resemblance/descriptive nature, failure not seen as a process), (3) Application focus (variable selection, selection of modelling method), (4) Other problems (use of a linear classification rule, use of annual account information, neglect of multidimensional nature of failure). The literature on Financial Credit Risk Assessment and business failure dates back to the 1930's [27]. Watson and Everett [3] described five categories to define failure: 1) ceasing to exist (discontinuance for any reason), 2) closing or a change in ownership, 3) filing for bankruptcy, 4) closing to limit losses and 5) failing to reach financial goals. When the Financial Credit Risk Assessment is negative, it is called business failure, which is a general term and, according to a widespread definition, it is the situation that a firm cannot pay lenders, preferred stock shareholders, suppliers, etc., or a bill is overdrawn, or the firm is bankrupt according to the law [4]. There is extensive literature in which this topic has been researched from the perspective of auditors or bankers. On the other hand, rare literature can be found about related literature from an information and decision perspective. The features (variables) which are relevant in the field of Financial Credit Risk Assessment will be analyzed in this paper. In this paper the focus will be on the auditor's, bankers and crediting rating firms, hence forward the term financial industry will be used to describe all three. A combination will be made between the financial industry and an information and decision perspective.

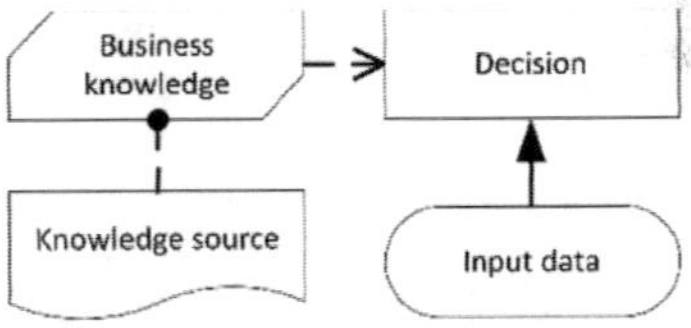

Figure 1. DRD-level elements

To do so, the DRD model will be used. The reason DMN is used is because it is currently the standard to model decisions. In September 2015, the Object Management Group (OMG) [5] released a new standard for modelling decisions and underlying business logic, DMN (Decision Model and Notation). The DMN standard is based on two levels; the Decision Requirements Diagram (DRD) level and the Decision Logic Level (DLL). The DRD level consists of four concepts that are used to capture essential information with regards to decisions: 1) the decision, 2) business knowledge, which represents the collection of business logic required to execute the decision, 3) input data, and 4) a knowledge source, which enforces how the decision should be taken by influencing the underlying business logic. The contents of the DLL are represented by the business knowledge container in the DRD level.

The remainder of this paper is organized as follows. Section II contains a description of relevant literature regarding features and feature selection with reference to Financial Credit Risk Assessment, from a combined perspective of both the financial industry and information and decision analysts, followed by the research method in Section III. In Section IV, our data collection and analysis will be reported. Subsequently, in Section V, a presentation of the results derived from the applied data analysis techniques will be given. The conclusion (Section VI) closes the article.

II. LITERATURE REVIEW

Feature selection is a critical step in Financial Credit Risk Assessment. Features (or variables or attributes) can be irrelevant, redundant or useful. There are several alternative methodologies for feature selection. Tsai [6] compares five well-known feature selection methods used in bankruptcy prediction, which are: 1) *t*-test, 2) correlation matrix, 3) stepwise regression, 4) Principle Component Analysis (PCA) and 5) factor analysis.

From a DMN perspective, a feature can either be a decision or an input data element. The choice between which element is used depends on one characteristic: derivation. Must the features be derived from other features then it is depicted as decision, for example expected market growth and, honesty in negotiation of human resources motivation. If the feature can be retrieved from a database or document, it is an input data element, for example retained earnings/total assets, or Total debt/total assets. Feature selection refers to the process that reduces the feature space and selects an optimum subset of relevant features. Three possible methods can be distinguished: human, statistical and hybrid. Statistically, there are two alternative approaches available. The first assesses the attributes in terms of measures independent of the learning algorithm that will be used. This is called the 'filter' approach. The second evaluates the subset according to the method that will ultimately be used for learning. This approach is called 'wrapper' [7]. There are two broad categories of techniques applied in Financial Credit Risk Assessment: statistical techniques and the (state-of-the-art) intelligent techniques. In the earliest research on Financial Credit Risk Assessment (FitzPatrick [27] and the well-known Altman models [8]) they used quantitative (hard) financial data. Besides these hard data, qualitative (soft) data are used [9]. The early studies for Financial Credit Risk Assessment were univariate (a specific statistical method applied) studies which had important implications for future model development.

These laid the groundwork for multivariate studies. Ravi Kumar and Ravi [10] identify statistical and intelligent techniques to solve the bankruptcy prediction problem. For each type of technique, they describe the way they work. Chen, Ribeiro and Chen [11] summarize the traditional statistical models and state-of-the-art intelligent methods. In terms of performances, an accuracy rate between 81 and 90% reflects a realistic average performance based on the results of the analyzed studies [7]. The top five bankruptcy models with accuracy level of more than 80 per cent are [9]:1) Altman [8], 2) Edmister [12], 3) Deakin [13], 4) Springate [28] and 5) Fulmer [29].

III. RESEARCH METHOD

The goal of this research is to identify and classify features that have been applied to determine Financial Credit Risk Assessment. In addition to the goal of the research, also, the maturity of the research field is a factor in determining the appropriate research method and technique. Based on the number of publications and identified features, the maturity of the Financial Credit Risk Assessment research field can be classified as mature. Mature research fields should A) focus on further external validity and generalizability of the phenomena studied or B) focus on a different perspective on the constructs and relationships between identified constructs [14].

Current studies have focused on selecting the best features to predict bankruptcy, while other studies have focused on comparing the efficiency and effectiveness of the different features identified. However, the analysis is always from a high-level and high latency perspective. Summarized, to accomplish our research goal, a research approach is needed in which the current features are explored, compared and mapped to the Financial Credit Risk Assessment Model. To accomplish this goal, a research approach is needed that can 1) identify features for Financial Credit Risk Assessment, 2) identify similarities and dissimilarities between features for Financial Credit Risk Assessment, and 3) map the features to the Financial Credit Risk Assessment Model. The first two goals are realized by applying a structured literature research and grounded theory. The purpose of the structured literature research is to collect the features. In addition, the purpose of grounded theory is to "explain with the fewest possible concepts, and with the greatest possible scope, as much variation as possible in the behavior and problem under study." Grounded theory identifies differences and similarities by applying eighteen coding families. However, in our specific situation, an a priori coding scheme has been applied.

IV. DATA COLLECTION AND ANALYSIS

As stated in the previous section, the goal of this a research is to 1) identify features for Financial Credit Risk Assessment, 2) identify similarities and dissimilarities between features for Financial Credit Risk Assessment, and 3) map the features to the Financial Credit Risk Assessment Model.

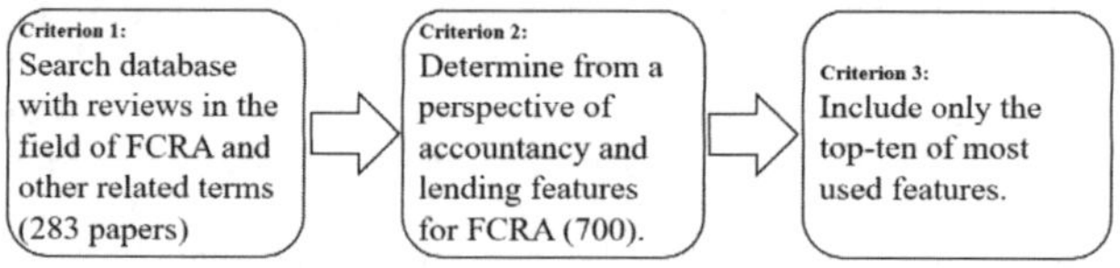

Figure 2. Feature Selection

The selection of the papers has been conducted via the link-tracing methodology [15], more specifically via snowball sampling. The snowballing was applied to take advantage of the social networks of identified respondents to provide a researcher with an ever-expanding set of potential contacts [16]. Snowballing is an effective and efficient form of contact tracing for use in diversity of research methods and designs, and apparently well suited for a number of research purposes [17] - [20]. In total, over 500 articles have been selected after which each paper was inspected for the inclusion of features. After this inspection, a total of 238 papers were included in the coding. For a study to be selected for coding, the study must explicitly address features for Financial Credit Risk Assessment (see Table I for details). This resulted in the identification of 700 features. Each of the 700 features have been added to a comparison table. After comparison, the features are coded. The unit of analysis for coding is a single feature, implying that one study can contribute multiple units of analysis.

Data analysis was conducted in one cycle of coding; the reason for one cycle of coding instead of three is the use of a priori coding scheme. The reason an a priori coding scheme was applied is because the concepts that needed to be coded were known upfront. To code the selected items the following question are asked: 1) is the feature a hard or soft feature? and 2) is the feature a relational or transactional feature? This process required inductive deductive reasoning. The inductive reasoning was applied to reason from concrete features to abstract elements. For example, the feature "net income/total assets" is a hard feature from a transactional perspective. Another feature is "the quality of management", which is a soft feature from a relational perspective. The coding was done by one researcher while the other researcher acted as reliability coder.

V. RESULTS

In this section, the results of the data collection are presented. As described in the previous section, first features from existing studies have been analyzed. Therefore, the descriptive statistics with regards to the results of our coding processes are presented. After that, the description of the features from a DMN perspective are presented. The extraction of the features resulted in the registration of 700 features from 283 papers. From this sample, the top ten features were identified and selected; see Table I. Analyzing the defined features showed three results: 1) from an existing ranking perspective, 2) from a DMN perspective, and 3) from an information availability perspective.

A. Results from an existing ranking perspective

As stated in the literature review section, research indicates that the Altman model for bankruptcy prediction [8] is the most applied one. From our analysis, it shows that 4 out of 10 features (indicated by an asterisk) are applied by Altman and that the fifth feature by Altman (Market Value of Equity/Total Liabilities) ranks thirteenth.

TABLE I. TOP TEN FEATURES

Feature 01: Net income/total assets	85 (papers)
Feature 02: current ratio	74
Feature 03: EBIT/total assets (*)	65
Feature 04: retained earnings/total assets (*)	62
Feature 05: working capital/total assets (*)	60
Feature 06: sales/total assets (*)	46
Feature 07: quick ratio	41
Feature 08: current assets/total assets	39
Feature 09: total debt/total assets	39
Feature 10: cash/total assets	32

B. Results from a DMN perspective

Analyzing the top ten features from a DMN perspective show four results. The first result: decision versus data input show that each feature is treated like a decision. The feature is derived from one or more conditions. For example, the first feature is derived out of two conditions: net income and total assets to which a mathematical formula is applied, in this specific case, net income divided by total assets. Each feature in the 10 retrieves the applied conditions from one data source, namely, the financial statements (the balance sheet and/or the profit and loss account).

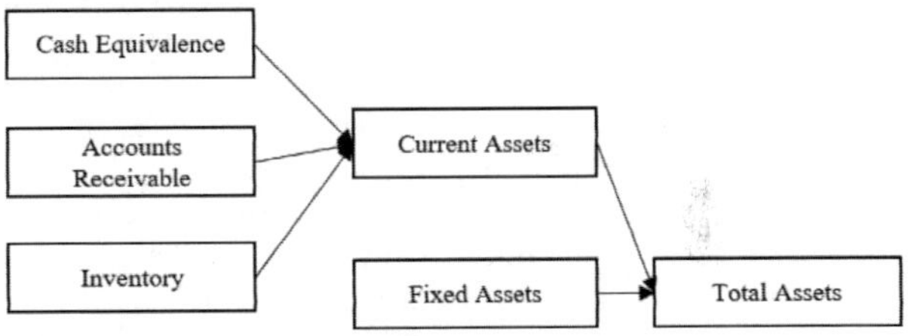

Figure 3. DRD-level elements

From the perspective of the financial statements, the conditions applied, e.g. net income, actually are data input since all are listed there. However, when analyzing one step deeper, each data input on the balance sheet or the profit and loss account is actually a decision. For example, total assets, is calculated as current assets plus fixed assets; see Figure 3. When analyzing all of the quantitative features selected, all features are derived from the balance sheet and/or the profit and loss account. A potential explanation of this phenomenon can be that the financial industry only looks at formal documents and formal statements. However, this raises the question if these combined features contain specific sub-decisions or specific input data elements that make them suitable for analysis. According to the researchers, this would be a subject to further investigate.

In addition, the features only apply information from the current financial statements. Formally, the balance sheet and the profit and loss account have to be created once a year. Most companies create this information more times a year, voluntarily or obligatory. Also, not comparing information from early years, thereby indicating that the patterns have no additional information value. By analyzing the deeper layers underneath the features described previously, the hypothesis is that a better and quicker Financial Credit Risk Assessment can be performed.

C. Results from an information type perspective

As stated in this section, most features are based on data from the financial statements. Financial statements are, in most organizations, created once or twice a year. Therefore, the data needed to calculate the features is available once or twice a year. This causes an information opacity problem thereby reducing the effectiveness of the features. Other organizations that also assess the financial credit risk of an organization are banks, credit assessors, etc. Both previously also had to trust numbers that are published once a year. Since this time period is too long for both parties they searched for solutions to address this problem.

The bank addresses this problem by applying lending technologies. A lending technology is *"a set of screening and underwriting policies and procedures, a loan contract structure, and monitoring strategies and mechanisms"* [21]. Examples of lending technologies they apply are: leasing, commercial real estate lending, residential real estate lending, motor vehicle lending, and equipment lending, asset-based lending, financial statement lending, small business credit scoring, relationship lending and judgment lending. The same conclusion is realized by Ju and Sohn [22] who proposed to update the credit scoring model based on new features like management, technology, marketability, and business and profitability. Kosmidis and Stavropoulos [23] even got one step further in their conclusion, as they state that factors such as economic cycle phase, cash flow information and the detection of fraudulent financial reporting can evidently enhance the predictive power of existing models. Altman, Sabato and Wilson [24] reach the same conclusion as they state: *"that qualitative data relating to such variables as legal action by creditors to recover unpaid debts, company filing histories, comprehensive audit report/opinion data and firm specific characters make a significant contribution to increasing the default prediction power of risk models built specifically for SMEs."* This leads us to the first conclusion that the financial industry should not only rely on hard features, which have a time delay, but also on soft information to assess the financial credit risk; see bottom left side in Figure 4.

To realize proper research in this area, the researchers have to go beyond the already cumulative features and look at the base data. E.g. no longer apply the cumulative feature: current assets but instead build features on the base information such as debtors information.

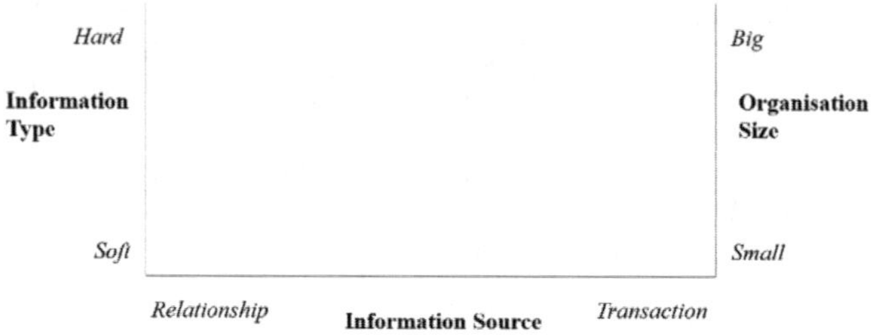

Figure 4. Financial Credit Risk Assessment Model

D. Results from an information source perspective

In addition to the type of information available, the data source and its fluidity are also factors. In financial literature, this phenomenon is called *"the hardening of information"* [21]. The concept *"the hardening of information"* states that because personal contact with the bank has decreased the banks rely more and more on hard quantitative information. However, if the model on which they base these conclusions is further dissected, two axes can be distinguished: A) the type of data and B) the manner in which the data is retrieved. The first axe describes the type of data that organizations retrieve to make a judgement about the financial credit risk. In the papers of Berger [21][25], the same distinction is made in an information type perspective: soft versus hard data. The second axe described the manner in which this information is retrieved. For example, two manners in which information can be collected are: 1) through face to face contact between a loan officers and the organization's owner and 2) through a form on a website or any other digital manner. Since more banks, credit organizations, and accountants rely on the second, the statement of "the hardening of information" is that only quantitative data is used. Thereby underlying the fact that the traditional features are the most useful features to analyze going concern assessment. The main reason they state to support their claim is the adoption rate of technology.

However, a counter claim can be made that through the adoption of technology soft information can be more easily collected. For example, through firehose access to social media websites. However, this will depend on the type of soft or hard information one wants to retrieve because not all soft information can be retrieved through social websites, some still might need to be retrieved face to face. Therefore, the bottom part of our model, see Figure 5, indicates the manner in which the information is retrieved.

E. Results from an organization perspective

In FCRA literature, from a banking perspective, a distinction is made between the manner in which small and big banks assess the risk. Small banks apply more of a relationship perspective to assess the risk while big banks apply the analysis of transactions to determine the risk. Although this specific distinction cannot be found in accountancy and lending (firms) literature, the hypothesis is that the same basic rules apply. Therefore, the right axe of the Financial Credit Risk Assessment Model contains the size of the firms assessing the risk; see Figure 4.

F. Overall Results

The overall analysis shows the following results. Most features are positioned in quadrant B, see Figure 5. The second most features are positioned in quadrant C. The other results show that none of the features are positioned in quadrant A and D, indicating a significant gap.

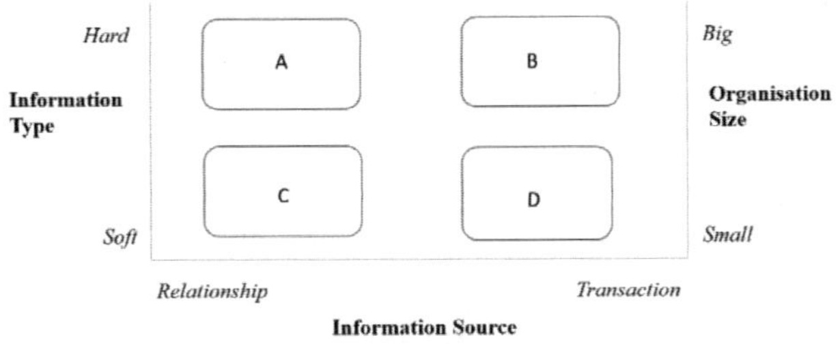

Figure 5. Overall Results with respect Financial Credit Risk Assessment Model

VI. CONCLUSION AND FUTURE WORK

In this paper, we aimed at finding an answer to the following research question: *"how to categorize financial credit risk features such that an integrative relationship is established with the information type applied and information sources used?"* To accomplish this goal, we conducted a literature study to identify features that have been designed and applied in previous research followed by coding the features based on an a priori coding scheme. The literature resulted in a total of 238 selected papers. From the selected papers, a total of 700 features were selected. Based on the a priori coding scheme, the features were mapped according to the following dimensions: A) the type of features applied, B) the information source applied and, C) the type of organization that applies the features. The results show that most features focus on hard information from a transactional source from official information with a high latency. In addition, the results show that most features still relate to the traditional Altman-Z score.

All the results have been mapped on the Financial Credit Risk Assessment Model, which is based on Wand and Weber [26], see Figure 4. The insights derived from this study provides a better understanding of the level on which the features are applied and where they score in the Financial Credit Risk Assessment Model. This will enable further exploration and identification of features that have a low latency but still have a proper predictive power. From a practical perspective, our study provides an overview of features that can currently be applied, and which further exploration should be taken into account.

While we provide an integrative overview of features for Financial Credit Risk Assessment, our study is not without limitations. The first limitation concerns the sampling and sample size. The sample group of features is drawn from the identified paper without taking into account the effectiveness of the features selected. The main reason for this choice is the fact that not all papers report on the effectiveness of the features applied. While we believe that for the purpose of this study this causes no problems, further refinement of the features selected is recommended. Additionally, our results should be further validated in practice.

We believe that this work represents a further step in research on classifying and creating new features for Financial Credit Risk Assessment. While this work has focused on classifying current features, future research should explore subcategories, reducing the high latency for hard information and to research more features from a relational/soft perspective and relational/transaction perspective.

Further research should focus on reducing the high latency for hard information and to research more features from a relational/soft perspective and relational/transaction perspective.

REFERENCES

[1] S. Cornee and A. Szafarz, "Vive la Difference: Social Banks and Reciprocity in the Credit Market," *J. Bus. Ethics*, vol. 125, no. July, pp. 361–380, 2014.

[2] S. Balcaen and H. Ooghe, "35 years of studies on business failure: An overview of the classic statistical methodologies and their related problems," *British Accounting Review*, vol. 38, no. 1. pp. 63–93, 2006.

[3] J. Watson and J. E. Everett, "Do Small Businesses Have High Failure Rates?," *J. Small Bus. Manag.*, vol. 34, no. 4, pp. 45–62, 1996.

[4] B. S. Ahn, S. S. Cho, and C. Y. Kim, "The integrated methodology of rough set theory and artificial neural network for business failure prediction," *Expert Syst. Appl.*, vol. 18, no. 2, pp. 65–74, 2000.

[5] T. Derriks, "A Business Process & Rules Management Maturity Model for the Dutch governmental sector," no. March, 2012.

[6] C.-F. Tsai, "Feature selection in bankruptcy prediction," *Knowledge-Based Syst.*, vol. 22, no. 2, pp. 120–127, 2009.

[7] E. Kirkos, "Assessing methodologies for intelligent bankruptcy prediction," *Artif. Intell. Rev.*, vol. 43, no. 1, pp. 83–123, 2012.

[8] E. I. Altman, "The Prediction of Corporate Bankruptcy: A Discriminant Analysis," *J. Finance*, vol. 23, no. 1, pp. 193–194, 1968.

[9] M. Aruldoss, M. L. Travis, and V. P. Venkatesan, "A reference model for business intelligence to predict bankruptcy," *J. Enterp. Inf. Manag.*, vol. 28, no. 2, pp. 186–217, 2015.

[10] P. Ravi Kumar and V. Ravi, "Bankruptcy prediction in banks and firms via statistical and intelligent techniques - A review," *Eur. J. Oper. Res.*, vol. 180, no. 1, pp. 1–28,

2007.

[11] N. Chen, B. Ribeiro, and A. Chen, "Financial credit risk assessment: a recent review," *Artif. Intell. Rev.*, vol. 45, no. 1, pp. 1–23, 2016.

[12] R. O. Edmister, "An empirical test of financial ratio analysis for small business failure prediction," *J. Financ. Quant. Anal.*, vol. 7, no. 2, pp. 1477–1493, 1972.

[13] E. B. Deakin, "A Discriminant Analysis of Predictors of Business Failure," *J. Account. Res.*, vol. 10, no. 1, pp. 167–179, 1972.

[14] A. C. Edmondson and S. E. Mcmanus, "Methodological fit in management field research," *Acad. Manag. Rev.*, vol. 32, no. 4, pp. 1155–1179, 2007.

[15] M. Spreen, "Rare Populations, Hidden Populations, and Link-Tracing Designs: What and Why?," *Bull. Méthodologie Sociol.*, vol. 36, no. 1, pp. 34–58, 1992.

[16] S. K. Thompson, "Adaptive sampling in behavioral surveys," *NIDA Res.Monogr*, vol. 167, no. 1046–9516 (Linking), pp. 296–319, 1997.

[17] K. Hjelm, P. Nyberg, Å. Isacsson, and J. Apelqvist, "Beliefs about health and illness essential for self-care practice: A comparison of migrant Yugoslavian and Swedish diabetic females," *J. Adv. Nurs.*, vol. 30, no. 5, pp. 1147–1159, 1999.

[18] M. N. Marshall, "Qualitative study of educational interaction between general practitioners and specialists," *BMJ*, vol. 316, pp. 442–445, 1998.

[19] T. R. Misener *et al.*, "National Delphi study to determine competencies for nursing leadership in public health.," *Image. J. Nurs. Sch.*, vol. 29, no. 1, pp. 47–51, 1997.

[20] J. H. Patrick, R. A. Pruchno, and M. S. Rose, "Recruiting Research Participants: A Comparison of the Costs and Effectiveness of Five Recruitment Strategies," *Gerontologist*, vol. 38, no. 3, pp. 295–302, 1998.

[21] A. N. Berger *et al.*, "Small Business Lending by Banks: Lending Technologies and the Effects of Banking Industry Consolidation and Technological Change."

[22] Y. H. Ju and S. Y. Sohn, "Updating a credit-scoring model based on new attributes without realization of actual data," *Eur. J. Oper. Res.*, vol. 234, no. 1, pp. 119–126, 2014.

[23] K. Kosmidis and A. Stavropoulos, "Corporate failure diagnosis in SMEs," *Int. J. Account. Inf. Manag.*, vol. 22, no. 1, pp. 49–67, 2014.

[24] E. I. Altman, G. Sabato, and N. Wilson, "The value of non-financial information in small and medium-sized enterprise risk management," *J. Credit Risk*, vol. 6, no. 2, pp. 1–30, 2010.

[25] A. N. Berger and L. K. Black, "Bank size, lending technologies, and small business finance," *J. Bank. Financ.*, 2011.

[26] Y. Wand and R. Weber, "An Ontological Model of an Information System," *IEEE Trans. Softw. Eng.*, vol. 16, no. 11, 1990.

Empathy Factor Mining from Reader Comments of E-manga

Eisuke Ito
Research Institute for IT
Kyushu University
Fukuoka, Japan 819-0395
Email: ito.eisuke.523@m.kyushu-u.ac.jp

Yuya Honda
Grad. School of Library Science
Kyushu University
Fukuoka, Japan 819-0395
honda.yuuya.128@s.kyushu-u.ac.jp

Sachio Hirokawa
Research Institute for IT
Kyushu University
Fukuoka, Japan 819-0395
hirokawa@cc.kyushu-u.ac.jp

***Abstract*—The digitization of manga (Japanese comics) is currently progressing. In the past, expressions of manga have evolved in a way that is suitable for printing on paper. With the spread of smartphones, the expression of e-manga is developing at present. In this research, we focus on reader comments on e-mangas in Comico. Comico is a popular e-manga service. Similar to other online contents services, such as YouTube, Comico implements a user comments system. Readers can post comments easily, and the comments quickly reach others, including the manga creator. Comico recognizes that reader comments may influence the creator and the story of e-manga. In this research, we try to mine the empathy factor of readers for the story and the characters of e-manga. We collect reader comments and apply feature selection of SVM (Support Vector Machine) to mine empathy factors among readers.**

Keywords–online contents; e-manga; user comments; interaction; feature selection; SVM.

I. Introduction

The digitization of manga (Japanese comics) is currently progressing. In the past, expressions of manga have evolved in a way that is suitable for printing on paper. With the spread of smartphones, the expression of e-manga is developing at present. In the past, most e-manga were digitized by image scanning from paper manga. At present, some smartphone-oriented expressions of e-manga are developing. Many e-manga applications for smartphones are being released.

The authors of the present paper are interested in online contents services. We analyzed a video recommendation method using comments for videos on nicovideo.jp [1], and proposed statistical analysis of video page views [2]. In addition, we have been studying the number of bookmarks and recommendation of novels using the link structure of bookmarks for the online novel site syosetu.com. Recently, we also analyzed the diversity trend of online novels [3].

In this paper, we focus on reader comments on e-mangas in Comico [4]. Comico is a popular e-manga service in Japan, and e-mangas in Comico are specialized for smartphone. Among the e-manga smartphone applications, the Comico app is the second most popular in Japan as of February 2017. Similar to other online contents services, such as YouTube, Comico implements a user comments system. Readers can post comments easily, and comments quickly reach to others including the manga creator. Comico recognizes that reader comments may influence the creator and the story of e-manga.

If a system can mechanically extract the factors readers empathizes with, it may become a good support tool for creation of e-manga. Toward realization of empathy factor extraction, we apply the SVM (Support Vector Machine) feature selection method [5] to reader comments, and extract important words.

The rest of this paper is organized as follows. Section II shows related work. In Section III, we describe the service and contents of Comico briefly, and show some statistics. Section IV shows comment crawler and preprocessing. In Section VI, we illustrate our feature selection method and some results of analysis. Section V presents in detail of "ReLIFE", which is an e-manga on Comico. We use comments for this e-manga as the first analysis. We describe the empathy factor extraction using feature selection of SVM in Section VI. Finally, Section VIII presents a brief summary and future work.

II. Related Work

Sentiment analysis of a story and of readers response is a hot topic of text mining. Murakami et al. proposed a method to associate characters in the story with frequently appeared words which represent character's personality [6]. They manually input character names and many co-occurred sentences in manga. Then they apply co-occurrence analysis. The readers response is out of their target of the analysis.

Emotional analysis of manga and manga readers is another new genre gaining much attention. Writers and readers can use a new style of visual communication different from textual words. In [7], Cohn and Ehly analyze the visual vocabulary appearing in the Japanese manga. They extracted 73 visual expressions that have been used in Japanese manga. It shows that these are also used in 20 volumes selected from boys and girls manga. In our case, many emojes (pictograms) are included in comments, but we are not addressing emotional expressions in this paper. When analyzing emotions, Cohn's study can be used.

Instead of using words in comments, stamps are gaining much attention in casual communication such as WathsApp [8] and LINE [9]. For example, Dharma et al. are studying how to use manga (cartoon) for communication in SNS (Social Network System) [10]. SNS is the world's largest community. It realizes various kinds of two-way communication and various news distribution. Dharma et al. proposed manga picture in SNS to improve their satisfaction in hobby fields. The Comico reader comment covered by this paper unilaterally describes the thought of the reader, so it is not used for interaction between readers or between authors and readers.

III. Comico

In this section, we describe our research target e-manga service "Comico".

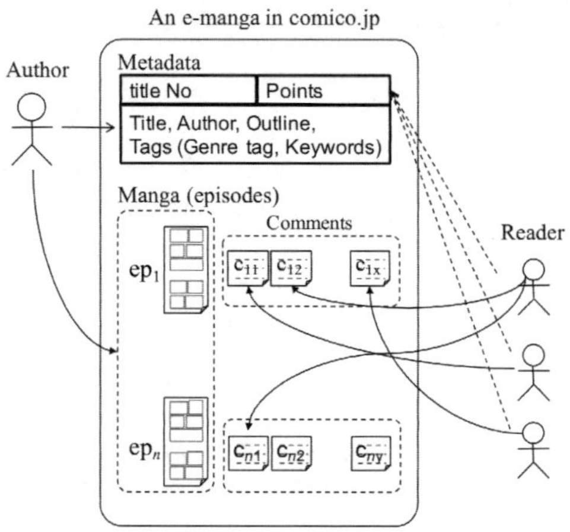

Figure 1. Data structure of an e-manga in Comico

A. Features of Comico

Comico [4] was established by "NHN comico" company in October 2013. According to a survey in February 2017 by Nielsen [11], Comico is the second largest user in Japan, and about 2.6 million people use it. (The first is LINE manga, 2.99 million users).

The most unique feature of Comico different from other e-manga services is that Comic only serves smartphone oriented original e-mangas. Almost all e-mangas on Comico are full-colored, and all e-mangas on Comico are able to browse just by swiping it from the top to the bottom. Comico does not serve e-manga which digitized past paper manga. For this reason, it does not need to move e-manga in the left-right direction, like a paper book.

Another feature is the use of reader comments. According to a news release from Comico, some e-manga creator used comments to measure reader's impression and used comments as a tool of interaction between readers and the creator.

Comico e-mangas are divided into three ranks: official, best_challenge and challenge. Newcomers' manga is serialized as a challenge work. When popularity comes out, then it is elected as best_challenge rank. When an e-manga in best_challenge rank is given quality and popularity, it arises to the official rank. Table I shows restrictions of comico e-manga in each rank, and Table II shows the number of e-mangas for each type.

TABLE I. RESTRICTIONS OF COMICO E-MANGA

Rank	Original	Min cuts	Color	New ep. freq.
official	Must	30	Must	Every two weeks
best_challenge	Should	15	Must	none
challenge	May	1	Should	none

B. Genre and tags

To improve searching and grouping, every e-manga on Comico is given tags by the manga creator. A tag represents genre, rank in Comico (official or challenge), and keywords. A tag is used like a hashtag in Twitter (a tag forms # and a word). Table III shows 12 genre tags used in Comico. Table

TABLE II. THE NUMBER OF E-MANGAS (OCT. 2017)

Type	Number
Continuing series	260
End series	188
Deleted series	9

IV shows the number of cartoon works with each genre tag attached. The total number of e-manga in Table IV is larger than the total number of works shown in Table II because most e-mangas are given multiple genre tags to hit a search query.

TABLE III. 12 GENRE TAGS (Oct.2017)

Drama, Gag/Comedy, Common life, School, Love romance, Fantasy/SF, Horror/Mystery, Action, History, Sports, Essay, Omnibus

TABLE IV. NUMBER OF E-MANGA FOR EACH TAG. (Oct.2017)

Genre tag	Num. of e-manga
Drama	167
Gag/Comedy	180
Common life	154
School	120
Love romance	136
Fantasy/SF	140
Horror/Mystery	43
Action	54
History	10
Sports	7
Essay	25
Omnibus	3

IV. COMMENTS ANALYSIS

A. Comment crawler

To collect comments mechanically, we made a comment crawler program using Python. This crawler accesses the comments page of Comico by specifying title ID and episode ID of the e-manga series, and gets HTML of the web page. It extracts comment text using XPath from the obtained HTML page.

The collected comments are reformed and put into a search engine for later analysis. We extract the comment author name, the date and time of comment post, and words in a comment using the morphological analysis tool MeCab [12]. We also implemented e-manga character name extraction function. Characters are often described by nicknames or abbreviations, so we assigned candidates of nicknames or abbreviations for each character.

B. Limitation of comments

As shown in Figure 1, any user can post a comment for an episode, if the episode is open. So, the older the episode is, the more comments are posted. We limited comments to 7 days posted comment for fair analysis. Let $\boldsymbol{C_i} =< c_1, c_2, ..., c_n >$ be the set of comments posted to i-th episode (ep.i). Posting date of c_n is 7 days later than the date of c_1.

C. Attention to characters

We believe that the reader's empathy for e-mangas influences manga. We focus on reader's response towards the characteristic of hero and heroines of the manga. Kazuo Koike, who is a famous story creator, said at the beginning of his book [13]. "Manga is character. If the character is catchy, the manga will be popular. If you create a catchy character, the character will be loved by many readers. And readers want to meet the character, then the manga will be sold and series of the manga will continue." We agree with his opinion and investigate whether the readers empathize with the characters of manga.

In this research, we consider that if a character name appears in a reader comment, then the commenter may have empathy with the character. In real world events such as sports, entertainments, and politics, people may show support for a person, team or party by using written placards which display their name. When a person empathizes with a person, a team, or a party, then they write their names on placard to show it. In other words, describing the name of an entity indicates that the descriptor may be interested in the entity.

D. Character frequency

We take $df(K)$ as the metrics of readers empathy to character K, where $df(K)$ is the document frequency of character K. In other words, $df(K)$ is the number of comments which include K's name at least one time in the comment. Most comments are short, and there are few comments which describes a character name multiple times. Also, there are few commenter who posts multiple comments to one episode.

We also count frequency of co-occurrence of character K and K', and we represent it as $df(K, K')$. In the story of manga (also novel or movie), the relation between two characters is important. There are cases where two characters become lovers, friends, or sports opponents. In manga dealing with love, the relationship between the two is important because readers are very interested and empathize with the progress of their relationship.

V. ReLIFE COMMENTS ANALYSIS

This section describes the analysis of ReLIFE comments. ReLIFE is an e-manga series on Comico, created by Yayoiso [14], and it is ongoing Japanese science fantasy high school drama [15]. ReLIFE is the most popular e-manga in Comico. Many users read it, and therefore many comments are posted. So, this is the best example for the first comments analysis.

A. Trend of the number of comments

Figure 2 shows the trend of $|C_i|$ for each episode. $|C_i|$ is the number of posted comments to ep.i ($i = 1..215$) of ReLIFE series.

Figure 2 is marked A – E for remarkable spikes. Until ep.24, the number of comments is small. ReLIFE was not popular in the early stage of the series, then a few readers posted comments. In period A (ep.25–27), an event to present gifts to commenters was held. So, a lot of comments are posted. In period B (ep.39–40), the author notified that the paper book of ReLIFE will release. At D (ep.118), the number of comments is the highest. The story reached its first climax. At E (ep.144), the author notified that ReLIFE will be made a TV animation drama. At F (ep.187), the author notified that ReLIFE will be made into a movie. So, we found that ReLIFE readers reacted to the climax of the story, announcements of TV animation dorama and movie, or to the event which the creator / the company prepared.

B. Trend of characters

Table V shows the main 6 characters of ReLIFE. They are high school students in the same grade and in the same class. They look like 17 years old, but characters 1 and 3 are adults (27 years old), because they are rejuvenated with a special medicine 'relife'.

TABLE V. MAIN CHATACTOERS OF RELIFE

No	Name	Sex
1	Arata Kaizaki	M
2	Chizuru Hishiro	F
3	Ryo Yoake	M
4	Rena Kariu	F
5	Kazuomi Oga	M
6	An Onoya	F

Figure 5 shows $df(K)$ of character K for each ReLIFE episode (ep.1–127). To quantitatively measure readers' empathy for characters, we consider frequency (the number of appearances) of character name in comments. Character 1 "Kaizaki" is the main character, then he is generally frequent. In ep.27, sub-character Oga (character 5) is rapidly increasing. The reason will be clarified in Section VII-A.

Figure 6 shows $df(K, K')$ for each episode (ep.1–127). $df(K, K')$ is document frequency of co-occurrence of character K and K' in comments. There are 15 combination pairs for the characters 1 to 6 in Table V, and investigated co-occurrence frequency of all 15 pairs. Figure 6 shows the highest co-occurring eight pairs.

VI. FEATURE SELECTION

In previous section, we understood what the reader empathized with, because we knew ReLIFE and checked the comments in detail. However, it is not efficient to apply manual analysis to all e-mangas. If a system can mechanically extract the factors of why reader empathizes, it may become a good support tool for creation of e-manga.

It is well known that SVM (Support Vector Machine) is a machine learning method that achieves good prediction performance compared with other methods. Moreover, SVM shows superior results when we combine it with feature selection. For example, Wariish et al. analyzed sales report using SVM, decision tree, and random forests [16]. The best result was obtained with SVM and feature selection.

Toward realization of the empathy factor extraction, we apply the SVM feature selection method [5] to reader comments and extract important words. We used SVM-light [17] with liner kernel, and with default parameters. We applied SVM assuming that all the comments containing a character K as positive data, and other comments are negative data.

A. Bag-of-words vectorization

To apply SVM, each comment must be vectorized. We vectorize comments using bag-of-words [18]. Figure 3 shows the outline of vectorization of documents (comments).

B. Extraction of feature words

We extracted feature words from the learning result of SVM [18]. SVM is a common method of machine learning for binary classification. Let input data be $\boldsymbol{x} = (x_1, x_2, \cdots, x_m)$,

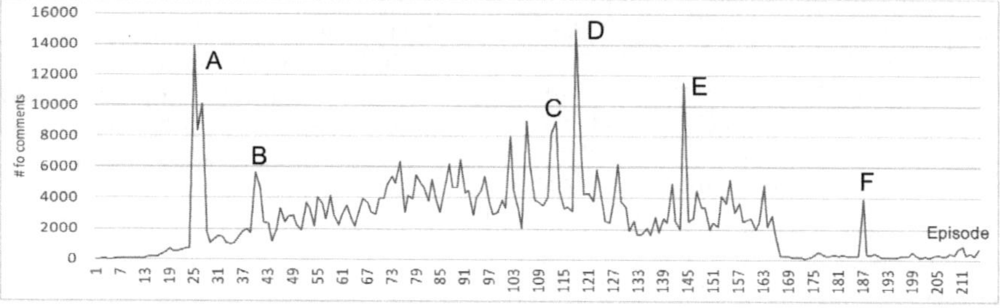

Figure 2. Number of comments for each ReLIFE episode (ep.1–ep.215)

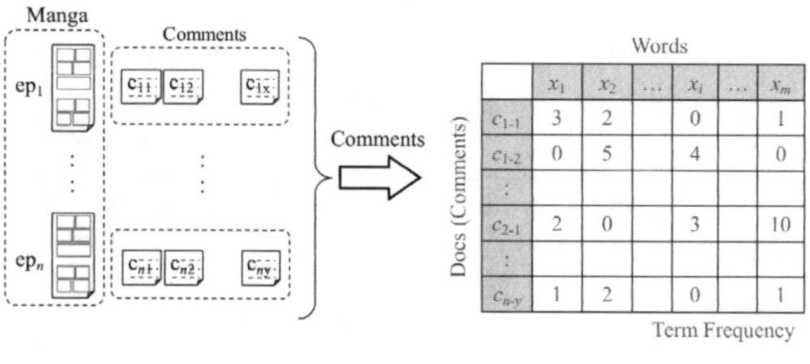

Figure 3. BoW vectorization of documents

and two classes be +1 (positive) and -1 (negative). Then boundary function $f(\boldsymbol{x})$ of SVM is described as follows:

$$f(\boldsymbol{x}) = \boldsymbol{w}^T \boldsymbol{x} + b, \tag{1}$$

where $\boldsymbol{w} = (w_1, w_2, \cdots, w_m)$ is weight vector and b is threshold. $\boldsymbol{w}$ and b are obtained by SVM machine learning.

Binary classification works as follows. Given a vector $\boldsymbol{x}$, and calculate $f(\boldsymbol{x})$ using obtained weight vector and threshold. If $f(\boldsymbol{x}) \geq 0$, then $\boldsymbol{x}$ is classified as positive, else classified as negative.

Next, we explain the method of feature words selection. At first, vectorize documents, and train SVM using training vectors. Next, give positive examples and negative example to the SVM. After that, calculate the importance of a word by using the weight for the word. The importance of word x_i is weight w_i in the weight vector generated by SVM training.

In [16], an experiment of feature selection is also performed. Let $S = (x_1, x_2, \cdots, x_m)$ be a set of words rearranged in descending order of the importance of words. m is the number of unique words which appear in documents. Then, the specific procedure is as follows:

I. Let $W' = \phi$ and $i = 1$.

II. While $i \leq N$, do the following steps.

- If i is even: $W' = W' \cup x_{m+1-i/2}$,
  If i is odd : $W' = W' \cup x_{(i+1)/2}$.
- Vectorize documets only using the words in W'.
- Train SVM and evaluate classification performance of SVM by using 5-fold cross validation.
- $i = i + 1$ and go back to II.

It is able to specify important words by comparing the classification performance in case of SVM of all words or a part of words.

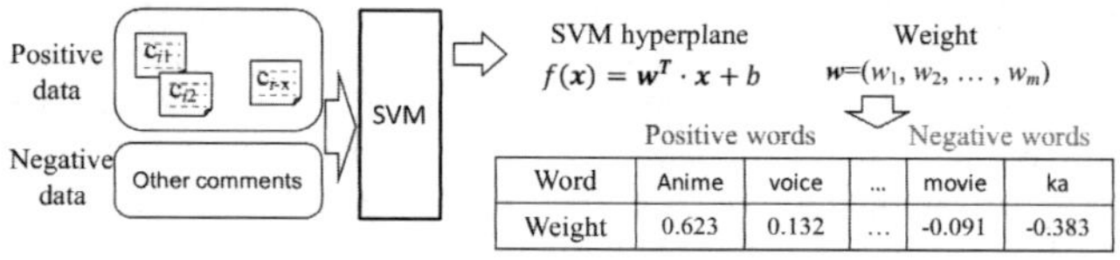

Figure 4. Feature words selection using SVM

VII. EXTRACTED EMPATHY FACTOR OF CHARACTERS

First, we vectorized all comments as shown in Figure 3. The number of all reader comments are 559,685, and the number of dimensions of a vector was 104,302. This means that there are 104,302 unique words in the set of comments.

SVM feature selection method needs to divide a document set into positive examples and negative examples. To extract the empathy factor of a character K, we set that positive examples are comments which include character K at least once, and other comments are negative examples. Extracting positive feature words are co-occurred with character K in reader's comments.

In [5], the score of a word is determined from the SVM model that separates the positive data the negative data. The score of a word represents the distance from the hyperplane. The characteristic words of positive data have positive scores, and those of negative data have negative scores. For feature selection, we choose top N positive words and bottom N negative words, as shown in Figure 4.

We applied feature selection method for reader comments of ReLIFE and extracted feature words from reader comments as the empathy factors for the character K.

A. Empathy factor by feature words selection

Table VI shows extracted top 20 positive words for each ReLIFE characters. Words in Table VI may illustrate what image or impression readers have for the character K. In Table VI, words starting with lower case letters are translated into English, but words beginning with capital letters remain in Japanese. Original results are Japanese single words because comments are written in Japanese.

Words for characters 2, 3 and 5 (Hishiro, Yoake and Oga) are easy to understand. These words express character's personality, appearance, and the role in the story of. In the row of character 5 (Oga), the word "Ogre" frequently appears because readers enjoy giving a nickname of "Ogre" to character 5 (Oga). On the other hand, characters 1, 4 and 6 (Kaizaki, Kariu and Onoya) are not easy. Character 1 (Kaizaki) is the main character, then he plays various roles in order to entered various situations. The role of character 6 (Onoya) is not yet decided in the story.

B. Performance of feature words selection

Table VII shows the results of classification performance of SVM. The 4th column in Table VII shows the number of words when F-measure becomes the highest. SVM classification accuracy may become highest when using all attributes. However, classification accuracy is higher when using limited effective attributes. So, we proposed a method to determine the optimum number of attributes in the SVM classification.

In Table VII, the number of words for max F-measure for characters 2 and 3 (Hishiro and Yoake) are both 8, and F-measure are 0.7900 and 0.8399. This means that characters 2 and 3 are able to present only 8 words. In other words, readers represent them using only 8 words. Actuary, the role of character 3 (Yoake) is facilitator of the story. Therefore, there are a few complicated topics for him. On the other hand, character 2 (Hishiro) is the main heroine. She is drawn as a cool beauty girl, and she does not act dynamically in the early part of the story. So, readers refer to her in simple expressions.

In case of character 4 (Kariu) in Table VII, the number of words for max F-measure is 20, and the value of F-measure is 0.8981. She is the highest F-measure in this analysis. Mr. Oga (character 5), his nick name is "Ogre" the number of words for max F-measure is 30, and the value of F-measure is 0.7924. In the first half of the story, their personality is clearly described, and the two will start dating as a lover. Readers were empathized in their life story and represented them in some words.

On the other hand, characters 1 and 6 (Kaizaki and Onoya) are not clear. Their F-measures are not high, and the number of words for max F-measure is 70.

VIII. Conclusion

In this paper, we focus on reader comments on e-mangas in Comico. We made a comment crawler program using Python, and collected a lot of comments from Comico. We showed statistical trend of comments and document frequency of characters. Human relations are important in stories, therefore we counted co-occurrence frequency of the two characters. We found that there are some spikes for the number of comments, and we estimated the reason for the rapid increase of comments.

Toward realization of the mechanical empathy factor extraction for support of e-manga creation of e-manga, we apply the SVM feature selection method to reader comments and extract important words. As the result of feature selection, we extracted words which represent each character. In other words, what the readers think about each character.

In the future, we want to expand empathy analysis to other e-mangas. More than 450 e-mangas exist on Comico. We hope to find a difference in empathy factors by genre. We also want to extract the transition of human relations.

Acknowledgment

This work was supported by JSPS KAKENHI Grant Number 15K00451.

References

[1] N. Murakami and E. Ito, "Emotional video ranking based on user comments," in Proceedings of iiWAS2011. ACM, December 2011, pp. 499–502.

[2] K. Noguchi, T. Iida, and E. Ito, "An analysis of cgm contents pageview using sir model and gbm," in Proceedings of ICCTD2017, March 2017, pp. 19–21.

[3] E. Ito and Y. Honda, "Keyword diversity trend of consumer generated novels," in Proceedings of ICESS2017, 2017, pp. 140–147.

[4] N. comico, "Comico," http://comico.jp [retrieved Dec. 2017].

[5] T. Sakai and S. Hirokawa, "Feature words that classify problem sentence in scientific article," in Proceedings of iiWAS2012. ACM, 2012, pp. 360–367.

[6] H. Murakami, R. Kyogoku, and H. Ueda, "Creating character connections from manga,," in Proceedings of ICAART 2011, 2011, pp. 677–680.

[7] N. Cohn and S. Ehly, "The vocabulary of manga: Visual morphology in dialects of japanese visual language," Journal of Pragmatics, vol. 92, 2016, pp. 17–29.

[8] "WhatsApp," https://www.whatsapp.com/ [retrieved Dec. 2017].

[9] "LINE," https://line.me/en/ [retrieved Dec. 2017].

[10] A. A. G. Dharma, H. Kumamoto, S. Kochi, N. Kudo, W. Guowei, C. Shu-Chuan, and K. Tomimatsu, "The utilization of social networking service and japanese manga in strategic user generated design," in Proceedings of ICEEI 2011, 2011, pp. 1–6.

[11] "Nielsen netrating," http://www.netratings.co.jp/news_release/2017/03/Newsrelease20170328.html, March 2017 [retrieved Dec. 2017].

[12] T. Kudou, "Mecab," http://taku910.github.io/mecab/ [retrieved Dec. 2017].

[13] K. Koike, Kazuo Koike's a new theory of characters. Goma Books (ISBN-10: 481491332X), August 2017.

[14] Yayoiso, "Relife," http://www.comico.jp/articleList.nhn?titleNo=2 [retrieved Dec. 2017].

[15] "Relife wiki," http://relife.wikia.com/wiki/ReLIFE_Wiki [retrieved Dec. 2017].

[16] N. Wariishi, S. Mitarai, T. Suzuki, and S. Hirokawa, "Text mining of daily sales reports," in Proceedings of AROB 2015, 2015, pp. 430–435.

[17] "SVM-Light," http://svmlight.joachims.org/ [retrieved Dec. 2017].

[18] T. Joachims, Learning to Classify Text Using Support Vector Machines: Methods, Theory and Algorithms. Kluwer Academic Publishers Norwell, 2002.

TABLE VI. EXTRACTED TOP 20 POSITIVE WORDS FOR EACH RELIFE CHARACTERS

No	Name	Top 20 positive words
1	Arata Kaizaki	KUN, SAN, SENPAI (elder person), out, Mr., &, HANNOU (reaction), follow, trauma, spokesman, nice, adult, reaction, KAI, cool, same age, reader, liked, cool, boomerang
2	Chizuru Hishiro	SHIRO, N, a subject, HI, growth, insensitive, SAN, KAWAII(pretty, in-Kanji), hair, KAWAII (in-Hiragana), HISHIRON, KAWAI-, No., incorrect, communi-, NITA (laughing), gum, smile, SETSU, action
3	Ryo Yoake	end, girl, time, S (sadistic), KOTO, child, boy, SAN, elder sister, AKE, CHAN, revenge, AKE-YO, charge, love, KUDASAI (please), looks, plain clothe, job, moment
4	Rena Kariu	SHIRE, game, KIRE, injured, RIU, TAMARAI, TAMA, effort, RARE, NARE, poor, KARI, return, gentle, claim, a big meeting, TSUN-DERE, practice, retire, CHAN
5	Kazuomi Oga	GA, pure_ogre, ogre_handsome, gap, cv, KUN, pure, sensitive, tone-deaf, dull_ogre, family, awake, annoy_ogre, CHARA, faint_ogre, or, sport, insensitive, ogre_pure
6	An Onoya	CHAN, you, ANMA, training, charge, ONO, combination, support, cv, outside, &, anti, pair, or, convenience store, go out together, doubtful, plan, gal, be stuck on

TABLE VII. FS RESULTS: MAX WORDS AND CLASSIFICATION PERFORMANCE

No	Name	sex	# of comments	Num. of words max F-meatsure	Precision	Recall	F-measure	Accuracy
1	Arata Kaizaki	M	79,323	70	0.5379	0.8854	0.6690	0.6987
2	Chizuru Hishiro	F	96,921	8	0.7084	0.8990	0.7900	0.8250
3	Ryo Yoake	M	56,788	8	0.8092	0.9040	0.8399	0.7675
4	Rena Kariu	F	46,352	20	0.8591	0.9419	0.8981	0.8217
5	Kazuomi Oga	M	35,152	30	0.7073	0.9043	0.7924	0.7304
6	An Onoya	F	39,066	70	0.4637	0.7487	0.5724	0.7587

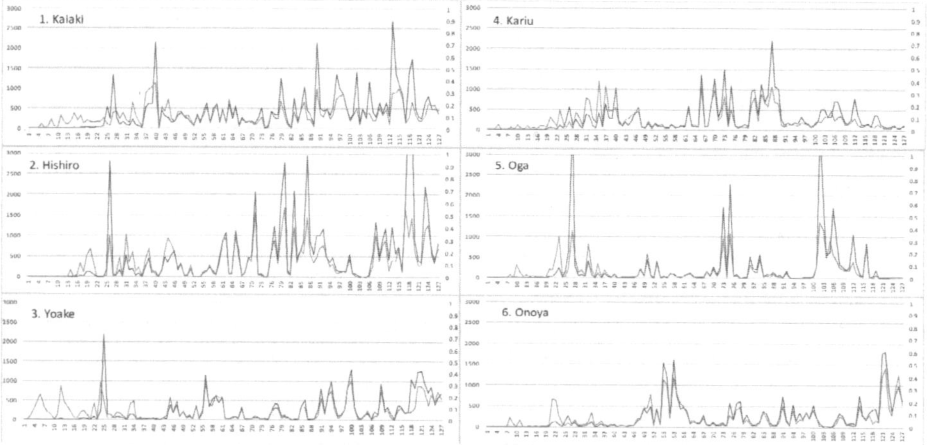

Figure 5. $df(K)$ of character K for each ReLIFE episode (ep.1–127)

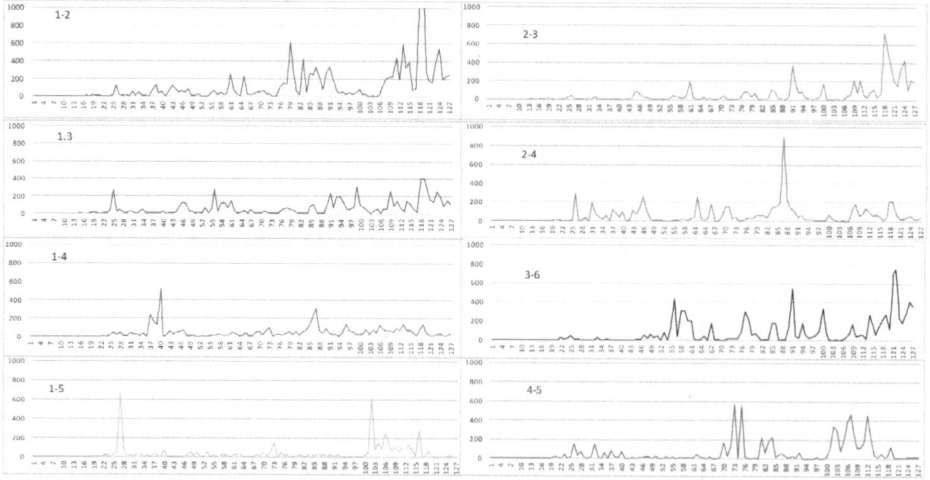

Figure 6. $df(K, K')$ of two charactors K and K' for each ReLIFE episode (ep.1–127)

Experiments to Verify How Robust the Collective Intelligence is When Summarizing Story Manga

Toshihiko Takeuchi
Faculty of Education
Tokyo University of Social Welfare
Tokyo, Japan
email: totakeuc@ed.tokyo-fukushi.ac.jp

Yuuki Kato
Faculty of Arts and Sciences
Sagami Women's University
Kanagawa, Japan
email: y-katou@star.sagami-wu.ac.jp

Shogo Kato
School of Arts and Sciences
Tokyo Woman's Christian University
Tokyo, Japan
email: shogo@lab.twcu.ac.jp

***Abstract*—We conducted experiments in which we asked large samples of Japanese students to read approximately 100 frames of story manga. We then requested that the students select between 5-20% of the frames necessary for the abstract. Once completed, we reviewed the n-th frames where the selectivity was the highest to see if it was an accurate summary, regardless of n. Our goal was to investigate whether it is possible to summarize comics by collective intelligence. In this experiment, we made the students read an English version of the Manga. We wanted to see if the collective intelligence still worked if read in a different language. The results obtained show that how robust the collective intelligence is.**

Keywords-collective intelligence; manga; summarizing; English.

I. INTRODUCTION

The authors previously proposed a method to summarize story manga as one of the test methods to measure intelligence. In the test, to summarize the story manga of about 100 frames, the subject selects about 5% to 20% of the frames. We conducted an experiment involving 113 female university students [1]. Hereafter, this experiment is called experiment A.

After Experiment A, we sorted each frame in descending order of the rate selected by the 113 students. Next, we rearranged the top k frames in manga frame order. Then, no matter what number k is, it became a good summary of the original manga. From this result, we concluded that collective intelligence worked very well in the summary of manga "The taste of that day".

We were interested in how robust collective intelligence is, so we conducted an additional experiment on another day [2]. The subjects were 60 university students. Other conditions are the same as in Experiment A. 30 are male and 30 are female. Hereafter, this experiment is called experiment B.

As a result of experiment B, the summary by collective intelligence also became a good summary overall.

Furthermore, compared with the result of Experiment A with respect to "The taste of that day", the selectivity of each frame is almost the same. The selectivity of each frame in Experiment A and Experiment B is shown in Figure 1.

When summarizing comics, collective intelligence was more effective than our expectation. So, we decided not to think that "summarizing manga with collective intelligence would be nearly a correct answer", but rather "think collective intelligence is the correct answer to manga summary". In other words, we assumed that "A person's summary ability can be measured by how alike it is to the summary of collective intelligence". Consequently, we proposed an index to measure the summarizing ability of story manga [1].

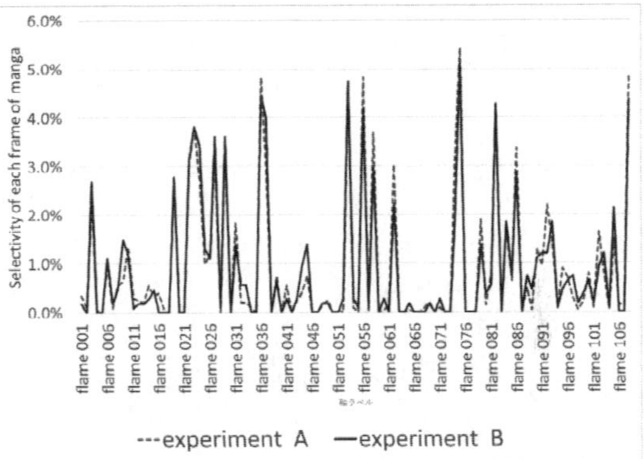

Figure 1. Selectivity of each frame of manga "The taste of that day" in Experiment A and Experiment B

II. PURPOSE

We translated the manga "The taste of that day" into English and we conducted experiments to have Japanese students read the manga under almost the same conditions as experiment A. We compared summaries of manga by collective intelligence between the English version and the Japanese version. The reason for doing the experiment is to investigate whether collective intelligence works even when Japanese students read the English version of manga.

III. METHOD

The experiment participants were 60 university students living in Tokyo.

The materials we used during the experiment are as follows.

(i) Preliminary survey questionnaire paper

(ii) English version and Japanese version of the manga booklet ("Today's Burger Volume 1" second episode "The taste of that day" first 108 flames)

(iii) Paper to fill in the selected flames number

(iv) Pre-questionnaire paper

(v) Post-questionnaire paper

The experiment schedule is shown in Table 1.

TABLE I. THE EXPERIMENT SCHEDULE

Time	Contents
5 minutes	Answer preliminary survey questionnaire and pre-questionnaire
25 minutes	Summary of manga
5 minutes	Write the numbers of the selected frames on the paper
3 minutes	Collect paper
2 minutes	Distribute Japanese version of manga
10 minutes	Read Japanese version of manga
10 minutes	Answer post-questionnaire

Figure 2 compares the selectivity of each frame in the experiments of this English version (Experiment C) and the past Japanese version (Experiment A + Experiment B). The difference in the selectivity of each frame is larger in Figure 2 than in Figure 1. This shows that when the subjects read the English version, they failed to select frames as accurately as they did for the Japanese version.

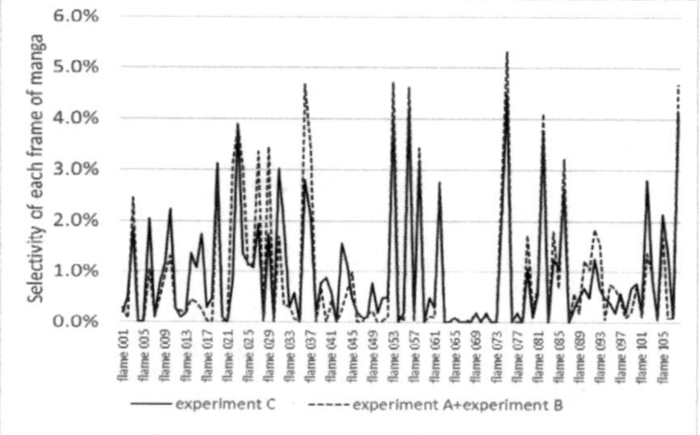

Figure 2. Selectivity of each frame of this experiment (English version) and "Taste of that day" in past two experiments A + B (Japanese version)

Figure 3 shows a plot of the frame numbers from 1st to 108th selectivity in Experiment A (Japanese version) with the horizontal axis and the plots corresponding to the frame numbers on the horizontal axis of Experiment B and Experiment C.

From the viewpoint of the order of selectivity of each frame in collective intelligence, as can be seen from Figure 3, there is no big difference.

Even in the English version, it was a good summary to rearrange the top k of the selectivity in the order of comics in manga. This means that collective intelligence works well even in the English version when summarizing comics. But for individuals, selecting frames to create a summary of the English version became more difficult than for the Japanese version.

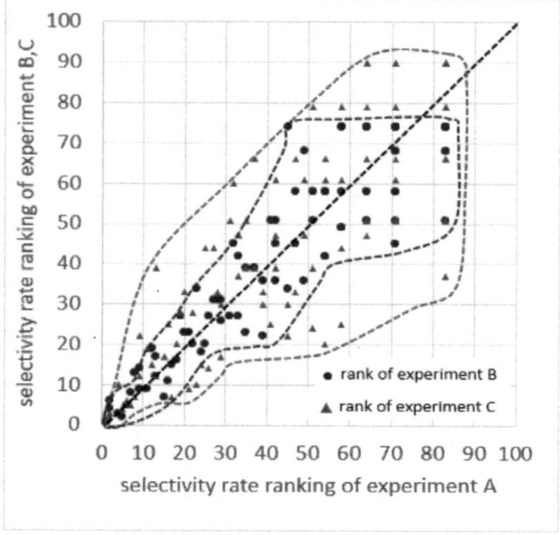

Figure 3. Selectivity ranking of each frame of Experiment B, Experiment C with the selectivity rate ranking of experiment A as the horizontal axis

IV. CONCLUSION

In order to verify the robustness of collective intelligence, we gave about 60 Japanese university college students the story manga, English version, which was about 100 frames in length. The students were asked to summarize the story using 5% to 20% of the frames. Then, we compared the result obtained here with the result of the Japanese version for the story manga from our previous studies.

Choosing the n-th highest selectivity resulted in a excellent summary of n. That is, in the summary of comics, collective intelligence also worked in the English version. However, the summary by collective intelligence was slightly less accurate in the English version than the Japanese version.

ACKNOWLEDGMENT

This research was funded by Grant-in-Aid for Scientific Research (foundation C "Establishment of manga summary test by collective intelligence and development of manga summary software using its evaluation criteria" assignment number 17K01142). Also, we got subsidies from CRET for our experiments. In addition to using the manga in the experiment, we also had the cooperation of Houbunsha Comics.

REFERENCES

[1] T. Takeuchi, Y. Kato, and S. Kato, "An experiment to investigate the relationship between the ability to summarize manga and collective intelligence", Proseedings of Japan Society of Educational Information, pp328-329, 2016a.

[2] T. Takeuchi, Y. Kato, and S. Kato, "Verification experiment on the robustness in measurement method for an ability of summarizing comics", Japan Association for Educational Media Study Proceedings of the 23rd Annual Conference, pp28-29, 2016b.

The Impact of SAP on the Utilisation of Business Process Management (BPM) Maturity Models in ERP projects

Markus Grube

University of Gloucestershire
Hamburg, Germany
email: markus.grube@voquz.com

Martin Wynn
The Business School
University of Gloucestershire
Cheltenham, UK
email: mwynn@glos.ac.uk

Abstract **– The SAP Enterprise Resource Planning (ERP) system is a leading software solution for corporate business functions and processes. Business Process Management (BPM) is a management approach designed to create and manage organizations' business processes. Both promise an improvement of business processes in companies and can be used together in organizations. In conjunction with the SAP ERP system and BPM approach, BPM maturity models can be used as diagnostic tools that allow an organization to assess and monitor the maturity of its business processes. This research analyses the complex relationships between SAP, BPM and BPM maturity models. The aim is to investigate and analyse the interaction between the use of the SAP ERP software package and the deployment of BPM maturity models. The research adopts a multiple case study approach, based on semi-structured expert interviews, and provides an in-depth insight into how a small number of organizations use SAP, BPM and BPM maturity models.**

Keywords – SAP; ERP; BPM; Business Process Management; Maturity Models; BPM Maturity Models.

I. INTRODUCTION

SAP (Systeme, Anwendungen und Produkte) is a German company created in 1972 and the world's largest provider of enterprise software that, in 2017, had more than 345,000 customers in over 190 countries [1]. The SAP ERP package provides software solutions for the full range of business functions in companies – from the processing of a leave request for employees in the human resource management function, to materials requirements planning in production and support for the full sales order processing cycle and commodity management [2]. SAP ERP is usually installed on a database platform that handles several different business functions within their respective modules, such as manufacturing, sales, finance and human resources. The implementation of an ERP system can often be seen as a form of technology innovation, and contributes to the technology maturity of a company. The capabilities of a company can often be improved by the implementation of an ERP system [3].

BPM is an approach to defining and operating company business processes, and can be used without any information technology (IT) systems or infrastructure [4]. In practice, companies often use IT software tools to administer the BPM of an organisation. Additionally, software such as SAP ERP can assist a company in standardizing and automating processes to make them as efficient as possible [5]. The basic idea of BPM is to think in terms of processes and to deal with the questions: "who does what, when, how and whereby?" [5]. BPM will usually start with a process analysis of the actual business processes [6] by the application of specific methods, techniques and tools [7].

A maturity model is described by Saco [8] as a diagnostic tool for an organization, which provides a framework to test, analyse and improve business quality [9]. For example, a maturity model analyses the quality of processes and classifies them as being at different levels of maturity. There are different maturity models for specific purposes – for example, for software development, for product manufacturing or for the business process management of a company [10] [11]. This latter type of maturity model offers a step-by-step guide, with goals and best practices, to support a more advanced use of BPM [12].

Figure 1 illustrates the various concepts that are shared by the SAP ERP system, BPM and BPM maturity models. On the one hand, the SAP ERP system includes its own business process models; on the other hand, BPM has the objective of improving business processes in an organisation; both have the same aim of optimizing an organisation's processes.

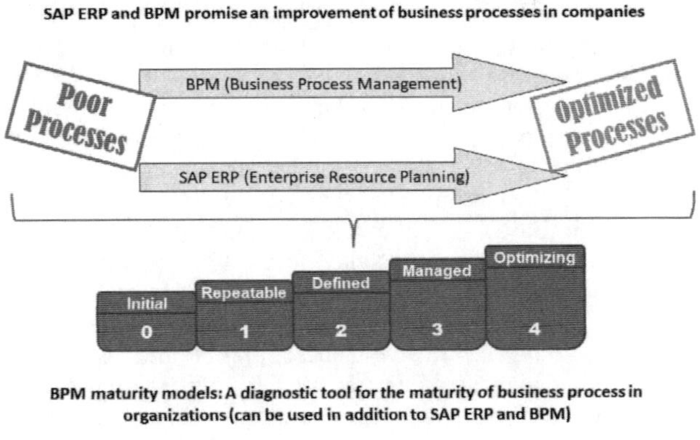

Figure 1. SAP ERP, BPM and BPM maturity models: overview

Then, there are BPM maturity models which have diagnostic tools to measure the effectiveness of processes in organisations. These tools can be used alongside SAP ERP and BPM. Van Looy [13] states that most BPM maturity models favour the use of an IT system (such as SAP ERP) to improve the BPM approach of an organisation [14].

Generally, a BPM maturity model analyses, through a set of tools and methods, the growth of BPM in an organisation. This study considers the relationship of these concepts and how these are used in practice.

Following this introductory section, Section 2 discusses relevant literature and puts forward three research questions. In Section 3, the research methodology is outlined, and this is followed in Section 4 by a summary of findings, in which the three research questions are addressed. Section 5 presents a further analysis of findings leading to the development of a number of principles to support the use of BPM maturity models within an SAP systems environment. Finally, in Section 6, the main themes of the paper are drawn together to provide overall conclusions regarding the research project.

II. LITERATURE REVIEW

BPM and process integration have been discussed for over 25 years [15], but existing literature is largely confined to general findings about the relationship between IT and the use of business processes, or about the relationship between ERP systems and business processes. For example, vom Brocke et al. [16] explain that the selection, acceptance and use of IT are a fundamental part of BPM. Business and IT need to connect with each other in order to realize better business value. Neubauer [17] also notes that ERP systems generally influence a company's business processes.

Saco [8] explains that a maturity model is a diagnostic tool for an organisation to improve its processes. This measuring tool can be used in conjunction with SAP ERP and BPM. Most authors view the use of an ERP system as a means of integrating business processes within one system which is used company-wide [17]. For example, an ERP system can hold all documents in relation to an invoice number or purchase order, and can show the document flow or action log for data changes that directly belong to a business transaction. Through the use of ERP systems, companies are expected to reduce costs by improving efficiencies and widening the availability of accurate and up to date business information, thereby enhancing overall company performance [18]. Antonucci et al. [19] indicate that ERP systems produce the data and information that are the basis for business decisions and strategies.

Overall the extant literature demonstrates that an IT application like SAP ERP can enable higher process maturity [13]. But these kinds of studies focus more on the general company level and IT systems as a whole, and do not address the question of which business process maturity model could be used if SAP is the central IT business system in the company. Van Looy et al. [20] suggest that further research could investigate the question of whether maturity models could be selected on the basis of IT business system alignment, or investigate the relationship between BPM maturity models and IT business systems on strategic, tactical and operational levels. The SAP company has its own BPM maturity model, this being a specific tool to model the business processes that underpin the design of the SAP package. One aim of this research is to explore this SAP maturity model in more detail, and assess its relationship with the SAP ERP software system.

There is nothing in the existing literature that addresses the question of whether SAP impacts on the utilisation of BPM maturity models. The best analogy is provided by Van Looy [13] regarding IT deployment for business process maturity. She outlines in her conclusion that most maturity models recommend IT to improve process modelling and optimization. She emphasises that, in general, IT usage enables higher process maturity. This research explores the dependencies between the use of SAP and BPM maturity models and addresses the following research questions (RQs):

RQ1. How are BPM maturity models used in the planning and implementation of ERP software projects?

RQ2. How does SAP impact upon the use of specific maturity models?

RQ3. To what extent (and how) is it possible to develop a comprehensive mapping of different maturity models to the SAP software system, indicating the implications for maturity model utilisation?

III. RESEARCH METHODOLOGY

Figure 2 presents the main elements of the research methodology used in this project, selected from a body of methods that can be used to gather and process data [21] [22].

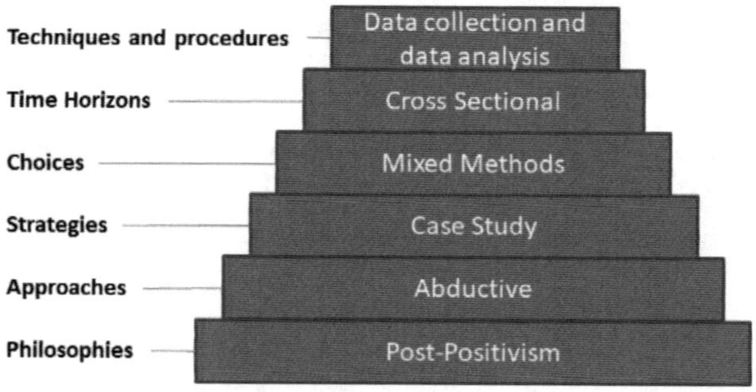

Figure 2. Research Methodology Layers [21] [22]

The research philosophy adopted here is post-positivist, based on the perspectives of Ryan [23] and Guba [24]. The goal of post-positivist research is the generation of "new knowledge that other people can learn from and even base decisions on" [25], which is relevant to this field of study where new maturity models in different specialized fields are generated with some regularity [26]. The post-positivist position supports the understanding that the world is much more complex than when the project was embarked upon, and that it is quite possible that the inclusion of other experts in the interview process would have led to different results. This research starts with a case study on organisations which use BPM maturity models, and concludes with a generalised theory regarding the behaviour in practice of different BPM maturity models in SAP ERP projects. As described by Thomas [27], this exploration uses the abductive approach in the form of a case study to collect facts from the examined cases, followed by a judgment about the best explanation of these facts. For this purpose, four different BPM maturity models are studied as separate cases with interviews relating to each case, before a generalised output is generated.

As an explanatory study [28], this research investigates the relationship between SAP and BPM maturity models in ERP projects. With a multiple case study approach, and based on semi-structured expert interviews, a small number of organisations are examined in depth. In line with the use of documentation of BPM maturity models, a qualitative research approach is pursued. According to Saunders et al. [22], the use of a case study strategy in combination with secondary data collection techniques allows a form of triangulation to confirm the obtained data from the case study. The aim of this work is to evaluate, in multiple cases with expert interviews, whether SAP can affect BPM maturity models.

Through the use of semi-structured interviews with experts in their field, and the analysis of secondary literature such as user manuals of BPM maturity models, this research uses mixed-methods to address the research questions, thereby providing greater depth in a complex environment [29]. The RQs were developed into a range of secondary questions for the first semi-structured expert interviews. The time horizon for this research is a cross-sectional snapshot study [22]. The research analyses the current SAP impact on BPM maturity models in practice, and evaluates the picture at the time of the study [30].

The interviewees were selected with the objective of gleaning the greatest amount of expert knowledge possible from practice. The semi-structured interviews allowed a degree of flexibility that engendered an understanding and explanation of the experts' opinions regarding important issues, events and patterns in the complex interaction of SAP and BPM maturity models in ERP projects [31]. The software tool MAXQDA was used for the qualitative data analysis and comparison of the interviews, and in arranging, organising and analysing all transcribed interviews, and also for analysing secondary literature sources. This allowed a special type of methodological triangulation through the use of more than one method to collect and analyse the data. A thematic analysis was used for the identification of topics. For this purpose, statements from the interviews were coded in order to recognize and interpret connections [31]. The amount and intensity with which a subject is mentioned and treated generally reflects the importance of the subject [32].

IV. FINDINGS

The search for potential interview partners was a difficult process and resulted in many rejections. The search utilised existing networks of business and personal contacts, resulting in 64 people in Germany, Austria and Switzerland being identified as potential experts, who were then invited for an interview. From this initial pool of 64 people, eleven people confirmed that they were willing to be interviewed for this research project. Most refusals were based on the fact that the experts did not have the necessary practical experience of the use of a BPM maturity model. Nevertheless, three of the experts interviewed are currently using no BPM maturity model, but perform some form of quality process assessment already at their company, or would like to apply a BPM maturity model in the future.

Baker and Edwards [33] explain that, within qualitative research, the attainment of a sufficient quantity of interviews cannot be set at a certain number. It is crucial to achieve saturation and try to gain new knowledge through additional interviews. In this research, there appeared to be a degree of saturation with the tenth interview, as no new knowledge surfaced.

The interviews revealed that the experts were familiar with four different BPM maturity models. These four models were already being used by the experts, and were described in more detail within the interviews. Each of these BPM maturity models was considered as a separate case. The accompanying documentation of the models was also analysed.

The models considered were:

- The eden maturity model. This model was developed by a working party called "Business Process Excellence" and has been updated and presented by the "BPM maturity model eden e.V. Association" [34] since 2009.
- Capability Maturity Model Integration (CMMI). CMMI was originally developed by the Carnegie Mellon University more than 20 years ago. Nowadays, the model is maintained and administered by the CMMI Institute [35].
- The Business Process Maturity Model (BPMM). This model was developed by the Object Management Group (OMG). Version 1.0 of the maturity model was released in June 2008 [36].
- The SAP maturity model. This model was developed directly by the SAP company. It was derived from the Process Enterprise Maturity Model (PEMM) developed by Michael Hammer and the CMMI [37].

Each expert was able to provide some key points for the implementation of BPM maturity models, when an SAP ERP system is used as the central IT system. The statements of the interviewees and the results of the documentation analysis were considered for each individual case, and then all statements were considered and reviewed as a whole. From this, generalised answers to the three research questions were developed.

A) RQ1: How are BPM maturity models used in the planning and implementation of ERP software projects?

In general, there are almost no prerequisites for the use of BPM maturity models. The BPM approach and BPM maturity models are usually introduced after the introduction of an ERP system. Only two experts reported an example when BPM maturity models were established before the BPM approach was introduced in the company. All experts reported that a typical approach is that an ERP system already exists, and only afterwards is a BPM approach and the application of a BPM maturity model required. An existing ERP system usually has to adapt to the requirements arising from the BPM environment and the application of a BPM maturity model.

All sources strongly indicate that the decision to implement a BPM maturity model should be carried out by the senior management with a top-down approach. A company gets the necessary support only if the management recommends the use of BPM maturity models. A bottom-up approach is also conceivable but much more difficult to accomplish successfully. The same applies to the introduction and use of ERP systems. For many companies, the use of a certain ERP system is a strategic decision taken by senior management. According to the experts, the ERP system is then often the most important and most valuable system within the company.

Both the practical experience of the interviewees, as well as the documentation, show that usually an ERP system already exists in a company before a BPM approach is adopted. In most cases, a BPM maturity model is only introduced once the practice of BPM is already established within the company. For most companies, the application of a BPM maturity model is only an add-on that does not have to be applied, and is the final step for the use of BPM in the organisation.

B) RQ2: How does SAP impact upon the use of specific maturity models?

For most companies, the use of SAP is a strategic decision. Senior management expect a stable and long term partnership if they use the SAP ERP system, which inevitably becomes the core IT system within the company. Some experts suggested that only a very few companies in their experience do not use SAP. There are industries where no one would consider not using SAP, reported one expert, because SAP is the market leader and the *de facto* standard.

The SAP system is usually implemented company-wide, and therefore has many touch points within a company. Theoretically, process definition can be done without any kind of IT system, but at a certain point in its growth, a company becomes of a size that requires an IT system for its effective operation and support. The SAP system provides some standard processes and some companies use these default SAP processes. A good maturity model should also draw attention to such standard processes, but not all BPM maturity models analyse processes which are provided by a standard system. Every company should critically question how much of a standard process is appropriate and necessary, in order to avoid a disproportionate amount of effort to achieve full module deployment and operation.

Some companies do not have the goal of achieving the highest possible maturity level. If the highest maturity level can only be achieved by adapting the SAP system, then a company must recognize that this can lead to a larger adaptation requirement in the future, as successive upgrades of the SAP product are released. A modified standard system means that the changed processes have to be fully tested and analysed every time the SAP system is changed, even if it is a standard system update or a simple system enhancement.

There are some other impacts and constraints that arise when an SAP ERP system is used within a BPM maturity model. The SAP system may not have the capability to display processes as a process map and how they are currently running within the SAP system. The continuous development of SAP functionalities, and the further development of a BPM approach in the company, create the risk that both will be further developed independently. The risk is that two independent process models will be developed for the same set of processes. Some experts pointed out that the application of SAP does not generally create an improved maturity level. SAP can be used without any business process orientation. If a process orientation is wanted, then a company must use its SAP system accordingly. Some experts reported that the intensive use of the SAP system will most likely lead to a higher maturity level if the system adheres to standard specifications and its underpinning process model.

A significant advantage when using the SAP system is that it has the functionality to determine key performance indicators (KPIs) for purposes of control and monitoring of business performance. Many SAP transactions already contain data like throughput times that can be used as KPIs for a more precise process analysis. These indicators can be determined directly from the financial transactions stored in the ERP database.

C) RQ 3: To what extent (and how) is it possible to develop a comprehensive mapping of different maturity models to the SAP software system, indicating the implications for maturity model utilisation?

All experts and available documentation suggested that the BPM models have no limitations and can be used in all companies. A link between the SAP modules used and the application of specific BPM maturity models was not evidenced by the experts' experiences. No correlation could be found which shows that certain SAP modules work more effectively with the investigated BPM maturity models. However, the four BPM models considered here demonstrate that quite different types of maturity model exist. Every company has to be clear regarding what it wants to achieve through the use of a maturity model and what is important, and what is not. For example, the eden maturity model with pre-defined questions behaves quite differently from the SAP maturity model which tries to establish as many standard SAP processes as possible. All of the four investigated maturity models can be used within an SAP environment, but there exist differences, and a company needs to know whether the model aligns with the company's goals, and if the analysis provided by the model matches their perceptions. The models can be broadly divided into three different categories:

- *Fixed models*

The eden model belongs to this category, and contains a questionnaire that is already fixed and does not require any adjustments to specific industry issues or interview partners. All questions are always the same. The application is relatively simple, because anyone who applies the model answers only these questionnaires.

- *Individual models*

The application of the CMMI or BPMM models is considerably more complex. Both are similar and require much more effort. The user has to think about what is important and what is not important for an organisation. For this purpose, individual topics and possible process objectives are defined by the models as a framework, and a user has to decide what he wants to use and how. The guidelines of the model should not be viewed as a pure best practice procedure, but must be adapted accordingly to individual circumstances.

- *Special interest models*

The SAP maturity model is also based on the CMMI model, but has significant differences and therefore can be classified in a third category. In contrast to the other models, the focus of this model is the use of best practices or standard SAP processes which originate from the SAP system. Within the maturity models examined here, it is the only one that deals with SAP-specific issues and characteristics, because other models view IT much more generally.

V. Analysis

Many BPM maturity models currently consider only a small range of IT applications, and do not analyse any kind of ERP system. But in many companies SAP is the dominant system, and for this reason a BPM maturity model should also consider relevant dependencies. Maturity models, such as BPMM or CMMI, are already very complex, but companies are often interested in guidelines that are less complex and require a smaller budget. Therefore, some principles have been developed in this research project to analyse the operation of the SAP ERP within a BPM application. The goal is not to develop a more complex and comprehensive maturity model; indeed the success of eden is due to the fact that the model has, in contrast to other models, less criteria and is easy to handle. The experts explained within the interviews that many companies prefer a checklist instead of a complex maturity model. For these reasons, it is not necessary to develop a separate and totally new BPM maturity model to understand and show possible dependencies.

On the basis of the three research questions, the following SAP specific principles have been developed to enable company management and all relevant stakeholders to determine and understand possible connections between an SAP system and a BPM approach. The principles can be employed to support the successful use of BPM maturity models within an SAP systems environment. These principles are not evident in any of the examined BPM maturity models in such detail.

- *Ensure that management fully support the use of SAP in the organisation to its full extent.*

The use of SAP ERP as the central IT software system within a company is usually a strategic decision. In this case, the company should decide how to integrate the system with the adopted BPM approach of the company. What does the SAP specification imply? Does that mean that only key figures have to be generated from the SAP system? Could there be other systems besides the SAP system? Should a company use as many standard SAP processes as possible? The company must determine who decides possible solutions or any adaptations of the SAP system. The successful implementation of an SAP system is only possible if the senior management are aware of and confront these issues.

- *Establish as many SAP ERP standard processes as possible at the company in order to minimize the complexity of system upgrades or enhancements.*

If the company wants to use SAP, and the management supports this, then companies should also decide whether, and to what extent, standard SAP processes should be used. The use of standard SAP processes reduces the time, cost, resources and other operational constraints, and supports the introduction of new SAP enhancement packages or release changes. Each change makes it necessary to test customised solutions and adjust the customer-specific programming to the upgraded SAP system. But it is important to prioritize when the standard SAP processes should be used, and when it is better to use self-defined solutions. A BPM team should not accept processes as given and must analyse which approach is best suited to a specific company environment. Not all standard processes are the optimal solutions for every company, and a company should not necessarily submit to the dictates of a rule-based IT system. But the use of standard process solutions could also be very helpful and reduce the budget required to operate an IT system. Regular consideration should be given to whether IT innovations in the system could lead to process improvements. For example, mobile device applications can now operate in conjunction with SAP modules, and thus such mobile functionality is now integrated into the standard SAP system.

- *Ensure that all processes have been documented, analysed and understood, even if they are pre-defined by the SAP system.*

The use of SAP standard processes does not absolve a company from the duty to document, analyse and understand each process. It can be the case that standard processes which run in a single system like SAP run with an optimised composition, and are better coordinated than other processes; but nevertheless, each process should be analysed. Unfortunately, it is not always obvious which data is being stored and used within an SAP process. Technically, it is currently not possible to get a fast and actual process flowchart from an existing SAP system, and see how customizing settings within an SAP system may change a process flow. Therefore it is very important to understand and analyse these SAP processes in detail. This is the only way to avoid incorrect or error-prone process operations. A company should know exactly how its processes are running, and therefore a company should not be dictated to by an IT system or by the opinion of an ERP system provider. An analysis of the pre-defined process should enable a company to decide whether the standard process is usable, or whether an individual process should be developed for their specific company environment.

- *Establish a procedure that ensures that all interfaces are analysed for their BPM relevance, regardless of whether they are used between different systems or from and to the SAP system.*

Interfaces between different systems often offer opportunities for systems optimization and process improvement. Many experts recommend considering the processes from an end-to-end perspective. They have learned from their practical experience that, especially in the case of system breaks and interface connections, data is often transmitted in a format that is different to that which is required. It is important to analyse the standard interfaces provided by the software provider, which may not be the best and optimal for the user organisation.

- *Ensure that all teams within a company, especially the BPM team and the SAP team, contribute to the development of the same processes and process maps, and that only one process map exists within the organisation.*

SAP is a very powerful tool that communicates with many different sub-modules and other systems. The early versions of SAP had a functional structure but with the application of BPM, the package is now more process-oriented in design. It is important to avoid different teams working in isolation and developing different process configurations within a company. The BPM team should consist of a variety of different stakeholders, to represent different requirements and knowledge inputs.

- *Ensure that all necessary key figures are generated directly from the SAP system.*

SAP provides many instruments for the generation and monitoring of KPIs and most BPM maturity models encompass the analysis of KPIs. For many experts in this study, the SAP system was often the leading financial system in their company contexts. This offers many advantages for the analysis of KPIs. Much financial information is already stored in the SAP system, which can be used to support the BPM approach. Some companies, when trying to implement quick solutions or consultancy generated analysis, may turn to creating Excel spreadsheets rather than using the "one view of the truth" available in the SAP system. SAP provides many predefined reports, and can also employ business intelligence tools to provide customised reports from the SAP database. It may take longer to determine the required fields for an analysis within the SAP system, but for frequent use it is much faster to retrieve the numbers directly from the SAP system.

VI. CONCLUSION AND FUTURE WORK

One view evident in the existing literature is that no specific IT system should determine the use of a BPM approach, but should simply support the business transactions of a company [38]. However, the practical experience of the experts interviewed in this research provides a different perspective. Neubauer [17] asserts that ERP systems can influence a company's business processes and this is confirmed by this research as regards the SAP ERP system. All the interviews, which involved many practitioners, have confirmed that the SAP and BPM concepts are closely related. Theoretically, there is often no such link found in the documentation, but in practice the SAP system is the leading ERP system in many companies, and therefore there is a practical connection. An IT system such as SAP ERP can influence a company and its processes. In many companies, SAP is the dominant system, and a BPM maturity model needs to accommodate this reality.

Unfortunately, many BPM maturity models currently consider only a small range of IT applications, and do not analyse any kind of ERP system. To this end, this research has developed some principles, which can be used as management guidelines for practising managers and other relevant stakeholders. They provide practical guidance for companies using SAP, BPM and BPM maturity models, and can lead to an improvement in business performance to the benefit of many stakeholders. It is evident that many maturity models do not consider any link between an SAP system and the BPM approach. The application of the principles discussed here can help develop interrelations between these topics. Further research could also examine whether such links also exist in other ERP systems or in other standalone software packages.

REFERENCES

[1] SAP, "SAP: The World's Largest Provider of Enterprise Application Software," SAP Global Corporate Affairs [retrieved: Feb. 2017]. [Online]. Available from: http://www.sap.com/documents/2016/07/0a4e1b8c-7e7c-0010-82c7-eda71af511fa.html

[2] SAP, "ERP System | Enterprise Resource Planning | SAP," [retrieved: Jan. 2018]. [Online]. Available from: https://www.sap.com/products/enterprise-management-erp.html

[3] D. E. O'Leary, "The Impact of Gartner's Maturity Curve, Adoption Curve, Strategic Technologies on Information Systems Research, with Applications to Artificial Intelligence, ERP, BPM, and RFID," Journal of Emerging Technologies in Accounting, vol. 6, pp. 45-66, 2009, doi: 10.2308/jeta.2009.6.1.45.

[4] H. Tscherwitschke, "What you need to know about business process management," Computerwoche. from FAQ zu BPM: Was Sie über Business-Process-Management wissen müssen. [retrieved: Jan. 2018]. [Online]. Available from: http://www.computerwoche.de/software/soa-bpm/1906638/, 2011.

[5] B. Heilig and M. Möller, "Business Process Management with SAP NetWeaver BPM," Bonn: SAP PRESS, 2014.

[6] P. Busch and P. Fettke, "Business Process Management under the Microscope: The Potential of Social Network Analysis," 44th Hawaii International Conference on System Sciences (HICSS), 2011.

[7] T. M. Bekele and Z. Weihua, "Towards collaborative business process management development current and future approaches," IEEE 3rd International Conference on Communication Software and Networks (ICCSN), 2011.

[8] R. M. Saco, "Maturity Models," Industrial Management, vol. 50, no. 4, pp. 11-15, 2008.

[9] E. Ericsson, P. Gustafsson, D. Höök, L. Marcks von Würtemberg, and W. Rocha Flores, "Process improvement framework evaluation," International Conference on Management Science and Engineering (ICMSE), 2010.

[10] T. De Bruin, R. Freeze, U. Kaulkarni, and M. Rosemann, "Understanding the Main Phases of Developing a Maturity Assessment Model," 16th Australasian Conference on Information Systems (ACIS), Sydney. [retrieved: Jan. 2018]. [Online]. Available from: http://eprints.qut.edu.au/25152/, 2005.

[11] C. Von Wangenheim et al., "Creating Software Process Capability/Maturity Models," IEEE Software, vol. 27, no.4, pp. 92-94, 2010.

[12] A. Van Looy, "Which business process maturity model best fits your organization?," Business Process Trends, vol. 2013, no. July, pp. 1-6., 2013.

[13] A. Van Looy, "Does IT matter for business process maturity? A comparative study on business process maturity models," Proceedings of the 2010 international conference On the move to meaningful internet systems, Hersonissos, Crete, Greece, 2010.

[14] S. Aeppli, "When SAP BPM calculates,“ Computerwoche. from Selbsttest für CW-Leser: Wann sich SAP BPM rechnet. [retrieved: Jan. 2018]. [Online]. Available from: http:// www.computerwoche.de/2503123, Jan 2012.

[15] A. Corallo, A. Margherita, M. Scalvenzi, and D. Storelli, "Building a process-based organization: The design roadmap at Superjet," International. Knowledge & Process Management, vol. 17, no. 2, pp. 49-61, 2010, doi: 10.1002/kpm.340,

[16] J. vom Brocke et al., "Ten principles of good business process management," Business Process Management Journal, vol. 20, no. 4, pp. 530-548, 2014, doi: 10.1108/bpmj-06-2013-0074.

[17] T. Neubauer, "An empirical study about the status of business process management," Business Process Management Journal, vol. 15, no. 2, pp. 166 – 183, 2009, doi: 10.1108/14637150910949434.

[18] R. Poston and S. Grabski, "Financial impacts of enterprise resource planning implementations," International Journal of Accounting Information Systems, vol. 2, no. 4, pp. 271-294, 2001, doi: 10.1016/S1467-0895(01)00024-0.

[19] Y. L. Antonucci, G. Corbitt, G. Stewart, and A. L. Harris, "Enterprise Systems Education: Where Are We? Where Are We Going?" Journal of Information Systems Education, vol. 15, no. 3, pp. 227-234, 2004.

[20] A. Van Looy, M. De Backer, G. Poels, and M. Snoeck, "Choosing the right business process maturity model," Information & Management, vol. 50, no. 7, pp. 466-488, 2013, doi: http://dx.doi.org/10.1016/j.im.2013.06.002.

[21] P. Cryer, "The research student's guide to success," 3rd ed., Maidenhead: Open University Press, 2006.

[22] M. Saunders, P. Lewis, and A. Thornhill, "Research methods for business students," New York: Prentice Hall, 2009.

[23] A. B. Ryan, "Post-Positivist Approaches to Research Researching and Writing your thesis: a guide for postgraduate students," pp. 12-26, MACE: Maynooth Adult and Community Education, 2006.

[24] E. G. Guba, "The Paradigm dialog," Newbury Park, Calif.: Sage Publications, 1990.

[25] Z. O'Leary, "The Social Science Jargon Buster," London, UK: SAGE Publications Ltd, 2007.

[26] J. Becker, R. Knackstedt, and J. Pöppelbuß, "Documentation quality of maturity model developments," vol. 123, [retrieved: Jan. 2018]. [Online]. Available from: https://www.wi.uni-muenster.de/sites/wi/files/public/research/arbeitsberichte/ab123.pdf, 2009.

[27] G. Thomas, "How to Do Your Case Study: A Guide for Students and Researchers," SAGE Publications, 2011.

[28] J. Collis and R. Hussey, "Business research: a practical guide for undergraduate & postgraduate students," Basingstoke: Palgrave Macmillan, 2009.

[29] R. K. Yin, "Case Study Research: Design and Methods," SAGE Publications, 2009.

[30] R. Kumar, "Research Methodology: A Step-by-Step Guide for Beginners," SAGE Publications, 2011.

[31] A. Bryman, and E. Bell, "Business research methods," Oxford University Press, 2007.

[32] G. Guest, K. M. MacQueen, and E. E. Namey, "Applied Thematic Analysis," SAGE Publications, 2011.

[33] S. E. Baker, and R. Edwards, "How many qualitative interviews is enough? Expert voices and early career reflections on sampling and cases in qualitative research," Southampton: ESRC National Centre for Research Methods, University of Southampton, 2012, [retrieved: Jan. 2018]. [Online]. Available from: http://eprints.ncrm.ac.uk/2273/4/how_many_interviews.pdf

[34] BPM Maturity Model EDEN e.V., "Who develop eden," [retrieved: Jan, 2018], [Online]. Available from: http://www.bpm-maturitymodel.com/eden/opencms/en/Who_do_eden/

[35] CMMI Institute, "About CMMI Institute," [retrieved: Jan, 2018], [Online]. Available from: http://cmmiinstitute.com/about-cmmi-institute

[36] Object Management Group Inc., "BPMM 1.0," [retrieved: Jan, 2018], [Online]. Available from: http://www.omg.org/spec/BPMM/1.0/

[37] DSAG-Arbeitskreis BPM, "DSAG-Guide - Business Process Management," vol. 112, 2013, [retrieved: Jan, 2018], [Online]. Available from: https://www.dsag.de/fileadmin/media/Leitfaeden/Leitfaden_Business-Process-Management/files/assets/downloads/publication.pdf

[38] C. Li, "Improving Business - IT Alignment through Business Architecture," (Doctorate Doctoral Dissertations), Lawrence Technological University, Southfield, MI, 2010, [retrieved: Jan, 2018], [Online]. Available from: https://search.proquest.com/docview/858204513

Alignment-free Sequence Comparison based on NGS Short-reads Neighbor Search

Phanucheep Chotnithi
SOKENDAI
The Graduate University for Advanced Studies
Tokyo, Japan
Email: phanucheep@nii.ac.jp

Atsuhiro Takasu
National Institutes of Informatics
Tokyo, Japan
Email: takasu@nii.ac.jp

***Abstract*—Next-generation sequencing (NGS) is becoming the mainstream format for genome-sequence data and creates new challenges in genome-sequence comparison. The multiple-sequence alignment approach is not suited to NGS data because of short-read assembly and computational resource problems. Therefore, alignment-free methods are needed for comparisons involving NGS data. Most alignment-free methods rely on k-mer-based distance measures. However, the characteristics of NGS data mean that k-mer-based alignment-free methods might not be optimal. NGS data contain substantial amounts of overlap among the NGS reads, which will affect the distances between the NGS sets for each input species as calculated by these methods. We propose a novel alignment-free sequence-comparison method, based on the number of neighbors in the NGS data, which aims to reduce the effect of the NGS-read overlap. We performed experiments that compared the proposed method with two existing methods. The results show that our method can distinguish the differences between diverse species better than the compared methods. Moreover, our method performs NGS data comparisons while showing robustness with respect to the k parameter, in contrast to the compared methods.**

***Keywords*–NGS; Phylogeny; Sequence comparison; Alignment-free**

I. INTRODUCTION

Next-generation sequencing (NGS) is a method used to transform data from genome samples to a digitized data sequence, achieving a rapid throughput compared with traditional sequencing processes. Instead of one long sequence of genome data, NGS produces large numbers of sequence fragments called *reads* per genome sample. NGS can be applied to many biological problems, including *de novo* whole-genome sequencing and RNA-seq [1].

For most genome-sequence analysis applications, *short-read* data is a new challenge [2], where sequence comparison and phylogeny analysis are issues that we are interested in. Normally, sequence-comparison algorithms use one long genome sequence, such as 16S rRNA in mitochondrial DNA (mtDNA), and the whole genome when measuring the distance between sequences [3], [4], [5]. Clustering and classification algorithms are applied via distance matrices to produce a phylogenetic tree from which evolutionary relationships among species can be inferred. The emergence of NGS short-read methods, with their new form for genome sequences, will challenge the approach to genome-sequence analysis. In fact, existing methods and algorithms are no longer efficient for this new type of genome data [6].

The traditional method for sequence comparison is the multiple-sequence alignment (MSA) method, which has trouble dealing with a large proportion of NGS short-read data. Its approach is to reconstruct the short reads into one long sequence. In a process called *assemble*, NGS reads are mapped onto the template sequence, which involves significant computational cost. To assemble the genome without template sequences is very challenging because the reads are mostly short and contain large numbers of repeated genome data. Recently, the alignment-free method for sequence comparison has attracted attention from researchers because of its processing efficiency compared with the alignment-based method [6]. This method does not require an assembly process, and is therefore scalable to large numbers of NGS short reads, which avoids the main problem with MSA. Most alignment-free methods rely on k-mer frequencies as the sequence profile used to measure the distance between profiles [5]. However, alignment-free methods remain less accurate than MSA.

Several studies have proposed techniques that focus specifically on NGS short-read data. $CVTree$ [7], [8] and d_2^S [9] have shown good results for distance measurements and phylogeny reconstruction with both NGS data and long genome sequences. For a given k, $CVTree$ and d_2^S calculate the distance between two NGS samples (or two DNA sequences) based on the normalized k-mer frequencies. Because these methods rely on k-mers, we need to consider the random overlaps between NGS short reads. These overlaps affect the frequency of occurrence of k-mers within NGS sets, which could lead to an inaccurate distance matrix. The random overlaps between NGS short reads can cause differences between the k-mer frequency profiles of any two NGS sets obtained from the same species sample.

In this paper, we propose an assembly-free and alignment-free sequence-comparison method for NGS data called d^{NS}. The main aim of d^{NS} is to reduce the effect of the overlap among NGS short reads in sequence comparisons. By grouping similar short reads together, we can assume that reads sharing the same overlap are likely to fall into the same group. Using a statistical assessment of the number of short reads included in the neighbor search with a set of queries, the method provides information about the similarity between NGS sets. We performed experiments with two simulated NGS datasets. According to the results using 29 mammalian mtDNA sequences [10], [11], d^{NS} performed well when reconstructing the phylogenetic tree of a diverse-species dataset, which indicates that d^{NS} can achieve sequence comparisons using NGS data. For a 29-member $Escherichia/Shigella$ whole-genome dataset [12], d^{NS} outperformed d_2^S and matched the performance of $CVTree$. In addition, the results showed that

d^{NS} is more robust with respect to various values for k than d_2^S and $CVTree$, which indicates that d^{NS} is robust against the effects of NGS short-read overlap on the k-mer frequency distribution. Because this neighbor-search-based alignment-free approach to sequence comparison is novel, there is plenty of scope for further development and possible improvements.

II. Background and Related Work

Two k-mer frequency-based alignment-free methods are considered in this paper, namely $CVTree$ [7], [8] and d_2^S [9]. Both $CVTree$ and d_2^S focus on normalized k-mer frequencies. The difference is that $CVTree$ calculates the distance between two genome sequences or NGS short-read sets by using their normalized k-mer frequency vector, called the composite vector (CV), whereas d_2^S is a statistical approach to modifying raw distance measures to produce measures better suited to NGS data.

A. $CVTree$: CV alignment-free method

The $CVTree$ process is as follows. For a fixed length k, count separately the number of substrings of length k, $k-1$, $k-2$ on each input sequence. The initial CV is the number of k-mer items, which is $N = 4^k$ total dimensions for DNA sequences and $N = 20^k$ for protein sequences in lexicographic order. Calculate the $subtraction\ score$ for the k-mer:

$$a_i(\alpha_1\alpha_2...\alpha_k) \equiv \frac{f(\alpha_1\alpha_2...\alpha_k) - f^0(\alpha_1\alpha_2...\alpha_k)}{f^0(\alpha_1\alpha_2...\alpha_k)},$$

where $f(\alpha_1\alpha_2...\alpha_k)$ is the frequency of k-mer $\alpha_1\alpha_2...\alpha_k$ and $f^0(\alpha_1\alpha_2...\alpha_k)$ is the predicted frequency of the k-mer, calculated by using a $(k-2)$-th Markov assumption.

Let $CV_A = (a_1a_2...a_N)$ and $CV_B = (b_1b_2...b_N)$ be the CVs for the species A and B, respectively. Finally, calculate the distance matrix for the modified CV:

$$D(A, B) = (1 - C(CV_A, CV_B))/2,$$

where

$$C(CV_A, CV_B) = \frac{\sum_{i=1}^N a_i \times b_i}{\sqrt{\sum_{i=1}^N a_i^2 \times \sum_{i=1}^N b_i^2}}.$$

B. d_2^S k-mer statistical alignment-free method

d_2^S statistics is a modified version of D_2, D_2^*, and D_2^S statistics [13], [14]. They are applicable to NGS data by considering the random processes of NGS data in terms of D_2, D_2^*, and D_2^S to model the correct k-mer distribution of NGS data. NGS short reads are small fragments from the original long sequence, which means that the method of sampling those reads will affect the k-mer frequency distribution. Another characteristic of NGS data relevant to d_2^S statistics is that an NGS short read can originate from the forward or reverse strand of the original genome, requiring consideration of not only the k-mer distributions of short-read data themselves but also their complementary sequences. d_2^S can be calculated by:

$$d_S^2 = \frac{1}{2}\left(1 - \frac{D_S^2}{\sqrt{\sum_{w\in A^k} \tilde{X}_w^2/\tilde{Z}_w}\sqrt{\sum_{w\in A^k} \tilde{Y}_w^2/\tilde{Z}_w}}\right),$$

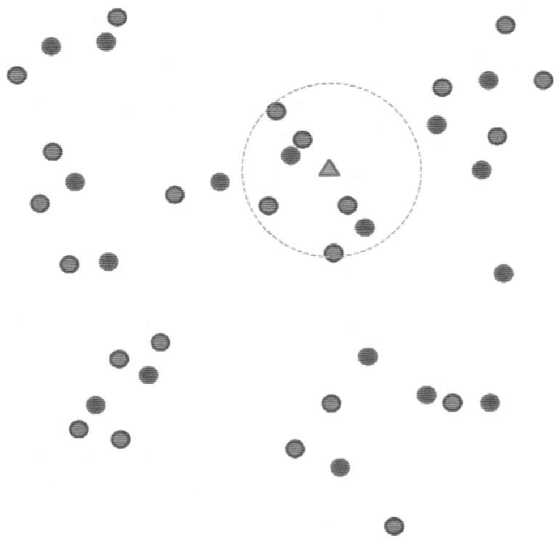

Figure 1. Neighbor search in NGS short reads

where

$$D_2^S = \frac{\tilde{X}_w\tilde{Y}_w}{\tilde{Z}_w}$$

and

$$\tilde{Z}_w = \sqrt{\tilde{X}_w^2 + \tilde{Y}_w^2}.$$

Suppose that M reads of length β are sampled from a genome of length n. Let X_w and Y_w be the numbers of occurrences of word pattern w in the M pairs of reads from the first genome and the second genome, respectively. We define $\tilde{X}_w^2 = X_w - M(b-k+1)(p_w + p_{\bar{w}})$ with $\tilde{Y}_w^2$ being defined analogously. Let $w = w_1w_2...w_k$ and $p_w = p_{w_1}p_{w_2}...p_{w_k}$, with $\bar{w}$ being the complement of word w. Consider two genome sequences taking L letters (0, 1, ..., $L-1$) at each position. For the null model, we assume that the two genomes are independent and both are generated by models with p_l being the probability of taking state l, l = 0, 1,..., $L-1$.

III. Proposed Method

The NGS data comprise a very large quantity of short reads that contain overlapping data. Particularly for whole-genome sequences, the number of overlaps and repeats can grow dramatically. Most existing research on alignment-free methods adopts k-mer frequencies to specify the profile of a sequence and when obtaining distances in NGS sets. However, the random overlap of short reads in NGS data will clearly affect the distribution of k-mer frequencies. This is the key problem we focus on in this research.

Because the problem is caused by the overlap and the repeating data, the key idea is to reduce their effect by grouping similar short reads. We can then use a statistical approach to calculate the evolutionary distance between NGS short reads. Fig. 1 shows a feature space spanned by the k-mers. (As mentioned above, the dimensionality of the space is 4^k, but, for readability, we show a 2-D space.) Each dot represents an NGS short read. Dots of the same color indicate that the corresponding NGS short read comes from the same genome sequence. For a given short read r, its set of neighbors is defined as the set of short reads whose distance from r is within a predefined threshold. The circle in Fig. 1 encloses the neighborhood of the short read represented by the triangle.

The assumption is that the short reads that are placed near each other in the feature space will have a high probability of sharing overlapping data. We define the difference between any two NGS sets by comparing the number of neighbor-search results that correspond to the same collection of search queries on their NGS short reads. Because this method does not consider k-mer frequencies in the similarity measures of NGS sets, any overlap effects on the final distance matrix are reduced.

A. Notations and equations

Denote $d^{NS}(X,Y)$ as the pairwise distance between NGS sets X and Y, where $X = \{x_1, x_2, ...x_n\}$ and n is the number of NGS short reads of X. Similarly, $Y = \{y_1, y_2, ...y_m\}$ and m is the number of NGS short reads of Y. For a query sequence q, let R^q_X denote the number of neighbors of q in X. $d^{NS}(X,Y)$ can then be calculated as follows:

$$d^{NS}(X,Y) = (D(X,Y) + D(Y,X))/2, \tag{1}$$

where

$$D(X,Y) = \sum_{i=1}^{n} \left(1 - \frac{min\left(\frac{R^{x_i}_X}{n}, \frac{R^{x_i}_Y}{m}\right)}{max\left(\frac{R^{x_i}_X}{n}, \frac{R^{x_i}_Y}{m}\right)}\right) \times \left(\frac{R^{x_i}_X}{\sum_{i=1}^{n} R^{x_i}_X}\right). \tag{2}$$

$D(X,Y)$ is a divergence measurement calculated by summation of the rational difference between the number of neighbors in NGS sets X and Y for all NGS short reads $x_1, x_2, ...x_n \in X$. The min to max ratio of two normalized values $\frac{R^{x_i}_X}{n}$ and $\frac{R^{x_i}_Y}{m}$ in Eq. (2) indicates the rational similarity between those two values. If the normalized numbers of neighbors for X and Y are the same, this term will be equal to 1. Subtracting the term from 1 makes it a divergence measurement. For each short read in X and Y, the distance is weighted by the normalized number of the neighbors for that query. Because $D(X,Y)$ is an asymmetric function, we define the distance $d^{NS}(x,y)$ as the average value of $D(X,Y)$ and $D(Y,X)$.

In the current implementation, we use locality-sensitive hashing (LSH) [15] for the neighbor search because of its lightweight nature. Minhash [16] was originally used to compare the similarity between documents. This algorithm provides a fast approximation of the Jaccard similarity between two sets by using their Minhash signatures and simply counts the number of components of the signatures that are equal. Let h be the hash function for mapping an integer to another different integer, with no collisions. Apply n hash functions in $H = h_1, h_2, ..., h_n$ to the set of integers. For each h_i from $i = 1$ to n, the minimum hash value produced by h_i will be assigned to the ith component of the Minhash signature. We use this process to obtain the Minhash signature of an NGS short read. The set of k-mers that appear in an NGS short read are transformed into a set of integers to enable the hash functions to be applied. These hash functions are randomly generated with various values for the parameters that produce different hash functions. LSH is a process for finding a group of items whose Minhash signature is similar to a query's signature. It separates the Minhash signature into a series of bands, each comprising a set of rows. For example, 200 Minhash signatures might be separated into 20 bands of 4 rows each. Each band is then hashed to a "bucket. If two sets have the same Minhash signature in a band, they will be hashed to the same bucket, and will therefore be considered candidate pairs. In our approach, utilizing LSH with Minhash enables us to search for similar NGS short reads easily. However, d^{NS} could adopt alternative neighbor-search algorithms because the distance measurements in d^{NS} are based on the results of neighbor search, rather than its method.

IV. Evaluations and Results

A. Experiment setup

Two datasets, comprising 29 mammalian mtDNA sequences [10], [11] and 29 $Escherichia/Shigella$ [12] genomes were used to evaluate d^{NS} by comparing it with two existing k-mer-based alignment-free methods, namely $CVTree$ and d_2^S. Because both datasets were originally made up of long sequences, we used a tool called $MetaSim$ [17] to simulate NGS short reads from long genome sequences. We used three error models, namely 454, Empirical(Illumina), and Sanger, which enabled us to simulate the NGS high-throughput sequencing results from three different NGS platforms. These sequenced the actual samples into NGS data. In the following discussion, the term "Exact" refers to the non-error case in simulating NGS short reads from long genomic sequences. We used sampling depths of 1, 5, 10, and 30, where the sampling depth means the average number of occurrences of the character at each position in the original sequences appearing in the NGS set. The length of NGS short reads was set to 100, with a default parameter for the error distribution for each model. For the parameter k, we considered using k values in the range 6 to 10. Although a larger k should give a better result, the processing time to map each NGS short read to the feature space would increase significantly. We planned our experiments to use this range of k values for several reasons. One reason was that $CVTree$ and d_2^S proponents have suggested it as a suitable range. Second, for d^{NS}, k values out of this range would affect the efficiency of the neighbor-search process.

MSA was used as the benchmark method for comparison with the alignment-free methods to evaluate their performance on phylogeny reconstruction. We used the $ClusterOmega$ tool [18], followed by the $dnadist$ tool in the PHYLIP package [19], on aligned sequences from MSA to calculate distance matrices.

For a distance matrix, either from MSA or from an alignment-free method, we used the $neighbor$ tool in the PHYLIP package to construct a phylogenetic tree using the neighbor-joining method [20]. We used the popular Robinson–Fould distance (RF) [21] for evaluation, as described in [22]. The RF value can be calculated by counting the internal nodes that appear in one tree but not in the other. A small RF value means that the shape of the trees is close to the benchmark tree. The values for RF range from 0, meaning two tree are exactly the same, to $2(n-3)$ where n is the number of leaf nodes.

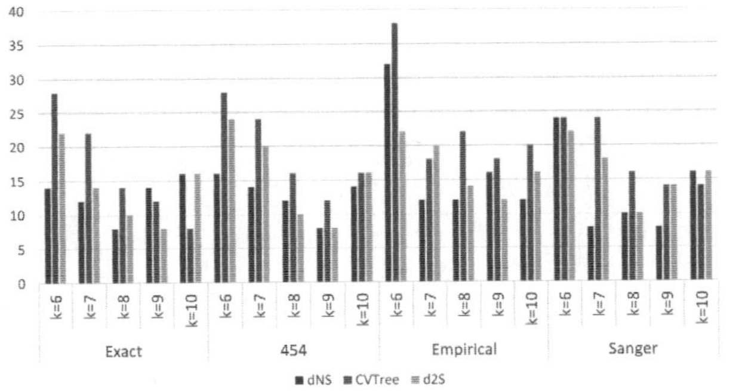

Figure 2. The RF of phylogenetic tree results for each method on NGS reads of 29 mammalian mtDNA sequences with a sampling depth of 5

B. Experimental results

1) The 29 mammalian mtDNA sequences: The 29 mammalian mtDNA sequences are a well-studied dataset, being widely used for the evaluation of existing sequence-comparison methods. The MSA tree for this dataset is therefore a reliable benchmark for our experiments. Because the evolutionary relation between each species in this dataset is diverse, a sequence-comparison method should be able to reconstruct a phylogenetic tree almost identical to that for MSA to offer confidence in the performance of the method.

We applied three alignment-free methods, namely d^{NS}, $CVTree$, and d_2^S, to simulated NGS short-read data. We compared the resultant phylogenetic trees with the benchmark tree obtained from MSA with mtDNA sequences. At a sampling depth of 1, the phylogenetic trees obtained from the three alignment-free methods were very different from the MSA benchmark tree because of the shallow sampling depth.

Fig. 2 shows the RF between the MSA benchmark tree and the phylogenetic tree obtained by d^{NS}, $CVTree$, and d_2^S on four types of NGS reads, using a sampling depth of 5 and various k parameter values. The figure shows that d^{NS} produces a more accurate tree than either $CVTree$ or d_2^S in most cases.

Table I summarizes the most accurate result for each alignment-free method shown in Fig. 2. Note that RF can be up to 52 for this dataset. The best RF result in the table among all three methods is 8, which means that the rational distance between the tree obtained via alignment-free methods and the benchmark tree is 8/52 = 0.154. We can therefore consider that d^{NS} and the other two alignment-free methods all perform well using this dataset. d^{NS} produced the best result among the alignment-free methods across all NGS error models. Regarding the sampling depth, we found no significant differences with 10 and 30 sampling, as shown in Fig. 3 for d^{NS}. The same result was found for $CVTree$ and d_2^S [22].

We investigated how parameter values affect the performance of d_{NS}. Fig. 3 shows the result of d^{NS} on NGS reads of 29 mammalian mtDNA sequences with a parameter setup that included four NGS error models, k values from 6 to 10, and sampling depths of 1, 5, 10, and 30. With a sampling depth of 1 for any NGS error model, d^{NS} could not produce an accurate phylogenetic tree for this dataset. The reason could be that the numbers of queries used in the neighbor search are too small to retrieve good distance measurements. According to this result for d^{NS}, we can infer that a more suitable value for the k parameter would be 8 or 9.

TABLE I. BEST RF RESULT FOR ANY K PARAMETER ON NGS READS OF 29 MAMMALIAN MTDNA SEQUENCES WITH A SAMPLING DEPTH OF 5

	d^{NS}	$CVTree$	d_2^S
Exact	**8**	**8**	**8**
454	**8**	12	**8**
Empirical	**12**	18	**12**
Sanger	**8**	14	10

2) The 29 $Escherichia/Shigella$ whole-genome sequences: We used this dataset to evaluate the performance of d^{NS} on the whole genomes of species that are close to each other in evolutionary terms. The 29 whole-genome sequences come from two main genera, namely $Escherichia$ and $Shigella$, which are from the same $Enterobacteriaceae$ family in the $Bacteria$ kingdom. Because the dataset is large, MSA's lack of scalability prevents it from being applied. We obtained the benchmark tree for this dataset from [12]. This involved concatenating the alignments of the 2034 core genes of the $Escherichia/Shigella$ genomes, then using a maximum-likelihood method to construct the phylogenetic tree for this dataset.

With the close evolutionary relationship between the $Escherichia$ and $Shigella$ species, all alignment-free methods tested in this experiment failed to obtain an accurate RF result when comparing their resultant trees with the benchmark tree. As shown in Table II, the best RF value was 16, with the rational distance between the result tree and the benchmark tree being 16/52 = 0.3. The performances of all three methods were below a satisfactory level. There was no significant difference among the d^{NS}, $CVTree$, and d_2^S methods. In fact, d_2^S performed better for the Exact error model, whereas d^{NS} and $CVTree$ performed better for the other error models.

A point to note is that d^{NS} appears more robust with respect to variations in the k parameter than $CVTree$ or d_2^S, as shown in Fig. 4. For most k, and for each error model, d^{NS}'s phylogenetic tree is more accurate than those of the other methods, with the RF value being at the same level. For example, although d_2^S performs best on the Exact model with RF of 18 when k = 9 and 10, the RF values are much bigger for other k values. Robustness against the parameter k is beneficial because it makes parameter tuning easier and we can optimize the processing efficiency by choosing a smaller value for k. The reason for this effect is that the k parameter does not directly affect how d^{NS} calculates the distance between each species. It uses the k value only for constructing the feature space. Because of limited computing resources, we examined only the case of the 1 sampling depth.

The main aim of this research is to introduce a novel approach to performing NGS data comparisons. It is to be expected that the computational efficiencies of $CVTree$ and d_2^S would exceed that of d^{NS} in its current implementation. Table III confirms that d^{NS}'s runtime is slower than the others. However, the k parameter value does not affect the runtime of d^{NS}, unlike those for $CVTree$ and d_2^S. In particular, d_2^S's runtime grows dramatically between k = 6 and k = 10. It is an

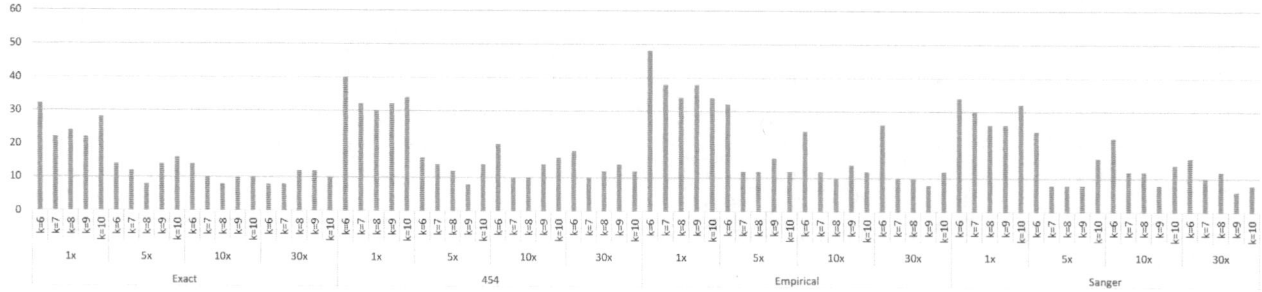

Figure 3. The RF of phylogenetic tree results for d^{NS} on NGS reads of 29 mammalian mtDNA sequences using four NGS error models, k = 6–10, and sampling depths of 1, 5, 10, and 30

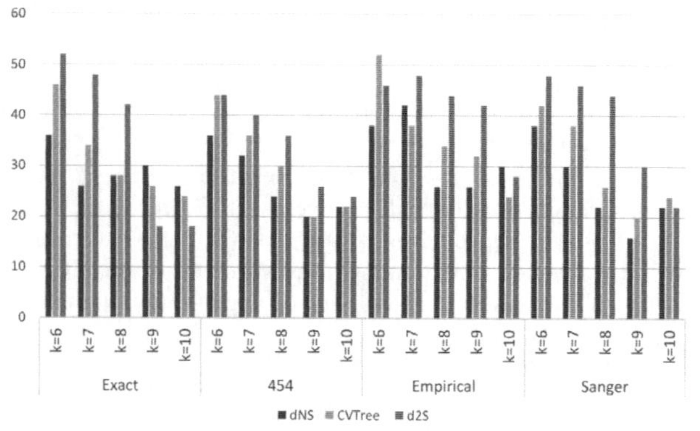

Figure 4. The RF results for NGS reads of 29 $Escherichia/Shigella$ whole-genome sequences with a sampling depth of 1

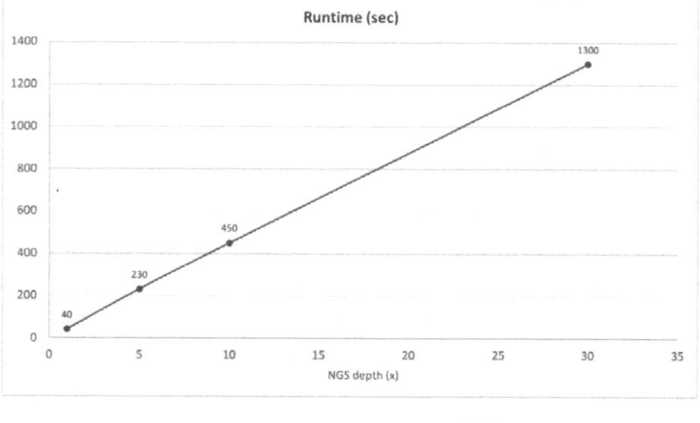

Figure 5. Computational runtime (seconds) for d^{NS} on the 29 mammalian mtDNA dataset with NGS sampling depths of 1, 5,10, and 30

TABLE II. BEST RF RESULTS FOR ANY K VALUE ON NGS READS OF 29 $ESCHERICHIA/SHIGELLA$ WHOLE-GENOME SEQUENCES WITH A SAMPLING DEPTH OF 1

	d^{NS}	$CVTree$	d_2^S
Exact	26	26	**18**
454	**20**	**20**	**20**
Empirical	26	**24**	28
Sanger	**16**	20	22

advantage that the k value has little effect on the runtime of our proposed method. In addition, the runtime of d^{NS} shows linear growth with varying sampling depth, as shown in Fig. 5

V. Conclusion and Future Work

In conclusion, we propose a novel approach for an alignment-free method d^{NS} that is focused on NGS short-read data and based on neighbor searching. Its main advantage is that it is an accurate alignment-free sequence-comparison method for reconstructing a phylogenetic tree more consistently than other k-mer-based alignment-free methods. Although it might lose significant information in the NGS data when ignoring the k-mer frequencies, the method is able to specify the distance between NGS sets with good accuracy when a sufficient number of queries is used.

According to our experimental results on mammalian mtDNA and $Escherichia/Shigella$ whole-genome sequences with simulated NGS short reads, the d^{NS} method can construct a phylogenetic tree that is almost as accurate as a benchmark tree. In addition, d^{NS} is able to deal with NGS short-read faults in the k-mer distribution, as shown in our results. However, the main drawback of d^{NS} is the computational inefficiency of the neighbor-search process, which consists of many NGS short-read comparisons.

Because this method is a novel approach to NGS short-read comparison, there are many aspects of it that we can develop to make the method more accurate and more computationally efficient. First, we should consider modifying d^{NS} toward a parameter-free approach. To improve the d^{NS} accuracy, we should consider applying different processes for mapping the NGS reads to a high-dimensional space during neighbor search, rather than using a k-mer frequency vector. This modification would seek to obtain more reliable grouping of overlapping NGS reads. Second, we should modify the equation for distance measurement used in this approach. We have noticed that calculating distances in the NGS data using only the number of neighbor query results might be insufficient to achieve better results. This information is quite coarse in comparison with normalized k-mer frequencies. We should consider combining our approach with other alignment-free methods to achieve higher accuracy. Finally, we need to optimize this method to be more scalable with respect to computational efficiency by considering alternative neighbor-search algorithms. In fact, we might consider a completely different approach, other than neighbor search, to the grouping of overlapping NGS reads.

TABLE III. COMPUTATIONAL RUNTIME FOR EACH ALIGNMENT-FREE METHOD (SECONDS) WITH 5 COVERAGE FOR MAMMALIAN mtDNA AND 1 COVERAGE FOR THE $ESCHERICHIA/SHIGELLA$ WHOLE-GENOME DATASET

	d^{NS}	$d_2^S(k=6)$	$d_2^S(k=10)$	$CVTree(k=6)$	$CVTree(k=10)$
29 mammalian mtDNA	230	4	780	2	5
29 $Escherichia/Shigella$ whole genome	8600	30	1050	25	180

REFERENCES

[1] M. L. Metzker, "Sequencing technologies–the next generation," Nature reviews. Genetics, vol. 11, no. 1, 2010, p. 31.

[2] A. Phillips, D. Janies, and W. Wheeler, "Multiple sequence alignment in phylogenetic analysis," Molecular phylogenetics and evolution, vol. 16, no. 3, 2000, pp. 317–330.

[3] M. S. Waterman, Introduction to computational biology: maps, sequences and genomes. CRC Press, 1995.

[4] R. Durbin, S. R. Eddy, A. Krogh, and G. Mitchison, Biological sequence analysis: probabilistic models of proteins and nucleic acids. Cambridge university press, 1998.

[5] S. Vinga and J. Almeida, "Alignment-free sequence comparisona review," Bioinformatics, vol. 19, no. 4, 2003, pp. 513–523.

[6] C. X. Chan and M. A. Ragan, "Next-generation phylogenomics," Biology direct, vol. 8, no. 1, 2013, p. 3.

[7] Z. Xu and B. Hao, "Cvtree update: a newly designed phylogenetic study platform using composition vectors and whole genomes," Nucleic acids research, vol. 37, no. suppl_2, 2009, pp. W174–W178.

[8] J. Qi, H. Luo, and B. Hao, "Cvtree: a phylogenetic tree reconstruction tool based on whole genomes," Nucleic acids research, vol. 32, no. suppl_2, 2004, pp. W45–W47.

[9] K. Song, J. Ren, Z. Zhai, X. Liu, M. Deng, and F. Sun, "Alignment-free sequence comparison based on next-generation sequencing reads," Journal of computational biology, vol. 20, no. 2, 2013, pp. 64–79.

[10] H. H. Otu and K. Sayood, "A new sequence distance measure for phylogenetic tree construction," Bioinformatics, vol. 19, no. 16, 2003, pp. 2122–2130.

[11] Y. Cao, A. Janke, P. J. Waddell, M. Westerman, O. Takenaka, S. Murata, N. Okada, S. Pääbo, and M. Hasegawa, "Conflict among individual mitochondrial proteins in resolving the phylogeny of eutherian orders," Journal of Molecular Evolution, vol. 47, no. 3, 1998, pp. 307–322.

[12] Z. Zhou, X. Li, B. Liu, L. Beutin, J. Xu, Y. Ren, L. Feng, R. Lan, P. R. Reeves, and L. Wang, "Derivation of escherichia coli o157: H7 from its o55: H7 precursor," PloS one, vol. 5, no. 1, 2010, p. e8700.

[13] G. Reinert, D. Chew, F. Sun, and M. S. Waterman, "Alignment-free sequence comparison (i): statistics and power," Journal of Computational Biology, vol. 16, no. 12, 2009, pp. 1615–1634.

[14] L. Wan, G. Reinert, F. Sun, and M. S. Waterman, "Alignment-free sequence comparison (ii): theoretical power of comparison statistics," Journal of Computational Biology, vol. 17, no. 11, 2010, pp. 1467–1490.

[15] A. Gionis, P. Indyk, R. Motwani et al., "Similarity search in high dimensions via hashing," in VLDB, vol. 99, no. 6, 1999, pp. 518–529.

[16] A. Z. Broder, M. Charikar, A. M. Frieze, and M. Mitzenmacher, "Min-wise independent permutations," Journal of Computer and System Sciences, vol. 60, no. 3, 2000, pp. 630–659.

[17] D. C. Richter, F. Ott, A. F. Auch, R. Schmid, and D. H. Huson, "Metasim: A sequencing simulator for genomics and metagenomics," Handbook of Molecular Microbial Ecology I: Metagenomics and Complementary Approaches, 2011, pp. 417–421.

[18] F. Sievers, A. Wilm, D. Dineen, T. J. Gibson, K. Karplus, W. Li, R. Lopez, H. McWilliam, M. Remmert, J. Söding et al., "Fast, scalable generation of high-quality protein multiple sequence alignments using clustal omega," Molecular systems biology, vol. 7, no. 1, 2011, p. 539.

[19] J. Felsenstein, "Phylip–phylogeny inference package (version 3.2) cladistics. 1989; 5: 164–166," DOI: citeulike-article-id, vol. 2344765.

[20] N. Saitou and M. Nei, "The neighbor-joining method: a new method for reconstructing phylogenetic trees." Molecular biology and evolution, vol. 4, no. 4, 1987, pp. 406–425.

[21] D. F. Robinson and L. R. Foulds, "Comparison of phylogenetic trees," Mathematical biosciences, vol. 53, no. 1-2, 1981, pp. 131–147.

[22] N. H. Tran and X. Chen, "Comparison of next-generation sequencing samples using compression-based distances and its application to phylogenetic reconstruction," BMC research notes, vol. 7, no. 1, 2014, p. 320.

Ranking Subreddits by Classifier Indistinguishability in the Reddit Corpus

Faisal Alquaddoomi
UCLA Computer Science Dept.
Los Angeles, CA, USA
Email: faisal@cs.ucla.edu

Deborah Estrin
Cornell Tech
New York, NY, USA
Email: destrin@cornell.edu

***Abstract*—Reddit, a popular online forum, provides a wealth of content for behavioral science researchers to analyze. These data are spread across various subreddits, subforums dedicated to specific topics. Social support subreddits are common, and users' behaviors there differ from reddit at large; most significantly, users often use 'throwaway' single-use accounts to disclose especially sensitive information. This work focuses specifically on identifying depression-relevant posts and, consequently, subreddits, by relying only on posting content. We employ posts to r/depression as labeled examples of depression-relevant posts and train a classifier to discriminate posts like them from posts randomly selected from the rest of the Reddit corpus, achieving 90% accuracy at this task. We argue that this high accuracy implies that the classifier is descriptive of "depression-like" posts, and use its ability (or lack thereof) to distinguish posts from other subreddits as discriminating the "distance" between r/depression and those subreddits. To test this approach, we performed a pairwise comparison of classifier performance between r/depression and 229 candidate subreddits. Subreddits which were very closely related thematically to r/depression, such as r/SuicideWatch, r/offmychest, and r/anxiety, were the most difficult to distinguish. A comparison this ranking of similar subreddits to r/depression to existing methods (some of which require extra data, such as user posting co-occurrence across multiple subreddits) yields similar results. Aside from the benefit of relying only on posting content, our method yields per-word importance values (heavily weighing words such as "I", "me", and "myself"), which recapitulate previous research on the linguistic phenomena that accompany mental health self-disclosure.**

Keywords–Natural language processing; Web mining; Clustering methods

I. INTRODUCTION

Reddit, a popular link-sharing and discussion forum, is a large and often difficult-to-navigate source of computer-mediated communication. Like most public discussion forums, it is distinct from other social networking sites such as Facebook or Twitter in that conversation largely occurs with strangers rather than members of one's explicit social graph (friends and followers, respectively). Unlike small topical discussion forums, Reddit is a vast collection of topical subforums (also known as "subreddits"), numbering just over one million as of January 2017 [1].

While Reddit is primarily a link-sharing website where users collaboratively filter content by voting, there is a significant portion of the site which is more social in nature. Many support subreddits exist in which the majority of posts are "self-posts", text written by users, rather than links to images or articles. A particularly interesting subset of these subreddits are the support and self-help subreddits where individuals spontaneously request and provide support to relative strangers. The ease of creating 'throwaway' accounts has encouraged the development of self-help subreddits where individuals can discuss possibly stigmatized medical conditions in relative anonymity. It has been shown that individuals who are anonymous tend to be less inhibited in their disclosures, and that Reddit users specifically make use of this feature when soliciting help (in the form of a self-post) more so than when providing it (in the form of a reply) [2].

The frankness and public accessibility of this communication makes it an attractive target for behavioral research, but as mentioned it can be difficult to navigate the vast number of subreddits, especially as existing ones change and new ones are introduced over time. It is infeasible to make use of user posting co-occurrence (a common and successful tactic for clustering subreddits) to study this subset of Reddit since users often do not maintain persistent accounts. This work presents a content-based subreddit ranking in which subreddits are ranked by the difficulty of distinguishing their posts from a "baseline" subreddit. We focus specifically on r/depression as the baseline subreddit in this work, since it is readily differentiable from average Reddit posts, as demonstrated in Section V. We explore the task of finding subreddits that are similar to r/depression based on this initial strength and compare our ranking results with other content- and user-based subreddit similarity measures. As an added benefit, our method provides weightings on the feature (in this case, words) that differentiate two subreddits, making the model's decisions more interpretable as a result.

The remainder of the paper is structured as follows. Section II provides a brief discussion of two fields which intersect in our work: mental health disclosure in social media, and clustering of forums by user and post attributes. We discuss the specific dataset, the Reddit corpus, in Section III. Section IV describes the methods we used to cluster subreddits, and Section V presents the results of our method and comparisons to others. Section VI discusses these results, with some high-level observations about the differences between prior results and potential problems with our current methodology. Finally, Section VII recapitulates the problem of clustering subreddits by post content, how we approached that problem, and what is left to do.

II. RELATED WORK

Since this work involves two separate topics, behavioral health as evidenced in online communities and subreddit clustering, they are presented below in two distinct sections.

A. Mental Health and Social Media

[2] examined the role of anonymity and how it affects disclosure in individuals seeking mental health support on reddit. They also automatically classified responses to these requests for help into four categories. While not directly relevant to the task of ranking subreddits by similarity, the context in which their study was conducted inspired this work, specifically in focusing on self-help subreddits in which individuals generally disclose anonymously. Their identification of the disparity between anonymous posters who are seeking help and often non-anonymous commenters providing aid influenced the decision to consider only self-post text in this work, as that is apparently more emblematic of people suffering from mental illness rather than individuals trying to help them. The ad-hoc process that they describe for collecting sets of related subreddits (a combination of knowledge from seasoned redditors and reading the information panel of their initial subreddits) motivated the need for an automatic method to find subreddits that requires only a "seed" subreddit from which to identify linguistically similar content. We hope that this work presents a possible solution in this context.

B. Clustering Subreddits

As far as we can tell, there has been little academic investigation into the problem of clustering subreddits. Instead, a number of individuals have informally explored the problem in blog posts and postings to Reddit itself. Their approaches fall into two groups: 1) user-based, and 2) content-based.

User-based methods focus on the users as the evidence linking subreddits. [3] computed a set of active users for each subreddit and used the Jaccard coefficient (the intersection of the users in common between two subreddits divided by their union) as a similarity score. [4], whose results we compare to our own in Section V, constructed a matrix of (normalized) user posting counts to subreddits, using the counts over all users posting to a subreddit as that subreddit's vector representation. Like the previous two approaches, [5], in an academic paper, also treated the same user posting a set of subreddits as evidence of their relatedness. They first built a graph weighted by this posting co-occurrence, then used a "backbone extraction" algorithm to eliminate edges that could be attributed to random chance.

Content-based methods focus on the text of comments and, to a lesser extent, posts to correlate subreddits. [6] used the top 100 words in the comments across 50 top subreddits (by commenting activity) to construct a (normalized) bag-of-words feature representation of each subreddit. They computed similarity by taking the Euclidean distance of all pairwise combinations of these subreddits, and performed clustering using affinity propogation. A second content-based method, [7], made use of term-frequency inverse-document-frequency (TF-IDF) and latent semantic indexing (with dimensions set to 2) on over 20 million comments to produce a plot of subreddits in a space where distance reflected their textual similarity.

III. Data

The dataset consists of posts from Reddit, a popular online forum. Reddit posts, unlike Twitter, are not length-constrained, and unlike Facebook are typically public but not necessarily identifying. Redditors (Reddit users) overwhelmingly prefer pseudonyms, and the site allows one to easily create throwaway accounts for one-off sensitive posts, something that is difficult to do on other services. This combination of public, lengthy, and often sensitive posts is a good source of data for studying the language with which individuals candidly express their symptoms or other circumstances surrounding their illnesses. (Despite being a publicly-available dataset, we acknowledge the sensitivity of these disclosures; none of the results or other data included in this work identify the individuals by name.)

The dataset was obtained from a public database of Reddit posts hosted on Google's BigQuery service [8]. Posts from 12-01-2015 to 7-31-2016 were considered in this analysis, although the corpus has been regularly updated since then.

A. Reddit Description

Reddit is made up of a large number of user-created special-interest fora, called subreddits, on which individuals post either links to content (images, news articles, etc. that are stored off-site) or self-posts, which typically consist of text entered by the poster. Subreddits are prefixed by an r/ in reference to their URL on the site, e.g., r/politics for https://reddit.com/r/politics. Each post on a subreddit is accompanied by a threaded comments section in which users can discuss the posted content.

Topics for subreddits include general interests, such as gaming or politics, or more specific interests such as particular television shows. Subreddits vary wildly in scale and activity, with some having thousands of subscribers and near-constant activity and others having been largely abandoned. Of particular relevance to this research are the social support/self-help subreddits, such as the ones around the management of chronic illnesses. This research in particular uses r/depression as a source of depression-relevant posts, although the method could be extended to other subreddits with a sufficient quantity of selfposts.

Content on the site is regulated through a community-driven mechanism of upvoting (or downvoting) both posts and comments on the site. Each user is able to provide one upvote or downvote for a particular element, and the aggregation of these votes (as well as other factors, such as age of the post or commenting activity) determines the order in which content is displayed, and thus its visibility. Elements that have a sufficiently negative score will be hidden by default, further reducing their visibility.

IV. Methods

Our objective is to differentiate depression-relevant posts – posts which are specifically about depression - from non-depression-relevant posts. Note that this is a separate task from identifying posts that were written by a depressed person, since they could write about many topics without a necessarily detectable influence on their writing. The general strategy was to start with a simple approach, then gradually work up to more complicated approaches should the simpler ones not provide sufficient accuracy. There are three high-level tasks that we addressed:

1) Discriminating a post from r/depression from a post selected from the entire corpus at random.
2) Determining if there are other subreddits which are measurably similar to r/depression based on the inability of the classifier to distinguish them

3) Identifying what features were most significant in the discrimination.

Tasks 1 and 2 can be performed with any binary classifier, but task 3 requires a classifier that assigns importance values to the features.

For task 1, 10,000 self-posts were uniformly selected from r/depression and 10,000 were uniformly selected from the corpus at large (potentially including posts from r/depression, although r/depression makes up a very small proportion of the total posts in the corpus.) Each post was labeled as originating from r/depression or not, and the sets were concatenated into a total dataset consisting of 20,000 labeled posts. These 20,000 posts were split into a 60% training, 40% test sets consisting of 12,000 training posts and 8,000 test posts. The classifier was trained using the training set, then validated by attempting to predict the labels of the posts in the test set.

For task 2, subreddits were selected that had a sufficient number of self-posts ($\geq$ 5000), which resulted in 229 candidate subreddits. 5,000 posts were selected uniformly from each candidate, and 5,000 posts were again selected uniformly from r/depression. The combined dataset of 10,000 labeled posts was constructed for each pairing of the 5,000 r/depression posts with the 5,000 posts from each candidate subreddit. The dataset was again split into training and test (6000 training, 4000 test) and the same process as described in task 1 was carried out for each pairing.

A. Sample to Feature-Vector Encoding

Most classifiers cannot directly accept samples, in this case a series of characters of arbitrary length, as input. Instead, the samples must be reduced into a set of features before use. Each post was encoded into a feature vector, a fixed-sized set of word counts, prior to being input into the classifier. To construct this feature vector, the entire training corpus was converted to lowercase and all punctuation except apostrophes were converted into spaces. The text was split on the spaces to produce tokens. The counts of each token were summed, then the 5000 most frequent tokens over the full set of posts (that is, including both r/depression and the other set of posts) were chosen as the elements of the feature vector.

Each post was then subjected to a similar tokenization and counting process, creating a 5000-element feature vector per post. Words that were present in the post but not in the feature encoding were ignored, and words which were not present in the post were given a count of 0. These per-post word counts were then scaled using TF-IDF, which in this case was the occurrence of the word within each post divided by the number of times it occurred within the full set of posts. No stemming or other collapsing of the token space was performed, with the intent being to capture idiosyncrasies in word choice.

Scikit-learn [9] was used to perform the above steps, specifically the `CountVectorizer`, `TfIdfTransformer`, and `Pipeline` classes.

B. Classification

We initially chose a naïve Bayes classifier as the simplest classifier to test the method. A naïve Bayes classifier considers each feature as an independent and identically distributed random variable and performs a binary classification on each sample into one of two possible classes (in this case, depression-relevant vs. not). After analyzing the performance on this classifier on the validation set, we moved on to a random forest classifier, which has many similarities to naïve Bayes, but also provides the importance values needed for task 3. (While feature importances can be derived from naïve Bayes' classifiers, according to [10] it is a good classifier, but poor estimator, so the importance values are apparently not robust.) A random forest classifier is an ensemble method which averages the performance of many decision tree classifiers to produce a more robust final estimate. Decision trees, as the name suggests, construct a tree of Boolean predicates on a feature (e.g., "feature #6 $<$ 563"), with the leaves of the tree consisting of the final classification for a sample that satisfies each Boolean predicate. The random forest constructs many of these trees on subsets of the training data, then averages them to circumvent the tendency for a single decision tree to overfit to the training data.

C. Comparison Methods

In the absence of a gold standard for subreddit clustering, we compare the rankings produced by our approach against several methods, described in detail in the following. The first two methods use the same feature representation for posts as described above, specifically 5000-element TF-IDF-scaled word counts. The last method's results were procured through the project's API by querying for subreddits related to 'depression'. We refer to the 5,000-post sample from r/depression as the **baseline set**, and each subreddit against which we are comparing r/depression as the **candidate set**.

1) Averaged TF-IDF Cosine Similarity: Cosine similarity is a popular choice in the field of information retrieval for determining the similarity of strings based on the angle between their feature representations [11]. In this case, we first compute a "subreddit vector" from its constituent posts in the sample, then determine the similarity of two subreddits by their angle. Specifically, for subreddit vectors A and B, the cosine similarity is defined as follows:

$$\text{similarity} = \cos(\theta) = \frac{\mathbf{A} \cdot \mathbf{B}}{\|\mathbf{A}\|\|\mathbf{B}\|} \tag{1}$$

Since our vectors all have positive components, the cosine similarity ranges from 1 (identical) to 0. The subreddit vectors are obtained by averaging the feature representations of each post in the baseline or candidate sample, respectively. We simply compute the cosine similarity between the baseline set's vector and each candidate set's vector to produce the final set of similarities, then order by descending similarity to produce the rankings.

2) Topic Vector Similarity: Prior to performing the similarity analysis, this approach first computes a 50-topic **topic model** over a co-occurrence matrix of the feature vectors for each post in the baseline set, performed using the software package gensim [12]. Specifically, we used a technique known as Latent Dirichlet Allocation (LDA) to produce a lower-dimensional 'topic' representation of the matrix. We apply this topic model of r/depression to transform each of the comparison subreddits' feature vectors into this lower-dimensional topic space. We employ gensim's `similarities.MatrixSimilarity` class to construct a data structure for efficiently comparing an input post's topic vector to every post in the baseline set. The comparison is performed via cosine similarity, but this time between the topic vector of the input post and the topic vectors of each post in the baseline set.

The topic model is then applied to each feature vector from the candidate set, producing a topic vector, then the similarity of every topic vector from the candidate post is compared to the topic vector of every post from the baseline set. The results of all of these comparisons are averaged, producing an average similarity score for the baseline-candidate pairing. The remainder of this method is the same as cosine similarity: the similarities for each candidate subreddit are ordered to produce a final ranking.

3) User-Centric Similarity: We did not directly implement this method; instead, we utilized the project's website to issue a query for posts similar to r/depression and downloaded the result. As described in its accompanying blog post [4], this method first constructs a user-subreddit matrix consisting of times in which each user has posted in each subreddit. The user list was drawn from participants in 2,000 "representative" subreddits and compared against 47,494 subreddits. These counts are adjusted by computing the positive pointwise mutual information for each. In this case, the subreddit vectors are the user-count vectors for each subreddit; similarity is once again computed as the cosine similarity between the subreddit vectors.

Note that this method's returned subreddits do not completely overlap with the 229 candidate subreddits of the other methods, since they were drawn from 47,494 subreddits instead.

V. RESULTS

Surprisingly, the naïve Bayes classifier performed extremely well on task 1. With no hyper-parameter tuning we achieved 89.9% accuracy on the test set. The random forest classifier achieved similar performance (89.1% accuracy.) As mentioned previously, we opted for the random forest classifier since we had reason to distrust the feature importances from naiïve Bayes.

A. Classifier Performance

Figure 1 depicts the receiver operating characteristic (ROC) curve for the random forest classifier, which shows the proportion of true to false positives as the decision threshold of the classifier is varied. The confusion matrix in Figure 2 demonstrates a relative scarcity of false-positive and false-negative errors compared to correct classifications in the test set.

To determine the feasibility of separating depression-relevant from non- posts, we also performed a principal component analysis (PCA) on the feature vectors of the samples in the test set. This was followed by a t-distributed stochastic neighbor embedding (t-SNE) of the first 50 principal components (derived from the 10,000 depressed vs. not set) to visualize the distribution of sample points in two dimensions, shown in Figure 3. Teal points are from the depression set, blue points are randomly selected from Reddit at large. The figure reveals distinct clusters of depression-relevant versus non-depression-relevant posts, which supports the argument that the classification task is inherently feasible.

The scattering of non-depressed points through a section of the depressed cluster could be due to those points being erroneously classified as non-depressed. For instance, they may belong to r/SuicideWatch or other such subreddits which are shown in task 2 to be difficult to distinguish from r/depression.

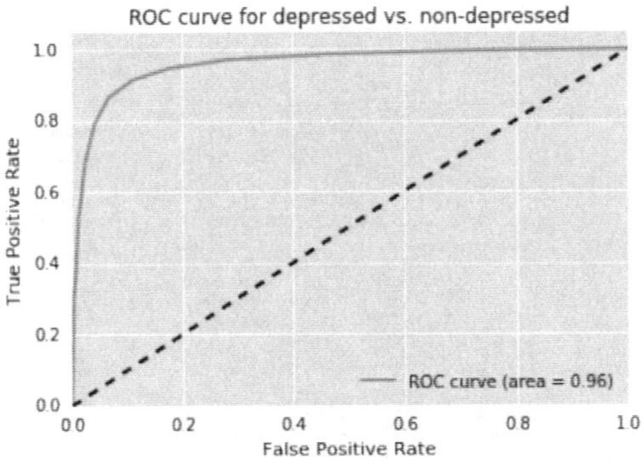

Figure 1. ROC curve displaying the performance of the random forest classifier in differentiating posts from r/depression from randomly-selected Reddit posts.

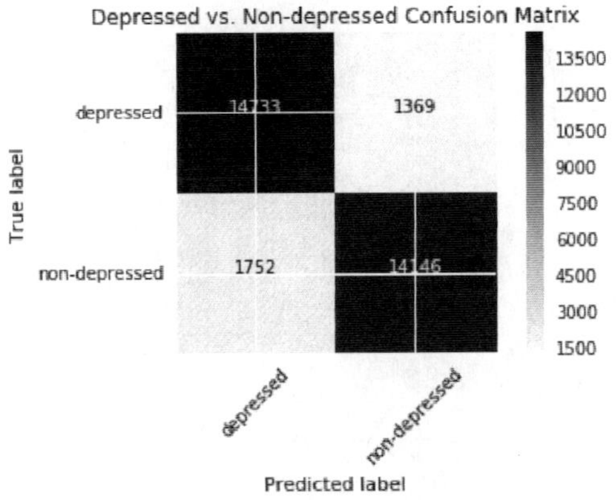

Figure 2. The confusion matrix in classifying r/depression posts versus posts randomly selected from Reddit.

B. Pairwise Comparisons

The performance of the classifier in task 1 could potentially be explained by the prevalence of easily-differentiated non-depression-relevant posts in the Reddit corpus. To test the hypothesis that some text is easier to differentiate from r/depression posts than others, we constructed a candidate set of 229 sufficiently popular subreddits with over 5,000 posts. We repeated the analysis in task 1 for each candidate, using the accuracy of the classifier to determine the similarity of that subreddit to r/depression. Table I shows an excerpt of the top 20 subreddits ranked by difficulty of discriminating them from r/depression. The accuracy column, by which the list is sorted, is the proportion of posts which were successfully classified as their true subreddit.

The least-distinguishable subreddits (r/SuicideWatch, r/offmychest, r/advice, r/Anxiety) are all within the support/self-help community of subreddits that relate specifically to depression and anxiety. This supports the hypothesis that the classifier has learned which posts are more likely to mention depression.

1) Alternative Rankings: In the absence of a gold standard for subreddit clustering, we compare the rankings produced by our approach against several standard and popularly-available methods. Tables II, III, and IV show rankings for the cosine

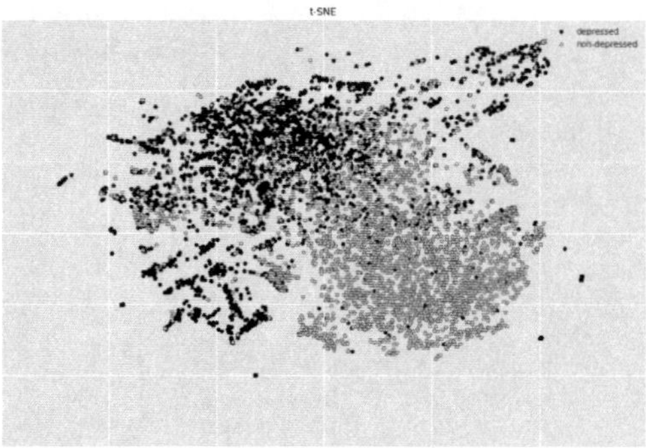

Figure 3. t-SNE 2-dimensional plot of the first 50 principal components.

TABLE I. TOP 20 SUBREDDITS THE RANDOM FOREST METHOD FOUND SIMILAR TO R/DEPRESSION.

accuracy	subreddit
0.628	SuicideWatch
0.703	offmychest
0.76825	Advice
0.7705	Anxiety
0.818	teenagers
0.8365	CasualConversation
0.84675	raisedbynarcissists
0.855	askgaybros
0.864	asktrp
0.871	asktransgender
0.8795	opiates
0.881	trees
0.88125	relationship_advice
0.88725	NoFap
0.888	NoStupidQuestions
0.8945	breakingmom
0.899	BabyBumps
0.901	Drugs
0.903	Christianity
0.90375	sex

similarity method, the LDA topic-vector method, and the user-centric method, respectively. For each of these tables, the distance column lists 1.0 − cosine_similarity to provide a consistent sorting order with table I.

In order to more rigorously compare these rankings to our method, we computed the Spearman's Rho [13] and Kendall's Tau rank correlation [14] coefficients over the top 40 subreddits for each method. Note that, since the user-centric method used a different set of candidate subreddits, subreddits not present in the 229 candidate subreddits were removed from that listing in the correlation. These coefficients and their respective P-values are listed in table V.

TABLE II. TOP 20 SIMILAR SUBREDDIT RANKING FOR THE COSINE SIMILARITY METHOD.

distance	subreddit
0.008156	SuicideWatch
0.026798	Anxiety
0.028122	offmychest
0.038478	Advice
0.049564	asktransgender
0.056973	stopdrinking
0.060631	teenagers
0.062695	NoFap
0.070161	raisedbynarcissists
0.074363	opiates
0.077625	CasualConversation
0.078701	BabyBumps
0.078729	askgaybros
0.079949	Drugs
0.081216	asktrp
0.087126	sex
0.09335	trees
0.094424	loseit
0.096255	breakingmom
0.099262	relationships

TABLE III. TOP 20 SIMILAR SUBREDDIT RANKING FOR THE LDA TOPIC-VECTOR METHOD.

distance	subreddit
0.077287	raisedbynarcissists
0.077868	relationships
0.078384	offmychest
0.082861	SuicideWatch
0.089728	Anxiety
0.089788	Advice
0.09074	tifu
0.093103	relationship_advice
0.100608	asktrp
0.101775	dirtypenpals
0.10187	stopdrinking
0.102771	exmormon
0.102937	breakingmom
0.106659	Drugs
0.109762	askgaybros
0.113361	asktransgender
0.114258	Christianity
0.116465	NoFap
0.116918	dating_advice
0.117696	legaladvice

TABLE IV. TOP 20 SIMILAR SUBREDDIT RANKING FOR THE USER-CENTRIC METHOD.

distance	subreddit
0.195466212	SuicideWatch
0.204685824	Anxiety
0.214096225	offmychest
0.226656993	socialanxiety
0.245376634	Advice
0.270127495	CasualConversation
0.273800743	BPD
0.281158627	bipolar
0.295523869	ForeverAlone
0.312207559	confession
0.321152875	BipolarReddit
0.321237547	raisedbynarcissists
0.321867951	relationship_advice
0.321882484	aspergers
0.323138283	ADHD
0.338704493	selfharm
0.341794481	OCD
0.345224437	ptsd
0.345228268	SeriousConversation
0.349653894	mentalhealth

All p-values are significant (≥ 0.05), but strangely none of the correlations are particularly strong. This is likely due to the length of the sub-lists that were compared, as only the first ten or so entries are strongly correlated across the lists.

C. Feature Importances

The random forest classifier assigns importances to each feature in terms of its ability to discriminate one label from the other. The list of words which best discriminated depression-relevant from non- posts reflects earlier research into the words

TABLE V. SPEARMAN'S RHO AND KENDALL'S TAU RANK CORRELATION COEFFICIENTS BETWEEN THE METHODS' LISTS.

	Cosine	LDA	User-Centric
Spearman	0.087	-0.175	0.104
P-Value	0.198	0.093	0.174
Kendall	0.049	-0.108	0.079
P-Value	0.219	0.109	0.157

TABLE VI. THE TOP 10 WORDS THAT DISCRIMINATE R/DEPRESSION FROM RANDOMLY-SELECTED POSTS.

importance	words
0.045848	i
0.040948	feel
0.038305	depression
0.032583	myself
0.022451	don't
0.021401	just
0.020019	depressed
0.01953	me
0.018206	but
0.017049	friends

that depressed people tend to use [15]. Specifically, they show a bias toward first-person personal pronouns (I, me, myself) in addition to the more obvious indicators of depression as a topic (e.g., depression, depressed).

Table VI is a selection of the 10 most important features in task 1, extracted from the 5000-element feature vector.

Figure 4 compares the importance of each word versus the rank of each word by importance. Importances, in accordance with Zipfs law, fall off at an inverse exponential rate.

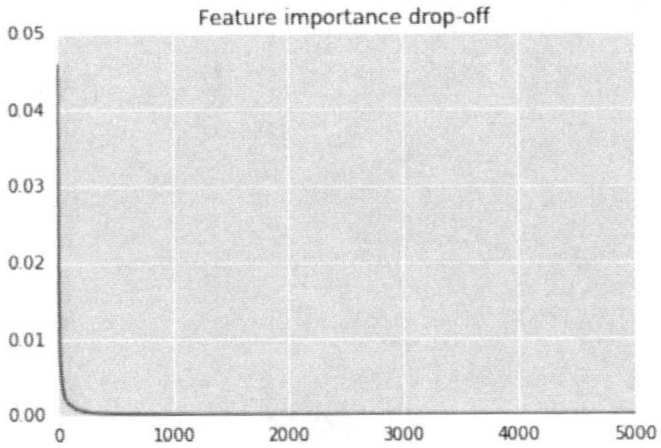

Figure 4. Feature importance declines at an inverse exponential rate in accordance with Zipf's law.

VI. DISCUSSION, FUTURE WORK

While the random forest method does seem to present reasonable similarity rankings that align with the other known methods, there is an alternate interpretation of the difficulty in discriminating between two subreddits. It could simply be that the model is not sufficiently robust to identify the actual differences between the subreddits or the input is not sufficiently rich; thus, the framework considers the two subreddits to be the same when in fact it is an insufficiency of the model or feature representation. It would be of interest to explore models that can perform better on the differentiation task for pairs of subreddits.

An additional open question is whether the method described here is applicable to other domains, as it is well-known that depression-relevant text overexpresses personal pronouns as well as contains obvious signifiers such as "depression" or "depressed". It would be of interest to apply the method to other subreddits, or ideally across all subreddits to identify ones which are less readily distinguishable from the mean. This question is inherently related to the above regarding model robustness – a more robust model might accurately capture differences between subreddits that are more subtle than the ones between depression-relevant and irrelevant text.

Finally, it is appealing that this method relies solely on post text due to the tendency for users to seek support anonymously, but that advantage breaks down outside the support context. It may be useful to construct a hybrid model that makes use of both user- and content-centric clustering methods in a way that would address their mutual limitations.

VII. CONCLUSION

In this work, we outlined the problem of exploring the relationships between self-help sub-forums on Reddit that are characterized by high self-disclosure, and consequently by anonymous posting behavior. We presented a method for ranking similar subreddits by the inability for a random forest classifier to distinguish between them, then compared its rankings to existing content-based and user-based subreddit similarity ranking methods. We present proposals to apply the approach to other corpora and to extend the framework with more sensitive classification on richer feature representations of the text, as well as hybrid user-content approaches that can circumvent anonymity by examining while still employing user data.

REFERENCES

[1] redditmetrics.com: new subreddits by month. [Online]. Available: http://redditmetrics.com/history/month (2017, accessed on 2018-02-01)

[2] M. De Choudhury and S. De, "Mental health discourse on reddit: Self-disclosure, social support, and anonymity." in ICWSM, 2014, pp. 71–80.

[3] J. Silterra, "Subreddit map," http://www.jacobsilterra.com/2015/03/10/subreddit-map/, 2015, (accessed on 2018-02-01).

[4] T. Martin, "Interactive map of reddit and subreddit similarity calculator," http://www.shorttails.io/interactive-map-of-reddit-and-subreddit-similarity-calculator/, 2016, (accessed on 2018-02-01).

[5] R. S. Olson and Z. P. Neal, "Navigating the massive world of reddit: Using backbone networks to map user interests in social media," PeerJ Computer Science, vol. 1, 2015, p. e4.

[6] A. Morcos, "Clustering subreddits by common word usage," http://www.arimorcos.com/blog/Clustering%20subreddits%20by%20common%20word%20usage/, 2015, (accessed on 2018-02-01).

[7] D. Wieker, "Subreddit clustering," http://dwieker.github.io/Reddit/, 2016, (accessed on 2018-02-01).

[8] F. Hoffa. 1.7 billion reddit comments loaded on bigquery. [Online]. Available: https://www.reddit.com/r/bigquery/comments/3cej2b/17_billion_reddit_comments_loaded_on_bigquery/ (2015, accessed on 2018-02-01)

[9] F. Pedregosa et al., "Scikit-learn: Machine learning in Python," Journal of Machine Learning Research, vol. 12, 2011, pp. 2825–2830.

[10] H. Zhang, "The optimality of naive bayes," AA, vol. 1, no. 2, 2004, p. 3.

[11] A. Singhal, "Modern information retrieval: A brief overview," 2001, pp. 35–43.

[12] R. Řehůřek and P. Sojka, "Software Framework for Topic Modelling with Large Corpora," in Proceedings of the LREC 2010 Workshop on New Challenges for NLP Frameworks. Valletta, Malta: ELRA, May 2010, pp. 45–50.

[13] C. Spearman, "The proof and measurement of association between two things," The American journal of psychology, vol. 15, no. 1, 1904, pp. 72–101.

[14] M. G. Kendall, "A new measure of rank correlation," Biometrika, vol. 30, no. 1/2, 1938, pp. 81–93.

[15] T. Brockmeyer et al., "Me, myself, and i: self-referent word use as an indicator of self-focused attention in relation to depression and anxiety," Frontiers in psychology, vol. 6, 2015, p. 1564.